The Literary *Angel*

The Literary *Angel*

*Essays on Influences
and Traditions Reflected
in the Joss Whedon Series*

Edited by
AMIJO COMEFORD *and*
TAMY BURNETT

McFarland & Company, Inc., Publishers
Jefferson, North Carolina, and London

LIBRARY OF CONGRESS CATALOGUING-IN-PUBLICATION DATA

The literary *Angel* : essays on influences and traditions reflected in the Joss Wheden series / edited by AmiJo Comeford and Tamy Burnett.
    p.   cm.
   Includes bibliographical references and index.

   ISBN 978-0-7864-4661-2
   softcover : 50# alkaline paper ∞

   1. Angel (Television program : 1999–2004)   2. Whedon, Joss, 1964– — Criticism and interpretation.   I. Comeford, AmiJo, 1979–   II. Burnett, Tamy, 1979–
PN1992.77.A588L58   2010
791.45'72 — dc22   2010015575

British Library cataloguing data are available

©2010 AmiJo Comeford and Tamy Burnett. All rights reserved

No part of this book may be reproduced or transmitted in any form or by any means, electronic or mechanical, including photocopying or recording, or by any information storage and retrieval system, without permission in writing from the publisher.

Front cover: Cast of *Angel*, from left to right: Spike (James Marsters), Lorne (Andy Hallett), Angel (David Boreanaz), Wesley Wyndham-Pryce (Alexis Denisof), Winifred "Fred" Burkle (Amy Acker) and Charles Gunn (J. August Richards) (The WB/Photofest); background ©2010 Shutterstock

Manufactured in the United States of America

McFarland & Company, Inc., Publishers
   Box 611, Jefferson, North Carolina 28640
      www.mcfarlandpub.com

For all the Whedon scholars out there
who still have colleagues and friends
raise an eyebrow when they mention
this field of study in a serious way

Table of Contents

Acknowledgments ix

Introduction: Los Angeles, City of Story
    AMIJO COMEFORD *and* TAMY BURNETT 1

One : Archetypes

Biting Humor: Harmony, Parody, and the Female Vampire
    LORNA JOWETT 17

Doyle as "The Passing Figure" and Nella Larsen's *Passing*
    ANGEL ANDERSON 30

Pylean Idol: L.A.'s De(con)struction of a Postmodern Bard
    JENNIFER HAMILTON 41

Lilah Morgan: Whedon's Legal Femme Fatale
    SHARON SUTHERLAND *and* SARAH SWAN 54

Two : Narrative & Identity

Fred's Captivity Narrative: American Contexts for (Re)Writing Community Identity from Mary Rowlandson to *Angel*
    TAMY BURNETT 69

Feminist Abuse Survivor Narratives in *Angel* and Sarah Daniels's *Beside Herself*
    ANIKA STAFFORD 85

Numero Cinco, Border Narratives, and Mexican Cultural Performance in *Angel*
    VICTORIA PETTERSEN LANTZ 98

Three : Theory & Philosophy

(Re)Negotiating the Dystopian Dilemma: Huxley, Orwell, and *Angel*
    MARY ELLEN IATROPOULOS 115

Angel vs. the Grand Inquisitor: Joss Whedon Re-imagines Dostoevsky
    KATIA MCCLAIN 130

Charles Gunn, Wolfram & Hart, and Baudrillard's Theory of
the Simulacrum
  K. SHANNON HOWARD 147
"It's a play on perspective": A Reading of Whedon's Illyria through
Sartre's *Nausea*
  CYNTHEA MASSON 159

Four : Genre

Helping the Helpless: Medieval Romance in *Angel*
  AMIJO COMEFORD 175
Whedon Meets Sophocles: Prophecy and *Angel*
  LAUREL BOWMAN 191
Detective Fiction/Fictionality from Asmodeus to *Angel*
  ALISON JAQUET 206
It (Re-)Started with a Girl: The Creative Interplay Between TV and
Comics in *Angel: After the Fall*
  STACEY ABBOTT 221

About the Contributors 233
Bibliography 237
Index 249

Acknowledgments

The editors are indebted to a wide range of individuals for the completion of this project. First, our families, who nurtured us throughout the process, especially the last-minute details, which fell during the holiday season; we are grateful for your generosity in understanding our commitment to this project, even when it took us away from you: Geri, Robert, Robby, Hollie, Tracee, Sondra, Loren, and John.

We were encouraged throughout the compilation of the manuscript by helpful colleagues and friends who supported and/or shared our interest in Whedon scholarship, assisted us with our own chapters for this collection, and reminded us to have faith in ourselves: Keri, Theda, Stephen, Amber, Regina, Alyson, Melissa, and Aimee.

This book would not be the fantastic volume you hold in your hands without the support of the wonderful, intelligent individuals who eagerly responded to our call for papers and contributed their superb essays, taking our editorial comments so graciously: Alison, Angel, Anika, Cynthea, Jennifer, Katia, Laurel, Lorna, Mary Ellen, Sarah, Shannon, Sharon, Stacey, and Vicky.

And, of course, this book would not have materialized without those who championed Whedon scholarship through their own writings, through establishing and coordinating academic events such as the Slayage conferences, and through facilitating publication opportunities for others, ranging from *Slayage* and other peer-reviewed journals to the "Buffy bookers" panels at the Slayage conferences. We are sure, in our effort to acknowledge and thank those who have contributed to this book's beginnings and fruition, to overlook some of you who contribute to and facilitate these important opportunities, so we limit ourselves here to Rhonda Wilcox and David Lavery, the founders of Whedon studies, as well as Stacey Abbott, whose work on *Angel* specifically made possible subsequent volumes such as this one.

Finally, though it may go without saying, we voice our appreciation to Joss Whedon, his creative team, and the cast and crew of *Angel* who devoted five years of their lives (more for those who also worked on *Buffy the Vampire Slayer*) to provide us with such great and nuanced text and literature. We also thank and acknowledge Brian Lynch and the illustrators at IDW Publishing whose work on the continuing story of these dynamic characters in comic book form has given us a new realm of visual and reading pleasure as well as a new medium with which to engage the complex and rich literary tradition begun in the television series.

Introduction
Los Angeles, City of Story
AmiJo Comeford and Tamy Burnett

At first glance, one might question the validity of considering a television series about a vampire detective in L.A. in terms of its engagement with literary concerns. After all, the series regularly features fast-paced action scenes and characters routinely solve an episode's conflict by killing the monster-of-the-week. Regular viewers know, however, that *Angel* is far more than simply an action show, or a vampire show, or even the "turgid supernatural soap-opera," as one character self-consciously calls his world and weekly adventures.[1] Indeed, *Angel* is a fantasy/horror/detective noir/drama/comedy show about a vampire cursed with a soul — a conscience — seeking redemption for the century and a half he spent as a sadistic, brutal killer. Angel and his friends do routinely fight supernatural creatures ranging from the average vampire to anti–Christ demi-gods to evil law firms. And those genre-based characteristics are exactly the type that so often cause the general populace and high-minded critics alike to dismiss just such a show without giving it a chance or even comparing it to previous vampire shows, to little positive effect. However, as a number of television and cultural critics have argued elsewhere, *Angel* provides viewers with a sophisticated, complex narrative and cast of characters, which together create a thought-provoking, high-quality, and, yes, entertaining television experience. And, as this volume also seeks to unequivocally prove, part of *Angel*'s appeal is that it draws on literary allusions and engages significant cultural narratives just as regularly as it depicts visually-stimulating fight scenes.

Angel's Los Angeles may be a world filled with blood-thirsty vampires, violent demons, evil law firms, and L.A.'s helpless in need of help, but it is also a world filled with books, texts, and other forms of literature. From the all-important Shanshu prophecy that predicts Angel's return to a state of humanity as a reward for heroic sacrifices (and thus raises questions about free will and the ethics of acting heroically for a promised reward) to the ever-present books that dominate the characters' research sessions into the latest demonic threat, texts are such an integral part of Team Angel's world that they are omnipresent, always in the background, as necessary as the blood Angel drinks to stay alive. However, a viewer paying close attention will notice that

Angel's creator, Joss Whedon, and the show's other writers place a premium on the role of texts in the series. Sometimes this manifests through complex and unusual representations of texts, as in the "holy" books of Pylea, the demon dimension the gang visits at the end of the second season, which take on a fascinating form: "Trionic," wherein one continuous text is written in three different volumes.[2] Instead of taking the form of a trilogy with the first third of the narrative in the first volume, the text shifts back and forth between the three with subtle textual clues that indicate when to switch volumes. Of course, upon closing the books and looking at the images on their covers, Angel's team — Wesley, Gunn, and Cordelia — discover another hidden message broken into three parts: the volumes' author — the wolf, the ram, and the hart — or Wolfram & Hart, the multidimensional evil law firm they regularly find themselves working against. Significantly, viewers find themselves in the same positions as the characters in their relationship to the show, with hidden messages and metaphors, which shift between episodes and seasons, between the present events and flashbacks, with layered meaning occurring even within a single episode.

Another example of the primacy of text in the series occurs in Season Four, when Angel's investigative team hires a shaman to temporarily remove Angel's soul in order to access information known only by his non-souled, evil alter ego Angelus. The unique use of texts here is two-fold. The monk's holy text is written upon his body so that he and the other members of his order are literally living embodiments of the teachings of their order,[3] in much the same way that viewers read the "text" of Angel's past as an evil vampire and use that backstory to shape understanding of the narrative present. At the same time, ironically, there is nothing embodied about the monk's actions in removing Angel's soul. The task is accomplished by producing a vivid fantasy of a perfect day within Angel's psyche — so perfect that Angel is overcome with his personal kryptonite, and the part of his curse meant to keep him suffering by remaining ever aware of his past sins is invalidated by the clause that releases his soul when he achieves a moment of perfect happiness. A fantasy spun through story causes Angel's soul to be released, reinforcing the power of belief in narrative, which functions here to manipulate audience response as well, since they are wrapped up in the same narrative, with no knowledge that the day is fictionalized until the closing moments of the episode, so powerful is the desire to believe the perfect fiction. Such erasure of the line between text and the power of that narrative to shape audience reaction reminds viewers to be cautious about what narratives they choose to believe and to evaluate not only the story being told but also the nature of that story's delivery. As critic Stacey Abbott has observed, *Angel* is notable for the ways in which it challenges traditional narrative conventions, as it does in the episode "Spin the Bottle," where the story is revealed through flashback and one character retelling the events at some future point, framing the viewers' understanding of the episode's plot and its connection to the continuing narrative arc.[4]

At other times, the series' preoccupation with literature shows up when the show's writers draw heavily on Western culture's literary traditions that help shape characters, episodic storylines, and larger narrative arcs. Examples of this range from the obvious re-telling of *Oedipus Rex* through the storyline for Angel's son Connor, to evil lawyer Lilah gifting Wesley with a copy of Dante's *Inferno* so that she can attempt to woo him to work for Wolfram & Hart after his estrangement from Angel Investigations. Lilah's recruitment technique attempts to shame Wesley into accepting her job offer, suggesting that his betrayal of Angel — he kidnapped an infant Connor to prevent the actualization of a prophecy predicting that Angel would kill the child — makes him no better than the greatest sinner in Western cultural and written history: Judas Iscariot, whose betrayal of Christ led to Christ's death and landed him in the lowest pit of Dante's hell.[5] References to hallmarks of Western literature are also strewn throughout the series in smaller ways. Lorne, the empathic demon who can foresee future events, references William Butler Yeats's "The Second Coming" to indicate the forthcoming series of events that will mimic and pervert the Christian story of the birth of Jesus through the birth of a people-eating demi-god.[6] And some of the most obvious references come from Angel/Angelus, whose allusions to narratives of cultural significance range from Shakespeare; to nineteenth-century French poet Charles Baudelaire, author of the poem "Le Vampyre"; to twentieth-century Charlton Heston movies.[7]

While Team Angel is more likely to consult non-fiction texts like religious documents or histories and encyclopedias of demons in pursuit of answers rather than fictional stories and poems — usually what one thinks of in response to the term "literature" — we here consider all texts to fall under the heading of "literature" since any text, even non-fiction ones, contribute to the formation of a larger cultural narrative. After all, history is nothing more than the story we, as a society, tell ourselves about how we arrived in the present, a story written by the winners, and all too often the presentation of "fact" is shaped by the author's socio-cultural-historical context. But, given that Team Angel often fights creatures of myth and legend, a reliance on older texts — those written during a time when such things were more widely accepted as fact rather than myth or legend — makes sense. After all, written history has far surpassed oral history within the framework of Western civilization as the most effective means of preserving knowledge and transferring cultural values and ideals from one generation to the next. All of Joss Whedon's works, especially *Angel*, are littered with literary allusions, references, and outright reproductions — and like any great author/auteur, he draws on the literary-cultural landscape to tell stories about life in America at the start of the twenty-first century, a place and time of cultural-historical location borne out of those older stories, shaped by their underlying messages and popular characterizations. What makes *Angel* truly unique in this regard is that audiences not only work through these allusions to discover narrative and experiential truth, but the text itself and the characters self-consciously engage in the same discovery inside the narrative, thereby reinforcing audience awareness of their own experience with Whedon's text and the texts he and his team of writers reference.

As teachers and life-long students of literary traditions in English, as editors of this collection, part of our interest in *Angel* stems from this central role literature and texts play in the series, in helping the characters conquer their foes and understand themselves and the world around them a little better—after all, one of the reasons we are drawn to the study of literature is that literature opens windows into other lived experiences, thereby providing insight into the human condition. Moreover, we are also fascinated by *Angel* itself as a cultural text. Our own love affair with the series grew out of a shared graduate school experience and a friendship that, in part, was nurtured through animated phone conversations following the nearly-weekly cliffhangers of *Angel*'s fourth season. To these conversations, AmiJo brought her background in American literature and history, especially that connected to the U.S. Civil War, as well as interests in literary theory and questions of gender representation. Tamy brought a background in American literature, as well as interests in popular culture studies and women's and gender studies. Simultaneously, over the next few years, the field of Whedon studies scholarship was born, and we have both slowly interwoven our personal and professional interests, introducing *Angel* and its parent show *Buffy the Vampire Slayer*, among others, into our classrooms and our scholarship.

The clear success of academic books devoted to *Buffy the Vampire Slayer*, intersecting themes in Whedon's *Buffy*, *Angel*, and *Firefly/Serenity*, and a recent collection devoted to *Firefly*, as well as the numerous article publications on Whedon's works in several peer-reviewed journals, indicates a continued academic and popular interest in Joss Whedon studies. Yet, the publications that support Whedon studies contain an obvious gap—books devoted to *Angel*, which ran for five seasons with a sixth season continued in comic book form in *Angel: After the Fall*, thereby engaging this creative world in another narrative genre. Though over a dozen full books devoted to *Buffy* have been published in recent years, only one edited collection has thus far been focused on its companion series, *Angel: Reading* Angel*: The TV Spin-off with a Soul*, edited by film professor and Whedon scholar Stacey Abbott.[8] However, some individual articles devoted to the characters on the show have also been published or presented as conference papers, and Abbott has recently authored a volume devoted to *Angel*.[9] This scholarship, as limited as it has been, has done much to highlight the complex and nuanced narratives that shaped *Angel* from its opening sequence in a dark alley in Los Angeles in the first episode, "City of," to its final sequence in that same dark alley in the conclusion of the show's televised run, "Not Fade Away."[10] Still, even with the variety of critical attention given to *Angel* in the past few years, a surprisingly small amount has surfaced in relative comparison to *Buffy the Vampire Slayer*. As Rhonda Wilcox and

David Lavery observed in a 2005 article, scholarly engagement with *Angel* has "lagged behind."[11] They go on, however, to reflect that "now we scholars of the Buffyverse have this rich collection [*Reading* Angel], we need not feel quite so outnumbered as Team Angel in that fatal alley behind the Hyperion. The work of investigating *Angel* has just begun."[12] *Angel* criticism thus far has engaged a variety of topics, including gender identity, film noir, the nature of evil, and the myriad ways in which *Angel* both adheres to and subverts traditional narrative, gender, and character structures. Some of the contributions to this volume build upon what others have begun in this area, while other chapters tread new ground, expanding the scope of *Angel* studies. Still, much remains to be done in regards to *Angel* as a show that can stand alone and outside of its parent series. Whedon scholars and *Angel* scholars specifically owe a particular debt to Stacey Abbott for her groundbreaking work on *Angel* and her continued support of *Angel* scholarship, including her chapter in this collection.

Often, our criteria for evaluating the quality of television draw heavily on the complexities of narrative structures and the reimagining of traditional tales or storytelling techniques. Whedon's works, including *Angel*, are rife with these types of older narrative structures and literary references, as a few scholars have noted in the past. This may be why Whedon's works serve as ideal springboards for professors and others to guide students into discussions of literary themes through a pop culture avenue that, for many students, is more familiar and accessible, since as David Lavery explains, "TV's allusions ... imply a mutual 'fund of knowledge.' When [such allusions] are merely to the rest of the vast cosmos of television, as they often are, they presume nothing more than the commonality of many hours before the small screen. But television's proliferating literary references stand as a testimony to the medium's increasing sophistication as it begins to partake in 'the conversation of mankind,' to the wider, deeper repertoire of its writers, and to new, much more flattering assumptions about the intellectual qualities of the Quality TV audience."[13] This volume works primarily with *Angel* as a text to be addressed in the wider field of narrative and literature, since critical analysis of visual narratives in our culture is often related to our literary history and cultural consciousness. As such, we hope this collection is useful not just for academics or scholar-fans interested in Whedon studies in general, but also for literature instructors and students.

To address these academic needs, our collection emerges out of two key motivations: (1) our attempt to bridge the gap in Whedon studies that exists in relation to materials devoted to *Angel*, and (2) our desire to draw attention to the uses of literary themes in current visual culture. As instructors of literature courses, we routinely examine new ways to help undergraduates, English majors and non-majors alike, to engage with literature and narrative in meaningful ways. In a world that is increasingly dominated by visual texts, how we approach students acculturated in this environment is crucial, and we believe that this volume exploring literary connections, references, and allusions within Joss Whedon's *Angel* will highlight the importance of historically canonized literary texts, narrative structures, and themes, as well as their continued relevance today.

For five seasons (1999–2004), Joss Whedon, *Angel* co-creator David Greenwalt, and their team of writers intrigued audiences weekly with the story of Angel (David Boreanaz), a vampire cursed with the return of his soul who regularly "helped the helpless" of Los Angeles, with some help from The Powers That Be (higher beings) and a team of misfits. Though *Angel* premiered to mixed reviews (detailed in Stacey Abbott's recent book *Angel*), what viewers witnessed over the next five seasons was nothing short of a creative masterpiece, engaging a range of social and philosophical themes that fans and academics alike have continued to discuss around water coolers, in coffee shops, at academic conferences, and in college classrooms.

As the show's title suggests, the central character is Angel, a guilt-ridden vampire who originated in the first season of *Buffy the Vampire Slayer*. For approximately 150 years, Angel marauded the world with his sadistic pleasure for tormenting and killing; when he became a vampire he no longer had a soul or conscience. Finally, he killed the wrong girl, and her family punished him by returning his soul. The re-ensouled vampire now had to live eternally with the memories of his past sins and a conscience so that he might eternally suffer in retribution for the suffering he caused. For three seasons he functions as Buffy's sidekick and love interest, leaving her show at the end of Season Three to move to L.A. and star in his own show, created by *Buffy*'s architect, Joss Whedon. In L.A., Angel is forced to form a new community, and various characters come to fight by his side, forming the core of what audiences come to know as Angel Investigations, or more familiarly, Team Angel.

Team Angel is comprised of several members over the years, ranging from the down-on-his luck half-demon Doyle (Glenn Quinn); to the wanna-be actress turned seer Cordelia (Charisma Carpenter); to the disgraced watcher (watchers train and guide slayers) Wesley Wyndam-Pryce (Alexis Denisof). Also joining the team over the years are the street fighter and vampire hunter Charles Gunn (J. August Richards); the taco-loving physicist Winifred "Fred" Burkle (Amy Acker), who is eventually transformed into Illyria, an ancient demon that takes over Fred's body; the karaoke bar owner/empathic demon Lorne (Andy Hallett); and even Spike (James Marsters), another souled vampire with whom Angel shares an evil past and a present antagonistic relationship. Each of these characters is united in Angel's fight, not only because they believe in "helping the helpless"—the motto of Angel Investigations—but because each has something of his/her own to atone for, past failures and mistakes for which they seek their own redemption.

In addition to these core characters, *Angel* is filled with a wealth of reoccurring characters who significantly impact Team Angel, for good or evil (usually evil). Team Angel's primary, long-term antagonist is Wolfram & Hart, a law firm dedicated to evil, which, ironically, the team takes over and runs during the show's fifth and final televised season. Of Wolfram & Hart's employees, Angel and company most often interact with Lindsey McDonald (Christian Kane), who constantly shifts between aligning himself with the firm and opposing it, and Lilah Morgan (Stephanie Romanov), a fiercely competitive, unrepentantly evil associate who, in later seasons, becomes embroiled in a tumultuous affair with Wesley. Also, in the series' frequent flashbacks, viewers see Angel, and sometimes Spike, with Darla (Julie Benz) and Drusilla (Juliet Landau), the female half of their vampire family foursome before Angel was cursed. Darla and Drusilla also show up in Angel's present, tempting him, even as their presence is a painful reminder of his past transgressions. In the third season, Darla bears Angel a son, Connor (Vincent Kartheiser), who, like any child, fundamentally alters Team Angel's world.

Whereas *Buffy* is often described as being a coming-of-age story centered on the metaphor that "high school is hell," *Angel* clearly engages questions of what it means to survive in the world as a young adult, a twenty-something making adult decisions and living with the consequences—all while fighting evil, of course. Throughout the show, characters struggle with defining and redefining themselves professionally and personally, learning to trust the family they have created at Angel Investigations, and discovering when to stand up to or apart from that same family. They grapple with adult responsibilities like parenthood and career decisions, as well as learning to face the (usually metaphorical) demons of their pasts. As Whedon and his creative team tell these stories, they draw upon older stories, significant narratives of Western and (mostly) English-speaking culture that situate Team Angel's adventures within the rich tapestry of Western literary tradition.

The essays in this volume are divided into four categories: Archetypes, Narrative and Identity, Theory and Philosophy, and Genre. The Archetypes group explores specific characters, illuminating the archetypes and stereotypes that help create the characters and viewers' understanding of them. The second set of essays, those concerned with questions of Narrative and Identity, examine ways in which the telling of stories about one's self helps shape and (re)define an individual. In the third grouping, contributors consider *Angel* through literary/cultural theories and philosophies, focusing on issues of reality and free will. The fourth and final set of essays examine the series by looking at both historical literary genres and the different genre forms that *Angel* utilizes throughout the run of the televised series and the subsequent comic book continuation. While most of the essays in this collection are as genre-blending as *Angel* and could fit into more than one category, we believe the arrangement we have chosen highlights the ways various authors' ideas work together, providing greater illumination to *Angel* as a whole.

To begin the Archetypes section, Lorna Jowett's chapter, "Biting Humor:

Harmony, Parody, and the Female Vampire," offers an insightful examination of the supporting character of Harmony, considering her in light of the conflicting stereotypes she represents—that of the female vampire and the dumb blonde. Jowett situates Harmony within a literary and filmic tradition of vampires in general and female vampires specifically, looking at how Harmony fulfills and ignores specific tropes like a predatory personality, hyper-sexualization/lesbianism, and the spectacle of monstrosity. Then, drawing on theories of feminist comedy, Jowett explores how Harmony's depiction as a "dumb blonde" complicates and subverts the female vampire characteristics through comedic parody and vice versa. Overall, Jowett's essay reveals multiple layers of gendered construction in Harmony's characterization and how the use of parody undermines the efficacy of the stereotypes.

Next, Angel Anderson's chapter, "Doyle as 'The Passing Figure' and Nella Larsen's *Passing*," situates Angel's first seer-sidekick within the historical and literary context of race-based "passing," the act of claiming a racial identity of higher social privilege by keeping hidden less-socially desirable aspects of one's racial heritage. For the half-demon Doyle, whose demon heritage becomes blindingly obvious whenever he sneezes and spikes pop out all over his face, passing as human allows him freedoms his full-blooded relatives cannot enjoy. Anderson compares Doyle's characterization and character arc to the main figures in Nella Larsen's *Passing*, a foundational classic of passing literature. Anderson's thoughtful analysis reveals that while Doyle is clearly cast in the literary and historical mould of the passing figure, the conclusion of his storyline offers a subversion to the expected tragic ending for such a figure.

In contrast, Jennifer Hamilton explores the character of Lorne in "Pylean Idol: L.A.'s De(con)struction of a Postmodern Bard," situating him within the legacy of bardic traditions that trace back to Celtic Scotland and Ireland. Hamilton identifies Lorne as a postmodern bard, one who fulfills the bardic role of being the interpreter of stories for his clan, weaving a cohesive narrative that shapes cultural identity while at the same time being constrained by postmodernism's reliance on contextuality. She traces Lorne's character development over the course of *Angel*, culminating in a fundamental shift in Season Five, when Lorne becomes more and more a participant within the narrative rather than someone on the edges who interprets and keeps the story. Ultimately, Hamilton concludes, Lorne's actions in the Season Five finale serve to fully sever him from the bardic role, as demonstrated by the subdued figure who exits the show, a sharp contrast to Lorne's early appearances on *Angel*.

Sharon Sutherland and Sarah Swan wrap up this set of essays with the thought-provoking chapter "Lilah Morgan: Whedon's Legal Femme Fatale." Like Jowett's consideration of Harmony, Sutherland and Swan position Lilah at the intersection of two major female archetypes—the femme fatale and the female lawyer. Drawing on literary and filmic traditions to highlight the femme fatale's characterization and filmic and televisual examples to typify the female lawyer in contemporary popular culture, Sutherland and Swan explore how Lilah conforms to, challenges, and redefines these archetypes. Moreover, they argue that Lilah's depiction is that of a feminist figure, one who is willing to fight for and then commit to her own—albeit evil—choices in life. Further, Sutherland and Swan consider Lilah as a femme fatale, female lawyer, and feminist in terms of traditionally gendered concerns like balancing career with family and narrowing one's area of specialization within a traditionally male career field, offering insight into not only Lilah's character but also larger cultural constructions of the femme fatale and the female lawyer.

The second section of the volume deals with narrative and identity creation, telling stories about the self in order to (re)form one's sense of self. Tamy Burnett's essay, "Fred's Captivity Narrative: American Contexts for (Re)Writing Community Identity from Mary Rowlandson to *Angel*," focuses on the distinct similarities that connect the Pylea story arc from *Angel*'s Season Two to Mary Rowlandson's captivity narrative from the seventeenth century. Not only does Burnett help to fill in the gap in *Angel* studies on the character of Fred, but she also contributes a provoking question about the ways in which *Angel* contributes to underlying racial stereotypes through its use of genre, in this case captivity narrative. Burnett approaches the argument through a compelling discussion of how, for both women, writing helps to filter and make comprehensible their captivity experiences for themselves and for the communities to which they return and into which they desire to integrate. From these comparisons, Burnett moves to her final discussion about the depictions in both Rowlandson's narrative and the Pylea arc that make American Indian images and customs "savage" and "primitive," effectively othering American Indian culture while at the same time privileging white society as the source of enlightenment. What makes Burnett's argument so unique is her claim that it is specifically through *Angel*'s development of Fred within the captivity narrative structure that these racial subtexts are revealed.

Anika Stafford writes the next chapter, "Feminist Abuse Survivor Narratives in *Angel* and Sarah Daniels's *Beside Herself*." This insightful essay compares Cordelia in "Rm w/a Vu" (1.05) and Bethany, the client Angel Investigations aids in Season Two's "Untouched" (2.04), to the primary character in feminist playwright Sarah Daniels's *Beside Herself*. Drawing upon feminist theories of the constructions and functions of abuse survivor discourse, Stafford examines Whedon's and Daniels's visual productions in terms of how they present the transformation of abuse victims into survivors in control of the agency necessary to stand up to and end abusive cycles. Specifically, Stafford examines the narratives in terms of how they present coping mechanisms like disassociative behaviors as legitimate responses to abuse rather than indicators of a troubled mental state (traditionally, displaying behaviors like disassociation results in one being labeled "mad" or "crazy"); how survivors can speak back to their abusers by reclaiming previously derogatory terms like "bitch"; and how positioning others as allies rather than experts allows them to help the survivor overcome abuse.

To finish up this set of essays, Victoria Pettersen Lantz's "Numero Cinco, Border Narratives, and Mexican Cultural Performance in *Angel*" provides a much needed study of the use of Latino representation in *Angel*, focusing specifically on the Season Five episode "The Cautionary Tale of Numero Cinco" (5.06) and its uses of the Mexican tradition of masking to address concepts of heroism. Lantz finds it especially troubling that in a show set in Los Angeles, in a city that has such a strong Latino presence, the narratives rarely engage either Latino characters or culture. Lantz uniquely approaches the topic through a comparison of this episode to the artistry of Chicano performance artist Guillermo Gomez-Peña. What Lantz argues effectively for in her essay is an assessment of the ways in which portrayals of Mexican culture in shows like *Angel* do in fact impact what she calls a "progressive Chicano/a identity" and viewers' engagement with it. She argues that though "The Cautionary Tale" does portray Mexican culture in comedic and at times exotic ways, which needs to be criticized, it nonetheless is a step toward a connection with the culture that seeks to show cultural isolation as dysfunctional.

In the third section, dedicated to considerations of theory and philosophy, Mary Ellen Iatropoulos brings to the collection her reading of *Angel* as a subversion of dystopian literature in her essay "(Re)Negotiating the Dystopian Dilemma: Huxley, Orwell, and *Angel*." Specifically, Iatropoulos finds the connections between Alduous Huxley's *Brave New World* and George Orwell's *Animal Farm* significant to a reading of the Jasmine story arc from *Angel*'s fourth season and the Circle of the Black Thorn storyline in the fifth season. Iatropoulos situates her fascinating argument in a tradition of dystopian novels that take characters through moments of enlightenment, disillusionment, and final rejection of that enlightenment. What she finds in *Angel*, however, is that though the narrative and the characters appear to follow the progression of these earlier novels in their dystopic attributes, in the final moments of the dystopic arc, the characters reject the dystopia, instead choosing to retain their own enlightenment and share that knowledge with others, thereby privileging individual choice over the pessimism of dystopia.

Katia McClain's "Angel vs. the Grand Inquisitor: Joss Whedon Re-imagines Dostoevsky" also joins the healthy dialogue in Whedon studies about how *Angel* and Whedon's other works engage questions of destiny and free will. A scholar of Slavic studies, McClain looks specifically at the Grand Inquisitor parable from the Russian classic, Fyodor Dostoevsky's *The Brothers Karamazov*, identifying a re-creation of Dostoevsky's scene in Angel's confrontation with Jasmine, the rogue higher power who attempts to create world peace through enslavement at the end of the Season Four primary story arc. McClain's examination of the two works in conversation with one another serves as a point of entry into a contrast of Dostoevsky and Whedon within their respective cultures and time periods, as well as illuminating previously unexplored aspects of Whedon's demonstrated existentialism.

K. Shannon Howard's unique contribution to this volume, "Charles Gunn, Wolfram & Hart, and Baudrillard's Theory of the Simulacrum," as the title suggests, contextualizes Gunn's development from vampire hunter on Los Angeles's streets to expert attorney at Wolfram & Hart as one not of simple liminality or displacement, as others have done, but rather one of progression toward postmodern absence. By taking the events of Gunn's involvement with Angel Investigations through the four stages of Baudrillard's concept of simulacrum, Howard argues that the images of Gunn in Season Five in the White Room and Gunn's imprisonment in Wolfram & Hart's hellish holding dimension are illustrative of Gunn's final projection as a simulacrum rather than as a character with solid presence. Howard reads Gunn's movement, however, not as the writers' attempts to present a nihilistic and ultimately despairing projection of reality, but rather as one filled with optimism, since in the face of his life as a simulacrum, Gunn nonetheless chooses to live by the principles embodied in his own self-vision.

Next, Cynthea Masson's contribution, "'It's a play on perspective': A Reading of Whedon's Illyria through Sartre's *Nausea*," engages a text that Joss Whedon has repeatedly referred to as one of his favorite novels. While critical analysis that focuses on Whedon's interest and use of existential philosophy in his work is not new, what is new is Masson's exploration of perhaps the most important of Whedon's existential models, Sartre's *Nausea*. Through a comparison between the novel's main character, Roquentin, and Illyria from *Angel*'s Season Five, Masson explores the questions that Whedon raises about the nature of the relationship between essence and existence, a focal point of existentialist philosophy. Masson's chapter is a compelling exploration of Whedon's revision and challenging of Sartrean existentialism through the existentialist journey of Illyria from her emergence at Fred's death, an essence that would seem to precede existence, to a character who consciously performs Fred at Wesley's death.

The fourth and final set of essays considers questions of genre, exploring both genres *Angel* pulls from and its expansion into various genre forms. AmiJo Comeford begins this section with "Helping the Helpless: Medieval Romance in *Angel*," a chapter that examines Angel, the character and the series, through the lens of medieval romances, such as the Lancelot story. She identifies thematic characteristics of the romance hero and the genre in general and applies them to *Angel*, especially in terms of how Angel's early characterizations on *Buffy the Vampire Slayer* and the long-term depiction of his and Buffy's ill-fated relationship even beyond *Buffy* and into his own series situates him as embodying courtly love. Comeford astutely argues that, unlike other conceptualizations of the Buffy/Angel doomed love, such as the comparison to *Romeo and Juliet*, considering it within the context of courtly love and the romance genre particularly raises questions about the reconciliation of sometimes-paradoxical values like love and duty. *Angel*'s engagement with romance is, according to Comeford, successful in part because it resists an easy resolution for this conflict, even as it elevates the romance hero and his love.

Laurel Bowman's thoughtful essay, "Whedon Meets Sophocles: Prophecy and *Angel*," explores the ways in which traditional concepts of tragedy are utilized in the early seasons of *Angel* but in the end are re-negotiated and made more complex for a modern audience. Bowman uses the lens of Greek tragic definitions and characteristics to contextualize the argument and then moves into the ways in which those same characteristics and definitions apply to the major and minor uses of prophecy in *Angel*, including the Shanshu prophecy. Bowman posits that because *Angel*'s audience is aware, if not intimately knowledgeable, about conventions of classical prophecy, the writers are able to manipulate those conventions in unique ways that lead to strong emotional engagement with viewers, subverting their understanding of classical use of prophecy, including the notion that relying on prophecy is the best and only way to achieve success, both in life and in detective work. Bowman reads *Angel*, its characters and its narrative arcs, as a negation of classical prophecy and its abnegation of individual responsibility and choice; rather *Angel* celebrates human reason and the choice to, in fact, choose rather than follow a destiny already prescribed.

Next, Alison Jaquet's "Detective Fiction/Fictionality from Asmodeus to *Angel*" examines the wealth of detective traditions that *Angel*'s characters and storylines draw upon, ranging from Asmodeus—a demon in sixteenth-century Spanish literature who removed the roofs from homes, literally revealing secrets—to the detectives of famous nineteenth-century British and American authors like Arthur Conan Doyle and Edgar Allan Poe, to modern approaches to mystery solving through scientific knowledge. In doing so, Jaquet successfully argues that *Angel* privileges detection as a collaborative act, reliant upon multiple, simultaneous approaches for success, highlighting one as effective in an individual situation but making clear that the detectives never know up front which mode of detection will provide results and thus must engage multiple models. Moreover, she contends that the show's concurrent representation of luck as a factor in effective detection is a commentary on the fictionality of the act of detection—making a cohesive narrative out of initially unexplainable phenomenon—on a metanarrative level.

Stacey Abbott's contribution to this collection, "It (Re-)Started with a Girl: The Creative Interplay Between TV and Comics in *Angel: After the Fall*," delves into the newest area of *Angel* narrative and investigation, the comics— *Angel: After the Fall*. Unlike many readers who see the comics as a mere narrative and visual extension of the television series, Abbott argues that the comics and television series are in dialogue with each other, a self-reflexive and self-referential system that reminds audiences about the "aesthetic challenges" posed by each medium. Abbott argues that not only do the comics refer back to and re-work the closing moments of Season Five's "Not Fade Away," but the reference process visually extends back to the opening episode from Season One, thereby complicating and intensifying the narrative intertextuality that is spread across the entire Angelverse, not just the final season, which at first glance appears to be the closest narrative arc to connect with *Angel: After the Fall*.

As Whedon studies continues to grow as both an academic pursuit and popular activity, we hope that *Angel* scholars particularly will find this collection of essays exploring literature and Joss Whedon's *Angel* a useful beginning for new questions as well as an answer to current questions about archetypes, narratives and identity, theory and philosophy, and genre. Like Team Angel who refuse to "fade away" from the L.A. they have established over five seasons of experience and growth, we expect the same will be said of *Angel* scholars who approach the series with a critical eye. In the words of the character who inspired fans and scholars alike, "Let's go to work."

Notes

1. "Players," *Angel*, DVD, written by Jeffrey Bell, Sarah Fain, and Elizabeth Craft, directed by Michael Grossman (2003; 20th Century–Fox, 2004).
2. "Through the Looking Glass," *Angel*, DVD, written and directed by Tim Minear (2001; 20th Century–Fox, 2003).
3. "Awakening," *Angel*, DVD, written by David Fury and Steven S. DeKnight, directed by James A. Contner (2003; 20th Century–Fox, 2004).
4. Stacey Abbott, *Angel*, TV Milestones Series (Detroit: Wayne State University Press, 2009), 90–95.
5. "A New World," *Angel*, DVD, written by Jeffrey Bell, directed by Tim Minear (2002; 20th Century–Fox, 2003).
6. "Slouching Toward Bethlehem," *Angel*, DVD, written by Jeffrey Bell, directed by Skip Schoolnik (2002; 20th Century–Fox, 2004).
7. "Soulless," *Angel*, DVD, written by Sarah Fain and Elizabeth Craft, directed by Sean Astin (2003; 20th Century–Fox, 2004); "She," *Angel*, DVD, written by David Greenwalt and Marti Noxon, directed by David Greenwalt (2000; 20th Century–Fox, 2002); "Carpe Noctem," *Angel*, DVD, written by Scott Murphy, directed by James A. Contner (2001; 20th Century–Fox, 2003).
8. Stacey Abbott, ed., *Reading* Angel: *The TV Spin-off with a Soul* (London: I.B. Tauris, 2005).
9. Stacey Abbott, *Angel*.
10. "City of," *Angel*, DVD, written and directed by Joss Whedon (1999; 20th Century–Fox, 2002); "Not Fade Away," *Angel*, DVD, written by Joss Whedon and Jeffrey Bell, directed by Jeffrey Bell (2004; 20th Century–Fox, 2004).
11. "The Depths of *Angel*," *Reading* Angel: *The TV Spin-Off with a Soul*, ed. Stacey Abbott (London: I.B. Tauris, 2005), 221–229 at 229. In the article Wilcox and Lavery give several statistics about the beginnings of scholarly work on *Buffy* in relation to the small attention paid to *Angel*.
12. Ibid., 229.
13. David Lavery, "The Allusions of Television," *Flow* 3, no. 10, http://davidlavery.net/writings/Television/Flow/Allusions_of_TV.pdf; Lavery attributes the phrase "fund of knowledge" to M. H. Abrams, quoting him at length as explaining that literary allusions "imply a fund of knowledge that is shared by an author and his audience" (*A Glossary of Literary Terms*, 5th ed. [New York: Holt, Rinehart, and Winston, 1970]); and he attributes "the conversations of mankind" to Richard Rorty, *Philosophy and the Mirror of Nature* [Princeton: Princeton University Press, 1981]).

One : Archetypes

Barney: You know, I just noticed it's 3:45 in the afternoon. If you're a vampire, why aren't you in your coffin?
Angel: Coffin. I hate that stereotype. You're a demon and you don't know anything about vampires?
Barney: Only what I learned from TV.

—"Parting Gifts"

Biting Humor
Harmony, Parody, and the Female Vampire
LORNA JOWETT

The way vampires blur boundaries (between life and death, for example) affords great potential for exploding fixed categories of identity, such as gender and sexuality. However, the female vampire has remained remarkably stereotyped, despite the nuances drawn out of different representations by previous scholarship. Deriving from "real life" vampires like Countess Elizabeth Bathory and a long line of vampire fictions, almost anyone knows how the female vampire is characterized: powerful, seductive, dangerous. Psychoanalytic theory suggests that the female vampire is abject and monstrous; she is frequently described as both masculinized and highly sexualized and is often lesbian or bisexual. These elements are developed from literary representations beginning with Sheridan LeFanu's novella *Carmilla* (1872) and the better-known Bram Stoker's *Dracula* (1897) and continuing onwards in a wide range of films depicting female vampires from Hammer's schlocky *The Vampire Lovers* (1970) to independent movie *Nadja* (1994).[1] Barbara Creed argues that the female vampire is a version of the monstrous-feminine and "driven by her lust for blood, she does not respect the dictates of the law which set down the rules of proper sexual conduct."[2] Thus for Creed, the female vampire has the potential to disrupt "the formal and highly symbolic relations of men and women essential to the continuation of patriarchal society"[3]; indeed this is why she is depicted as monstrous, though her monstrosity is also her attraction as a transgressive figure. Certainly, LeFanu's *Carmilla* lays the foundation for the female vampire's lesbian sexuality; Stoker's character Lucy Westenra in *Dracula* provides a template for her monstrosity. The female vampire, as exemplified by Lucy, "undergoes many transformations (from good to bad, from weak to strong, from victim to predator, and from pure to sexual),"[4] thereby inverting stereotypes of femininity.

This much is common knowledge to vampire scholars and fans. Similarly, any horror fan knows that horror and comedy are closely related. Theory explains this in terms of the carnivalesque, the grotesque, or transgression and subversion, all of which feature as regularly in comedy as in horror. Horror films have often contained humor and there has been a long tradition of horror-comedy (like *Shaun of the Dead*, 2004) and comedy-horror (such as *Dracula: Dead and Loving It*, 1995).[5] Horror on television operates rather differently than on film and, perhaps, draws on humor more consistently to achieve its effects and success with its audience. Television drama, like serial fiction, also has more room for extra, peripheral characters and for development of its characters than a one-off cinematic release or classic novel, enabling it more scope to use both comedy and horror as ways of offering new stories or angles on a familiar premise and cast.

Although there are various ways horror might incorporate humor, which is an obvious characteristic in shows like *Buffy the Vampire Slayer* and *Angel*, Stacey Abbott notes that there has been surprisingly little discussion of comedy in *Buffy* and *Angel*. Perhaps this is because of value judgments about the nature of comedy and tragedy, judgments that go back to the inception of literary criticism and mean that comedy has not always been named or recognized as such in order to assign it some artistic value. David Marc notes, for instance, that "comedy has certainly been valued and admired by critics when 'properly' presented as drama, satiric poetry, or (in recent times) the novel," and in terms of cinema, Andrew Horton observes that comedies never win Academy Awards despite their box office success.[6] Such comments serve to explain why even with such a hybrid form as television drama and with shows like *Buffy* and *Angel*, which draw on action, fantasy, horror, science fiction, and melodrama, critics and scholars have chosen to focus on more "serious" elements in order to elevate the importance of the text as a form of "quality" television.[7]

In today's popular fictions, and perhaps especially in television drama, it is increasingly the case that "any plot is potentially comic, melodramatic, or tragic, or perhaps all three at once"[8] and much mainstream drama incorporates comic moments, comic lines, comic characters, and even whole comic episodes. *Buffy* and *Angel* do all of these things, using comedy for tonal variation (lightening the mood), or for sheer entertainment (Wilcox and Lavery note how *Angel* managed to deliver some highly memorable comic moments in its five-year run[9]), but here humor additionally functions to underline thematic issues. Thus in her discussion of Wesley, Angel, and masculinity, Abbott argues that in *Angel* "comedy allows for a space in which the conventions of masculinity can be undermined, challenged and redefined."[10] Parody is a type of comedy that makes fun of conventions, and Abbott's discussion of Wesley demonstrates how it is used to deconstruct masculinity. Here, a slightly different form of parody will be explored through the character of Harmony. Harmony is funny because she does not act like a conventional vampire, much like Spike. But Harmony does not act like a conventional *female* vampire, mainly because she acts too much like another stereotypical female, the dumb blonde.

On YouTube a montage found at the time of writing encapsulates this perfectly (in the spirit of *Angel*'s karaoke bar, Caritas, you can even sing along).[11] Like much of the content on YouTube, this brings together clips and images of a specific character from the show with music providing structure or meaning.[12] In conflating images of human Harmony and vampire Harmony, and moments from both *Buffy* and *Angel*, the clip presents Harmony as a dumb blonde using key images and its chosen song (Julie Brown's "Cause I'm a Blonde"), neatly showing in around two minutes exactly how her character has been defined and constructed through this stereotype. This montage highlights how comedy is about what Steve Neale and Frank Krutnik refer to as the deformation of stereotype.[13] Clearly all kinds of comedy from satire to sitcom use stereotypes and self-consciously present them *as* stereotypes. Along similar lines, Steve Wilson notes that a show like *Buffy* "lampoon[s] the clichés it embraces," both perpetuating and mocking those clichés or conventions.[14] Of course, genre works rather like this too, since certain conventions must be apparent for a text to be identified as part of a genre (vampires only go out at night, for instance), even if these are revised as a means of producing novelty and development (many recent vampire fictions from action movie *Blade*, 1998, to teen Gothic romance *Twilight*, 2005 and 2008, explain that vampires might be able to move around during the day so long as they are not exposed to direct sunlight).[15] Genre fictions are thus easy to parody since there are already a set of conventions structuring the narrative that can be attacked, mocked, or subverted.

A character like Harmony, who appears in *Buffy* and in Seasons Two and Five of *Angel*, is both a stereotype (of the dumb blonde) and a direct challenge to a stereotype (the female vampire). While Harmony may superficially resemble Lucy from *Dracula*, in that both are privileged beauties who thrive on male attention, Harmony's transformation into a vampire has none of the high contrast that characterizes Lucy's. On the contrary, through the comic figure of Harmony, the typical female vampire's power, competence, and seductive nature are overturned, and the combination of adherence to type and subversion of convention that her character embodies allows *Buffy* and *Angel* to reveal another side to the glamorous, outsider icon of the vampire. As a vampire who is also a dumb blonde, Harmony exposes the conventional masquerade of femininity, what Kathleen Rowe describes as the distance between the woman and the feminized gestures that are understood to denote or construct gender.[16] Many of the examples Rowe discusses in her examination of "unruly women" in popular culture display excessiveness, a feature of both the comedy and horror genres and one that provides entertainment and, in visual media, spectacle for the reader/audience. This may position such characters as somewhat problematic since an excessive and unruly female like Miss Piggy from *The Muppet Show* "provides the occasion for laughter at women. Yet at the same time, she mobilizes laughter against the posturing and illusoriness of a femininity that encourages such silliness as diminutive names ('Piggy') and girlish ways for full-sized, fully grown women. It is this masquerade more than the feisty and funny 'woman' who plays it that she renders ridiculous."[17] Vampire Harmony is no more a "real" woman than Miss Piggy, and the markers of extreme femininity that surround her (pink and pastel clothing, the collection of unicorns, a childish voice and language) are juxtaposed with her vampire strength, bloodlust, and narcissism which contrast the passivity, softness, and self-sacrifice of stereotypical femininity. Horton describes the comic mode as "plural, unfinalized, disseminative, dependent on context and the intertextuality of creator, text and contemplator. It is not ... just the content of comedy that is significant but also its 'conspiratorial' relationship with the viewer (reader)."[18] Indeed, Harmony is not necessarily unruly in her actions, unlike many of the characters Rowe discusses. Rather unruliness or subversive comedy arises from the collision of stereotypes and conventions that is highlighted for the viewer by the way her character is presented, thus forging exactly the kind of intertextuality Horton identifies. In this way, she consistently contributes to key themes of power, otherness, gender, and sexuality on *Angel*.

"Cover the boring stuff": Harmony and the Female Vampire

An integral aspect of the vampire as classic and contemporary icon is alienation. In older literary and film texts, the vampire was an outcast from society, a monster, if an alluring one. The "lure of the vampire" so effectively described by Milly Williamson in her book of that title becomes, in more contemporary representations that focus on vampire subjectivity, the lure of the outsider. In situating the vampire as deriving from more than one literary tradition, Williamson notes how this alienation works in conjunction with gender ambiguity: "sympathy and personal rebellion are the twin attractions in the construction of the vampire for the surrounding fan culture. However, while the vampire's rebellion draws on bohemian themes, its sympathy is structured as pathos, which is as much derived from the heroine of the Gothic novel and melodrama, as from the bohemian outcast. Rice's vampires, like the heroine of the Gothic novel ... suffer from circumstances they did not choose even if, at times, they revel in their outsiderdom."[19] Thus the vampire tends to be a marginal figure whose very marginality is appealing; vampires from Dracula, through Rice's Louis and Lestat, to action hero Blade are presented as the liminal Other, the lone wolf.

Harmony is *so* not cut out to be a lone wolf: she is a sheep, a follower, not a leader. In *Buffy* she was one of the Cordettes, part of Cordelia's high school in-crowd, and the desire to fit in, to conform, persists after she becomes a vampire. When she tries to set herself up as "totally Buffy's archnemesis" in Season Five of *Buffy*,[20] it is a failure because Harmony has none of the qualities or competence required of a leader. Yet her vanity will not allow her to become a henchvamp, the obvious position for a vampire who is not a leader (these appear in vampire novels and movies as well as on television and function like the red-shirted crew members of the 1960s television show *Star Trek*; disposable nobodies, stake fodder). Harmony still wants to be somebody.

But Harmony's desire to fit in does not negate the conventional alienation of the vampire, especially since she is a *female* vampire. Key scenes of female bonding with Cordy when Harmony enters *Angel* in "Disharmony" (2.17) turn around the usual alienation of the vampire, converting it into the nostalgia of someone whose best years were in high school, as Harmony also mentions in Season Five.[21] "Disharmony" is partly designed to establish how much Cordelia has changed since high school, how she has largely abandoned her selfishness and vanity and her ambitions of fame and wealth for the satisfaction of helping the helpless.[22] Harmony clearly cannot quite grasp this change, but tells Cordelia, "You've got friends. I don't have anyone who understands what I'm going through." The fact that Cordelia does not know at this point that Harm is now a vampire suggests that Harmony is alienated *because* she is a vampire, and in "Harm's Way" (5.09) she articulates this clearly to Fred (Winifred), in another girl-to-girl chat, telling her that she used to be "way popular" in high school but admitting, "since I got vamped at my graduation, I've had trouble connecting with people."[23] Visually, this is often conveyed through images of Harmony isolated among other Wolfram & Hart employees in the break room (as in "Harm's Way") or via long shots of her at the reception desk outside Angel's office.

This can be read as the typical self-involvement of the immortal vampire, which some critics have interpreted as a form of narcissism (Rob Latham suggests that contemporary vampire stories work by "conflating relations based on voyeurism, narcissism, and homoeroticism with specifically consumerist desires and pleasures"; lesbianism has also been read as narcissism, as mentioned by Creed).[24] Angel and Spike, vampires with souls, are Champions because they try to help others. Harmony apparently never thinks of others before herself, and this is partly explained by the fact that she has no soul, that is, she is a typical vampire. When she asks Fred for advice in interacting with men, Fred tells her to ask about work and interests. "Cover the boring stuff," Harmony responds immediately and Fred winces at her self-centeredness, advising that she pretend it is not boring.[25] Significantly, Harm's girl time with Cordy in "Disharmony" is about pampering and image: they are shown in fluffy robes with towels round their hair and later manicuring each other's nails.

Here, the narcissism of the vampire is conflated with the narcissism or, arguably, the necessary image maintenance of the female (the masquerade of femininity) and the result is not alienation but bonding. Other female vampires, like LeFanu's Carmilla, also attempt to form bonds with women: Carmilla develops a relationship with Laura and, as Nina Auerbach argues, this is something that seems to distinguish her from later male vampires: "everything male vampires seem to promise, Carmilla performs: she arouses, she pervades, she offers a sharing self."[26] The story's domestic setting lends itself to this female bonding, though it can also be read as sexualized, and Auerbach acknowledges the "erotic, interpenetrative" nature of these female attachments,[27] elements that are heightened in subsequent female vampires. Thus while Carmilla and Laura spend time brushing each other's hair, it is hard to imagine the glamorous Miriam Blaylock from *The Hunger* (1981 and 1983) in a fluffy purple robe or painting her chosen partner Sarah's toenails.[28] Their female bonding is more intense, more serious, and more sexualized, in line with the now established conventions of the female vampire. Based on LeFanu's novella, the film *The Vampire Lovers* includes an early scene where Carmilla shares girl time with her latest victim, offering sophisticated dresses for the naïve country mouse to try. Here, though, it is an excuse for a topless bedroom chase scene, the lesbian desire of the vampire displayed as titillation for the audience. Of course, the bonding between Harmony and Cordelia can be read in this way too, especially given what happens next.

In *Sex and the Slayer*, I suggested that in *Buffy* vamp Harmony displays an enhanced sexuality, like other female vampires,[29] and this is achieved through her brief relationship with Spike. On *Angel*, however, Harmony is positioned more ambivalently. Her entrance into the show deliberately invokes the conventions of the female vampire as lesbian predator and plays on the audience's knowledge and characters' ignorance that Harmony is now a vampire. She appears in Season Four of *Buffy* as a vampire, having been vamped at graduation in the Season Three finale, so characters in *Buffy* know she is now a vampire, but Cordelia, having left Sunnydale after graduation, is none the wiser. Thus, when, in "Disharmony," Harmony appears at the premises of Angel Investigations and is reunited with Cordelia, regular viewers of *Buffy* already know that Harmony is a vampire (the "previously on" segment does not remind us, however). Delighted to see her old friend, Cordy invites Harm to stay at her apartment and they spend an evening reliving shared happy memories. On retiring to bed, Harmony enters Cordy's bedroom and stares at her friend's neck, licking her lips. When the door slams unexpectedly (helped by resident ghost Dennis, Cordelia's self-appointed protector) Cordelia confronts Harmony and a major comic misunderstanding ensues as Harmony apologizes for not being able to control her "urges" in the face of her "luscious" friend. Cordelia reprimands Harmony for thinking her "narrow-minded" when she confesses that she thought Cordy would react violently if she admitted "what I was," but they agree that this incident will remain their "secret."

The scene immediately following shows Cordelia mid-call to Sunnydale, asking why she was never told "about Harmony" complete with ensuing confusion about whether Harmony is a lesbian or a vampire. Given that Cordelia is talking to Willow, who has recently come out as a lesbian on *Buffy*, the comic misunderstanding works on all kinds of levels, as when Willow clarifies that

Harmony is a vampire and Cordy responds, "Oh, my God, I'm so embarrassed! All this time I thought she was a great big lesbo!— Really?— Well, that's great! Good for you." The joke here is that Harmony is *not* a lesbian vampire, yet elsewhere in the show the language of homosexuality continues to be used to refer to vampirism, as when she tells Fred in "Harm's Way" that the men they can see in the bar are all "straight. Non-vamps," and therefore not her type.[30] Ken Gelder has suggested that across literary and other representations, the secret of the vampire parallels the secret of homosexuality.[31] Arguably Harmony is queer because of her vampire sexuality, even when she is feminized and heterosexualized; again she is both atypical and typical. Gelder notes that the vampire myth "involves a narrative structure which depends upon the tension between knowing and not knowing, recognition and secrecy — where the vampire both 'stands out' ... and mingles unobtrusively,"[32] and Harmony epitomizes this, highlighted from her very first appearance on *Angel*.

In *Angel*, Harmony is again heterosexualized via Spike, telling him, when he suggests that returning alive from his heroic self-sacrifice (in the series finale of *Buffy*) will dampen the possibility of reuniting with Buffy, "Girls don't care about stuff like that. Just one look at you, and she'll forget herself, and she'll get all tingly, and it won't matter how horribly you treated her in the past and how you took her for granted, and —" at which point Spike, with the typical self-involvement of the (male?) vampire, continues to talk about Buffy until he belatedly realizes that Harmony is describing how she feels about him.[33] When Spike is recorporealized in "Destiny," one of his first acts is to kiss Harmony, and tell Angel he needs to "borrow" her.[34] While Harm starts to protest, "You think that just because —" she trails off and is soon persuaded to leave with Spike.[35] This speedy acquiescence may involve the fulfillment of her own desire, but nevertheless Spike is the active agent who instigates their physical relationship. He uses Harmony without acknowledgement and her sexuality is reinscribed here as passive, in contrast to the active domination of the typical female vampire. Subsequently, Hamilton, the high-powered liaison to Wolfram & Hart's Senior Partners, also uses Harmony sexually, presumably as a way to get to Angel at the end of Season Five. Here too, Harmony is shown to enjoy the physicality of their relationship (during the fleeting glimpse offered of them together she sucks his thumb sensually),[36] but Hamilton's status with the firm suggests that he is in charge. There is a further moral aspect to their relationship since it leads to Harmony's betrayal of Angel, though Angel lets her go before his showdown fight with Hamilton. In doing so, Roz Kaveney suggests that "he judges her according to her nature, both as vampire and as selfish child, rather than for her personal betrayal."[37] Harmony's selfish vampire nature cannot encompass the self-sacrifice of the conventional loyal and supportive personal assistant (PA), a self-sacrifice that is part of conventional femininity, seen as an adjunct to active, achieving masculinity.

"Something in a rodent": Normalization and the Dumb Blonde

It is already clear that using stereotypes, whether of the female vampire or the dumb blonde, in Harmony's character construction is partly about familiarity and normalization. Comedy in the classical sense was considered to be low (in comparison to high tragedy or other forms) because it deals with ordinary people. Harmony, like other vampire or demon characters in *Buffy* and especially in *Angel*, normalizes the vampire, makes it ordinary and she does it through comedy as much as through becoming a regular character in Season Five (Mercedes McNab as Harmony was included in the show's opening credit sequence as a regular beginning with "Underneath," 5.17).[38] Notably, we never see her bite or feed on a human: though she kills Tamika in "Harm's Way" this is allowable because Tamika is a vampire who is framing her for murder, plus killing her saves an important demon summit from breaking down by fulfilling cultural customs that demand a sacrifice before proceeding to negotiation.[39] Nikki Stafford observes that throughout Season Five Mercedes McNab does a "great job of maintaining the comic element of the series while being a constant thorn in Angel's side."[40] In this sense, she also normalizes Angel by being his annoyingly cheerful and incompetent assistant ("You're the boss, Boss!"[41]), and it is largely through their interactions that his dark hero status comes into conflict with his positioning as just another perpetually grumpy high-powered CEO.

Both the comedy and the normalization are partly achieved through Harm's stupidity, the dumbness of the dumb blonde contrasting sharply with the heightened instincts and rapier wit of the conventional vampire. "The dumb blonde," Rowe argues, "domesticates the earlier unruly heroine by tying her out-of-bounds behavior to dimness rather than to liberating eccentricity or disregard for convention," and Stafford suggests that in contrast to the bitchy Cordelia, "Harmony is as clueless as Anya was on *Buffy*, and she doesn't realize she's actually insulting people,"[42] as when she identifies listening to men talk about their work or hobbies as "cover[ing] the boring stuff." Still, Harmony's dumbness, however it distinguishes her from other plain-speaking characters in *Buffy* and *Angel*, allows her to say things that might be otherwise considered tactless or painful, and since they are mostly true, she is a wise fool. Neal and Krutnik, drawing on Aristotle's theory of comedy, ascribe this foolish truth-speaking to "comic insulation" where "ugliness" and "error" become comedy and therefore painless, and, similarly, Rowe suggests that "Like the fool figure, the dumb blonde can enjoy a supreme detachment from the world."[43] Thus in "Life of the Party," Harmony is the only character prepared to tell Angel that most of the Wolfram & Hart employees think he "sucks" as their CEO, perhaps because of Angel's own alienation — always a feature and often parodied itself. Harmony, despite her self-centeredness, takes a more professional attitude and at least knows colleagues' names, even when they don't know hers (as with vampire employee Eli in "Harm's Way").[44]

Minor characters thus clearly allow for multiple points of view, providing other angles on more central characters, as already described, in a strategy typical of ensemble cast television and some types of serial fiction. Even during her first appearance on the show in "Disharmony," Harm alerts Angel to truths about his existence as a "good" vampire. Having offered her pig's blood ("that's gonna go straight to my hips") she asks him how he can stand it, offering a sensual description of drinking human blood ("rich, warm, human blood — flowing into your mouth — bathing your tongue — caressing your throat with its sweet, sticky—") that mesmerizes Angel until Gunn's entrance snaps him out of it. Harmony both is and is not a normal vampire; Angel clearly is not (and is).[45] Here Harmony's conventional nature highlights his difference, demonstrating that he is still attracted to the physicality of vampire feeding, while choosing to forgo it for moral reasons. (Later the whole plot of "Harm's Way" revolves around whether Harmony is off the wagon regarding the No Human Blood policy enforced by Angel at Wolfram & Hart). At times this shift in perspective allows the tone to diverge from comedy. Following Spike's casual "borrowing" of Harmony for sex, she turns on him with vampire aggression and tells him some home truths: "You! You don't want me! You want your slayer whore! I'll kill you!"[46] That this happens under magical influence makes it no less true, and it allows a startling glimpse below the surface of her acquiescence to Spike's attitude, even as her "cover the boring stuff" comment exposes as tedious the convention of the supportive, listening female: the conjunction of vampire and dumb blonde subverts gender stereotypes.

The vampire's bloodlust is part of its physicality and, along with the sexualization of female vampires, means that they are often depicted, even in the nineteenth century, as having high "vitality" and "corporeality," as Auerbach notes[47] as seen, for example, in Stoker's Lucy. This inevitably overturns feminine passivity and makes the female vampire physically active as well as sensual. Perhaps especially in visual forms like film and television, the vampire is involved in action and violence and, increasingly, female vampires take on these roles. Harmony is both differentiated from and aligned with typical vampires in these respects too. She admits she is bad at being bad ("I tried being out on my own, all independent and evil. I'm just no good at it," she tells Fred in "Harm's Way"). Yet on *Angel* she graduates from the hilarious slap fighting we see in Season Four of *Buffy* (included in the YouTube montage),[48] a scene designed to undercut opponent Xander's masculinity as well as Harmony's status as a super-strong vampire: the parody is intensified by the use of slow motion. "Harm's Way" gives us a very different extended fight scene with Tamika, the jealous co-worker who tries to frame Harmony for murder-by-vampire-feeding, allowing Harm to show off her vampire strength and fighting skill. This slips into parody at various points, though, as when they strike martial arts poses with their chopstick-stakes.

Comic parody here allows the masquerade of femininity to become visible, highlighted by the ease with which Harmony moves from a day at the office as Angel's perky and supportive PA to a life and death struggle involving smashed furniture and a staking in the board room. In her fascinating discussion of Miss Piggy, Rowe notes that "Miss Piggy only barely conceals the power, coarseness, and aggressiveness of her physicality beneath a simpering and submissive mask of femininity, which she drops the moment her own interests are threatened."[49] As a vampire, Harmony at times functions in almost exactly the same way. Her lack of a soul and enjoyment of physicality make her useful to Team Angel: in two episodes she is ready to torture information out of characters on their behalf,[50] a moral loophole that tells us much about the compromises the team makes in becoming Wolfram & Hart, however comically conveyed.

Stafford suggests that "like Xander, Harmony is never appreciated by the others for the work she does every day, even though she deals with all the little things so the rest of them don't have to."[51] Despite her apparent self-involvement, she does this often, as when she distracts the Fell Brethren from Angel's late arrival by persuading them to accept "organic cola" while waiting, or when she explains the No Human Blood policy to the vampire aide of an important client, offering him "something in a rodent" and recommending the "fruity, unassuming vole."[52] Professionally, then, Harmony does think about and work for others. In these instances, she contrasts Angel, who overlooks Harmony's efforts as his employee, while Lorne fosters his PA (foregrounded in "Harm's Way"). Both Kaveney and Meyer point out that Harmony is the only one who visits Gunn in the hospital after an unwitting bargain he strikes leads to Fred's death,[53] even showing him compassion, though arguably her visit is simultaneously a sign of her low status since she tells him she has "stuff you need to sign."[54]

It is surely no coincidence that Harmony becomes a regular character in Season Five, which is all about little people and power/lessness. "Harm's Way," the episode focused on Harmony that Stafford compares to *Buffy*'s "The Zeppo" because it follows the path of a minor character while others are involved in more "important" action,[55] starts with a promo spot for the made-over Wolfram & Hart. This explains the Zero Tolerance policy on vampire behavior that will be important to the narrative but it also reinforces corporate mentality and the disposability of employees. If Harmony is proved to have killed the man she finds in her bed, she would be a victim, not just of Wolfram & Hart but specifically of Angel's adoption of corporate policy. The episode reveals that she was plucked from the steno pool to be Angel's PA, and while it ends with Spike reminding Harmony that she must matter if someone cared enough to kill her, it persistently shows how she is ignored by everyone higher up and seems to lead directly to her betrayal of Angel to Hamilton in the final episode. Kaveney notes that "Angel's decision to spare her to pursue what might be her redemption is based partly on recognition of the lost humanity they have in common, and on a ruler's sense of justice,"[56] though it also proves that she is so insignificant she is allowed to live every time she is caught, even after a major betrayal.

The Last Laugh?

The constant evocation and subversion of stereotype in Harmony demonstrates exactly the kind of active intertextuality Horton identifies as typical of the comic mode. She is still the butt of jokes on *Angel*, as she was on *Buffy*, but here the way she operates as a foil to the title character is fundamentally changed. Angel's overly-serious demeanor means that he also functions as the object of humor much of the time, and some of the recurring jokes at his expense focus on vampire conventions (such as sexuality or image), just as with Harmony. As an ordinary vampire (one without a soul) Harmony is a perfect contrast to Angel. As a female vampire she is a refreshing, comic change to the convention of the powerful, threatening dominatrix. To laugh at Harmony is to laugh at the conventions of both the female vampire and the dumb blonde. As Rowe noted of other excessive female characters, our laughter may not be entirely untroubled by the gendered nature of these stereotypes, but *Angel* exposes the stereotypes *as* conventions—laughable ones. The death of Harmony's predecessor Lucy in *Dracula* is one of the novel's most memorable and debated scenes. Lucy's tragic transformation established the female vampire as a monster whose transgressive nature requires punishment. Comic Harmony is able to parody these conventions of genre and morality and get away with it. When Angel allows her to leave Wolfram & Hart in the final episode, he even tells her (after she asks) that he has written her a recommendation so she can find another job. The very fact that she lives, provides the last laugh.

Notes

1. James B. Twitchell reconstructs a lineage of the female vampire that includes earlier works like Coleridge's unfinished poem "Christabel" and John Keats's "Lamia." See James B. Twitchell, *The Living Dead: A Study of the Vampire in Romantic Literature* (Durham: Duke University Press, 1981). *The Vampire Lovers*, directed by Roy Ward Baker (1970); *Nadja*, directed by Michael Almereyda (1994).
2. Barbara Creed, *The Monstrous-Feminine: Film, Feminism, Psychoanalysis* (London: Routledge, 1993), 61.
3. Ibid.
4. Lorna Jowett, *Sex and the Slayer* (Middleton: Wesleyan University Press, 2005), 71.
5. *Shaun of the Dead*, directed by Edgar Wright (2004); *Dracula: Dead and Loving It*, directed by Mel Brooks (1995).

6. David Marc, *Comic Visions: Television Comedy and American Culture*, 2d ed. (Malden, MA: Blackwell, 1997), 14; Andrew Horton, ed., *Comedy/ Cinema/ Theory* (Berkeley: University of California Press, 1991), 2.

7. "Quality" here is used to refer to certain characteristic markers, not as a term indicating value. "Quality" television is often described as being literary, partly because it usually involves serial narrative, complex plots, and detailed, sustained development of character and theme, among other elements. See, for instance, Jane Feuer et al., ed., *MTM Quality Television* (London: BFI, 1985); Robert J. Thompson, *Television's Second Golden Age: From Hill Street Blues to ER* (Syracuse: Syracuse University Press, 1997); Mark Jancovich and James Lyons, ed., *Quality Popular Television* (London: BFI, 2003); Janet McCabe and Kim Akass, ed., *Quality TV: Contemporary American Television and Beyond* (London: I. B. Tauris, 2007).

8. Horton, *Comedy/ Cinema/ Theory*, 1.

9. Rhonda V. Wilcox and David Lavery, "Afterword: The Depth of *Angel* and the Birth of *Angel* Studies," in *Reading* Angel*: The TV Spin-off with a Soul*, ed. Stacey Abbott (London: I.B. Tauris, 2005), 221–29 at 223.

10. Stacey Abbott, "'Nobody Scream ... or Touch My Arms': The Comic Stylings of Wesley Wyndam-Pryce," in *Reading* Angel*: The TV Spin-off with a Soul*, ed. Stacey Abbott (London: I.B. Tauris, 2005), 189–202 at 201.

11. "Cause I'm a Blonde — Harmony," YouTube, http://www.youtube.com/watch?v=xD85NlE5blw (accessed May 2009).

12. Here, a few diegetic sounds remain on the audio track for comic emphasis, such as the beeping alarm clock it opens with and the cigarette smoke–induced coughing that wraps it up.

13. Steve Neale and Frank Krutnik, *Popular Film and Television Comedy* (London: Routledge, 1990), 92.

14. Steve Wilson, "'Laugh, Spawn of Hell, Laugh,'" in *Reading the Vampire Slayer*, ed. Roz Kaveney (London: I. B. Tauris, 2001), 78–97 at 89.

15. *Blade*, directed by Stephen Norrington (1998); the novel *Twilight*, by Stephenie Meyer (2005), the film of the novel, directed by Catherine Hardwicke (2008).

16. Kathleen Rowe, *The Unruly Woman: Gender and the Genres of Laughter* (Austin: University of Texas Press, 1995), 6.

17. Ibid., 30. *The Muppet Show* (1976–81).

18. Horton, *Comedy/Cinema/Theory*, 9.

19. Milly Williamson, *The Lure of the Vampire* (London: Wallflower, 2005), 39.

20. "Out of My Mind," *Buffy the Vampire Slayer*, DVD, written by Rebecca Rand Kirshner, directed by David Grossman (2000; 20th Century–Fox, 2002).

21. "Disharmony," *Angel*, DVD, written by David Fury, directed by Fred Keller (2001; 20th Century–Fox, 2003).

22. For more on this, see Janine Harrison, "Gender Politics in *Angel*: Traditional vs. Non-Traditional Corporate Climates," in *Reading* Angel*: The TV Spin-off with a Soul*, ed. Stacey Abbott (London: I.B. Tauris, 2005), 117–131 at 127.

23. "Harm's Way," *Angel*, DVD, written by Sarah Fain and Elizabeth Craft, directed by Vern Gillum (2004; 20th Century–Fox, 2004).

24. Rob Latham, *Consuming Youth: Vampire, Cyborgs, & the Culture of Consumption* (Chicago: University of Chicago Press, 2002), 100; Creed, *The Monstrous-Feminine*, 69.

25. "Harm's Way."

26. Nina Auerbach, *Our Vampires, Our Selves* (Chicago: University of Chicago Press, 1995), 38.

27. Ibid., 39.

28. The novel *The Hunger* by Whitley Strieber (1981); the film directed by Tony Scott (1983).

29. Jowett, *Sex and the Slayer*, 83.

30. "Harm's Way."

31. Ken Gelder, *Reading the Vampire* (New York: Routledge, 1994), 63; see also Auerbach on the use of the homosexual euphemism "strange" to describe the relationship between Carmilla and Laura, *Our Vampires*, 40.

32. Gelder, *Reading the Vampire*, 63.

33. "Harm's Way."
34. "Destiny," *Angel*, DVD, written by David Fury and Steven S. DeKnight, directed by Skip Schoolnik (2003; 20th Century–Fox, 2004).
35. Ibid.
36. "Not Fade Away," *Angel*, DVD, written by Joss Whedon and Jeffrey Bell, directed by Jeffrey Bell (2004; 20th Century–Fox, 2004).
37. Roz Kaveney, "A Sense of the Ending: Schrodinger's *Angel*," in *Reading* Angel*: The TV Spin-off with a Soul*, ed. Stacey Abbott (London: I.B. Tauris, 2005), 57–72 at 69.
38. "Underneath," *Angel*, DVD, written by Sarah Fain and Elizabeth Craft, directed by Skip Schoolnik (2004; 20th Century–Fox, 2004).
39. "Harm's Way."
40. Nikki Stafford, *Once Bitten* (Toronto: ECW Press, 2004), 296.
41. "Power Play," *Angel*, DVD, written by David Fury, directed by James A. Contner (2004; 20th Century–Fox, 2004).
42. Rowe, *Unruly Woman*, 176; Stafford, *Once Bitten*, 312.
43. Neal and Krutnik, *Popular Film and Television Comedy*, 69; Rowe, *Unruly Woman*, 176.
44. "Life of the Party," *Angel*, DVD, written by Ben Edlund, directed by Bill Norton (2003; 20th Century–Fox, 2004); "Harm's Way."
45. "Disharmony."
46. "Destiny."
47. Auerbach, *Our Vampires*, 49.
48. "The Initiative," *Buffy the Vampire Slayer*, DVD, written by Douglas Petrie, directed by James A. Contner (1999; 20th Century–Fox, 2002).
49. Rowe, *Unruly Woman*, 29.
50. "You're Welcome," *Angel*, DVD, written and directed by David Fury (2004; 20th Century–Fox, 2004), and "Shells," *Angel*, DVD, written and directed by Steven S. DeKnight (2004; 20th Century–Fox, 2004).
51. Stafford, *Once Bitten*, 310.
52. "Time Bomb," *Angel*, DVD, written by Ben Edlund, directed by Vern Gillum (2004; 20th Century–Fox, 2004); "Power Play."
53. Kaveney, "A Sense of the Ending," 61; Michaela D. E. Meyer, "From Rogue in the 'Hood to Suave in a Suit: Black Masculinity and the Transformation of Charles Gunn," in *Reading* Angel*: The TV Spin-off with a Soul,* ed. Stacey Abbott (London: I.B. Tauris, 2005), 176–88 at 184.
54. "Shells."
55. Stafford, *Once Bitten*; "The Zeppo," *Buffy the Vampire Slayer*, DVD, written by Dan Vebber, directed by James Whitmore Jr. (1999; 20th Century–Fox, 2002).
56. Kaveney, "A Sense of the Ending," 70.

Doyle as "The Passing Figure" and Nella Larsen's *Passing*

ANGEL ANDERSON

The good fight, yeah? You never know until you've been tested. I get that now.
— Doyle, "Hero"[1]

She wished to find out about this hazardous business of "passing," this breaking away from all that was familiar and friendly to take one's chance in another environment, not entirely strange, perhaps, but certainly not entirely friendly.
— Nella Larsen, *Passing*[2]

The boy turns to Doyle, the half-human, half-demon sidekick of the title character in *Angel*. The boy looks to be an average teenager, clad in jean jacket and backpack — all except for his raised cheekbones, prominent brow line, and clearly distinguishable pale green skin. "You wouldn't get it," Reef says bitterly, glaring into Doyle's human face, free of demon attributes.[3] "You're passing. My mother was the same way. You can walk down the street."[4] Reef then tells Doyle about the day he was finally able to go out with his mother, the day he could be out in the neighborhood with the other children. "You know what day it was?" Reef asks pointedly.[5] Doyle hesitates, despite knowing Reef's response immediately. After a moment, Doyle replies sadly, "It was Halloween."[6]

The physical differences characterized here between Doyle and Reef illustrate the physical markers that distinguish any race from another. Some markers, like the color of Reef's skin and prominent facial features in this instance, make it impossible for the bearer of these traits to pass for another race. Doyle struggles with a choice that people like Reef are not afforded; Doyle must decide, quite literally, which face he will wear.

Allen Francis Doyle is introduced in *Angel*'s pilot episode, a comical yet mysterious figure who delivers messages to Angel from The Powers That Be, higher beings that seek to direct Angel's heroic power. Despite Doyle's short-lived run in the series, his character left a lasting impact on the show; moreover, Doyle promises to leave a lasting impact on an American literary genre as well, through his act of passing, which links him to a long-standing history of cultural and racial difficulties in America. Beginning with the early literature of slave narratives, progressing through the Harlem Renaissance, and continuing beyond, writers have told stories about racial passing. Passing texts share many established tropes, several of which are laid out in Juda Bennett's *The Passing Figure: Racial Confusion in Modern American Literature*, which uses Nella Larsen's *Passing*, a novel about two women who struggle with the consequences of their racial identities, as the primary example.[7] Doyle's character exhibits each of the five standard tropes of a passing text, as outlined by Bennett, and, more importantly, offers an alternate ending for the traditionally tragic passing figure — one that portrays the passer as heroic, making it possible to embrace all aspects of the character's mixed heritage, rather than forcing the character to choose between the two. Furthermore, this chapter fills a long-standing void of critical scholarship on Doyle. While much attention has been given to Angel, to the series as a whole, and even to many other characters throughout the show's five seasons, little attention, if any, has been paid to Doyle and his character's unique complexities.

The term "passing" has a long history — one that defines and redefines both action and person. The original usage most likely comes from "the 'pass' given to slaves so that they might travel without being taken for runaways."[8] A person's ability to pass stems from a mixed heritage, which provides the opportunity for others to mistake them for a heritage of greater social privilege. Bennett stresses, however, that passing "refers more easily or logically to an 'act' than a person," clarifying the definition of passing as "that phenomenon of light-skinned blacks allowing and even encouraging people to mistake them for white."[9] While the initial idea of passing involved crossing the color line, other ideas and definitions of passing have formed over the decades, broadening the concept into areas that Elaine Ginsburg explores when she writes that passing involves a "move from a category of subordination and oppression to one of freedom and privilege."[10] It is the act of passing, then, that Doyle participates in, which allows others to assume he is fully human. Doyle may not lead a life of privilege as far as other humans are concerned, but living as human certainly has its perks over the life offered to those whose demon heritage marks them as visibly non-human.

As Doyle demonstrates, the situational act of passing is utilized in order to escape some form of social injustice and judgment, thereby becoming a performative act, since the role of an identity is assumed depending on the identity's potential reception. Doyle's passing is intriguing since he was not aware of his demon heritage until he turned twenty-one; therefore, he legitimately lives as human until that point. After discovering his demon characteristics, however, he continues to live as human and does nothing to persuade others to believe that he is anything other than human. In Doyle's case, this tactic only works for the human population since other demons can detect his demon blood. This situation identifies an important characteristic of passing, illustrating that passing relies on how the passer is perceived rather than how she or he may try to live. If Doyle were in the same situation as Reef, for example, he would not have the ability to pass because no one would mistake him for fully human.

Another aspect of passing, Bennett notes, "not only explores the strain of 'black' passing for 'white' but 'primitive' passing for 'civilized.'"[11] In *Passing*, Clare and Irene both pass in order to gain access to a lifestyle they could not participate in otherwise. Their chance meeting on the rooftop of the Drayton Hotel is a perfect example. This high-brow white restaurant does not serve blacks; however, because both Clare and Irene are fair enough, they can pass as white to enjoy the luxuries the Drayton Hotel has to offer. Doyle's life is certainly far from high-brow, but at least he does not wear a wreath of intestines around his head or ceremoniously eat the brains of his fiancé's former lover, both of which are depicted in *Angel* as primitive and barbaric customs of demon tribes.[12]

In order to fully examine Doyle in the act of passing, I will juxtapose him with Larsen's *Passing* using Bennett's five standard tropes as points of comparison. The first of Bennett's characteristics of a passing text is the use of a Manichean style, which deals in dualisms, presenting the world primarily in black and white.[13] The dualisms in *Angel* focus on good and evil, and, more specifically for Doyle, non-demon and demon. These binaries blend in Doyle's case, where "good" is synonymous to human, and "evil" is synonymous to demon. While the overall intention of the series seeks to obliterate these binaries, as the main hero of the show is a vampire, Doyle also destroys these binaries on a personal level through self-acceptance and harmony of both heritages.

In *Passing*, Larsen emphasizes both the importance of eye color and differences in skin color in order to complicate the ability to "read" race.[14] Irene studies Clare's dark eyes, and her pale skin, but still cannot determine Clare's racial identity. In their first meeting on the roof of the Drayton hotel, Irene wonders if the staring stranger (Clare) knows from a distance that Irene herself is passing. Irene finally concludes that Clare cannot know, since "white people were so stupid about such things for all that they usually asserted that they were able to tell; and by the most ridiculous means, finger-nails, palms of hands, shapes of ears, teeth, and other equally silly rot."[15] While Irene laughs at those who use such physical characteristics to determine race, she herself makes conjectures according to Clare's appearance. Ironically, she proves her own theory because, at first, she cannot tell that Clare is passing.

For Doyle, reading the demon race certainly seems an easier task. Green skin and spikes covering one's face tend to be significant clues. However, Doyle's ability to morph from human form to demon form, and do so largely voluntarily, further complicates the issue of reading race. When Angel first meets Doyle, Angel demonstrates other options for detecting race. Angel says, "You don't smell human," when Doyle first approaches him,[16] to which Doyle replies, "Well that's a bit rude. As it happens, I'm very much human," accompanied by a sneeze which causes his horns to appear, "on my mother's side."[17] Angel, who also displays human and demon attributes, uses his demon senses to detect other demons. Cordelia, however, does not share that luxury. Cordelia cannot "read" Doyle's racial heritage, despite her awareness that there is something different about Doyle. Because Doyle is interested in pursuing a relationship with Cordelia, he wants to hide his demon form from her out of fear that she might reject him. Cordelia does not help matters much in "Lonely Hearts" (1.02) when she exclaims, "Ugh! Demons! Is there anything more disgusting?"[18] Doyle's response provides insight into his difficulties with self-classification, since his first real statement about himself in the series declares himself as human first. He asks Cordelia, "You think so? ... I think some demons can be nice, given the opportunity. You'd have to get to know them, yeah?"[19] As with most passing figures, Doyle keeps his past a secret and does not offer personal information that might jeopardize his portrayed racial status. Likewise, Clare does not share any personal childhood information with her husband that might lead him to discover her true race.

Doyle's "silence" after Cordelia's remark about demons furthers the comparison to *Passing*. Cordelia unknowingly attacks Doyle, and rather than come forward, Doyle chooses to keep his demon half hidden in order to protect his relationship with Cordelia. Similarly, Clare allows her husband, John, to attack her heritage as well. John playfully calls her "Nig" because he believes she is Caucasian. John continues to berate African Americans in front of Irene and Gertrude, who choose to keep silent as well, partially for Clare and partially for themselves. This silence is most important to Clare, however, since John's ignorance allows Clare to pass safely between races. Clare must protect her marriage to John because she lacks certain proof of her whiteness without him. Doyle, however, chooses silence to protect his relationship with Cordelia not because she enables him, but because passing in her perception truly matters to him.

The second of Bennett's tropes involves the controversy surrounding racial justice in the plot.[20] The idea of racial justice calls into question both racial loyalty and cultural betrayal, where racial loyalty suggests that the characters are faithful to their most predominant race, and cultural betrayal suggests that the character must deny some part of his/her cultural identity in order to build a more socially acceptable self. In *Passing*, both Clare and Irene struggle with racial loyalty and cultural betrayal. In order for Clare to fully pass as white, she must deny her black roots and lie about her past. Irene feels it a danger to associate with Clare because of Clare's betrayal to her race. After Clare and Irene make plans to meet again following their first chance run-in at the Drayton, Irene decides that she has no desire to meet someone who "held so low an opinion of her [Irene's] loyalty, or her discretion."[21] By associating with Clare, who is identifiably white, Irene runs the risk of appearing to deny some part of her "blackness." The loyalty struggle is so great for Irene because she, too, passes as it conveniences her. Irene's varying degrees of whiteness are pushed further into question by her keeping a black servant, Zulena, in her home. Irene expresses her confusion on the subject with her husband, Brian: "It's funny about 'passing.' We disapprove of it and at the same time condone it. It excites our contempt and yet we rather admire it. We shy away from it with an odd kind of revulsion, but we protect it."[22] Still, somehow Irene lacks sympathy for Clare. Because Clare chooses to deny her black heritage in order to pass, Irene has no interest in forgiving Clare, despite Clare's desire to return to her roots. Like Clare and Irene, Doyle also walks this dangerous line — capable of suffering rejection from both sides. His fear of not being fully accepted by anyone causes him to be constantly aware of his actions in front of every audience. Doyle is neither demon enough for the full-breed demon population, nor human enough should he reveal his demon side to the human population. Each character relies on images and perceptions, and it seems best for everyone to turn a blind eye. When Irene thinks to inquire about Clare's past years, she decides that it is best if she does not know. Similarly, Doyle only provides personal information on a need-to-know basis and tells Angel that he will reveal only what he feels is necessary.

Doyle's struggle with racial loyalty stems from being unaware of his demon heritage for so long. As Doyle reveals in "The Bachelor Party" (1.07), he was raised human by his mother. He never knew his father and did not discover his demon heritage until the age of twenty-one when his demon attributes literally sprouted with a sneeze.[23] At this point, Doyle had already spent twenty-one years being unknowingly loyal to his human half. His racial loyalty is called into question when Lucas, a fellow Bracken demon, comes to him for help escaping the threat of the Scourge.[24] Having only been newly introduced to his demon side, he turns Lucas away, stating that he is not interested in "exploring [his] roots," thereby exhibiting cultural betrayal by denying his demon half.[25] Because Doyle is unable to initially accept his demon roots, his fellow Bracken demons are killed at the hands of the Scourge.

A more literal notion of racial justice occurs throughout the series and is exemplified in "Hero," in the saving of the half-demon clan. Angel consistently proves that he is willing to save anyone in need of saving; Doyle, while hesitant at first to participate by any other means than his visions, ultimately shares Angel's enthusiasm. When the half-demon clan tells Doyle and Angel of their attempts to escape from the Scourge, Doyle must face his past dealings with the Scourge and the death of his fellow Bracken demons. Doyle is eager to make sure a massacre such as this does not happen again. The conversation Doyle has with Cordelia when she first arrives to help move the half-demon family to safety demonstrates the polemics of racial justice exactly. Cordelia, who represents a doctrine of binary racial biases, says, "Hey, Doyle, you did notice that these folks are demons?"[26] Doyle's response exemplifies the conflict he feels between the continued denial of his racial heritage — especially to Cordelia —

and his commitment to not repeating his earlier cultural betrayal: "Yeah, I know that. It doesn't make them bad people."[27] Doyle's emphasis on changing Cordelia's term of "demon" into "people" speaks to the heart of his conflict and the questions raised by the idea of passing.

A return home is the third characteristic of a passing text.[28] Like Doyle, Clare's return to her roots is both muddled and problematic. Clare must reintroduce herself to the black community carefully because of her husband's clearly racist attitudes and the bitterness felt from her loyal black peers. Irene doubts the sincerity of Clare's return, suggesting that Clare feels no affection for her race, but merely "belong[s] to it."[29] Even more troubling, as Irene suggests, is "not only that she [Clare] wanted to have her cake and eat it too, but that she wanted to nibble at the cakes of other folks as well."[30] Clare's desire to return to her race is not a wholly passionate one, but rather one driven by some magnetic pull, or a "mysterious calling of race," as Bennett asserts.[31] Clare is not interested in gaining a deeper level of self-understanding; rather, she desires to participate in what she assumes to be the best of both worlds. Her interests in passing become an interest in "having," which Larsen frequently emphasizes. At first, Doyle shares Clare's "having" desires. Doyle passes in order to have a normal life — to be accepted by society — and more importantly for Doyle, to have a relationship with Cordelia. Doyle ultimately differs from Clare, however, because Doyle realizes that he can have what is important to him, namely Cordelia, without passing.

Doyle's return also differs from Clare's because he does not physically seek out the place of his roots; instead, his return comes in the form of self-acceptance as he reveals and openly embraces the nature of his demon heritage in order to rescue his friends. Bennett clarifies that the return is not always necessarily physical and is often atavistic in nature.[32] While Doyle's demon characteristics do not fully demonstrate an atavistic return, as they do not reappear after several generations of absence, there is an atavistic quality about the appearance of his demon characteristics because they do not surface until Doyle turns twenty-one.

Doyle's return begins with a surprise visit from his wife, Harriet, known as Harry throughout the series.[33] When Harry comes to Doyle for a divorce so she can marry another half-demon, Doyle is forced to relive the initial cause of his separation from Harry. Doyle reveals that it was he who could not come to terms with his demon form, rather than his wife, much like Doyle's relationship with Cordelia where he passes more for fear of rejection than to protect his love interest. His struggle to accept this new part of himself results in his separation from his wife — something he associates with becoming demon — and, therefore, prevents him from accepting his demon half sooner.

Doyle takes a big step forward when he agrees to go to the bachelor party of Harry's fiancé for Harry's sake. The bachelor party serves Doyle in several ways: it begins the process of coming to terms with his divorce, it is his first demon social function, and it is his first time choosing to fight in demon form. Even though Doyle spends most of the evening in human form, significantly so do Richard (the fiancé) and his family, negating the idea that Doyle's choice of human face is an attempt to pass in this instance. While fighting seems to support the barbaric stigma associated with demons, fighting in demon form is actually a big step for Doyle toward accepting his demon strengths. After a previous fight, Angel asks Doyle why he doesn't fight in demon form when he knows that he is stronger that way; Doyle replies that it is not his style. In fact, Doyle consciously suppresses his demon form while fighting, suggesting that Doyle has internalized fear of stereotypes even while fighting alongside another demonic and "passing" figure — Angel. Doyle associates his demon form with his divorce, anger, and aggression. However, after Doyle realizes that Harry truly did accept him as he was, and that it was he who rejected himself, he slowly eases into self-acceptance. Using his demon attributes for good helps Doyle progress towards a balance of the strengths of both halves.[34]

Another similarity Doyle shares with the women of *Passing* is displayed in their fear of an atavistic return in their children. Clare and Gertrude both express their fear of having children due to the suspense of not knowing how they may turn out. Gertrude explains, "No ... no more for me either. Not even a girl. It's awful the way it [racial characteristics] skips generations and then pops out."[35] Likewise, Doyle's discussion with Harry about having children of their own came to an abrupt halt once they learned of Doyle's demon heritage. Both Doyle and the women of *Passing* long to protect their children from the possibility of a forced return, suggesting fear of their own exposure should their children display any closeted racial characteristics.

The fourth trope Bennett discusses focuses on moments of secrecy and exposure in order to create elements of surprise.[36] Irene and Gertrude suffer both surprise and humiliation at the hands of Clare and her husband. Clare knowingly risks exposure by having the two women over while her husband is home. Not only is this dangerous for Irene and Gertrude should John be able to tell that the two women are black, but it is a greater danger for Clare who only casually assumes that Irene and Gertrude will not say anything about their race in front of John. Irene's run-in with John in the street, however, most surprises her. Irene is shopping with her friend Felise, who is identifiably black, when they meet John. Irene brushes off John's polite greeting as he puts the pieces together. Irene's new moment of suspense involves wondering what will happen to Clare should John figure out that Clare is passing as well. Both Clare and Irene fear John finding out because of his blatant hatred for their race. Not only must the women be concerned about rejection, but they must also worry about other consequences and punishments that would arise from the wrong people learning the truth of their passing.

Moments of secrecy and exposure plague Doyle in a similar fashion. Doyle's first major risk of exposure comes with Harry's arrival. Harry's return surprises Doyle because he has not seen or spoken to her in years; her sudden, unannounced appearance not only reveals his hidden marriage, but it also jeopardizes Doyle's passing should Harry unknowingly share Doyle's secret with Cordelia. In "Hero," Doyle attempts to tell Cordelia about being part-demon when he is violently interrupted by a vision, creating yet another moment of suspense ultimately left to secrecy. Furthermore, Doyle leaves Cordelia to learn of his secret, not from Doyle himself, but from the half-demon father expressing his appreciation for their help later in the episode.

Doyle also creates moments of suspense that could have ended in unintentional exposure of his demon form. In the episode "In the Dark" (1.03) Doyle uses his demon sense of smell to locate a mystical ring for which he and Cordelia are searching.[37] In order to do so, he must turn demon while Cordelia's back is turned, risking exposure in order to save Angel. There is a similar incident in "The Bachelor Party" when Cordelia and Harry arrive at the restaurant to rescue Doyle. Cordelia finds the green-skinned, spiky demon and proceeds to beat him with a serving tray. The demon runs off screen to return moments later as Doyle in human form. If Angel had not distracted Cordelia long enough for Doyle to change, Cordelia may have discovered Doyle's secret in a much more shocking manner. Thankfully for Doyle, his news is well-received. Cordelia is only angry that Doyle chose to hide his secret for so long.

The final trope, death of the hero or heroine, fittingly brings a tragic character to a tragic end. Bennett suggests that the passing character's death is partially linked to the desire to return to one's roots, noting that "the cost of this return, which is usually too late, is dramatic."[38] Indeed, Clare's death is both tragic and dramatic. While the reader may anticipate Clare's death, there is no resolution in the act because the reader is not certain who is responsible. Larsen weaves such a muddled scene that the reader is left questioning the basic plotline. In the final scenes of *Passing*, John bursts in on a gathering that Brian, Irene, and Clare are attending. John has finally realized that Clare is indeed passing as white and storms in to confront her. Clare, standing by the window, is suddenly approached by both Irene and John, but before anyone can process the transpiring events, Clare tumbles out of the window. The story ends with the characters wondering if Clare's death was an accident, suicide, or a murder.[39] Bennett explains, "This 'dark' ending plays with the expectations of the reader, for though we know that Clare, the novel's significant passing figure and tragic mulatto, must die, we are surprised when Irene, who has also been passing, must die a figurative death."[40] The focus is shifted from Clare to Irene, who only vaguely recalls the order of events after she faints. Irene's fainting serves as her own figurative death, not falling from any height, as Bennett notes, but rather she falls deep within, losing her self-identity.

Doyle's major contribution to the passing paradigm stems from the final trope. For Doyle, the end is not only dramatic, but heroic as well.[41] By this time, Doyle receives the acceptance he has been searching for from Harry and Cordelia. He comes to understand that it was he who so fervently rejected his demon form, and now it is he who must come to accept it. Doyle realizes that his demon strength will be what saves Angel, Cordelia, and the demon family they are trying to protect. Not only does his selfless act save his friends, but it gives Doyle a greater sense of purpose by becoming a martyr for "the good fight."[42] Indeed Doyle is tested, tried, and comes out victorious. Unfortunately for Doyle, his victory is also his self-sacrifice. After kissing Cordelia, he tells her that it is "too bad [they'll] never know if [his demon visage] is a face [Cordelia] could learn to love."[43] For the first time, Doyle shows his demon form proudly, using his demon strength to leap to the beacon and diffuse it. There is something fascinating about the scene where Doyle diffuses the beacon. He must use his demon form in order to have the ability to reach it, as well as the strength to pull the plug. However, the beacon's light kills any form with human blood, so as the light is killing Doyle it turns him human. In essence then, Doyle dies in human form. While this may seem problematic at first, it is important to realize that Doyle's strengths come from both sides. Without both his human and demon qualities, Doyle would not be the type of person he inevitably becomes. If it were not for the attributes from each heritage, it is probable that Doyle would not have chosen to sacrifice himself for the lives of others, nor may he have been able to.

Unfortunately for many passing figures, a part of their tragic demise involves their inability to reach some sort of comfortable conclusion about themselves. Clare only knows that she would do anything, hurt anyone, to get what she wants. "Having" becomes Clare's replacement for genuine happiness. Irene, who may have believed she was happy, loses a part of herself through her unsettled relationship with Clare. Doyle separates himself from other passing figures, however, because he is able to reach a sense of self-understanding and acceptance, something that neither Clare nor Irene possess. Doyle knows—as he explains to Reef—that "losing yourself somewhere, hoping it all goes away ... never works."[44] Doyle is able to interfuse his multiple selves into one entity, whereas Clare and Irene are unable to coalesce the multiplicity of their identities into something they can understand and accept as themselves.

The culmination of Doyle's experiences allows him to understand and appreciate the significance of his heritage. Doyle is no longer afraid that the acceptance of his demon self means the denial of his humanity. Doyle's ability to reach this level of self-understanding makes him capable of placing himself into a bigger picture—the good fight—which allows him to embrace the importance of his life, as well as his death. Whedon's re-envisioning of the passing figure as heroic alters the trajectory of passing characters in the American literary genre and allows for a positive, alternate ending that reinforces the notion that we all should embrace our differences.

Notes

1. "Hero," *Angel*, DVD, written by Howard Gordan and Tim Minear, directed by Tucker Gates (1999; 20th Century–Fox, 2002).
2. Nella Larsen, *Passing* (New York: Dover, 2004), 15.
3. "Hero."
4. Ibid.
5. Ibid.
6. Ibid.
7. Nella Larsen's *Passing* is widely received as a staple text among passing literature; Juda Bennett, *The Passing Figure: Racial Confusion in Modern American Literature* (New York: Peter Lang, 1996).
8. Bennett, *The Passing Figure*, 36.
9. Ibid.
10. Elaine K. Ginsburg, "Introduction: The Politics of Passing," in *Passing and the Fictions of Identity*, ed. Elaine K. Ginsburg (Durham: Duke University Press, 1996), 1.
11. Bennett, *The Passing Figure*, 24–25; I would like to take a moment to note that I am in no way suggesting that "black" passing for "white" is synonymous to "demon" passing as "human." I am only trying to apply the theories of standard passing texts to Doyle's situation throughout the series.
12. "Lonely Hearts," *Angel*, DVD, written by David Fury, directed by James A. Contner (1999; 20th Century–Fox, 2002); "The Bachelor Party," *Angel*, DVD, written by Tracy Stern, directed by David Straiton (1999; 20th Century–Fox, 2002).
13. Bennett, *The Passing Figure*, 48. The term "Manichean" originated from the belief in religious dualism brought about by Manes, a Persian prophet of the third century A.D. One aspect of this religious dualism focused on the conflict between light and dark, or good and evil. *Merriam-Webster's Collegiate Dictionary*, 11th ed., s.v. "Manichean," 755.
14. Bennett, *The Passing Figure*, 49. The notion of "reading" race is also emphasized in a number of other passing texts. The most readily accessible example is Hughes's "Who's Passing for Who?" In this short story, the narrator, presumably Hughes, and two friends try to "read" their supposedly white companions. When the couple suggests that they are passing for white, the narrator and his friends' personalities are completely altered because they now believe their company is also black. At the end of the evening, just as the couple is driving off, they yell to the narrator that they were only joking and just wanted to try passing as black for a little while. Because the narrator initially read the couple as white, he treated them differently than when they stated they were only passing as white. Mis-reading race can also be found in William Faulkner's *Light in August*, Philip Roth's *The Human Stain*, Art Speigelman's graphic novel *Maus: My Father Bleeds History*, and many other texts.
15. Larsen, *Passing*, 8.
16. "City of," *Angel*, DVD, written and directed by Joss Whedon (1999; 20th Century–Fox, 2002).
17. Ibid.
18. "Lonely Hearts."
19. Ibid.
20. Bennett, *The Passing Figure*, 48.
21. Larsen, *Passing*, 21.
22. Ibid., 43.
23. Doyle's discovery of his demon half reflects the narrator's discovery of his black roots in James Weldon Johnson's *Autobiography of an Ex-Colored Man*. The discovery is both startling and unexpected. The narrator learns of his race by the principal asking the white students in his class to stand. When the narrator stands, his teacher quietly asks him to sit back down. The narrator learns of his heritage in front of his entire class, a shocking discovery for someone who was allowed to believe he was white. Doyle's sneeze, equivalent here to the teacher's command, also comes as a painful surprise. Much like the narrator is allowed to believe he is fully white up until this moment, Doyle is allowed to believe that he is fully human. Furthermore, Doyle does not feel like a demon after his discovery, just as the narrator does

not feel like he is black. James Weldon Johnson, *The Autobiography of an Ex-Colored Man* (New York: Penguin Books, 1990).

24. The Scourge is a neo–Nazi group who sets out to purify the demon race. "Hero."
25. Ibid.
26. Ibid.
27. Ibid.
28. Bennett, *The Passing Figure*, 48.
29. Larsen, *Passing*, 38.
30. Ibid.
31. Bennett, *The Passing Figure*, 51.
32. Ibid. Atavism, in this instance, references the reappearance of characteristics which have been removed from previous generations, such as darker shades of skin color or demon horns.
33. "The Bachelor Party."
34. As previously discussed, other demon attributes also work in Doyle's favor. The day after Doyle rescues Cordelia from the vampire in "The Bachelor Party," Cordelia explains to Angel that she thought her date would run at the first sight of a demon, and he did, a moment played for comedic value as Cordelia remains unaware of Doyle's half-demon heritage. Angel tells her running is a part of "human" nature. Doyle's determination to rescue Cordelia, then, must come from somewhere else — namely — his demon nature. This action ultimately leads Cordelia to acknowledge her desire for Doyle, by recognizing that he possesses what Cordelia calls "really hidden depths."
35. Larsen, *Passing*, 26.
36. Bennett, *The Passing Figure*, 48.
37. "In the Dark," *Angel*, DVD, written by Douglas Petrie, directed by Bruce Seth Green (1999; 20th Century–Fox, 2003).
38. Bennett, *The Passing Figure*, 51.
39. Larsen, *Passing*, 90–94.
40. Bennett, *The Passing Figure*, 53.
41. Doyle's most significant episode, "Hero," alone exemplifies all of the elements of a passing text. This perhaps is the most important example of passing because it so closely mirrors the type of passing necessary during the Holocaust — the Scourge symbolic for the Nazi movement. This, of course, leads to a number of connections to Holocaust literature.
42. "Hero."
43. Ibid.
44. Ibid.

Pylean Idol
L.A.'s De(con)struction of a Postmodern Bard
JENNIFER HAMILTON

> *I know I'm going to regret this. In fact, being prescient, I'm sure of it.*
> — Lorne, "The Trial"[1]

In worlds of decentralized identity, there is great need for the rehearsal of history. History — the essential analepsis (flashback) of a culture — defines a people and provides the necessary psychological underpinnings by which decisions are made both individually and as a collective. When considering "group identity," the story of an entire group must necessarily be fictive or take on mythological proportions at some level, for no matter how inclusive that narrative strives to be, embracing the often disparate truths of individuals within a larger narrative is bound to surpass the limits of some people's "truth." Oral tradition cultures well understood this concept, and as a result, key cultural figures such as the bard evolved. In the television series *Angel*, Lorne's character immediately emerges as a type of this traditional bardic figure. Viewers first encounter Lorne in "Judgment" (2.01), when he "reads" Angel through Angel's song, offering insight (though not prescriptive) into the dilemma which Angel will soon face.[2] Throughout the series, Lorne's demeanor keeps him peripheral to most of the action, allowing him the interpretive distance necessary for a bard, and he is often the one to whom the group at Angel Investigations turns to rehearse the narrative. Early in *Angel* Lorne functions as a bardic figure (keeping stories, interpreting situations, and offering future outcomes to conflicts); however, toward the end of the series, continual contact with dark forces and moral compromises seemingly required in the fight against evil result in the erosion of Lorne's bardic function, transforming this character from a more traditional bardic figure — albeit with a postmodern twist — into a figure who can no longer serve that purpose either for the other characters or for the series as a whole.

Bardic Tradition

The nature of story and the function of the bard are dynamic, responding to the culture of origin. In the world of *Angel*, Lorne, known for most of Season Two as "the Host," exhibits these essential qualities of the bard (keeping story, interpreting story, foretelling), though these qualities are adapted to the time and setting of the Angelverse, impacting the narratives within *Angel*. Noteworthy in this examination is the way in which Lorne, as bard, departs from traditional expectations. Rather than maintaining an overarching narrative to which all adhere, in postmodern fashion Lorne as bard interprets and reads individuals and allows their stories to manifest contextually. Challenges arise when competing narratives vie for pre-eminence and sometimes hide themselves from the Host; however, the interplay of individual story and the larger narrative of an episode (and even a season or the entire series) allows for a complex presentation of both individual and communal narratives.

Storytelling, the creation of narrative which defines identity and purpose, is vital to the human condition because we must create stories to understand ourselves and our place in the world. Through established and accepted narrative we have history, we make sense of current paths in light of the past, and, as well-trained hearers (inheritors of an oral bardic tradition), we are able to anticipate and/or discern the future. Bardic traditions, established primarily in Celtic Scotland and Ireland, rely on the power of storytelling to inform culture and people, to take what might be competing narratives and order them into a coherent plot that makes sense of the situation in which a people find themselves. Katie Trumpener states in *Bardic Nationalism*: "For nationalist antiquaries, the bard is the mouthpiece for a whole society, articulating its values, chronicling its history, and mourning the inconsolable tragedy of its collapse.... English poets, in contrast, imagine the bard (and the minstrel after him) as an inspired, isolated, and peripatetic figure."[3] As a figure peripheral to the action and often traveling between narratives, the bard is able to connect what others are unable to see, situating him with a unique authority to provide social commentary in his stories.

Often, the bard's abilities to see ties between events, weave them into story and song, and lead the hearers to understanding were credited to supernatural gifts or to the "chosen" nature of the bard himself. Born with artistic gifts of music and poetry, the bard was able to take events and mythologize them, venerating leaders in a heroic fashion, inspiring confidence in followers, and creating a strong cultural mythos upon which people within that culture could rely. Strong national leaders inspire a strong nation, one bold enough to act confidently (even when in error) and swiftly, making those people influential (one could even argue primary) actors, in creating the narrative of the future. In "The Narrative Creation of Self," Jerome Bruner writes, "However much we may rely on a functioning brain to achieve our selfhood, we are virtually from the start expressions of the culture that nurtures us. And culture itself is a dialectic, replete with alternative narratives about what self is or might be. The stories we tell to create ourselves reflect that dialectic."[4] Story, then, no longer occupies benign bedtime space between events of the day and dreams of the evening: collection, coordination, and construction of narrative offer a powerful, sobering position of influence to the bard, even if the bard (Lorne) is often seen sipping a Sea Breeze.

Lorne as Bard

Joss Whedon's *Angel* gives viewers a bardic figure in the character Krevlornswath of the Deathwok Clan (Lorne), a demon from the dimension Pylea. According to Jes Battis, Lorne is "a green-skinned empathy demon who can read people's emotions by listening to them sing karaoke. Lorne is a bit of a Fred Astaire throwback, wearing a lot of silk bathrobes, but his ambivalence around fighting doesn't stop him from acting as a critical source of information for the [Angel] Investigations crew."[5] Lorne fits Trumpener's description of the bard in that he is certainly peripatetic, negotiating not only interdimensional existence, but also life between humans and demons. Just as his character is interdimensional, he is also multidimensional. Being an empath, he is able to read characters through their song; he is prescient, and he is empathetic in ways that transcend the demon/human barrier. When introduced in Season Two, Lorne is peripheral to all action, an incidental character who runs a karaoke bar for demons. The bar, Caritas (Latin for "mercy"[6]), is protected by a spell, allowing demons of all kinds a place to come together peacefully. As a pacifist, Lorne's desire is to provide a respite from the conflict of the outside world,[7] a place where all can come and experience the beauty of music, though viewers soon learn that the "beauty" depends on who is performing. Coming from the dimension of Pylea, Lorne is dragged to Los Angeles when an interdimensional portal opens. He arrives from a world devoid of music and art where he was little more than a disgrace to his family, for his gift of song was and continues to be considered a curse there, even after he left. In L.A., Lorne finds a way to fulfill his dream of being a lounge singer while utilizing his talents as an empath demon.

Beginning with the first time Team Angel enters Caritas and interacts with Lorne in "Judgment,"[8] Lorne learns that his abilities are both helpful to them and, at times, potentially harmful to him. His abilities to read characters, foretell events (regardless if he reveals his knowledge), and bring together competing stories assist in the formation of the overarching narrative in which all characters, including himself, participate. In postmodern fashion, assimilation of narrative requires particular context, and Lorne acknowledges at different points the ability for the story to take divergent directions, all dependent on the context of interpretation.[9] Since Lorne is often interpreting *in medias res*, he speaks in broad strokes allowing for freer participation of characters in their choices of action.[10] Indeed, as cognitive psychologist Jerome Bruner writes, "We more often tell stories to forewarn than to instruct. And because of this, stories are a culture's coin and currency."[11] The culture into which Lorne is channel for story is a particular family construction of Whedon's design: Angel Investigations.[12]

Taking into account Bruner's notion that stories are more often told to forewarn, and keeping in mind that, in Whedon's world, fate is tempered by the will of the characters, it is to Lorne's advantage not to be predictive. There is great irony when one considers the notion of scripted characters with "free will," but that very irony is explored by Thomas Flamson in "Free Will in a Deterministic Whedonverse": "The characters in Whedon's worlds are not free in the strict sense of being completely undetermined. In fact, they are eminently determined, making choices that can be predicted in advance with knowledge of their personality and the surrounding circumstances when they make that choice. However, this determinism cuts both ways, and means that the characters are also capable of predicting their opponents' behavior, and this capacity presents new information which changes those circumstances."[13] Within the context of stories told to warn and characters acting within many levels of "scripting," it makes sense that Whedon's team often only allows Lorne to speak with sparse detail, which allows characters to work out fuller understanding through their own paths, though always with Lorne's forewarning in front of them.

At times, warnings present themselves in the form of the Host's own songs, often sung before the action unfolds in the episode. In his first appearance,[14] he sings his way into the show with the opening lines from the song "I Will Survive."[15] Considering what is about to unfold not only in this episode, but also throughout Lorne's participation in later episodes, this is an apt foreshadowing, both in terms of the vocalized lyrics and the song's ultimate message about triumph over adversity. In this episode, viewers learn that upon entrance to the karaoke bar Caritas, patrons see a sign that no violence or weapons are allowed. This sign subtly signifies a fundamental character trait: Lorne is a pacifist. Throughout Lorne's interactions with Angel Investigations, he uses song and his interpretive abilities to contribute to the fight against evil by reinforcing his chosen community. He doesn't fight; he uses his gifts to carve out a niche. As he becomes more of a regular character on the show, he becomes one of the crew, necessarily impacting his bardic role.

Lorne on the Team

Just as bards served particular function within their spheres of reference, in Lorne's character we find a postmodern reconstruction of the bardic form. Whedon's writers exploit various facets of Lorne's character to frame episodic narrative and larger, more overarching themes which often span seasons. In "Postmodernism and Television," Jim Collins posits:

> There is no short definition of *postmodernism* that can encompass the divergent, often contradictory ways the term has been employed. One reason for this divergence is that the term is used to describe: (1) a distinctive style; (2) a movement that emerged in the sixties, seventies, or eighties, depending on the medium in question; (3) a condition of milieu that typifies an entire set of socioeconomic factors; (4) a specific mode of philosophical inquiry that throws into question the givens of philosophical discourse; (5) a very particular type of "politics"; and (6) an emergent form of cultural analysis shaped by all of the above.[16]

For the purposes of this exploration, multiple elements of Collins's definitions are profitable, especially the notion that a mode of inquiry can "[throw] into question the givens of a philosophical discourse." The reuse of the bardic trope, with minor adaptation, can shed light on a new situation in profound ways. Essentially, Lorne's character has fundamental bardic traits that manifest in extremely unusual ways, most of which require interpretation and understanding within the very particular context of the Angelverse. Lorne's bardic functions serve communal purpose, but he simultaneously interacts and responds to individuals within the narrative. At times Lorne challenges the culture of the Angelverse by bringing together disparate points of view and causing the crew at Angel Investigations to see situations and characters in an unconventional way, demonstrating a unique and significant adaptation of bardic form.

Analyzing Lorne's participation with Angel Investigations over the seasons reveals an interesting pattern. Lorne's powers are useful and employed successfully when matters are minor. However, when a major plot twist arises, and humanity finds itself torn between The Powers That Be and the demonic law firm Wolfram & Hart's Senior Partners (between good and evil), Lorne's powers often are inadequate to the task. In the Angelverse, characters cannot act out of their realms of power. Some characters are ushered between realms of abilities (e.g., Cordelia's shift from regular human to supernaturally gifted seer and Fred's transformation from sweet-natured woman into dominating god-king Illyria); however, regardless of any character's given power, they are necessarily limited. Characters in the Angelverse, like us, can only do so much.

Facing this type of limitation becomes a more familiar occurrence for Lorne, for in the episode "That Vision Thing,"[17] Lorne's abilities are put to the test and found lacking. Cordelia's visions begin to have physical manifestation, and she finds herself sliced by claws, infected with boils, and severely burned due to successive visions. Wesley calls on Lorne to read Cordelia to see if they can "trace the calls" to find out who or what is tormenting Cordelia. Lorne offers this disclaimer: "Way outside my area of expertise, I should caution. But hey, who knew William Shatner could sing? Okay, bad example."[18] Rather than have Cordelia sing, he puts his hands on her temples; while Lorne attempts to read her, she receives a vision that knocks him unconscious. His powers are not ineffectual; however, using them causes him physical harm. He is eventually able to report to the crew what he learned, but he admittedly is meddling in powers greater than his, reinforcing his position as postmodern bard because, unlike traditional bards, his ability to interpret the narrative — in this case, Cordelia's visions — is not guaranteed; it is contextualized.

Later in this same season, viewers witness Lorne's powers pushed beyond his limitations. In the episode "Offspring,"[19] a pregnant Darla returns, and what the team doesn't know is that Angel is the sire. In order to determine what kind of demon Darla is carrying, since vampires cannot reproduce, the team decides she should sing for Lorne. The characters assemble at the remains of Lorne's karaoke bar, which was destroyed in the previous season. Although Caritas is in disrepair, the non-violence spell remains in place, so the crew brings Darla to Lorne. She grabs Lorne's face and barks out the first line of "Danny Boy." Lorne immediately declares: "This is way beyond my ken — and my Barbie and all my action figures."[20] Rather than construct a narrative which might or might not be helpful, he concedes that he is inadequate to this task of interpretation. Lorne is only able to confirm what the gang knows: a child born of two vampires cannot bode well.

Lorne again finds his powers tested in Season Four when Cordelia returns in "Slouching Toward Bethlehem," an allusion to William Butler Yeats's poem "The Second Coming."[21] When she appears at the Hyperion, she has little recollection of her past (though elements of her teen years remain in her memory), barely even recalling having been a higher power during her absence. The team tries to decipher the meaning of her return while simultaneously slowly gaining her trust, which to them means not disclosing the "abnormal" aspects of their shared life: Angel being a vampire, fighting demons for a living, etc. As Cordelia encounters the truth of their messy existence, she is understandably distraught. She is talked into singing for Lorne, having been told that he can read her and fill in the gaps in her memory. Clearing her throat, she badly sings Whitney Houston's "The Greatest Love of All," the same song she sang for talent show tryouts at Sunnydale High in the episode "The Puppet Show."[22] As she sings, Lorne becomes increasingly disturbed. His reading has revealed something so dense, intense, and frightening, that he leaves the room mid-sentence. When Angel confronts Lorne, Angel must work to get any details from the reading, demanding, "Come on, Lorne. You gotta give me something!"[23] Lorne, still disoriented from the overpowering nature of the reading, says, "Do the words 'Slouching toward Bethlehem' ring a bell? Or how about 'despair, torment, terror?'"[24] Recognizing that Angel is relying on his interpretation (his function as bard), Lorne continues, "What I saw was jumbled. It was pieces, flashes. It was enough to make my skin crawl away and scamper under the bed. Evil's comin', Angel, and — and it's planning on staying."[25] Lorne is able to foreshadow, through mood, key words, and literary allusion to Yeats's poem what lies ahead, but even with his powers, he isn't able to lay out details of what the world will face in the coming apocalypse. He is even unable to foresee his own torture at the hands of Wolfram & Hart as they send in a demon to extract the knowledge he gained by reading Cordelia. The bard references poetry to order the chaos he experienced in

Cordy's reading. Calling on a pre-existing literary tradition, Lorne weaves what might be an older, familiar tale with story as yet unwritten. Viewers begin to see more overtly that the characters are simultaneously limited in what they can accomplish while being held at the mercy of pernicious powers. The world of *Angel* is complex; a world in which even heroes, including those with talents like Lorne's, aren't always adequate to the task.

Recognizing that his powers are limited, Lorne incorporates the use of magic to reveal the mystery of Cordelia's lost memory. The most creative narrative venture in the run of the show is the episode "Spin the Bottle,"[26] in which Lorne recounts the failed attempt to recall Cordelia's memory through magic. The primary narrative is expressed through Lorne; he is seated at the piano at Caritas, and the episode opens with him singing the aptly-chosen "The Way We Were."[27] Lorne's recitation of events recalls a comedy of errors in the execution of a spell. Uniquely, the writing in this episode departs from familiar formulas, with the tale told in remembered pieces, with the primary narrative being Lorne recounting the mishap to his audience at Caritas and the secondary narrative being the actual event itself, rather than a more linear plot. Lorne is able to recount, interpret, and set the stage for successive episodes. He confesses, "It's my job to read people, but nobody in this clan was exactly singing."[28] So he resorts to magic, and when the magic largely makes a mess, Lorne sums up to his audience, "So all's well that ends well, right, kiddies? But since nothing ended all that well, I guess I gotta say that, well, nothing *was* well. See, none of us knew it then, but the sequence of events was a little different than what we thought.... Well, it's been a long night for everyone, and I hope you've all enjoyed my little tale so much that you tip your waitress with obnoxious abandon...."[29] As storykeeper to the clan, he takes disparate recollections from characters and sums up the story, all the while acknowledging his limitations. In this episode, a subtle transition begins in Lorne's bardic role. He not only is the storyteller, but he is embroiled in the tale which he tells. His peripatetic posture is compromised, and this begins to affect his ability to maintain a bard's perspective as an outsider who interprets. An audience member shouts out, "Finish it!" but being wise, even if not all powerful, Lorne merely responds, "Always leave 'em wantin' more, kiddo, that's the rule."[30]

De(con)struction of a Bard

Any precedence set for Lorne's participation as bard gets broken in the final televised season of *Angel*. In Season Five, the Angel Investigations team takes over Wolfram & Hart, the evil law firm which they have battled since the first season. What the team has yet to learn is that their engagement with evil will unravel all they have accomplished with one another; tenuous truces between characters will erode, individuals will make compromises which fundamentally alter their motivations and interactions, and ultimately in the final season, all overarching themes which have garnered attention during the run of the show will take a backseat to Whedon's continuous inquiry into the tension between determinism and free will. As their world seems doomed to slouch toward apocalypse, and as characters fight against compromising their ideals, Lorne's abilities to interpret, keep story, and foretell disintegrate.

As often happens in Whedon's creations, one can find literary inspiration for fundamental plot lines. Seasons Four and Five follow this pattern, for an attentive viewer notes Lorne's overt reference to William Butler Yeats's poem "The Second Coming." The literary allusion most resonates in these lines:

> Things fall apart; the centre cannot hold;
> Mere anarchy is loosed upon the world,
> The blood-dimmed tide is loosed, and everywhere
> The ceremony of innocence is drowned;
> The best lack all conviction, while the worst
> Are full of passionate intensity.
> ...
> The darkness drops again; but now I know
> That twenty centuries of stony sleep
> Were vexed to nightmare by a rocking cradle,
> And what rough beast, its hour come round at last,
> Slouches towards Bethlehem to be born?[31]

The tone set by Yeats's poem continues not only through Season Four but also through to the end of the show. Cordy's return sets in motion several key events which precipitate the disintegration of Angel Investigations. Connor and Cordelia's mystical pregnancy indeed vexes Los Angeles "to nightmare by a rocking cradle" when the evil demi-god Jasmine is born.[32] Destroying Jasmine also destroys the veneer of peace and happiness which the world was enjoying, and the team realizes that false happiness is an evil of its own kind, no matter how intoxicating its appeal. As the Angel team engages Wolfram & Hart, the centre indeed falls apart, and things cannot hold. Each character begins to make his or her way through the moral quagmire of working for ultimate evil while simultaneously attempting to combat it. This tension, which continues and goes unresolved until the final episode of the series, mounts throughout the final season as the team is fragmented into areas of their expertise. Lorne takes over the Entertainment Division, where he learns that just about everyone famous has made a Faustian bargain of some sort with Wolfram & Hart. Now his responsibility is to negotiate between those with whom the firm has contracts, no matter how evil, and Team Angel. Characters working to their strength is not a new concept to the show; however, as the team begins working for the Senior Partners, they find themselves separated physically (and consequently emotionally, intellectually, and spiritually) from each other. The sheer size of Wolfram & Hart forces each character into new space which they attempt to make their own, despite continual friction with forces outside their control.[33]

With their own staff to supervise, their own projects, and their own moral quandaries, the characters become divided, and the strength that they derive from each other wanes. Lorne's most successful venture while at Wolfram & Hart is his initial reading of the employees. In the opening episode of Season Five, "Conviction," Lorne reads all the current employees of Wolfram & Hart to determine who can be trusted. This provides some comic relief, but also stands as one of the last times that Lorne is really able to utilize his powers effectively. Interestingly, in this episode, Lorne doesn't read Knox (Fred's right hand man in the Science Division). Fred has Knox working on a case, and when Knox volunteers to sing for Lorne, Fred naïvely expresses her trust in him, a mistake that will cost her life. Later in "A Hole in the World" (5.15),[34] it is Knox who has a sarcophagus delivered which releases Illyria (precipitating Fred's demise). In the following episode, "Shells" (5.16),[35] Lorne expresses remorse that he misread Knox, clearly misremembering that Knox never sang. The suggestion surfaces that Lorne's abilities to interpret have decayed within the walls of Wolfram & Hart through overwork and compromise. This disintegration signals a shift in Lorne's role: he begins to detach himself from the team, and his role as bard fades in significance. Lorne no longer interprets or keeps story, for within the chaotic walls of Wolfram & Hart, he has lost the plot.

The appearances of Lorne's character lessen in significance throughout this season, and in the context of the dismantling of the team, putting Lorne in charge of Entertainment merely serves to distract him from his previous roles. Attentive viewers witness a familiar tension in Lorne: he is busy, but his preoccupations are menial and quotidian, and his character exhibits frustration in losing sight of what was once a much simpler narrative: Get the Bad Guys. Lorne is relied on less and less to interpret pivotal moments, project a future, or maintain a narrative, for he no longer is a *worker*. Along with everyone else on the team, he is now *management*.

In the role of management, Lorne and the other characters begin to compromise in ways they wouldn't have when working as Angel Investigations. At Wolfram & Hart, their physical separation facilitates individual bargains which would never have been considered when working together. Separated into their own spaces, the Angel Investigations Team becomes easier to dismantle. As characters become overwhelmed with new duties, they allow Wolfram & Hart to meddle in their minds as well. Gunn does so in "Conviction"[36] when he allows the Senior Partners to grant him heightened mental abilities, thus ameliorating his own discomfort about moving in circles incredibly *other* from his experience as a hardened street-fighter. Likewise, Lorne allows Wolfram & Hart to meddle in his physical and mental makeup in an attempt to become increasingly effective, to do *more*.

"Life of the Party"[37] is a pivotal episode that illustrates Lorne's disintegration. In this episode, Lorne has his sleep removed in order to work around the clock to pull off the annual Halloween Party. Unknowingly, this choice splits his psyche; his powers as a Pylean empath demon alter through sleep deprivation; as a result, through his speech, he *writes* destiny rather than merely predicting it. In frustration, Lorne directs Gunn to "mark his territory," suggests that Angel and Eve "get a room," and tells Wesley and Fred that they "need to get drunk."[38] All of the characters begin to behave strangely, manifesting the behaviors suggested by Lorne's remarks. In the episode, this twist provides some humorous moments as Gunn goes about Wolfram & Hart marking his territory in the most animal of ways, but viewers see the potential harm in scripting action through speech rather than merely interpreting. Previously as bard, Lorne would interpret or advise; however, we see that within Wolfram & Hart, his powers have been distorted and become tainted. Lorne's transmogrification into a Hulk-like beast signifies that his internal character has shifted through his interactions with the Senior Partners. No longer keeper or interpreter, Lorne is now the director of actions. Lorne has sacrificed something elemental, signifying a reversal of how his character functions.

The ultimate destruction of Lorne as bard comes about in the final two episodes of Season Five, "Power Play" and "Not Fade Away."[39] As the final season reaches denouement, Angel has distanced himself from the rest of the crew by giving the appearance of turning evil in order to gain the trust of the Black Thorn secret society. In so doing, Angel alienates his closest friends and creates much confusion in the ranks about their direction. Most significant to this discussion is the way in which Angel and Lorne's relationship is compromised. When Angel is able to explain his final plan to the crew, they all realize precisely how final this act will be. Most of the characters welcome the return to action; however, Lorne exemplifies the breaking point when he tries to excuse himself from the action: "Oh, I'm not a fighter, Angelwings. Never had the stomach for it. Looks like I'm your weak link."[40] Angel's reply belies the true nature of what he asks of Lorne when he says, "I just need you to back up Lindsey."[41] As the action unfolds, viewers realize that Angel has asked Lorne to kill Lindsey, an act that violates Lorne's pacifist nature as well as his role as bard, as observer who weaves the community narrative; in this instance, however, rather than shaping the historical narrative through interpretation and language, he contributes to it through violent action. Along with sacrificing a foundational part of his nature for the good of everyone, he sacrifices his relationship with Angel and the rest of the crew.

Lorne is clearly aware of the cost of agreeing to Angel's request, as he explicitly articulates the consequences of taking on the role of participant rather than shaper of the narrative: "Hey, uh, Angel, I'll do this last thing for you, for us, but then I'm out. And you won't find me in the alley afterwards. Hell, you won't find me at all. Do me a favor. Don't try."[42] When functioning as bard, Lorne remains outside the stories, weaving them together and providing continuity. As his character continues that function, the inevitable intertwining of his self with the stories brings Lorne to a moment of truth. Killing Lindsey requires Lorne's full participation, nullifying his role as bard, and in this significant identity shift, Lorne realizes that all is irrevocably changed; the centre cannot and did not hold. In following through with this final act for the good of the team, Lorne detaches himself from the group.

The fight scenes in "Not Fade Away" show all of the crew returning to early form, fighting evil in "old school" ways. Spike, Gunn, Wesley, and even Fred's presence, in the form of Illyria, take on members of the Black Thorn, and they accomplish their missions. Lorne is with Lindsey, and when Lindsey is done killing, he and Lorne have a significant exchange showing that in Lorne's transition from storykeeper to actor in the story, Lorne is transformed. Lindsey says to Lorne, "You don't trust me. You don't think a man can change?" and Lorne, in full knowledge of Lindsey's character replies, "It's not about what I think. This was Angel's plan."[43] While simultaneously distancing himself from the ensuing violence and preparing to participate, Lorne avoids direct answer to Lindsey's question. Seeing that he hasn't convinced Lorne, Lindsey pleads, "Come on. I could sing for you."[44] Clearly Lindsey has forgotten that Lorne is prescient. Lorne replies, "I've heard you sing."[45] He then fires two shots, ending the discussion. Mortally wounded, Lindsey expresses outrage that he is killed by Lorne, "a flunkey,"[46] rather than Angel. In Lindsey's estimation, dying at the hands of the hero is his fitting end because he once was a prominent, major player at Wolfram & Hart and he took on the Senior Partners. For Lindsey, this is a most dissatisfying death; for Lorne, it is a necessary evil done to thwart greater evil, for, as he explains, "You're not part of the solution, Lindsey. You never will be."[47] The pacifist has turned killer.

When a peripatetic figure becomes embroiled in the heart of the action, his role fundamentally changes. In order to keep perspective, to maintain the view, the bard must remain above the minutia of the moment. Lorne's final action in the series shows that he no longer is peripheral to the action; he is now someone new. He no longer foretells, interprets, or keeps the story; instead, he helps write a narrative to which he cannot reconcile his previous self. Lorne is most changed in this final episode. Fulfilling Angel's last request permeates him with an intense sadness unfamiliar to his character. No longer the bard, this Pylean Idol has indeed been de(con)structed in Los Angeles. True to his first melodic utterance in Season Two, Lorne does survive, but now his song is silenced. Proving the extent to which his character has altered, Lorne makes his final exit from the television series *Angel* quietly, with a simply spoken "Good night, folks."[48]

Notes

1. "The Trial," *Angel*, DVD, written by David Greenwalt, teleplay by Tim Minear and Douglas Petrie, directed by Bruce Seth Green (2000; 20th Century–Fox, 2007).
2. "Judgment," *Angel*, DVD, written by David Greenwalt and Joss Whedon, directed by Michael Lange (2000; 20th Century–Fox, 2007).

3. Katie Trumpener, *Bardic Nationalism: The Romantic Novel and the British Empire* (Princeton: Princeton University Press, 1997), 6.
4. Jerome Bruner, *Making Stories* (New York: Farrar, Straus and Giroux, 2002), 87.
5. Jes Battis, *Blood Relations: Chosen Families in* Buffy the Vampire Slayer *and* Angel (Jefferson, NC: McFarland, 2005), 5.
6. "Judgment."
7. Lorne creates a similar space in L.A. in the *After the Fall* comics, which only validates his continual function in the bardic role, even in a hell dimension. However, in this essay, I am focusing on Lorne's characterization in the televised aspects of the *Angel* narrative only; I leave a study of Lorne as he is portrayed in the comics for another essay.
8. "Judgment."
9. This contextuality is evident in Lorne's interactions with several characters in various episodes. In the episode "First Impressions" (2.03), Angel sings for Lorne, and Lorne tells him he faces a "bend in a personal road, whether it slows you down is up to you." "First Impressions," *Angel*, DVD, written by Shawn Ryan, directed by James A. Contner (2000; 20th Century–Fox, 2007). In "Dear Boy" (2.05), Lorne acknowledges, "I set people on their paths," implying that what happens after his input is up to the character in his/her context. "Dear Boy," *Angel*, DVD, written and directed by David Greenwalt (2000; 20th Century–Fox, 2007). In "Over the Rainbow" (2.20), Lorne visits a medium for his own benefit, signifying that within his own context, he needs direction at times. "Over the Rainbow," *Angel*, DVD, written by Mere Smith, directed by Fred Keller (2001; 20th Century–Fox, 2007). In "Calvary" (4.11), Lorne reads Angel/Angelus, and mistakenly identifies Angel as being in control, showing that even the bard can be tricked by evil. "Calvary," *Angel*, DVD, written by Jeffrey Bell, Stephen S. DeKnight, and Mere Smith, directed by Bill L. Norton (2003; 20th Century–Fox, 2007). In "Supersymmetry" (4.05), Lorne recovers from being assaulted by Wolfram & Hart, and he states, "I wish I could tell you what was coming and when...." Yet he refuses to re-read Cordy, possibly out of fear, and denies his bardic role. "Supersymmetry," *Angel*, DVD, written by Elizabeth Craft and Sarah Fain, directed by Bill L. Norton (2002; 20th Century–Fox, 2007). These are but a few examples of how the bard might at times command the narrative, but at other times, the story is wholly dependent on the context of the character being read and the situation into which the bard attempts to see the future.
10. At this point, one might be tempted to digress into discussions of free will versus fate in the characters and the series; however, that topic is well treated in works such as K. Dale Koontz's *Faith and Choice in the Works of Joss Whedon* (Jefferson, NC: McFarland, 2008); Thomas Flamson's chapter "Free Will In a Deterministic Whedonverse" in *The Psychology of Joss Whedon: An Unauthorized Exploration of* Buffy, *and* Firefly, ed. Joy Davidson (Dallas: BenBella, 2007), 35–50; Gregory Stevenson's *Televised Morality: The Case of* Buffy the Vampire Slayer (Dallas: Hamilton Books, 2003), and J. Michael Richardson and J. Douglas Rabb's *The Existential Joss Whedon: Evil and Human Freedom in* Buffy the Vampire Slayer, Angel, Firefly *and* Serenity (Jefferson, NC: McFarland, 2007). Further, Katia McClain's chapter in this volume adds to that conversation.
11. Jerome Bruner, *Making Stories* (New York: Farrar, Straus and Giroux, 2002), 15.
12. In the DVD collector's box set (2007), Joss Whedon writes a letter to fans, and in it, he describes the family construction in *Angel* as set apart from the Scooby Gang in *Buffy the Vampire Slayer*: "We lived on the edge of chaos, personally, narratively ... even as Angel surrounded himself with more and more of a family (and we found more and more wonderful actors for David Boreanaz to play against), that central core of warmth and safety that Buffy enjoyed was missing." The family construction is there, but it's a family of misfits in a way that is both heartwarming and distressing. The crew at Angel Investigations forges their own community, but it is well-earned through hard work, ruination of relationships, and tenuous repairs.
13. Flamson, "Free Will," 43.
14. "Judgment."
15. Most famously preformed by Gloria Gaynor, "I Will Survive," *Love Tracks*, written by Freddie Perren and Dino Fekaris (Polydor, 1978).
16. Jim Collins, "Postmodernism and Television," in *Channels of Discourse, Reassembled: Television and Contemporary Criticism*, ed. Robert C. Allen (Chapel Hill: University of North Carolina Press, 1992), 327.

17. "That Vision Thing," *Angel*, DVD, written by Jeffrey Bell, directed by Bill L. Norton (2001; 20th Century–Fox, 2007).
18. Ibid.
19. "Offspring," *Angel*, DVD, written by David Greenwalt, directed by Turi Meyer (2001; 20th Century–Fox, 2007).
20. Ibid.
21. "Slouching Toward Bethlehem," *Angel*, DVD, written by Jeffrey Bell, directed by Skip Schoolnik (2002; 20th Century–Fox Film Corporation, 2007); William Butler Yeats, "The Second Coming," in *Yeats's Poetry, Drama, and Prose*, ed. James Pethica (New York: Norton, 2000), 76.
22. Whitney Houston, "The Greatest Love of All," *Whitney Houston*, written by Michael Masser and Linda Creed (Arista, 1985); "The Puppet Show," *Buffy the Vampire Slayer*, written by Rob Des Hotel and Dean Batali, directed by Ellen S. Pressman (1997; 20th Century–Fox, 2002).
23. "Slouching Toward Bethlehem."
24. Ibid.
25. Ibid.
26. "Spin the Bottle," *Angel*, DVD, written and directed by Joss Whedon (2002; 20th Century–Fox, 2007). For more on this episode, see Stacey Abbott, *Angel*, TV Milestones Series (Detroit: Wayne State University Press, 2009), 90–95.
27. Most famously preformed by Barbra Streisand, "The Way We Were," written by Alan Bergman and Marilyn Bergman (1973).
28. "Spin the Bottle."
29. Ibid.
30. Ibid.
31. Yeats, "The Second Coming," 76.
32. "Shiny Happy People," *Angel*, DVD, written by Elizabeth Craft and Sarah Fain, directed by Marita Grabiak (2003; 20th Century–Fox, 2007).
33. When the team goes to Wolfram & Hart, Angel is CEO and often harried due to the enormous clientele, his preoccupation with the Shanshu prophecy and Spike's return, and his own struggle with his quest for redemption; Fred takes over the Science Division; Wesley heads up Research, in charge of a library that would leave the most meticulous of researchers drooling; Gunn (in a moment redolent of *The Matrix*) gets legalese and a "messload of Gilbert and Sullivan" ("Standard. Great for elocution.") uploaded into his mind to become the premier lawyer in the firm; and all of these diverse activities serve to splinter their efforts, thereby precipitating friction on the team. "Conviction," *Angel*, DVD, written and directed by Joss Whedon (2003; 20th Century–Fox, 2007).
34. "A Hole in the World," *Angel*, DVD, written and directed by Joss Whedon (2004; 20th Century–Fox, 2007).
35. "Shells," *Angel*, DVD, written and directed by Steven S. DeKnight (2004; 20th Century–Fox, 2007).
36. "Conviction."
37. "Life of the Party," *Angel*, DVD, written by Ben Edlund, directed by Bill L. Norton (2003; 20th Century–Fox, 2007).
38. Ibid.
39. "Power Play," *Angel*, DVD, written by David Fury, directed by James Contner (2004; 20th Century–Fox, 2007); "Not Fade Away," *Angel*, DVD, written by Joss Whedon and Jeffrey Bell, directed by Jeffrey Bell (2004; 20th Century–Fox, 2007).
40. "Not Fade Away."
41. Ibid.
42. Ibid.
43. Ibid.
44. Ibid.
45. Ibid.
46. Ibid.
47. Ibid.
48. Ibid.

Lilah Morgan
Whedon's Legal Femme Fatale
Sharon Sutherland and Sarah Swan

Joss Whedon has described his penchant for creating shows which combine genres in unusual ways as "both my gift and my curse. I am never satisfied with one genre."[1] Within *Angel*, that mixing of genres includes the mixing of stereotypes to create individual characters. In this regard, Lilah Morgan is a particularly interesting combination of two seemingly opposed literary and filmic stereotypes, the femme fatale and the female lawyer. The character of Lilah successfully combines these two stereotypes in a manner that emphasizes the often overlooked commonalities between the two types and creates a powerful and arguably feminist character.

"Don't you ever get tired of the whole femme fatale act?"[2]

The figures of the femme fatale and the female lawyer share rich histories. The femme fatale, in particular, is an archetypal figure, both ancient and ubiquitous. She crosses temporal and cultural boundaries and occupies diverse media. She is found in folklore and early mythology, morphing through early civilizations as the Sumerian Ishtar, the Biblical Eve and Salome, the Greek Helen of Troy, and the Sirens. In China, the historical figure of concubine Yang Guifei may be included in this tradition. The femme fatale has continued to appear in literature throughout the ages, having particularly strong showings in periods when gender roles were most rigidly enforced, where she acted as an exemplar of "the threat to traditional female gender roles."[3] While her fundamental nature as a transgressor of social norms means that her character changes somewhat in relation to the social values of each time, she notably flourished as a figure in Gothic novels and their Victorian descendants. In the twentieth century, the femme fatale has made a very successful transition to the filmic and televisual forms, especially during the *noir* period of American film in the 1940s and 1950s (a genre heavily referenced in *Angel*).[4]

The figure of the female lawyer has been much less widely used than that of the femme fatale, but she too has an ancient history. In dramatic literature, the female lawyer appears in such older works as *The Eumenides* and *The Merchant of Venice*. That said, the legal profession remained largely closed to women until the twentieth century, so the female lawyer's character has developed chiefly in the visual media of film and most especially on television. In both literature and the visual arts, the female lawyer has represented intelligence, and, like the femme fatale, her form has adapted over time in response to social norms. In her case, the most important of these norms in defining her character has been the relative prevalence of females within the real world bar.[5]

We see the fusion of these two archetypes in Lilah's first scenes in *Angel*. As is clear in the femme fatale tradition, this woman is exceptionally beautiful, making her very attractive to men and distinguishing her from the average woman: "She often has a majestic, provocative aura about her, and her physical appearance is uniquely captivating. She generally has pale or white skin with a translucent quality which symbolizes an inexplicable, ethereal presence. The color of her hair and eyes is typically dark, contrasting with the skin's paleness. Her eyes are captivating to the male; also, her hands fascinate the male character, who notices their positions and movements. The colors red and black are symbolically used to represent the type's power."[6] When we first meet Lilah in *The Ring* (1.16), she perfectly portrays this image. Played by former model Stephanie Romanov, Lilah is a dark-haired beauty, with pale skin and red lips, seated at a dimly lit bar. Her hand movements are important: we notice her twirling a finger around a glass of red wine and later swirling a glass of scotch. Lilah's wine, lipstick, and nail polish contrast with her dark hair and the darkened background of the bar, creating a black and red palette. Her voice is a low, seductive purr. In early episodes, Lilah's hair is styled to reflect a 1940s wave, emphasizing her connection with the noir era and by extension her association with the era's femme fatales.[7] These visual cues all clearly announce that Lilah is a dangerous woman, a fact underscored by her very presence in the audience of an illegal demon-fighting establishment.

Lilah introduces herself as Lilah Morgan, a name which aurally connects her with at least three famous femme fatales: Delilah from the *Book of Judges*; Lilith, Adam's first wife; and Morgan Le Fey, the enchantress of the Camelot tales. Despite her name and physical connections to the femme fatale, Angel's first observation of her, as he sees her seated in front of an array of legal texts, is that she's "a lawyer." And, in fact, Lilah's beauty also announces her to be a lawyer in the tradition of most of television's female attorneys.

On television, the female lawyer is almost always both beautiful and brilliant. Her beauty is often closely connected to contemporary beauty standards. In the 1980s and 1990s, for instance, actresses Susan Dey, Calista Flockhart, and Lara Flynn Boyle all drew heavy media criticism for playing lawyers with unhealthily tiny figures, though undoubtedly they reflected the image of beauty portrayed in the fashion magazines of their time. Similarly, the female lawyer has always been fashionably dressed: the power suits of *L.A. Law*, the pant suits of *The Trials of Rosie O'Neill*, and the mini-mini skirt of Ally McBeal all marked the female lawyers as trendy and fashion conscious. That one of the main characters in *Sex and the City*, a show that made fashion one of its primary topics, is a lawyer, is unsurprising given the fashion sense with which female lawyers are almost always endowed in television. Lilah, of course, has perfect noir style in her early appearances, but by Season Three we understand that she is, in fact, "fashion forward." When Lilah and Cordelia have a heated discussion about the need to kill the viciously misogynistic Billy, Cordelia implies that Lilah's shoes are less than perfect. Lilah quickly responds, assuring Cordelia that these shoes are not only designer but are also from the next season's collection, marking Lilah as superior in her fashion awareness.[8]

Physical beauty as a commonality between the femme fatale and the female lawyer creates a ready visual connection to each tradition for Lilah: she draws her color palette from the femme fatale and her fashion sense from the female lawyer for a stunning physical form well suited to the role of seductress/negotiator discussed below.

Wearing the Mantel of "vicious bitch"[9]

The literary femme fatale typically moves "outside the boundaries of convention" and "creates controversy in society."[10] The femme fatale is villainous and morally corrupt, as, of course, Lilah is, and one aspect of the femme fatale's villainy has traditionally been her unwillingness to play by society's rules. The femme fatale resists socially defined roles for women, and in especially morally restrictive periods, she suffers notably brutal ends for her resistance to "proper" roles. In this respect, Lilah's occupation as a lawyer is ironically utilized to position her outside society's bounds. Whereas the typical female lawyer challenges social norms only insomuch as she appears with much greater frequency in television than in real life and occupies, in significant numbers, roles that are much more commonly held by men in the real legal community, in *Angel*, Lilah's occupation as a lawyer sets her far outside of conventional norms. Lawyers in *Angel* represent ultimate evil. The Senior Partners of Wolfram & Hart stand in direct counterpoint to the forces of good, The Powers That Be, in the ongoing battle between evil and good. So simply choosing to be a lawyer in this world marks Lilah as occupying a position of moral corruption. Beyond that, of course, Lilah has knowingly entered into a literal pact with the devil, exchanging morality for power and money. Lilah is not just a threat to social norms as a figure moving outside the boundaries of convention but a person who has explicitly chosen to fight to destroy society.

Within the conventions of the female lawyer, Lilah also occupies an unusual position. While television series have, since *L.A. Law*, frequently sought to reflect a legal community in which women pursue traditionally male practice specialties in numbers far beyond the real world average, it is still unusual to see powerful female corporate lawyers. Many of the women on television law shows work in what might be called female practice specialties — areas of law that emphasize personal relationships over the power and money of corporate practice. *Judging Amy*'s Amy Grey and *Family Law*'s Lynn Holt are two good examples of smart women choosing to work in relationship-based areas of practice. Lilah's contemporary, Ally McBeal, becomes a partner in a commercial litigation firm, but even in that context she often engages in traditionally female areas of practice like mediation and takes on relationship-based work. Lilah is, therefore, further outside the social norm as an up-and-coming associate at Wolfram & Hart. Even within the usually female-friendly Whedonverse, Lilah is almost exclusively surrounded by male lawyers. Within the prestigious "Special Projects Division," Lilah is the only woman.

Nonetheless, Lilah brings the femme fatale to her work style. Most high-powered female lawyers on television are shown to be at their best when they mimic male lawyers' aggressive, cutthroat litigation styles and adopt a coldly dispassionate approach to their work. Lilah, to the contrary, employs sneak attacks, subterfuge, and her exceptional powers of persuasion to accomplish her tasks. One consequence of her quiet and manipulative approach to her tasks is that Lilah often plays a secondary role to Lindsey in the early seasons: her skillfulness is overshadowed by his courage and risk-taking. She fears reprisals from the Senior Partners and is openly afraid of their wrath, whereas Lindsey is unconcerned. She shows her fear of reprisals when she asks Lindsey, "Remember when Robert Price let the Senior Partners down, and they made him eat his liver? I don't know what made me think of that."[11] While she is certainly ambitious, Lilah does not necessarily want to step into the full glare of leadership but prefers to see someone else's head on the chopping block. Lilah, however, gains confidence through her relationship with Wesley in Season Four, and takes on some of the characteristics Lindsey previously represented, though in this case as a foil not to Angel's heroism but to Wesley's increasingly morose vigilantism.

Lilah does cultivate a lawyer's objectivity and cold dispassion as a sign of strength and revels in the title "bitch" and its variations. Lilah is variously referred to as "an evil bitch" (by Angel in "That Vision Thing" [3.02]), a "backstabbing traitorous bitch" (by Sahjahn in "Sleep Tight" [3.16]) and a "succubitch" (by Lorne in "Calvary" [4.12]).[12] But it is Cordelia's comment in "Billy" (3.06) that explicitly recognizes the power in the epithet. Cordelia tries to persuade Lilah, who has been physically abused by the misogynistic Billy, that Lilah should help Angel Investigations rid the world of Billy. Cordelia does not make the mistake of appealing to Lilah's good nature but instead talks of the feeling of being abused and declares, "No woman should ever have to go through that, and no woman strong enough to wear the mantel of 'vicious bitch' would ever put up with it."[13] Here Cordelia grasps an essential aspect of Lilah's character: Lilah is a strong woman in the male world of Wolfram & Hart, and she has inevitably attracted the title of "bitch" as a result of this strength. Rather than attempt to appease her male colleagues with less powerful behaviors, however, Lilah, like Cordelia, "wears the mantel" with pride, knowing that it reflects upon her strength.

Lilah grows into her mantel over the early seasons of *Angel* as she secures her place within Wolfram & Hart and develops the power to be more overt in her dealings with her colleagues. Initially, Lilah faces many of the struggles which plague real female lawyers in practice: she is disrespected and overlooked in favor of her male colleagues. In her time as a junior associate, Lilah is often criticized by supervising partner Holland Manners, even though she is obviously dedicated to her job and good at it. Holland compares her to Lindsey (in what is undoubtedly his own version of manipulation), yet the discussions are often explicitly gendered, as for example, when he informs her that her girl (Bethany) is "finger painting" all over Lindsey's big plan.[14] She works harder than Lindsey, as even he acknowledges, and yet she does not receive the recognition her work deserves until Lindsey tells their male colleagues that she's the "guy."[15] As Lilah comments herself, she has had to be "better, smarter, quicker than every man at Wolfram & Hart" in order to succeed.[16] Angel suggests to Lilah that her hard work and drive for success is a "feminist thing," but Lilah does not accept his glib analysis.[17] "It's a survival thing," she retorts, explaining, "I've made a lot of devil's bargains and I stuck to them.... My mother, who no longer recognizes me, has the best room at the clinic. I get up every morning, put on my game face, and do what I have to do."[18]

No matter her successes, Lilah must continually compete to bring down her colleagues in order to succeed. Within the world of the law firm, Lilah's competitive drive forces her to be even more evil than her male counterparts. She makes it clear, however, that she chose the game and has committed to play by its rules: whatever the gender inequalities in her world, she is not a victim. The very fact that she cares so much more passionately about her job security than men like Lindsey is an extension of the commitment and sacrifices she knowingly made to succeed in this world: at the core of Lilah's character is the fact that she chose evil and considers it morally repugnant to pretend that she did not know the consequences of that choice. Repentance and redemption — essential themes for most characters in *Angel*— are for the weak.

"Is Lilah worried we're going to hurt the itty bitty baby?"[19]

Given the fact that the femme fatale has suffered varying degrees of ostracism as a result of her role outside society, it is perhaps not surprising that she is rarely given the role of mother or nurturer. In fact, she is generally seen as a poor mother, often lacking the "natural" feminine impulses to care for others. Similarly, despite their successes in the courtroom and judicial realm, most of television's female lawyers are remarkably unsuccessful in their own personal relationships and parenting. One might argue that the femme fatale and female lawyer share an inability to lead rewarding personal lives as a punishment for their choices in occupying positions outside social norms. Certainly the femme fatale tradition has explicitly demonstrated the dangers of women leading untraditional lives. In the case of the female lawyer, her creators may show her struggles with conscious feminist goals in mind, but the repetition of the image of the successful career woman unable to maintain a relationship or to successfully mother does not send a message of female empowerment. Lilah certainly begins as a character who reflects these characteristics, but her development over the seasons suggests greater potential for empowerment constrained primarily by her early career decision to join the forces of evil, rather than a social impossibility of combining successful personal relationships with career. Lilah chooses her lot in life: it is not the inevitable result of seeking to have a successful professional life, but the result of choosing a career in evildoing.

Similarly, Lilah has a complex relationship with motherhood, as we see in her responses to the few children we meet in the series. In the episode "Blind Date" (1.21), for example, an assassin is hired to murder three children with the ability to see into people's hearts. Lindsey is so disturbed by this plan that he allies himself with Angel and nearly defects from the evil law firm.[20] Lilah plays no role in the development of the project, but given that she makes it a point to always know what her colleagues are doing, we can safely assume that she is aware of it. It is interesting, then, that Lindsey, not Lilah, objects to the infanticide.

We do see Lilah bond with a young woman, Bethany, in "Untouched" (2.04).[21] Having delivered a motivational speech at the girl's high school, Lilah allows Bethany to stay with her and acts as her mentor. We finally see Lilah in a domestic setting, engaged in a domestic chore, the laundry. However, Lilah has an ulterior motive for her kindness: she wants to harness the girl's psychic powers for the use of the firm. In this episode, Lilah's cruelty is particularly shocking as she exploits the girl's history of childhood sexual abuse. Lilah watches, almost smirking, as the girl relives that abuse in a dream, and she arranges for two men to attempt to rape Bethany in an alley. Eventually, Lilah brings in Bethany's abusive father, knowing that both will likely be destroyed. The cruelty inherent in these actions is completely at odds with even the potential for Lilah to become a nurturing, mothering figure.

Lilah also seems unmoved by the baby Connor, in contrast to her male colleague, Linwood, who baby talks to the surveillance video of the child and confesses that he likes children. In fact, when Gavin makes the sexist accusation that she is worrying about the cute little baby, Lilah convinces us that her only fear is that the baby will be killed before Wolfram & Hart have a chance to "cut him open while he's still breathing and find out how the hell he's alive in the first place."[22]

While Lilah shows no interest in children, she does have a family connection, a mother in a care facility whom she supports, at least financially. Lilah ensures that her mother has the "best room at the clinic."[23] We learn in "Loyalty" (3.15) that her mother may not even remember her, yet it is clear that even this family connection is a liability in the world of Wolfram & Hart.[24] Linwood makes the risk explicit in "Forgiving" (3.17) after learning that Lilah has been secretly meeting Angel: "It's not like I'm going to get my feelings all bruised and yank your mother out of that very expensive clinic you have her in."[25] The message is clear to Lilah, and also clear to the audience: no one at Wolfram & Hart can afford to have family they want to protect. The choice to join Wolfram & Hart is a choice to leave behind the prospect for family connections.[26]

"This is the offer of a lifetime. Just not, you know ... mine."[27]

Perhaps the most dangerous aspect of the femme fatale is her ability to seduce and persuade. Literature's most notorious of femme fatales are its most persuasive: we need only look to Eve convincing Adam to taste the fruit and Delilah persisting in pushing Samson to reveal the secret of his strength for examples of the temptress who tempts not just through her physical beauty and availability, but also through her persuasive skills of debate and her treacherous ability to lie. In the Angelverse, where lawyers represent the ultimate evil, Lilah's femme fatale qualities combine with her legal training to make her an exceptionally persuasive negotiator. As she points out in "Home" (4.22), her name not only identifies her with a long line of femme fatales, but it also tells us that she is a liar. "Lie. Lah. Lie-lah," she purrs.[28]

Lilah is certainly the smooth-tongued lawyer, persuading and tempting her enemies with a mix of promises and threats. She is Wolfram & Hart's first choice for virtually all negotiations. It is Lilah who convinces the Senior Partners to buy Angel's contract in her first appearance in "The Ring"; she negotiates with Faith when the firm seeks to hire her as an assassin; and she convinces Angel and his team to join Wolfram & Hart.[29]

Lilah utilizes a variety of techniques in her negotiations: she seduces; she prepares thoroughly, obtaining secret information on all of her opponents and her colleagues; and she identifies each individual's interests and motivations and plays directly to those. In fact, as she tells a colleague in Season One, she has "people skills."[30] Her varied techniques make Lilah a particularly flexible negotiator, able to entice and threaten simultaneously. This skill is demonstrated in "Judgment" (2.01) where she tells a business associate: "You have every right to review the contract. I encourage it. We'll talk on Monday. Course if you don't sign, we'll sue your ass off and kill your children. Just kidding, Donald. Nobody wants a lawsuit."[31] As a result of her prowess as a negotiator, it is Lilah who returns—despite her intervening death—to negotiate the most important of contracts for the Senior Partners in "Home." Lilah is the temptress able to convince each and every one of Angel's friends, and eventually Angel himself, to accept a role in the management of the recently massacred, and clearly evil, Wolfram & Hart. As she does in all of her negotiations, Lilah reads her individual targets well and makes her offers based on what will most surely tempt them. She divides and conquers in the team's tour of the firm—even while the team is explicitly suspicious of this very ploy. Lilah's final appearance as a resignedly willing part of the Wolfram & Hart machinery captures her role throughout as the loyal and fearful retainer, reminding us again and again of how difficult it would be for anyone to fight Wolfram & Hart—especially from within. Despite the glaring message her very presence should be sending, she succeeds in enticing everyone to enter into a pact with the evil law firm. The episode is a brilliant example of Lilah's greatest power—a combination drawn from her joint heritage of femme fatale and brilliant lawyer—seduction entwined with cool logic and objectivity.

"So it's a feminist thing?"[32]

Lilah is clearly not a particularly sympathetic character: she has made a willing bargain with the devil which requires her to participate in, and indeed instigate, numerous despicable acts in exchange for power and survival. Nonetheless, Lilah is arguably a strong feminist character as she unapologetically pursues her own goals, paying little heed to social conventions or restrictions. Lilah is evil, but she is evil on her own terms, having made an informed decision to follow this path. We never see Lilah as a victim of any form of trickery. In fact, Lilah despises those weaker individuals who regret their choices and seek to renege on their obligations. While she may have some understanding of Angel's search for redemption—he did not make a choice to be evil, but was turned evil—she sees most others as weak in their inability to accept all of the consequences of their choices. Choice, after all, is precisely what women have been seeking; the ability to make choices to live their lives by the rules they choose rather than respond to gendered notions of appropriate choices is fundamental to feminism. Lilah makes a choice that we might not like, but we know she made it from a position of sufficient power to say "no" and that she was fully informed of all consequences (and perpetuity clauses). That Lilah insists on honoring her obligations to Wolfram & Hart is a further choice she makes: she entered into the agreement willingly, and she sees it as dishonorable to seek to back out.

Given the emphasis on male characters in *Angel*, strong feminist themes do not receive the same lengthy treatment in most episodes as they do in the more feminine *Buffy the Vampire Slayer*. Nonetheless, Lilah is central to the most overtly feminist episode in the series, "Billy" (3.06).[33] This episode deals with demonically exaggerated misogyny in virtually all of the male characters leading to frighteningly real encounters of male-to-female violence and intimidation. Very early in the episode, we see another lawyer, Gavin, physically attack Lilah when he wants her to be quiet. At this point, the narrative is not clear that Gavin has been changed by Billy, and his violence is deeply disturbing. Throughout the episode, we see scenes of violence and misogyny between police officers and a dream sequence of domestic violence between spouses. Most frightening of all, however, is seeing Wesley seek to murder Fred, and Gunn's near participation in the same act. These acts, committed by mortal men against women, carry a horror of realism that is absent from most of the demonic attacks in the series: these episodes are reflections of real gendered violence occurring every day.

Lilah's role in fighting this misogyny is an essential aspect of her role in the series: cowed as she may be by physical abuse, she is the one who ultimately kills the demon. "Billy" begins with a woman, Cordelia, learning how to fight in order to protect herself if Angel is not there and ends with Lilah shooting Billy to reclaim the power he has taken from her. This is the only time we see Lilah act against the will of her employers. She does not stop the murder of children or deter the use of rape to intimidate incest victims when those acts are in the best interests of Wolfram & Hart, but she refuses to allow a man to make her a victim. Critic Jennifer Stoy argues that this act makes Lilah morally ambiguous, as it is not the act of a "villain."[34] However, the act is entirely in keeping with Lilah's villainous character. She is not motivated by any sense of "goodness" or drawn to the "rightness" of the act, as Cordelia is when she threatens to kill Billy; Lilah simply refuses to allow someone to strip her of power. Cordelia is right to appeal to the "vicious bitch" in Lilah as the aspect of her character that cannot be beaten into submission.

"Standard perpetuity clause..."[35]

Throughout the series, Lilah is an active and willing agent of evil, a fact which makes her late series relationship with Wesley meaningful in what it says about his moral and psychological state at the time, while underlining yet again Lilah's role as temptress. While Lilah clearly has genuine feelings for Wesley, even in this relationship she remains committed to her goals and seeks to bring him over to Wolfram & Hart. The relationship remains immensely complicated by the fact that neither Lilah nor Wesley is moveable on their fundamental values. In fact, some of the attraction between the two may be the fact that they recognize and respect each other's deep and unbending commitment to the choices they have made. Stoy writes: "The moral and romantic entanglement between Wesley and Lilah, ending as it does in a heartbreaking stalemate, is both satisfying and disappointing: satisfying because the moral difference between Wesley and Lilah, as well as Lilah Morgan's status as one of the few creative moralists in the shared *Buffy/Angel* universe, remains intact and beautifully rendered, disappointing because Lilah's punishment—damnation eternal at the hands of a truly unbreakable contract—seems uncharacteristically harsh for both Wesley and Lilah as characters, and for an ethical universe that allows love to equal redemption."[36] It may be that the rest of the Angelverse does allow love to equal redemption, but Lilah is a very different character than Angel: she is past redemption. Angel has committed appalling acts of cruelty, but did so without a soul and entered into his life of evil without choice. Similarly, the other characters who seek various forms of redemption—Cordelia, Gunn, Wesley, Faith, Spike, and others—have all made mistakes which they want to believe can be balanced against the good they choose to do. In contrast, Lilah knowingly and entirely willingly became an agent of evil and continues to choose evil at every opportunity. Even her act of killing Billy is not done out of altruism; it is an act of power reclamation. We see Lilah engage in horrific atrocities: she sends near-fatal visions to Cordelia, helps bring Darla back from the dead to torment Angel, and even feeds Angel his own son's blood, in order to create a craving to drink it.[37] Lilah's frequent references to her own evil status are not a case of a lady protesting too much; rather, they are simply restatements of her clarity of purpose. Lilah is unique in the Angelverse as a character who does not seek to change her past. Lilah is Lilah's own creation.

Conclusion

Throughout *Angel*, Lilah succeeds in combining the characteristics of femme fatale and female lawyer to create a brilliant, beautiful, and devastatingly manipulative villain. She both looks and acts the part of the femme fatale: her dark hair and pale skin mark her as the physical embodiment of that figure, and her seductive powers, lack of conformity to standard social and feminine norms, and numerous cruel acts are the typical features of the femme fatale. Interestingly, many of these same features, her beauty, seductive skills, and position outside normal societal conventions, connect her to another figure, the female lawyer. Whedon combines these two figures to create an evil, yet arguably strongly feminist character. The fact that Lilah is truly villainous and still compelling is a tribute to the writers and actress, of course, but also to the fascination of the femme fatale and the female lawyer figure.

Notes

1. Serenity: *The Official Visual Companion* (London: Titan, 2005), 24–25.
2. "Sleep Tight," *Angel*, DVD, written by David Greenwalt, directed by Terrence O'Hara (2002; 20th Century–Fox, 2003).
3. "The Femme Fatale Throughout History," *History Television*, www.history.ca/content/ContentDetail.aspx?ContentId=73.
4. Stacey Abbott has explored film noir in *Angel* in "Kicking Ass and Singing 'Mandy': A Vampire in L.A.," in *Reading* Angel: *The TV Spin-Off with a Soul*, ed. Stacey Abbott (London: I.B. Tauris, 2005), 1–13, and "Walking the Fine Line Between Angel and Angelus," *Slayage: The Online International Journal of Buffy Studies* 3, no. 1 (August 2003), www.slayageonline.com.
5. On television, the female lawyer first became an important figure on *L.A. Law*. Premiering in 1986, the series starred women attorneys in significant roles. The advent of these women on television corresponded with the increasing numbers of women in the legal profession. Prior to the 1970s, women made up only a tiny minority of the profession. Only 3 percent of American attorneys were women in 1975. From the 1970s on, though, the number of women entering law school swiftly increased. By the time *L.A. Law* premiered, women made up 50 percent or more of most incoming classes.
6. Ghada Suleiman Sasa, *The Femme Fatale in American Literature* (New York: Cambria Press, 2008).
7. Rita Hayworth, Barbara Stanwyck, and Gene Tierney are examples of actresses who wore their hair in this style.
8. "Billy," *Angel*, DVD, written by Tim Minear and Jeffry Bell, directed by David Grossman (2001; 20th Century–Fox, 2003).
9. Ibid.
10. Sasa, *The Femme Fatale*.
11. "To Shanshu in L.A.," *Angel*, DVD, written and directed by David Greenwalt (2000; 20th Century–Fox, 2002).
12. It is worth noting that she is also referred to less frequently by terms related to her femme fatale role, such as "femme fatale" by Angel in "Sleep Tight" and the noir-ish "cheap brunette" by Fred in "Carpe Noctem," *Angel*, DVD, written by Scott Murphy, directed by James A. Contner (2001; 20th Century–Fox, 2003). "That Vision Thing," *Angel*, DVD, written and directed by Jeffrey Bell (2001; 20th Century–Fox, 2003); "Sleep Tight"; "Calvary," *Angel*, DVD, written by Jeffrey Bell, Stephen S. DeKnight, and Mere Smith, directed by Bill L. Norton (2003; 20th Century–Fox, 2004).
13. "Billy."
14. "Untouched," *Angel*, DVD, written by Mere Smith, directed by Joss Whedon (2000; 20th Century–Fox, 2003). Bethany, a young woman with telekinetic powers which Lilah hopes to harness, is instead befriended by Angel's team.
15. "Dead End," *Angel*, DVD, written by David Greenwalt, directed by James A. Contner (2001; 20th Century–Fox, 2003).
16. "Sleep Tight."
17. Ibid.
18. Ibid.
19. "Dad," *Angel*, DVD, written by David H. Goodman, directed by Frederick King Keller (2001; 20th Century–Fox, 2003).
20. "Blind Date," *Angel*, DVD, written by Jeannine Renshaw, directed by Thomas J. Wright (2000; 20th Century–Fox, 2002).
21. "Untouched."
22. Ibid.
23. "Sleep Tight."
24. "Loyalty," *Angel*, DVD, written by Mere Smith, directed by James A. Contner (2002; 20th Century–Fox, 2003).
25. "Forgiving," *Angel*, DVD, written by Jeffery Bell, directed by Turi Meyer (2002; 20th Century–Fox, 2003).

26. Angel must also, in some sense, leave his family when he joins Wolfram & Hart, though his motivation for the union is to save Connor.

27. "Home," *Angel*, DVD, written and directed by Tim Minear (2003; 20th Century–Fox, 2004).

28. Ibid.

29. "The Ring," *Angel*, DVD, written by Tim Minear, directed by Nick Marck (2000; 20th Century–Fox, 2002); "Five by Five," *Angel*, DVD, written by Jim Kouf, directed by James A. Contner (2000; 20th Century–Fox, 2002), and "Sanctuary," *Angel*, DVD, written by Tim Minear and Joss Whedon, directed by Michael Lange (2000; 20th Century–Fox, 2002); and "Home."

30. "Five by Five."

31. "Judgment," *Angel*, DVD, written by David Greenwalt and Joss Whedon, directed by Michael Lange (2000; 20th Century–Fox, 2003).

32. "Sleep Tight."

33. "Billy."

34. Jennifer Stoy, "'And Her Tears Flowed Like Wine': Wesley/Lilah and Complicated (?) Role of the Female Agent on *Angel*," ed. Stacey Abbott, *Reading* Angel: *The TV Spin-Off with a Soul* (London: I.B. Tauris, 2005), 166.

35. "Home."

36. Stoy, "And Her Tears," 164.

37. "That Vision Thing," *Angel*, DVD, written and directed by Jeffrey Bell (2001; 20th Century–Fox, 2003); "To Shanshu in L.A.," *Angel*, DVD, written and directed by David Greenwalt (2000; 20th Century–Fox, 2002); "Sleep Tight."

Two : Narrative & Identity

Let me tell you a little bedtime story.
— Doyle, "City of"

Fred's Captivity Narrative
American Contexts for (Re)Writing Community Identity from Mary Rowlandson to Angel

TAMY BURNETT

> *I've been trying to make an enchilada out of tree bark.*
> — Fred, "There's No Place Like Plrtz Glrb"[1]

The story arc that concludes Season Two of Joss Whedon's *Angel* ends with the overthrow of a corrupt regime that has been controlling the residents of Pylea through a species-based slavery system and false religion. Cordelia wishes good luck to Groo, the Pylean hero Team Angel has installed as ruler of the newly-freed land, but warns him that "you've got a long road ahead. Slavery has ended, but reconstruction has just begun."[2] When Groo questions her use of the unfamiliar term "reconstruction," Cordelia passes the responsibility of further explanation to one of her teammates, Gunn. Although all four regular characters—Cordelia Chase, Charles Gunn, Wesley Wyndam-Pryce, and Angel—contribute to the revolt against the corrupt authority, significantly, Cordelia and Gunn are the two who speak about the aftermath of abolishing slavery, for they are the only two (at this point) American members of Angel's investigative and demon-fighting team. Moreover, Gunn's explanation of "reconstruction," that "saying people are free don't make 'em free,"[3] is voiced by the only African American member of the team, suggesting that he has more authority to speak to the topic than his white, European or Euro-American teammates. The clear situating of the legacy and aftermath of slavery in an American, race-based context is the culmination of the slavery metaphor in the Season Two story arc.[4] This moment is one of many that situates the slavery in Pylea as allegorical, but, even more significantly, it establishes clear and obvious connections to slavery in an American context, highlighting connections between *Angel*'s Pylea story arc and American history and culture. In turn, the scene asks viewers to consider other cultural-historical influences which are uniquely American and which offer a deeper, more complex understanding of the construction of Pylean society, its residents, and the newest member of Team Angel rescued from this demon dimension: Winifred "Fred" Burkle.

At present, little critical attention has been paid to Fred; most scholars interested in her have instead focused on Illyria, the ancient demon who overtakes her body in *Angel*'s fifth season. Of the scholarship looking at Fred, the vast majority focuses on how events related to her character affect the show's other characters, rather than on Fred herself. Most of this criticism concentrates on exploring her death/transformation into Illyria and the impact of this event on the other characters—an important moment to consider, but one far removed from Fred's origins on the show.[5] In a similar vein, of the limited scholastic engagement with the Pylea story arc, most of it examines the demon dimension in relation to characters other than Fred, especially Angel, Lorne, and Cordelia.[6] Jes Battis does suggest that Fred's captivity in Pylea parallels Illyria's experience in L.A., but his commentary is limited to a footnote on a larger discussion of Illyria.[7] This essay addresses the hole in the world of *Angel* scholarship left by the absence of critical explorations and close readings of Fred, especially the earliest characterizations of her during and immediately after her captivity in Pylea.

When Team Angel meets her, Fred is an escaped human slave living in Pylea, having been sucked through a mystical portal from Los Angeles five years previously. Though one might observe that her story closely resembles the experiences of slaves in American history, the slave metaphor in the Pylea story arc is fairly obvious. In fact, while the slave metaphor makes for an inspiring storyline when Team Angel overthrows the unjust regime, little insight deeper than "slavery is wrong" is immediately apparent in the historical allegory. In contrast, a significantly more illuminating and complicated comparison comes from considering the influences of one of the oldest American literary genres: the captivity narrative, made popular by Mary Rowlandson's account of her time as a captive among the Nipmuc, Narragansett, and Wampanoag American Indians in 1676. In calling upon the captivity narrative tradition, *Angel*'s writers both subvert the genre's expectations and participate in a subtle cultural racism that underpins the foundations of American cultural identity.

The Captivity Narrative Genre

As a genre, the captivity narrative has far-reaching influences in American cultural and literary history. The earliest examples of memoirs written in this genre served as a testament to Puritan religious beliefs, detailing the hardships white captives endured while living with American Indians after being captured. The trajectory of early captivity narratives consistently worked towards the final conclusion of professing the captive's moment of revelation, providing an assurance to the writer and future readers that the endured hardships and the captive's continued/renewed faith in (the Christian) God meant the captive was among the Elect chosen for eternal life in Heaven. This belief in one's own election was a crucial foundation for the captivity narrative, as Puritans believed only a select few would be allowed entrance to Heaven upon their death and that God had already chosen those individuals.

One of the earliest and, arguably, most famous captivity narratives is Mary Rowlandson's *The Sovereignty and Goodness of God*,[8] published in 1682, six years after her release from captivity. Rowlandson's tale details the attack by New England-region American Indians upon her settlement and the subsequent three months during which she lived amongst the Indians as a captive. Rowlandson's narrative was immensely popular during her lifetime and came to be considered a classic of American literature by the middle of the eighteenth century; moreover, it continues to be taught in college classrooms today. As proof of Rowlandson's popularity in her own time, James D. Hartman notes that "Mary Rowlandson's captivity narrative was one of only seven books that sold more than one thousand copies during any decade between 1660 and 1690," and Kathryn Zabelle Derounian-Stodola and James Arthur Levernier claim that, when it was published, Rowlandson's text "was second in popularity among American readers only to the Bible."[9] To further contextualize the popularity of the captivity narrative and Rowlandson's narrative in particular, Richard VanDerBeets explains that "the immense popularity of the Indian captivity narrative in its own time is unquestionable; first editions are rare today because they were quite literally read to pieces, and most narratives went through a remarkable number of editions. There are some thirty known editions of the Mary Rowlandson narrative"; new editions of Rowlandson's text were spread out over the three centuries subsequent to its original publication, being printed "a dozen times in the eighteenth century, several dozen in the nineteenth, and a dozen or so in this [the twentieth] century."[10] Moreover, literary critics have traced Rowlandson's influence on defining American literary culture to several famous subsequent literary figures ranging from Edgar Allan Poe and Herman Melville to the nineteenth-century transcendentalists.[11] This essay adds Joss Whedon and his group of writers to that list.

The Captivities of Mary Rowlandson and Fred Burkle

On first glance, Rowlandson's story seems to line up with Fred's captivity in Pylea only slightly. While Mary Rowlandson is a captive, she is not a slave in the most common conceptualization of the term in American history. Other than shouldering the same kind of pack everyone, tribe members and captives alike, carries when the tribe moves its encampment, her work is limited to domestic tasks like knitting and sewing for Indians other than her owner — and she is paid for this work in English money, food, and other goods. In fact, the first time she receives a commission (a shilling) for sewing a shirt, she offers the money to her master, who "bade [her] keep it."[12] That is not to say, however, that readers will not notice some limits to her agency. For example, when another Indian man pays her with a knife, her Master "ask[s] [her] to give it him"[13]; that she is not allowed to keep a weapon when she is allowed to retain money speaks more to the inadvisability of any captor allowing his captive to possess a weapon than of specific limitations of Rowlandson's captivity (or perhaps the more practical use her master saw for a good knife than an English shilling). Overall, although she does not have the freedom to leave, Rowlandson is afforded some agency by her captors, which she uses to barter for food or money. In contrast, since viewers only see Fred in actual enslavement for a short period (after she has been captured and is awaiting execution), viewers' understanding of Fred's work while in captivity are inferences drawn from Cordelia's experiences when first enslaved: serving the role of pack mule for her master's shopping and performing menial labor like "shoveling demon horse poop."[14] Cordelia is not even afforded the agency of speech; when she tries to protest that she has rights (in part because she is American), Cordelia's master gives her an electric shock, saying, "Cows [humans] aren't for talking. They're for doing their job if they know what's good for them."[15] These inferences add up to Fred's Pylean masters treating her and other slaves as "beasts of burden"[16] without individual agency or worth beyond their physical labor.

Another significant difference between Rowlandson's and Fred's experiences lies in the outcome of the two women's captivity. Rowlandson's narrative primarily details her time with the American Indians, while viewers witness Fred in Pylea living alone in the woods as an escaped slave, separate from those who would enslave her. Rowlandson's captivity ends when she is ransomed back to her husband, a common practice of the New England Indian tribes during this time period, whereas Fred is rescued by Angel, and his team is reliant on her scientific knowledge about portals to facilitate their return to L.A.

Yet Rowlandson's and Fred's experiences do share important similarities — primarily the inability of either woman to fully escape her captivity. While Rowlandson's agency extends, at times, to being granted permission to travel to a nearby encampment to visit her son (also a captive) by herself, she understands that she cannot actually escape, since she is ignorant of the terrain and her location in relation to white settlements (in fact, she becomes lost while traveling the mile between her camp and her child's, and when her master finds her, his response is to show her the way to her son's location rather than assume she is attempting to flee and punish her).[17] Further, during her time as a captive, Rowlandson is repeatedly threatened with violence. For example, when she complains that the pack she carries each time the tribe travels has rubbed the skin off her back, she relates that she is told "*that it would be no matter if*

[her] *head were off too*,"[18] and when Rowlandson first balks at working on the Sabbath, her captors "answered [her], they would break [her] face."[19] In addition to these threats, she hears detailed stories of extreme violence enacted upon captives, such as the fate of a woman captured the same day as her, who is stripped naked, beaten, and eventually burned to death as punishment for her continued requests to be released.[20] On another occasion, Rowlandson meets an American Indian from another encampment and asks after her son; he tells her (falsely) that her son's master "roasted" the boy and he (the man speaking) had eaten a piece of her son's flesh, which he assured her "was very good meat."[21]

Comparably, Fred cannot escape her captivity in Pylea. Much like Rowlandson's limitations through ignorance of the landscape, although Fred figures out how to disable the electric shock collar used to control slaves and escapes to live alone in the woods, she does not have the full knowledge necessary to create a portal that would return her to Los Angeles. Similarly, viewers both infer and witness the use of physical punishment to deter disobedience in slaves. This punishment ranges from the low-grade electrical shocks used on Cordelia to the full power of the collar, which can cause a slave's head to implode. Further, when the slave trader and the Pylean citizen who buys Cordelia are haggling over the purchase, the slaver acknowledges that Cordelia is "maybe a little talkative," before assuring his client "but you can whip it out of her."[22] And, of course, viewers witness Fred's near execution via beheading.

A less immediately obvious but important similarity between the two captivity narratives is the preoccupation with food the women share and how this preoccupation colors their behaviors. In nearly every one of Rowlandson's "removes" (short chapters), she includes commentary on the lack of food available to her or the poor quality or quantity of that food. Initially she characterizes her relationship to the American Indians's different eating habits by saying, "The first week of my being among them, I hardly ate any thing; the second week, I found my stomach grow very faint for want of something; and yet it was very hard to get down their filthy trash: but the third week, though I could think how formerly my stomach would turn against this or that, and I could starve and die before I could eat such things, yet they were sweet and savory to my taste."[23] This preoccupation with food and her changed attitudes toward it culminate late in the narrative when Rowlandson demonstrates her desperation-driven hunger by stealing food from another captive, a young child.[24] While this example is especially shocking, Rowlandson offers it as representative of the "savageness" she wishes to convey about herself in this environment, a temperament her time among the Indians forced her to adopt. More generally, Rowlandson's named diet consists of nuts and bear meat, although she offers a list of various foods designed to impress upon her audience a sense of Otherness in describing her captors' eating habits: "They would eat Horses guts, and ears, and all sorts of wild Birds ... Bear, Venison, Beaver, Tortois, Frogs, Squirrels, Dogs, Skunks, Rattle-snakes; yea, the very Bark of Trees."[25]

Her emphasis on food is unsurprising, given the role adequate food access played in the survival of all individuals at this time, especially English colonists separated from aid by an ocean and attempting to survive in the harsh New England winters. More than this cultural preoccupation, though, Rowlandson's focus on food reveals her authorial style and talent, underpinning her captivity with a metaphor of sustenance: "In a double irony, while she is physically well fed before her capture, she is spiritually malnourished, and while she is poorly fed and almost always hungry during her captivity, she is spiritually replete."[26] Her preoccupation with eating is a rhetorical move that emphasizes the hardship of her captivity experience, a necessary maneuver for the goal of turning her narrative into a testament of her religious devotion and revelatory experience, thereby asserting to herself and her reader her identity and position within the Puritan community following her captivity.

A preoccupation with food, especially the familiar foods Fred could easily access when living in L.A. and her home state of Texas, is one of Fred's early defining characteristics, both in Pylea and after her return to L.A., and Fred's reactions to food (or the thought of food) mirror Rowlandson's own reactions to food while in captivity. For example, in Pylea Fred asks Angel if the "oatmeal" she has made of "crug-grain and thistles" tastes good and then, in the next breath, shouts, "Tacos!"[27] echoing some of Rowlandson's more desperate reactions to food while in captivity. While Rowlandson's recollections are moderated by being written after her experience (and with a specific rhetorical purpose in mind), Fred is, in this moment, still fully ensconced within her captivity experience and cannot yet fully believe in the possibility of returning home, disallowing her the possibility of talking about food as a rhetorical strategy. Fred's exuberant shout startles Angel, and when she sees his surprise, she apologizes, saying, "I love tacos. Do they still have them?"[28] Angel assures her of her favorite food's continued existence, yet when the group returns to L.A., viewers again witness the centrality of familiar food to Fred. The scene opens with the characters mid-conversation as they walk back into the old hotel that serves as Angel Investigations's home base. Not yet able to believe (or fearful of getting her hopes up), Fred asks tentatively, "Are, are you sure about that?" and Cordelia replies, "Trust me. Tacos everywhere."[29] While Fred's love of tacos becomes an endearing quirk in later episodes, it initially serves to reinforce her extended separation from the familiar and her lack of resources during her captivity; here *Angel* engages in the same rhetorical maneuver Rowlandson utilizes with her extended emphasis on the common and often taken-for-granted acts of satisfying hunger and enjoying familiar foods. For Rowlandson, absence or abundance of food serves as a reminder of her past states of spiritual fulfillment; for Fred, access to tacos becomes representative of access to agency and a free life.

While the shared elements of inability to escape, threat of brutal physical punishment, and a preoccupation with food clearly establish a connection between Rowlandson's captivity experience and Fred's, a thoughtful reader might note that these are also elements likely to appear in all narratives of captivity or enslavement. After all, denial of resources—ranging from autonomy to basic necessities—is a key component in the oppression and subjugation of any individual or group. However, Rowlandson's and Fred's experiences share one other important element that conclusively links their experiences: the act of writing about captivity and the role that writing plays in helping each woman establish her position within her community post-captivity.

In Rowlandson's time, publishing one's own writing, especially if one were female, raised questions about vanity, a cardinal sin in Puritan society. To counter that potential for public sinning, Rowlandson's text engages in a standard practice for captivity narratives; its authenticity is established through a preface written by someone other than the author, who testifies to the truthfulness of the narrative and the author's reasons for publishing—namely that she does so only at the urging of friends who believe the text may be instructive to others, not because the author is vain enough to think so herself. Rowlandson's work is rhetorically framed, then, as being something written for private edification—for Rowlandson to more fully understand the spiritual lessons of her captivity—and subsequently published only at the urging of friends who believed her work could be religiously instructive to others. However, a thoughtful reader of Rowlandson's work cannot overlook additional cultural influences and rhetorical strategies in which the narrative engages, factors that suggest other motivations for writing and publishing.

As Neal Salisbury notes, "There are suggestions in her narrative and elsewhere that Rowlandson also wrote in order to clear her name with respect to a number of rumors and innuendo," such as a (forced) marriage between her and one of her Indian captors, as well as the celebrity she enjoyed as one of the more well-known Puritan captives, "especially near the end [of her captivity] when she was the focus of English efforts at redemption and was in fact the first to be freed."[30] Further, the size of the ransom raised for Rowlandson's release may have been a cause for resentment among her peers. The ransom amount, £20, was set by Rowlandson herself at her captor's prompting and specifically justified in her narrative.[31] While Salisbury cites various formulas to argue that the amount was equivalent to $437 in 1991 U.S. currency, Derounian-Stodola and Levernier claim that the ransom "equaled the annual income of a middle-class worker" in Puritan New England.[32] In contrast to Rowlandson's £20 ransom, her narrative does offer the comparison of her fifteen-year-old son's ransom of £7 and her nephew's release for £4, suggesting that Rowlandson's ransom price was exorbitant.[33] In addition to responding to rumors and re-establishing her own modesty, Rowlandson's text undoubtedly also served the religious purpose that more generally characterizes Puritan captivity narratives: "The autobiographical act sought constantly to persuade both writer and reader of God's favor toward that one individual. In [her narrative], Rowlandson deepened her religious sensibility and recovered her conviction that she was one of the Elect."[34] While Rowlandson's text may have worked to address more earthly concerns, such as the jealousies and gossip of her neighbors, it also served to establish Rowlandson's position in her community as one chosen for salvation. Further, while the narrative functions in clearly political ways, it may also, as the preface and various scholars claim, have first privately allowed Rowlandson to make meaning of her captivity and help her (re)establish her faith and understanding of her own role in her community.

Like Rowlandson, Fred engages in writing as a coping and clarifying mechanism as she processes her captivity experience. Of course, Fred's writings are not nearly as collected or polished as Rowlandson's; most of them occur on the walls of her cave in Pylea or her room in Angel's hotel.[35] Fred's initial scribblings are mathematical formulas as she attempts to figure out how to open a portal back to L.A. from Pylea. While this goal is not something she accomplishes on her own, Team Angel's escape from Pylea does rely on her scientific knowledge. Given their disorderly and gibberish-like appearance, the writings on her cave's walls first imply a level of mental instability; however, the act of writing and trying to work through the scientific problem of interdimensional travel undoubtedly helps Fred retain her grasp on sanity when she lives alone in hiding in Pylea. Further, her repetition of this behavior after her return to L.A. facilitates her transformation from the traumatized, escaped captive living in a cave into the young woman who overcomes her fear and joins Team Angel in their fight against evil. Fred initially latches onto Angel as her rescuer, and his absence for three months immediately following the group's return from Pylea (when he leaves to deal with his grief over Buffy's death) is a setback in her recovery. During this period, she remakes her room at the Hyperion into a new cave, a protected space with walls once again covered in writing. Instead of cracking the portal puzzle, Fred's writings are now an attempt to make sense of her captivity, of the horrors and loneliness she experienced when she "got lost" from the world she understood.[36] Fred explains to Angel that the writings on her walls are "a story": "Once upon a time, there was a girl who lived all alone in a horrible cave, so far from home it made her chest hurt. And every day ... the girl tried to figure out a way to escape. None of her plans ever succeeded."[37] Fred then characterizes her rescue in terms of the traditional fairy tale trope where the valiant knight rescues the damsel in distress, acknowledging in her rhetorical construction the unrealistic expectations she pinned upon her rescuer, Angel, and the passivity of the role in which she cast herself, concluding that after her rescue, "the handsome man went away again. And even though she didn't mean to, didn't want to ... the girl just built herself another cave, hoping he would save her again."[38] Fred's writings on her room's walls are her attempt to write a captivity narrative, to make sense of her experience so that she can understand who she is and what her place is now that she has been freed from captivity, recognizing that her captivity has altered her.

The episode "Fredless" (3.05) is a turning point for Fred, offering her the opportunity to return to her childhood home and the comfort of her family, leaving behind Team Angel, Los Angeles, and other reminders of her captivity. Fred's transition begins when she explains her narrative to Angel, an explanation that ends with the sad realization that "you can't save me this time, can you?"[39] While Fred initially understands this revelation to mean she should leave L.A., by the episode's ending, she realizes that instead of a narrative in which she relies on others to save her, Fred can transform herself into a contributing member of the team of demon fighters who rescued her — she can be part of that community and use her experiences to help others who find themselves in some way captive to evil's influence. The episode's final scene reinforces the role that Fred's writings about captivity play in her recovery and how they help establish her position in her new community, even as the scene twists captivity narrative expectations. Team Angel, plus Fred's parents, are painting Fred's room at the hotel, covering up her various writings on the wall. Cordelia enters the room with pizza for a dinner break and offers some to Fred. The former captive responds, "In a minute. I just want to finish this section,"[40] and turns to a drawing of a horse and two people — herself and her rescuer Angel — atop it. She deliberately paints over the image, erasing the false fairy-tale narrative that characterizes her as a victim in need of rescuing, an act that "signif[ies] her empowerment," as Janine R. Harrison notes.[41] Whereas Mary Rowlandson published the narrative that she wrote to make sense of her captivity, Fred erases hers, signifying that she is ready to create a new narrative for her life, one separated from her past role as an escaped captive living alone in the woods. The twist to this literary tradition is appropriate for a television series that repeatedly subverts and reinvents various tropes, genres, and character archetypes.

Genre Implications and Cultural Biases

While captivity narratives like Rowlandson's initially functioned as religious texts, the genre influenced more than Puritan culture and was adopted in later centuries by white Americans held captive by American Indian tribes in other parts of the United States and its territories. The basic construction of colonist/pioneer identity became a construction of American identity — one which clearly situated white, Christian (mostly Protestant) Americans against the non–Christian people of color who struggle to maintain their own culture rather than assimilate into dominant American ideology and practice. As Rebecca Blevins Faery observes, "In the popular-culture history of the United States, conflicts between Indians and whites have acquired epic and archetypal dimensions and have served as a universal definition of [white] American identity and history."[42] Faery's observation, of course, refers to American identity as synonymous with the white, Anglo-European identity that has dominated the construction of so much of American history.

In fact, several scholars cite an evolutionary progression for the captivity narrative genre that begins with its roots as a "straightforward and generally unadorned religious" text in Rowlandson's time, which "attempted to synthesize the Puritan religious outlook of the late Reformation with the merging scientific spirit of the early Enlightenment. In such a union, these tales heralded the future discourse of the new nation and served as a formative crucible in which that discourse and culture could develop."[43] From this point, the American captivity narrative transitioned, by the mid–eighteenth century, into a "means for spreading propaganda against those nations and powers that blocked Anglo-American westerly settlement. Accordingly, this propaganda was directed against the French, the English, and the American Indian, all of whom at different times and in different degrees were seen as enemies."[44] In the nineteenth century, the genre transformed into one that "reminded white Americans of their past, which could in turn be used to inspire patriotism and national pride. Captivity accounts also ... became a means ... for preserving historical and ethnological information about the Indian and for illustrating frontier heroism."[45] Overall, "accounts first became stylized and romanticized for literary 'effect,' then rendered overtly sensational and melodramatic though still grounded largely in fact, and finally highly fictionalized — culminating in the outright novel of sensibility with the context of Indian captivity employed as a fictive device for narrative management."[46]

Angel's parallels to the captivity narrative genre, then, also call to mind the genre's troubling history and impact on American national identity and the cultural racism in which the genre so often participated. Given the centuries since Rowlandson's captivity and the changes the captivity narrative has undergone, one might be skeptical of the connection that I have just outlined. However, from the first moment Pylea is pictured, when Cordelia wakes up after being pulled through a portal, the suggestion of Cordelia's position in the demon dimension as allegorical to being lost in the wilderness amongst American Indian tribes is inescapable. Cordelia wakes in a wooded area; as she stands up, she is framed in a close-up and strange noises reminiscent of the horns of a hunting party echo around her. The camera abruptly shifts to a long-distance shot in which Cordelia becomes a tiny figure framed by stretched animal skins and furs hung from trees.[47] In addition, the first creature Cordelia encounters is an animal that growls menacingly and chases after her; while the "hellbeast"[48] turns out to be more like a friendly dog than a dangerous lion, its initial appearance and threatening manner reinforce the "primitive" quality of Pylea and the threat such an environment poses to the unarmed (white) woman. Cordelia is shortly thereafter captured by a slaver, and her experiences cause Lorne's comments about his home dimension to take on a fearful, and fearfully familiar, rhetorical bent — of the Other (in this case demon) as savage, in need of a civilizing influence provided by a more enlightened society.

Lorne's descriptions of his home as a place with "screwed up values ... a world of only good and evil, black and white, no gray. No music, no art" and his lack of desire to return — "I'd rather have a hydrochloric acid facial. I'd rather invite a hive of wasps to nest in my throat. I'd rather sit through a junior high school production of *Cats!*"[49] — foreshadow Pylea's characterization as an uncivilized, savage place, especially in light of the way that the possession and valuing of arts — like music — have traditionally represented a society's level of cultural advancement. Further, the native Pyleans offer a sharp visual contrast to the viewer's or Team Angel's expectations, suggesting that they are different in the same kind of fundamental ways that Anglo-American culture has, in the past, believed American Indians to be. First, Lorne's cousin Landok is the quintessential primitive warrior, interested only in proving his bravery and hunting his prey, and Angel's acceptance into Pylean society is predicated on Landok's testimony of Angel's warrior abilities (in spite of Angel's "cow-like" appearance). Aside from the fierce warrior stereotype, many Pyleans, like Lorne, are green-skinned with red horns and eyes, reinforcing their difference from Team Angel's appearances, while others are less different, but still visibly Other.[50] Also, Lorne's people are anatomically different from humans; their hearts are found not in their chests, but in their left buttocks, and decapitation does not kill them as they must also be dismembered. To further reinforce the Otherness of this demon species, Lorne's mother's gender performance contrasts with expectations; she is, by modern American gender conventions, more lumberjack than loving mother. When Lorne's headless body is smuggled to his family before it can be dismembered following his decapitation, his mother's action of placing it on the "lice pile instead of the maggot heap"[51] is depicted as a kindness, but the "incivility" of either option reinforces the difference between Team Angel's world and Lorne's home society.

Of course Team Angel's further experiences in Pylea complicate the underlying "savage Other" trope. Angel first revels in the freedoms this alternate dimension offers him before realizing that he is all the more savage in his demon form, refuting the direct analogy of Pyleans equaling "bad" and humans (or former humans) equaling "good." The slave metaphor clearly reframes at least part of Pylean society in terms of a more-charged racial (species) metaphor for modern American viewers, as does the revelation that slavery in Pylea has been orchestrated by representatives of the evil law firm Wolfram & Hart (suggesting that the Pyleans are, to some degree, dupes of a false religion that endorses slavery). Moreover, the "testing" that Cordelia (unwillingly) undergoes to prove the divine origin of her visions recalls the sort of trials witches were subjected to during the Early Modern period in Europe and the Salem witch trials in America, which occurred about fifteen years following Mary Rowlandson's captivity. Such complications are a hallmark of Joss Whedon and company's genre-blending approach to storytelling, but they do not erase or override the impact of the unavoidable "Pyleans as Indian" comparison, particularly when the similarities of the captivity narrative genre are so clear between Fred and Mary Rowlandson.

The presence of this comparison is especially troubling as it offers more evidence of Whedon and company's weakness in representing racial differences with the same empowering and captivatingly positive force and skill with which they engage questions of gender and sexuality in *Angel* and other television series. The iconic and archetypal nature of the Indian/white man (savage/civilized) conflict in American history, literature, and culture means that (mis)representations of American Indians are particularly tricky and fraught with pitfalls. Indeed, of all racial or ethnic minority groups, American Indians are the minority most (consistently) problematically represented (literally and allegorically) in Whedon's shows, ranging from the vengeful Indian spirit Hus in the *Buffy the Vampire Slayer* episode "Pangs" (4.08) to the suggestion of *Firefly*'s Reavers as the savage Other waiting to attack those who venture too far away from "civilized" society.[52] While various critics have engaged these representations of American Indians within the context of their respective series, Fred's captivity experience, and the attendant comparison of Pylean society to American Indians, adds a third point of comparison and helps identify a troubling pattern, one which is not exclusively representative of Whedon and company's conceptualization of the racial Other but rather also speaks to larger implications for American culture. A deeper study of this topic is the purview of another essay, however.

Conclusion

Overall, Mary Rowlandson's captivity narrative, *The Sovereignty and Goodness of God*, offers a fruitful comparison to *Angel*'s Pylean story arc and the early Season Three episodes that introduce Fred and establish her place on Team Angel. Not only do the two captivity narratives share several significant characteristics, but Rowlandson's and Fred's acts of writing about captivity as a means of processing their experiences and further establishing their places in their respective communities also makes clear the value of considering the two narratives side-by-side. Further, the conventions of the captivity narrative genre — the earliest uniquely American literary form — highlight troubling cultural biases and archetypes that underpin American cultural and literary history and *Angel*'s depiction of Pylean society. Bringing to light the allegorical suggestion of Pyleans as the archetypal "savage Indian" further reveals a pattern of problematic representation of American Indians through Whedon's television series, opening the door for further inquiry about this pattern and larger questions about representations of the racial Other in *Angel*, other works by Joss Whedon, and contemporary American culture and literature at large. Although the fantasy element of Pylea is emphasized by episode titles alluding to fantasy stories well known in contemporary American society—*The Wizard of Oz* and *Alice in Wonderland* are referenced by the episode titles "Over the Rainbow" (2.20), "There's No Place Like Plrtz Glrb"(2.22), and "Through the Looking Glass" (2.21), respectively—the clear situating of the slavery metaphor within an American context at the story arc's ending also demands that viewers consider other American cultural texts and genres contributing to the construction of Pylea and Fred's experiences there. While the motto "There's no place like home" is undoubtedly meaningful during captivity, once the captive returns, she finds, as Mary Rowlandson and Fred both do, that home is no longer the same place it once was because the captive is no longer the same person she once was. However, the restored captive may find a means of reconciling these differences and (re)asserting her place within her home community through writing about her captivity.

Notes

1. "There's No Place Like Plrtz Glrb," *Angel*, DVD, written and directed David Greenwalt (2001; 20th Century–Fox, 2003).
2. Ibid.
3. Ibid.
4. Other connections to this legacy are made in a number of ways, ranging from the clear species-based means of differentiating slaves from free citizens (humans as slaves, the Pylean demons as free citizens) to Groo's comment in "Through the Looking Glass" that his human-like appearance demonstrates that he has "cow's [human] blood." Groo's comment alludes to the "one-drop rule," which dictated individuals in America who could be proven to have "one drop" of African ancestry through cross-racial procreation were considered "black" and treated as such regardless of their physical appearance, and to the idea of atavism, the reappearance of biological features in a child that the parents (or possibly more generations past) did not display—both means of distinguishing one's value in society based on one's physical appearance. The act of situating the slavery context in relation to American history calls upon knowledge most American (and possibly other) viewers would possess, providing an obvious historical corollary for viewers. "Through the Looking Glass," *Angel*, DVD, written and directed by Tim Minear (2001; 20th Century–Fox, 2003).
5. Most critical scholarship, including Stacey Abbott's *Angel*, TV Milestones Series (Detroit: Wayne State University Press, 2009) and various essays in Abbott's edited collection *Reading* Angel: *The TV Spin-off with a Soul* (London: I.B. Tauris, 2005), pays only passing attention to early characterizations of Fred or her role on Team Angel, focusing instead on the impact of her death and transformation into Illyria on the other characters or on Illyria herself.
6. For more on Angel in Pylea, see Stacey Abbott, "Kicking Ass and Singing 'Mandy,'" in *Reading* Angel: *The TV Spin-off with a Soul*, ed. Stacey Abbott (London: I.B. Tauris, 2005), 1–13. For more on Lorne and/in Pylea, see Matthew Mills, "Ubi Caritas? Music as Narrative Agent in *Angel*," in *Reading* Angel: *The TV Spin-off with a Soul*, ed. Stacey Abbott (London: I.B. Tauris, 2005), 31–43; and Stan Beeler, "Outing Lorne: Performance for the Performers," in *Reading* Angel: *The TV Spin-off with a Soul*, ed. Stacey Abbott (London: I.B. Tauris, 2005), 87–100.
7. Jes Battis, *Blood Relations: Chosen Families in* Buffy the Vampire Slayer *and* Angel (Jefferson, NC: McFarland, 2005), 174n3.
8. Mary Rowlandson, "The Sovereignty and Goodness of God," in *The Sovereignty and Goodness of God, Together with the Faithfulness of His Promises Displayed: Being a Narrative of the Captivity and Restoration of Mrs. Mary Rowlandson and Related Documents*,

ed. Neal Salisbury (Boston: Bedford Books, 1997), 62–112. In reference to the question of critical merit and timeline, Frances Roe Kestler asserts that "the majority [of critics] agree that Rowlandson's work was the first and best example of the genre" in her introduction to *The Indian Captivity Narrative: A Woman's View* (New York: Garland Press, 1990), xxiii.

9. James D. Hartman, *Providence Tales and the Birth of American Literature* (Baltimore: The Johns Hopkins University Press, 1999), 16; Kathryn Zabelle Derounian-Stodola and James Arthur Levernier, *The Indian Captivity Narrative, 1550–1900* (New York: Twayne Press, 1993), 14.

10. Richard VanDerBeets, *Held Captive by Indians: Selected Narratives 1642–1836* (Knoxville: University of Tennessee Press, 1973), xi; Derounian-Stodola and Levernier, *Indian Captivity Narrative, 1550–1900*, 94.

11. Hartman, *Providence Tales*, 34.

12. Rowlandson, *Sovereignty*, 83. All quotes herein from Rowlandson's narrative reflect spelling, grammar, and emphasis used by Rowlandson in the second edition reprinted in Salisbury's critical edition.

13. Rowlandson, *Sovereignty*, 84.

14. "Over the Rainbow," *Angel*, DVD, written by Mere Smith, directed by Fred Keller (2001; 20th Century–Fox, 2003).

15. Ibid.

16. Ibid.

17. Rowlandson, *Sovereignty*, 84.

18. Ibid., 87.

19. Ibid., 79.

20. Ibid., 77–78.

21. Ibid., 87. Rowlandson's recounting of enacted violence presents an interesting conundrum for readers in terms of the authenticity of her claims. Although the threats of violence she details are often horrific and shocking, it is notable that she does not witness any such violence other than that enacted in the initial raid upon her settlement. However, Derounian-Stodola and Levernier suggest that the lack of direct violence Rowlandson witnessed may be at odds with captives' experiences generally: "One way in which Indians purportedly avenged themselves against their enemies involved burning a prisoner at the stake. This activity, usually presented in gruesome detail though almost certainly not as frequently or flagrantly practiced as many captivity authors would have their audience believe, appears with such regularity in the captivity narratives that it becomes almost a stock feature. Other ritualistic forms of torture and death that Indians reportedly practiced on their captives included mutilation, dismemberment, decapitation, and cannibalism" (*Indian Captivity Narrative, 1550–1900*, 3). However, on multiple occasions in her narrative, Rowlandson notes (albeit in wonder) how her safety and personage were largely respected while in captivity. During the Ninth Remove, when Rowlandson becomes lost while attempting to visit her son at a neighboring encampment, she comments, "Though I was gone from home, and met all sorts of *Indians*, and those I had no knowledge of, and there being no Christian soul near me; yet not one of them offered me the least imaginable miscarriage to me" (*Sovereignty*, 84). Likewise, during the Twelfth Remove she states, "*I have been in the midst of... [the American Indians] ... by night and day, alone and in company: sleeping all sorts together, and yet not one of them ever offered me the least abuse of unchastity to me, in word or action*" (Ibid., 107). Further, the editor's note on this passage claims that "while most colonists feared otherwise, there is no record of any sexual violation of captive women by Native Americans anywhere in Eastern North America" (*Sovereignty*, 107n82).

22. "Over the Rainbow."

23. Rowlandson, *Sovereignty*, 79.

24. Rowlandson writes: "Then I went to another *Wigwam*, where there were two of the *English Children*; the *Squaw* was boyling *Horses feet*, then she cut me off a little piece, and gave one of the *English Children* a piece also. Being very hungry I had quickly eat up mine, but the Child could not bite it, it was so tough and sinewy, but lay sucking, gnawing, chewing and slobbering of it in the mouth and hand, then I took it of the Child, and ate it myself, and savory it was to my taste" (*Sovereignty*, 96).

25. Ibid., 106.
26. Derounian-Stodola and Levernier, *Indian Captivity Narrative, 1550–1900,* 107.
27. "There's No Place like Plrtz Glrb."
28. Ibid.
29. Ibid.
30. Neal Salisbury, "Introduction: Mary Rowlandson and Her Removes" in *The Sovereignty and Goodness of God, Together with the Faithfulness of His Promises Displayed: Being a Narrative of the Captivity and Restoration of Mrs. Mary Rowlandson and Related Documents,* ed. Neal Salisbury (Boston: Bedford Books, 1997), 1–60 at 43.
31. Rowlandson explains: "I thought if I should speak of but a little, it would be slighted and hinder the matter; if of a great sum, I knew not where it would be procured" (*Sovereignty,* 98). Salisbury notes that "Rowlandson's elaborate explanation of the ransom price she sets suggests that she may have been criticized for it by some colonists" (Ibid., 98n64).
32. Ibid., 98n63; Derounian-Stodola and Levernier, *Indian Captivity Narrative, 1550–1900,* 4.
33. Rowlandson, *Sovereignty,* 110.
34. Derounian-Stodola and Levernier, *Indian Captivity Narrative, 1550–1900,* 102.
35. One could argue that the physics paper Fred publishes and presents at a conference in the fourth season is another means of captivity-inspired writing. "Supersymmetry," *Angel,* DVD, written by Elizabeth Craft and Sarah Fain, directed by Bill L. Norton (2002; 20th Century–Fox, 2004).
36. "Fredless," *Angel,* DVD, written by Mere Smith, directed by Marita Grabiak (2001; 20th Century–Fox, 2003).
37. Ibid.
38. Ibid.
39. Ibid.
40. Ibid.
41. Janine R. Harrison, "Gender Politics in *Angel*: Traditional vs. Non-traditional Corporate Climates," in *Reading* Angel: *The TV Spin-off with a Soul,* ed. Stacey Abbott (London: I.B. Tauris, 2005), 118–131 at 129.
42. Rebecca Blevins Faery, *Cartographies of Desire: Captivity, Race, and Sex in the Shaping of an American Nation* (Norman: University of Oklahoma Press, 1999), 7.
43. Richard VanDerBeets, *The Indian Captivity Narrative: An American Genre* (New York: University Press of America, 1984), ix; Hartman, *Providence Tales,* 2.
44. Derounian-Stodola and Levernier, *Indian Captivity Narrative, 1550–1900,* 23.
45. Ibid., 36.
46. VanDerBeets, *Indian Captivity Narrative: An American Genre,* 25.
47. "Belonging," *Angel,* DVD, written by Shawn Ryan, directed by Turi Meyer (2001; 20th Century–Fox, 2003).
48. "Over the Rainbow."
49. "Belonging"; "Over the Rainbow."
50. In fact, the residents of Pylea who do not look like Lorne are red-skinned demons or they have Caucasian coloring but their facial features appear deformed by "human" standards—invoking either radicalized depictions of "redskins" as evil or old beliefs and stereotypes wherein physical deformity is equated with evil or damnation.
51. "There's No Place Like Plrtz Glrb."
52. "Pangs," *Buffy the Vampire Slayer,* DVD, written by Jane Espenson, directed by Michael Lang (1999; 20th Century–Fox, 2003). For more on the depiction of Hus in *Buffy,* see Ewan Kirkland, "The Caucasian Persuasion in *Buffy the Vampire Slayer,*" *Slayage: The Online International Journal of Buffy Studies* 5, no. 1 (June 2003), www.slayageonline.com; and Sally Emmons-Featherston, "Is that Stereotype Dead? Working with and Against 'Western' Stereotypes in *Buffy*" in *The Truth of* Buffy: *Essays on Fiction Illuminating Reality,* ed. Emily Dial-Driver, Sally Emmons-Featherston, Jim Ford, and Carolyn Anne Taylor (Jefferson, NC: McFarland, 2008), 55–66. Also, to be fair, the comparison of Reavers to American Indians is more obvious early in *Firefly* and somewhat reduced by the revelations about the Reavers's origins in *Firefly*'s sequel feature film *Serenity.* Further, various critics have argued both in favor and against the "Reavers as Indian" comparison. For more, see J. Douglas Rabb and J.

Michael Richardson, "Reavers and Redskins: Creating the Frontier Savage," in *Investigating Firefly and* Serenity: *Science Fiction on the Frontier*, ed. Rhonda V. Wilcox and Tanya R. Cochran (London: I.B. Tauris, 2008), 127–138; and Agnes B. Curry, "'We Don't Say "Indian"': On the Paradoxical Construction of the Reavers," *Slayage: The Online International Journal of Buffy Studies* 7, no. 1 (Winter 2008), www.slayageonline.com.

Feminist Abuse Survivor Narratives in *Angel* and Sarah Daniels's *Beside Herself*

ANIKA STAFFORD

A girl being chased down an alley; the tear-streaked face of a woman recounting memories of abuse; a dark room with a female character about to turn on a light only to find attackers lurking around a corner — these images are a common feature of television today. In popular cultural portrayals of abuse, such images are too often trivialized, used to move a plot forward, or included to incite an exotic/dangerous feeling for the viewer. These images starkly contrast with the reality of the devastating effect abuse has on individuals' lives. Joss Whedon's television shows (to date: *Buffy the Vampire Slayer*, *Angel*, *Firefly*, and *Dollhouse*), however, offer a markedly different portrayal of abuse. Though full of violent, dangerous, and scary images, Whedon's creations also provide viewers with and engage them in serious social commentary about abuse and its ramifications for society and individual survivors. Women experiencing abuse are not portrayed as hapless victims, and the abuse is not shown for lurid titillation. Rather, in Whedon's shows, survivors of abuse possess great survival skills and ingenuity within a context of social violence, offering an alternative construction to mainstream television's portrayal of those who have experienced abuse.

Dominant discourse surrounding abuse in institutions such as mainstream media, education, and medicine, has created insidious social frameworks that shape cultural understandings of gender, sexuality, and mental health. Discourse that disregards survivor narratives of women, children, and disenfranchised others classified as "mad" often serves to perpetuate a cultural climate in which abusers are not held accountable for their actions. In turn, this creates social norms in which abuse thrives without consequence. The past thirty years have witnessed a proliferation of feminist scholarship seeking to uproot said norms and create alternative, feminist abuse survivor discourse to counteract the pervasive and abuse-perpetuating mainstream. Such alternative discourse is employed by many genres of literature, each with tools for illustrating abuse survivors' struggles to validate their memories and move away from abusive dynamics.

One genre that offers a unique representation of feminist abuse survivor discourse is contemporary theatre, which provides a striking medium wherein survivors' journeys are brought to life in front of the audience, embodying both survivors and the effects of abuse. One prime example of theatrical engagement with feminist narratives concerning trauma recovery is Sarah Daniels's *Beside Herself*, a play that brings feminist abuse survivor strategies to life in theatrical form through the main character Evelyn and her alternate persona Eve.[1] The majority of the scenes in *Beside Herself* alternate between St. Dymphna's housing for people with mental illness, where Evelyn volunteers, and the home of George, a doctor who is also Evelyn's abuser/father. These settings situate Evelyn in the centre of institutional/medical discourses surrounding abuse. In *Beside Herself*, Evelyn is shadowed in every scene by Eve, a character embodying the part of Evelyn who is constantly engaged with survival mechanisms, such as covering up abuse and disassociating. The play follows Evelyn's stages from accepting self-blame to standing up to her father.

Like drama, the visual nature of television brings feminist literary themes to life, and like *Beside Herself*, *Angel* furthers feminist theatrical conventions, specifically through the primary character Cordelia and through Bethany, the guest character in "Untouched" (2.04).[2] Both Daniels and Whedon illustrate disassociation through visual means, giving form to this abuse survival technique. Cultural stigmas attached to mental illness dismiss survivors who engage in disassociative behaviors. By validating the cause of a survivor's disassociation, Daniels and Whedon help to alleviate this trend. For Evelyn/Eve, Cordelia, and Bethany, the on-going struggle to survive the violence in their lives is given respectful acknowledgment as opposed to being reason for related characters and viewers to denigrate the survivor according to notions of "madness." Moreover, through their theatrical depictions of disassociation and survivors overcoming the effects of abuse, both *Beside Herself* and *Angel* highlight key components of feminist abuse survivor discourse: (re)claiming power from abuse and the function of allies in helping survivors (re)claim that power.

Abuse survivor discourse focuses on how people can recover from abuse. Feminist abuse survivor discourse argues that recovery of agency and sense of self occurs through specific speech acts, such as reclaiming derogatory terms and privileging conversation with peer allies over speech by experts. The idea of speech acts functioning to reclaim power, especially from pejorative terms used to perpetuate abuse, is based on the understanding that specific societal hierarchies utilize language to invalidate women and children's experiences, especially experiences of abuse. As Linda Alcoff and Laura Gray summarize, "A variety of discursive strategies have operated to pre-empt or to dismiss the speech of women and children generally and survivors in particular."[3] Because these hierarchies use language to remove power and agency from those most often abused, they create a climate in which abuse flourishes. In order to break the cycle of abuse, survivors often use one of the tools of oppression — language — to challenge and destroy these social constructions of power. Feminist discourse places importance on survivors finding their own voices to break isolation and see their abuse as part of social structures rather than an incident unique to their lives alone.

Many theorists, like Carol E. Barringer, frame abuse survivors' speech acts in unequivocally positive terms.[4] However, authors such as Alcoff and Gray draw on a Foucauldian analysis to warn about how discourse can recreate rather than subvert dominant systems of power. They caution that the incitement to speak can take place within an oppressive framework, invalidating the speaker: "Before we speak we need to look at where the incitement to speak originates, what relations of power and domination may exist between those who incite and those who are asked to speak, as well as to whom the disclosure is directed."[5] When feminist discourse in which the "incitement to speak" takes place in a survivor-controlled context, the speech act can be subversive and healing, rather than perpetuating the social structures which allow abuse.

To facilitate survivors' ability to use speech acts in a way that is amenable to rebuilding senses of self and breaking isolation, feminist writings on abuse have drawn on "consciousness raising" models from the 1980s that focused on women becoming allies in articulating their experiences of oppression in order to link violence in their lives to the larger society and fight abuse on a systemic level. Changing the authority of speech acts can shift relations of power from women being objects of study by professionals (an "expert" model) to being seen as autonomous subjects of their own making. Expert models, as often found in mainstream institutions, have a tendency to view individual behavior as a deficit of the person, as opposed to seeing their struggles in a larger social context. The result is that effects of abuse, such as disassociation, are seen as individual problems, not as a survival strategy in the face of trauma. Additionally, expert models have often dictated how survivors tell their stories (e.g., what information is deemed important to a medical model in making a psychiatric diagnosis) as opposed to speech acts that a survivor deems relevant for the recovery process. Instead of pathologizing individuals whose speech acts transgress social norms, epistemological validity is afforded to the ways survivors incorporate effects of trauma, including those effects classified as mental illness, into reshaping their futures. Ally approaches are often framed with attention to individual strengths and resilience, including those developed in order to live through abuse. Feminist abuse survivor discourse has stressed the importance of survivor-controlled dialogue — that the survivor, more than a medical professional, has the capacity to discern what is useful to speak of for one's own recovery.

Writing feminist abuse survivor discourse necessitates a strategic balance between recognizing survivor agency and strength without minimizing violation. One way in which this can occur is through the reclamation of language used to disempower those who have been abused. Both *Beside Herself* and

Cordelia's actions in "Rm w/a Vu" (1.05) portray a respectful negotiation of balance between illustrating survivor resilience, without erasing the harm of violence through the rejection of victim-blaming rhetoric, and the reclamation of derogatory terms used to victimize targets of abuse.[6]

In Act One: Scene Two of *Beside Herself*, Evelyn attends a meeting where male colleagues discuss childhood sexual abuse. One man frames such abuse as a case where "the man [of the heterosexual, nuclear family] is looking for affection and nurturing, albeit inappropriately, and therefore the whole family, starting with the mother, need re-educating into their appropriate roles,"[7] placing the blame for the abuser's actions on those who are oppressed by them. Another man states that survivors are all "naughty precocious girls who certainly had no doubts about their attractiveness to men,"[8] again illustrating the totalizing power of victim-blaming discourse. For the duration of the scene, Evelyn, with Eve's prompting, escapes this discourse by listing colors she could repaint her bathroom. Through this task, Evelyn disassociates from the moment, relying on old patterns that enabled her to survive abuse as a child — disconnection from her body and preoccupation with "covering up" the situation. Evelyn is not yet ready to vocally reject the victim-blaming discourse and instead separates herself from it. Significantly, Daniels does not pathologize Eve's presence or actions in *Beside Herself*. Instead, the theatrics of depicting disembodiment through interactions with another character validate disassociation, an understandable response to victim-blaming discourse that can trigger survivors' memories of abuse.

Evelyn makes the shift from internal rejection of victim-blaming discourse to outward reclamation of harmful terms in Act Two: Scene Ten when she confronts her father about his abuse of her. Eve is present in that scene, but instead of turning on Evelyn (herself), she turns against the perpetrator of her abuse (her father) calling him a "fucking liar" and a "bastard."[9] Evelyn and Eve have become allies, rejecting lies they were told about themselves and their situation. After confronting her father and exposing him as an abuser in his personal and professional life, Evelyn's father calls her a "stupid bitch."[10] Instead of this silencing her, or retreating into disassociative habits of "covering up" the abuse, Evelyn names her father's actions unforgivable. She now believes that she need only forgive herself and does not need to accept him after the pain that he caused in her life. Daniels frames Evelyn no longer being vulnerable to the threat of being called a "bitch" as a milestone in her progression toward recovery. *Beside Herself* illustrates feminist abuse survivor discourse that stresses the need to (re)claim power through the repudiation of victim-blaming discourse and the salvaging of derogatory terms (be it the threat of being "mad"/"crazy" or that of being a "bitch") for the survivor's benefit. Eve's presence and influence on Evelyn's actions here are not pathologized but theatricalized as an integral part of Evelyn's recovery, which (literally) gives voice to the hidden nature of her abuse, making it observable, hearable, and knowable.

Similarly, in *Angel*, Whedon's creative team demonstrates an understanding of feminist abuse survivor discourse through the rejection of victim-blaming dialogues and the reclamation of pejorative terms. "Rm w/a Vu" is a defining episode in which Cordelia claims (feminist) control over violation in an abusive situation by reclaiming previously abusive and oppressive discourse. In this episode, Cordelia moves into an apartment haunted by the ghost of a murderous mother. Maude Pearson died of a heart attack after killing her adult son, Dennis, in order to keep him from marrying a woman she classified as a "tramp."[11] In the years following Maude's death, several "suicides" occur in the apartment. Each victim is a woman who Maude believes to be another "slut,"[12] and therefore unworthy of her son. Since Maude can not physically kill the women, she emotionally abuses them in order to convince the women that they are worthless, culminating in each woman's act of suicide. Significantly, Maude killed her son by burying him alive in the apartment wall. The fact that Dennis's corpse — the proof of Maude's abusive nature — remains covered by a literal wall parallels the ways in which abuse is all too often covered up in society through social structures that diminish or dismiss survivors' claims. So long as Dennis remains hidden, women moving into the apartment remain vulnerable to Maude's abuse. As asserted within feminist abuse survivor discourse, the culture of secrecy leaves a legacy of vulnerability for women until the abuse can be exposed, ending the cycle of (gendered) shame.

When Cordelia moves in, the apartment holds particular significance to her as it symbolizes the comfortable life Cordelia once led but has since vanished because her family lost their fortune. On Cordy's first night in the apartment, Maude begins throwing items across the room and causing tornados throughout the house. Like many who experience domestic violence, Cordelia initially minimizes the gravity of her situation, by insisting that she is fine and asserting to the ghost that she has already survived one hell(mouth) in Sunnydale and can do it again. But, Cordelia's denial of abuse only feeds the abuser's power, and parallel to the cycle of abuse, the hauntings escalate. Maude tells Cordelia that she is unworthy of the house and that no one will ever care about her. As with Evelyn in *Beside Herself*, Cordelia's inability to access support in this moment results in her internalization of the abuse being directed at her.

To further establish her power in the situation, Maude's ghost employs gendered messages of female value/valuelessness drawn from dominant culture. For example, she capitalizes on messages that sexually "deviant" women have no value. Maude calls Cordelia "a cheap, small town tramp trying to be better than she is."[13] She continues, "You don't have any friends. Why would anyone care about you? You don't deserve to live here. You don't deserve anything."[14] Although Cordelia's friends, Angel and Doyle, try to help her, Cordelia's acceptance of Maude's victim-blaming strategies and internalization of the abuse prevent the men from being ultimately successful.

As the violence reaches a peak, the parallel to violence against women is reinforced through a visual reference to sexual abuse and rape. Cordelia is forced toward the bedroom by an unseen power, her arms outstretched in protest. Once inside the bedroom — a domestic space more likely to be a site of abuse — Cordelia is even more trapped, isolation being a key means through which abusers maintain control over those they abuse. Cordelia pleads with Maude, offering to leave the apartment if the ghost will release her. While driving Cordelia away was Maude's initial goal in tormenting her, now that Maude has complete control over Cordelia, she replies that Cordelia has ruined her "nice home," implying that Cordelia deserves to be punished for that transgression, saying, "You know what happens next" and "You'd better be sorry, you stupid little bitch," before instructing Cordelia to make a noose out of the bed sheets.[15] *Angel* breaks the traditional abusive cycle at this point. When Maude calls Cordelia a "bitch," Cordelia stops crying because she realizes that the qualities for which she is being shamed are, in fact, the tools for her own resistance. Cordelia stands up and reiterates, "I'm a bitch."[16] This moment is a powerful turning point for Cordelia as she realizes that she is not a helpless victim, but rather "the nastiest girl in Sunnydale history"; she warns Maude to get ready to leave because, "Lady, the bitch is back."[17]

When Cordelia acknowledges the abuse while infusing her survival mechanisms with pride, she is able to reject Maude's victim-blaming strategy and take back her home and sense of self. This is done through contesting derogatory meanings in pejorative terms used against women, in this case the term "bitch," claiming them as a site of power. Feminist abuse survivor discourse also positions victims, while facing trauma, in a place to possess the agency with which to challenge the abuse in their lives and end the cycle of violence. When she reclaims the term "bitch," Cordelia defeats Maude and the malevolent ghost is cast out of her apartment. Just as Eve's presence as an embodiment of Evelyn's coping strategies is not pathologized in *Beside Herself, Angel* celebrates rather than stigmatizes Cordelia's embrace of the identity of being a "bitch," a term often used to degrade and belittle women. In fact, throughout the series, Cordelia continues to develop an unabashed, brazen sense of self, a "bitchiness" that is paramount to her ability to fight significant attacks. Though further assaults overpower her by the end of the series, she is not a helpless victim and demonstrates considerable agency and resistance. As is often advocated within feminist abuse survivor discourse, Cordelia's sense of self, gained through fighting her own abuse, is later used to challenge abuse on a systemic level.

Cordelia goes on to use the reclamation of the word "bitch," not only for herself but to hold other women accountable for allowing the perpetuation of abuse in others' lives. When she is trying to find a man, Billy, who is rampantly spreading violence against women (enabled by an evil law firm), she confronts Lilah, a lawyer who has been attacked by Billy and yet refuses to aid Cordelia in stopping him. Cordelia refers to the violence she has experienced from the law firm as well as to Lilah's situation. She states, "It's not the pain. It's the helplessness. The certainty that there is nothing you can do to stop it, that your life can be thrown away in an instant by someone else. He doesn't care. He'll beat you down until you stay down because he doesn't even think of you as alive — no woman should ever have to go through that, and no woman strong enough to wear the mantel of 'vicious bitch' would ever put up with it."[18] Though previously in their conversation "bitch" was used to criticize Lilah's actions, Cordelia uses it (even critically) as recognition of a person's strength and resilience. In this instance, the word itself is a site of resistance to violence. Cordelia's reclamation of the word from its silencing potential is so complete that calling Lilah a bitch is Cordelia's leverage to convince Lilah to end violence.

Although *Beside Herself*'s theatrical construction of Eve as a separate person from Evelyn dramatizes the disassociative state, Daniels's work ultimately offers a synthesis of the two selves, reinforcing what viewers of this drama understand: Evelyn and Eve are the same person. In that regard, both Evelyn/Eve and Cordelia draw on internal strength to resist their abusers. However, feminist abuse survivor discourse recognizes that individual resistance is but one piece of ending and recovering from abuse. Another equally important part of this approach is the support provided by allies in resisting the cultural messages that codify abusive behaviors. Both *Beside Herself* and *Angel* are illustrative of an understanding by their respective creators of the power of allies in fighting abuse.

In *Beside Herself*'s previously referenced scene, in which Evelyn's colleagues callously dismiss the seriousness of abuse with victim-blaming discourse, viewers see Evelyn retreat from her body as discourse espoused in the workplace causes Evelyn to feel unsafe, as she did during her abuse. Eve encourages Evelyn to dwell beside, rather than inside, herself. The popular association of being "beside" one's self is that of being "crazy." Daniels visually reframes this notion, de-pathologizing individuals coping with trauma, rather than viewing "madness" as an individual deficit. This switch is consistent with feminist abuse survivor discourse that shifts blame from survivors to larger social contexts that enable abuse. Eve becoming an ally when Evelyn finds the strength to confront her abuser illustrates the way survivors can cease to view survival mechanisms as something "wrong" with them and instead seek supportive social networks, in this case represented by a supportive colleague of Evelyn's.

Reinforcing this message is Daniels's choice to posit a moment of "madness" as a pivotal turning point toward Evelyn moving from abusive dynamics to social alliances that enable her to see herself as an active agent in her life. Evelyn discovers a resident died in the house where she works. While Evelyn remains detached from the situation, Eve attempts to engage Evelyn. Evelyn directly acknowledges Eve for the first time and, in doing so, defies the learned behavior of remaining distant from how devastating events impact her life. Eve vocalizes: "While they stand and point and tell each other you're to blame, I am smashing my fist, splitting my skull. Inside my head someone is wielding an axe. I am smashing all the things in my father's house. Everything is splintering around me. Every stick of furniture lies useless and broken. I am crashing my way through the brickwork and plaster, the rendering and the mortar until nothing, nothing is left of my father's house but rubble and dust. And it goes on and on and it will never stop."[19] At this point Evelyn grabs scissors and holds them against her arm. Significantly, the only employee who notices is Nicola Adams, who is also an abuse survivor but has taken steps toward her own healing and ending abusive patterns in her life. By acknowledging Eve, Evelyn externally demonstrates how the abuse in her life has affected her (as opposed to internalizing messages of her own worthlessness that she received during the time of her abuse). Through the external expression of her distress, she begins meaningful dialogue with Nicola regarding recovery.

In the subsequent scene, titled "Exodus," Nicola discusses how she was silenced by the abuse in her childhood and supports Evelyn in telling her story in a way that will help Evelyn see she has choices as to how she lives her life in the future (e.g., not needing to spend time with her abusive father out of a sense of familial obligation). The scene ends with Evelyn ready to talk openly with Nicola about her abuse. Stage directions make clear the peace Evelyn has found as a result of Nicola acting as an ally: "They leave the supermarket. Open air. Early evening. Silence."[20] The peaceful description is in sharp contrast to the previous scene of the play, where the employees at the group home framed Evelyn's distress as pathologized madness, suggesting that Nicola's acknowledgement of Evelyn's history facilitates an exodus from cycles that kept her stuck in abusive dynamics. Similarly, the next scene, "Genesis," asserts the possibility of a beginning after exodus. Allegorically, this change in biblical chronology shifts associations with the loss of Eden away from being something for which Eve (Evelyn) is at fault, away from victim-blaming behavior, and into a position from which there can be a new beginning. Nicola *Adams*'s name has a similar suggestion that the shadow character Eve is in need of an ally to complete the work of creation of self (as opposed to the biblical Adam, who blamed his counterpart — the biblical Eve). As a result of Nicola's support, Eve urges Evelyn to change the helplessness she is enacting in her life, suggesting that Eve can now support Evelyn's recovery, not merely encourage coping mechanisms like learned patterns of disassociation. Evelyn's relationship with Eve has shifted from one of re-enacting abusive messages to acting out against abuse. Due to the allies Evelyn finds in Eve and Nicola, who encourage her to recognize the social frameworks that perpetuate the after-effects of abuse, she is able to reclaim her "madness" (her disassociative behaviors) as dialogue leading to the reclamation of self, rather than seeing it only as a pathologized illness.

Likewise, *Angel*'s characters' response to abuse utilizes a network of allies for abuse survivors, rather than stigmatizing survivors' responses to abuse as "madness." This is especially apparent in Team Angel's treatment of Bethany, a guest character in the second season episode "Untouched."[21] The episode opens to two men threatening a teenage girl, Bethany, with a knife and about to rape her. In a moment of panic, she telekinetically moves a heavy, industrial dumpster, crushing the men between it and a wall, killing them. As the dumpster moves, the visual picture on the screen becomes blurry, as if the viewer is watching through the haze of Bethany's fear. This visual choice brings the viewer into Bethany's disassociative perspective. Whereas Evelyn escapes into conversation with Eve, Bethany's disassociation is illustrated through visual blurring; she is no longer able to connect to and see her surroundings clearly. In Bethany's case, disassociation is visually depicted not only as a trauma survival mechanism but also as raw and unfocused power. When Angel finds Bethany in an abandoned warehouse and touches her arm, we see the same distortion of vision that moved the dumpster, and a metal rod flies toward Angel, piercing him through the chest. While Bethany's survival mechanism has the power to save her from further attack, she neither embraces nor controls that power. Rather, she fears that the power her disassociation offers to her also makes her dangerous, and that fear prevents her from either resisting the abuse directly or from finding support in opposing the abuse. Like Daniels's depiction of Evelyn's disassociation as an understandable strategy for survival rather than as something to be pathologized, Whedon's depiction of Bethany's telekinetic power is not as a sign of illness to be overcome. Instead Bethany's disassociation is framed simultaneously as a result of abuse she has faced and a tool that will enable her to end abusive dynamics and take control over her life. The development of Bethany's ownership over her telekinetic abilities is paralleled with self-reclamation from abuse, albeit as an action which requires the intervention of allies for Bethany to achieve.

In "Untouched," Angel Investigations is presented as an ally in breaking abusive cycles. When Bethany first approaches Angel for help, she expresses a fear of vocalizing her disassociative state and its accompanying psychic phenomenon because she worries that Angel will think her crazy. He calmly replies that if she is, in fact, crazy, then things will go more smoothly if he knows upfront. In this response Angel functions as an ally as he disempowers the silencing potential of the label "crazy." Angel clearly conveys that "crazy" is no reason to dismiss a survivor's memories and experience of abuse. Bethany's response is to defer to Angel, saying, "I don't know, you're the expert, right?"[22] He does not agree that he is an expert but rather states that he has experience dealing with out-of-control power (referencing his own struggle with his vampiric powers). As stressed by feminist abuse survivor narratives, Angel does not engage with "expert discourse" but validates "personal experience and emotional pain,"[23] thereby enabling him to act as an ally rather than one who even inadvertently disempowers the abuse victim within a framework of, in this case, masculine hierarchy.

Angel's success at establishing himself as an ally rather than an expert is clear, given Bethany's response that she doesn't want to control her telekinetic power but wants it gone. That she feels comfortable expressing an opinion differing from Angel's suggestion that she may want to learn to deal with the power clearly shows her acceptance of his rejection of the expert position. Here, Bethany's desire to rid herself of the power reflects the social stigma of "madness" and mental illness she connects to her abilities—a connection viewers later learn is engendered by her abusive father's perspective. In fact, Bethany fears the power becoming an extension of her agency because she views it as a disease. As with Eve/Evelyn in *Beside Herself*, fitting the status quo is not a goal that is positioned as indicative of healing; rather healing occurs through the use of strategies that enable survival through reclamation of an embodied self. Bethany's telekinetic abilities are not an illness from which she must recover; rather, she is able to become less vulnerable to abuse when she stops being silenced by the fear of being "sick" and aligns her power with an awareness of her surroundings, including her allies. As an ally, Angel attempts to reframe the ways in which Bethany views her telekinetic power, offering her a new understanding. He reminds Bethany that the men in the alley tried to hurt her but that she stopped them, emphasizing her agency in the situation rather than emphasizing what she sees as the negative consequences of that agency.

Although Angel functions here as an ally, he is often represented in the series as the narrative knightly hero who "helps the helpless," often in the form of young "distressed damsel" women like Bethany. Images in the opening credits that depict his gallant walk down the street to save the day and numerous episodes in which he sweeps in to help women who are about to be murdered, who are being stalked, or who are running from abusive partners, all play on the image of the masculine "rescuer" archetype. However, as is typical of Whedon's work, this archetype is engaged critically throughout the series, simultaneously referenced and challenged to illustrate the archetype's potential flaws and shortcomings. For example, the women Angel "saves" generally come into their own power on their own terms; e.g., a woman being stalked states that she is "tired of crying" (1.04),[24] and, despite Angel's protection, her moment of fighting back against her attacker is framed as a pivotal turning point in her situation. The production choice to problematize Angel's construction as the hero-knight is important, as the "damsel in distress" myth reduces the woman in need of rescue to one incapable of saving herself, reliant on an outside hero for her salvation. Such an approach to abuse survivor narratives is anything but feminist. However in "Untouched," Cordelia recognizes that Angel cannot completely break away from this archetype and explicitly critiques the "heroic knight/damsel in distress" discourse. She situates herself as another ally for Bethany, one who will not risk thinking Bethany requires rescue.

As in *Beside Herself*, allies have the potential to aid survivors in seeing themselves as active agents, and in a scene between Cordelia and Bethany,

Cordelia urges her to see that she has the agency to make deliberate choices about her abilities. Cordelia tells Bethany that Angel "sees you as pretty much the damsel in distress. I think it's a little more complicated than that. I think you're kind of dangerous ... you come on all helpless, and people who thought you were helpless before have died. You could have flown them away or spun them until they puked. You squashed them."[25] Drawing upon her own experiences as a survivor of Maude's abuse in "Rm w/a Vu," Cordelia stresses that in the moment of attack, Bethany must make a decision. While emphasizing that she does not want harm to befall her or her friends, Cordelia urges Bethany to see the power she has to take control over that moment of decision and the aftereffects of trauma in her life. Like Angel, Cordelia speaks from personal experience. Rather than taking an expert position, she tells Bethany about her psychic vision wherein she felt everything that Bethany felt and knows how scary it was. Although Cordelia is not gentle with Bethany when stressing her belief in Bethany's power, she is an empathic peer as opposed to an "expert." As Cordelia does not see Bethany as weaker than herself, she does not have to work against an impulse to rescue her. Instead Cordelia speaks as one who has a shared experience of fear and whom Bethany can understand as a peer; she urges Bethany to see her psychic reaction as a strength (as opposed to diagnosing, controlling, or pathologizing it).

Through the peer support offered by Angel and Cordelia acting as allies, Bethany is able to take control when her abusive father meets her at Angel's hotel. In *Beside Herself*, when Evelyn has support from Nicola (and Eve becomes an ally), she ends the relationship with her father that is prohibitive to her recovery. Evelyn goes to her father's house and tells him the shame from the abuse that she has been living with is not hers, but his to live with now, thereby removing the power he has had over her life. Likewise, Bethany's removal of her father from Angel's hotel removes the shame he has given her (by investing shame in her understanding of her telekinetic power) and used to control her life.

When Bethany's father arrives at the hotel, all of the windows in the building simultaneously explode. This event is depicted from the outside of the hotel where the viewer can see the extent to which the force of Bethany's devastation is "shattering." The beginning of Bethany's interaction with her father re-enacts a nightmare scenario depicted earlier in the episode wherein Bethany's father finds her in the attic. The room shakes, nails fly out of walls, and plaster cracks while Bethany's father talks. He narrates, "I know what you can do ... you don't mean to hurt anyone ... you're a good girl, Bethany ... I promise it will be just like it was before."[26] In the background, Angel attempts to remind Bethany to take control. He states, "You have the power here, don't let [him] touch you."[27] At this moment, Bethany stops the room from shaking. Interpreting this as an act of compliance, Bethany's father reaches out to bring her downstairs. However, as Bethany then focuses her gaze on her father, the shaking moves from general and out of her control (risking the safety of herself and those who are helping her) to being focused on her father. He is lifted into the air, choking. She says "good bye" and sends him hurtling out the window and down many stories. Just as he is about to land on the pavement below, she suspends him in the air and stops the impact of the fall enough that he will survive.[28] The closing image of him lying winded on broken glass, however, suggests that while surviving the impact of the fall, his power over her has been eliminated. Because of the help she receives from Angel Investigations, specifically the ally status Angel and Cordelia adopt in encouraging her to (re)claim agency, Bethany embraces her non-normative identity. This move enables her to take power away from her abuser, thus ending the perpetuation of abuse in her life.

As evidenced in the characters of Evelyn/Eve, Cordelia, and Bethany, Daniels's and Whedon's engagements with abuse survivors' "madness" and power/powerlessness utilize feminist abuse survivor discourses that stress self-advocacy through speech acts that (re)claim agency and power and that emphasize the value of allies against abuse and abuse-proliferating societal hierarchies. While both depict characters without analysis of how whiteness, heterosexuality, and other presumed social locations can create normative assumptions as to survivors' experiences that are not universally applicable, these writers contributions to feminist abuse survivor discourse is substantial and deserves recognition. Dominant culture has often dismissed accounts of abuse from oppressed members of society due to social stigmas that discount these individuals based on normative notions of acceptable expressions of mental health. However, feminist discourse exposes norms that pathologize individual survivors, subverting the social structures that enable abuse. Such rhetoric has become emblematic of feminist writing on abuse recovery. This discourse stresses the importance of trusting the gravity of one's pain while taking control over the ability to tell one's story. Many survivors believe that challenging structures in society that foster high incidence of abuse is an essential outcome of working toward their recovery processes within a feminist framework. Feminist playwright Sarah Daniels and feminist television auteur Joss Whedon both illustrate how the media of contemporary theatre and popular television, respectively, can provide space for unique theoretical and visual strategy to engage in feminist traditions that contest mainstream abuse discourse. As *Beside Herself* works to theatricalize "crazy" behaviors like disassociation in order to destigmatize their place in abuse survivor strategies, *Angel* illustrates the subversive potential of television to promote survivor-centered and community-focused narratives that aid in feminist abuse survivor discourse.

Notes

1. Sarah Daniels, *Beside Herself* in *Daniels Plays: 2: The Gut Girls, Beside Herself, Head-Rot Holiday, and The Madness of Esme and Shaz* (London: A&C Black, 2003), 95–188.

2. "Untouched," *Angel*, DVD, written by Meredyth Smith, directed by Joss Whedon (2000; 20th Century–Fox, 2002).
3. Linda Alcoff and Laura Gray, "Survivor Discourse: Transgression or Recuperation?" *Signs: Journal of Women in Culture and Society* 18, no. 2 (1993): 284.
4. Carol E. Barringer, "The Survivor's Voice: Breaking the Incest Taboo," *NWSA Journal* 4, no.1 (1992): 15.
5. Alcoff and Gray, "Survivor Discourse."
6. "Rm w/a Vu," *Angel*, DVD, written by Jane Espenson, directed by Scott McGinnis (1999; 20th Century–Fox, 2002).
7. Daniels, *Beside Herself*, 134.
8. Ibid., 138.
9. Ibid., 184, 182.
10. Ibid., 182.
11. "Rm w/a Vu."
12. Ibid.
13. Ibid.
14. Ibid.
15. Ibid.
16. Ibid.
17. Ibid.
18. "Billy," *Angel*, DVD, written by Tim Minear and Jeffrey Bell, directed by David Grossman (2001; 20th Century–Fox, 2003).
19. Daniels, *Beside Herself*, 173.
20. Ibid., 176.
21. "Untouched."
22. Ibid.
23. Nancy Naples, *Feminism and Method: Ethnography, Discourse Analysis, and Activist Research* (New York: Routledge, 2003), 169.
24. "I Fall to Pieces," *Angel*, DVD, written by Joss Whedon and David Greenwalt, directed by Vern Gilum (1999; 20th Century–Fox Home Video, 2002).
25. "Untouched."
26. Ibid.
27. Ibid.
28. Ibid.

Numero Cinco, Border Narratives, and Mexican Cultural Performance in *Angel*

VICTORIA PETTERSEN LANTZ

> *It used to be that I would don my Mexican wrestling mask and my prosthetic "low-rider suit," paint my chest with the words "Don't Discover Me," and climb into the metaphorical combatant's ring to wrestle with social complacency, artistic stagnation, and, not least, my own personal demons.*
> — Guillermo Gomez-Peña

> *Wearing that mask doesn't exactly hide your past.*
> — Angel to Numero Cinco

One of the main ways in which audiences connect with a fantasy series like *Angel* is when the show draws on Western traditions and Eurocentric myths to establish recognizable plots and characters. Arthurian legends, American film noir, and Greek/Norse mythology make up the foundation of *Angel*'s title character and the trials he endured weekly from 1999 to 2004.[1] The show's creators, Joss Whedon and David Greenwalt, both utilize and challenge Western folklore to create a complex world where heroes, champions, villains, and demons have neither a clear identity nor a predetermined path; in doing so, they offer audiences introspective, rather than escapist, fantasy. Perhaps the most obvious and discussed dismantling of stereotypes Whedon offers in all his television series to date (*Buffy the Vampire Slayer, Angel, Firefly,* and *Dollhouse*) is that of gender. Scholars like Lorna Jowett, Sara Buttsworth, AmiJo Comeford, and Susan A. Owen, to name only a few, view the Buffy/Angelverse through a feminist lens.[2] However, most scholars of Whedon's shows do not offer the same treatment for issues of race, mostly because of the way ethnic identity is under-examined in the shows themselves.[3]

The Buffy/Angelverse omits discussions of ethnic identity/cultural difference in part because within Whedon's fantasy world, difference is mythological rather than racial. Demons in the shows take on the role of the "other," focusing the audience's introspection on issues of good and evil rather than issues of race. Even so, the minority characters are equally othered by their lack of presence in the shows' plots/stories. The often confrontational work of Chicano performance artist Guillermo Gomez-Peña, as highlighted in this chapter's epigraph, aims to combat the idea that racial minorities can be pushed into obscurity. His position as a "social wrestler" and his writing gives us a means through which we can begin to see why a Latino presence in *Angel* is necessary to the setting of and representations in the show. In *Buffy* and *Angel*, a few black actors were cast as supporting characters, along with a few Asian and Latino/a actors who function as secondary characters or background visuals. This oversight is of particular concern in regard to *Angel*, a show centered on the troubled vampire hero roaming Los Angeles, a city with pronounced ethnic diversity and a long history of race-based conflicts.

Los Angeles is a city composed of less than 30 percent non–Latino white Americans and an over 40 percent Latino population. Yet Team Angel is about 80 percent white (of European decent) and 20 percent non-white (not factoring the non-human Lorne into the mix). Until the final season of *Angel*, the overwhelming Latino presence in L.A. is barely acknowledged. Indeed, before Season Five, any references to Hispanic L.A. are merely passing jokes, such as when Cordelia announces in the first season that due to her impoverished state, she is living in "the barrio."[4] However, roaming around the first half of the fifth season is a company mailman wearing a Mexican wrestler mask. At first glance, the man appears as just another quirky member of Whedon's sizeable Buffy/Angelverse until episode six, when writer/director Jeffery Bell creates a storyline dedicated to this background figure. The episode, "The Cautionary Tale of Numero Cinco" (5.06), blends Mexican traditions of *lucha libre mascaras* ("free wrestling" masks), Spanish language scenes, and Mayan mythology in order to explore typical Whedon themes of problematic hero figures through a Latino frame.[5] This chapter examines the characters and language of "The Cautionary Tale" and the writings of Guillermo Gomez-Peña in order to assess how the mainstreaming of Mexican culture affects a progressive Chicano/a identity. My exploration of the hybrid space in both *Angel* and Gomez-Peña's writing demonstrates the importance of Los Angeles to the narratives, the nature of masking, and marginalization of culture in the show and the importance of literature from the margins.

On the surface, comparing a mainstream television show like *Angel* to the work of Gomez-Peña seems a theoretical stretch, but a deeper examination of the latter's language and self-styled characterization exposes a unique overlap between *Angel* and Gomez-Peña's radical art. Gomez-Peña was born in Mexico City and moved to California in the late 1970s, an experience that is foundational for much of his art. Beginning in the late 1980s, he developed a writing and performance style that aggressively examines U.S. neocolonialism and xenophobia emanating from the U.S.–Mexico border culture and his position as a Mexican American. His poetry, critical essays, and theatrical texts infuse multiple forms of Spanish, "Spanglish," and English to emphasize cultural hybridity in the border areas, like Los Angeles. In performance, he portrays a number of different characters that fuse multiple stereotypes, be it a motivational speaker dressed to resemble the Mexican flag or El Aztec High-Tech, a radio personality and spokesman for the "New World Border." According to theatre scholar Lisa Wolford, through his work, Gomez-Peña "articulates the complex range of tensions and projections, desires and fears that characterize U.S./Mexican relations at the end of the twentieth century."[6] While Wolford accurately depicts the cultural sophistication of Gomez-Peña's characters and writing, his work continues to extend into the twenty-first century as it represents a modern performance response to new border politics in the Internet age.

Where, then, do *Angel*'s "The Cautionary Tale" and the writing of Guillermo Gomez-Peña meet? In fact, the connections between the artist and the show are more than just the Mexican American frame of one episode. Gomez-Peña's work connects to many aspects of the show's themes, characters, and writing. Specifically, the writing of Gomez-Peña and the *Angel* series highlight the fallacies of and society's reliance on pop culture because they both tend to satirize cultural trends to ease the tension of the more serious situations unfolding on screen or on stage. Most of all, both the title character Angel and Gomez-Peña explore the foundations of their "pensive, wounded" identities,[7] the former in terms of his crimes and the latter in terms of the crimes committed against his people (and himself). While the show's usual form of border exploration is between the human and the mythic (i.e., a vampire with a soul), "The Cautionary Tale" confronts cultural, as well as mythic, intersections. Gomez-Peña and Numero Cinco both share personal experiences, set in Los Angeles, through bilingual storytelling frames that illustrate life from a Chicano-American perspective. In this sense, *Angel* and Gomez-Peña, though varied in style, attempt to translate border relations into a communal cultural hybridity, and while Gomez-Peña is a more effective "border narrator," *Angel* offers the idea of border narratives to a mainstream, American audience.

Mapping Lost *Angeles*

One of the most dominant reoccurring themes of Gomez-Peña's work is his fixation on Los Angeles, a place that serves as an epicenter of border-culture conflicts. The ethnic demographic alone reinforces his focus on the city, given that almost half of the population is Latino. From its Spanish name and Mexican history to the current tourism of Olvera Street, L.A. is firmly identified as part of Mexican American culture. However, popular representations of the city splinter L.A. into two parts: one glamorous and rich (often dominated by white Americans) and the other dangerous and poor (categorized by black and Hispanic Americans). Out of this troubling split-personality comes

Gomez-Peña's "Lost Angeles."[8] In his epic poem, titled "The Last Migration: A Spanglish Opera," he illustrates the two versions of L.A.:

> a day in the life of Califas
> we'll be back after you leave
> with more asbestos, colera, teluride
> HIV, nasal sex, pesticides
> mexi-cide, other-cide,
> the other side,
> Riverside, Topanga, Malibu
> Hollywood in shock
> another day in the life of Califas
> L.A. mansión de L.A. muerte[9]

The structure of his language reiterates the city's amalgam of peoples and cultures. His blend of idioms, along with his idiosyncratic neologisms, in his description of the city points to the tension of ownership and the fight between the whitewashed version of L.A. and the real traumas that the greater (non-white) population suffers. For Gomez-Peña, to be in Califas, Chicano slang for Southern California (a portmanteau of California and Sur, Spanish for south), means to be lost in a crisis.

This same idea is easily translated into the Buffy/Angelverse's L.A. From the moment Buffy runs away to L.A. after "killing" Angel,[10] L.A. is established as a place for lost souls. The series *Angel* drives this point home, particularly in the first season. Angel wants to lose himself in the city after leaving Buffy, but instead finds himself a magnet for people facing supernatural trouble in a big city where things like bodies can easily disappear. More than a border between the magical and human realms, *Angel*'s L.A. transforms into a shared space where the lines between good and evil, light and dark, found and lost are blurred. *Angel*'s L.A. backdrop fits with Gomez-Peña's characterization of "Lost Angeles Diabólicos" and his claim, "I'm not really back in Los Angeles / for this pinche city does not really exist."[11] His description of the city highlights how easy it is for writers to fictionalize L.A. as Whedon does in *Angel*. While in reality, L.A. averages over 300 days of sunshine per year, Whedon transforms L.A. to fit Angel's personality, another form of "Lost" Angeles. The dark setting emphasizes the ambiguity between good and evil that Angel continuously questions and challenges. He can only guard the darkest corners of sunny L.A. and hope he is on the right path for salvation (his own and that of Angelinos in general). Angel epitomizes the loneliness of Lost Angeles in his battles over personal and professional demons.

Whedon's fictional L.A. is not without pockets of reality, and in the moments that real L.A. intersects with *Angel*, a social commentary of the city's crises begins to emerge. In *Blood Relations: Chosen Families in* Buffy the Vampire Slayer *and* Angel, Jes Battis states, "The fact remains that L.A., unlike the mythical Sunnydale, is a real locus of economic inequality, and a space within which multiple poor neighborhoods compete with each other."[12] In a number of episodes, Angel discovers that the complex socioeconomic challenges of the city are not solved by killing a demon or two. In particular, the theme of segregated self-help follows the demographics of the city; minority and economically-disadvantaged communities are left to fend for themselves. For instance, in a city where whites are the minority, Angel spends most of his time saving white victims. In contrast, Gunn originates from a group of black Angelinos who keep vampires out of their "hood." Likewise, the titular Numero Cinco of "The Cautionary Tale" worked to keep "monsters and gangsters. Vampiros" out of East L.A., a predominantly Latino area.[13] Episodes like "The Thin Dead Line" (2.14) and "That Old Gang of Mine" (3.03) highlight the idea of designated areas, often defined by ethnicity, where people deal with demons in their own way.[14] In these moments, the show offers audiences a glimpse of real L.A., where ethnic communities struggle to connect with one another and suffer hardships in isolated groups.

Beyond racial lines, Angel and Gomez-Peña both see L.A. in general as a violent space whose ownership is contentious and whose citizens are traumatized. The conflict for Angel is the line between good and evil, with both forces trying to stake their claim to the city. In the case of Gomez-Peña's L.A., the fight is still a binary split, but here it is a split between whites and non-whites and the battle itself is over acceptance. He is waiting for the time that L.A. will embrace, rather than deny, its Mexican heritage and "bi-dentity" (bilingual, bicultural, biracial). Both of these battles for ownership are marked by violence in general. Gomez-Peña summarizes this violence in "The Last Migration": "A black man passes by on skates whistling 'L.A. Marsellaise' / 'typical, typical Los Angeles,' he says / violencia sin antecedentes."[15] Roughly translated as "violence without antecedents," the statement defines L.A. as a place of unprovoked violence where crises and cruelty have turned the city into a war zone. Angel's L.A. is built of the same tensions, though the violence surrounding Angel almost always has a demonic source. The city, struggling with the battle of ownership, becomes a magnet for different forms of evil (be they fictional demons or real poverty and ethnic tension). In order to redefine L.A., characters in *Angel* have a similar cause to that of Gomez-Peña; they are working to alleviate violence through their actions—artistic, heroic, or otherwise. In order to do so, however, both Gomez-Peña and Angel work to develop their "champion" personas.

Masking Heroes

The central theme of "The Cautionary Tale" is Angel's struggle to come to terms with what it means to be a champion. With the aid of the disgraced Numero Cinco, Angel faces off against an Aztec demon who hunts for the hearts of heroes. Angel forces Numero Cinco, the only living member of Los Hermanos Numeros (a fraternal group of Mexican American warriors), back into fighting to defeat once again the demon that killed his brothers. The episode has Angel destroying the demon, Tezcatcatl, who has taken the heart of all heroes in East L.A. except Angel's. The location, a predominantly Latino area, the demon's faux-Aztec history, and the presence of Numero Cinco firmly cement the episode in Hispanic L.A., outside of Angel's comfort zone. The only shared space for Angel and Numero Cinco is their complex hero/warrior identity. Both have the strength of a demon-fighting warrior but struggle to prove they have heroic hearts. Numero Cinco acts as a guide in this episode, navigating Angel through the "foreign" territory of East L.A., providing the means for Tezcatcatl's demise and steering Angel back to his heroic destiny with the Shanshu prophecy. As a guide, Numero Cinco confronts his own hero status and disappointments with life. Together, the two parallel each other's weaknesses and highlight each other's potential as champions, which is defined in the context of this discussion as a warrior who accepts the role and responsibilities of a hero.

The idea of warriors, heroes, and champions runs throughout the episode, as with many *Angel* episodes, but in this instance, Numero Cinco and Angel struggle with the concept of being a champion, something with which Gomez-Peña has less trouble. The latter finds strength in his art and creates a persona, named the Warrior for Gringostroika, to support his own champion status. In a *New York Times* article, Gomez-Peña notes, "The 'Warrior for Gringostroika' is a self-proclaimed 'social wrestler,' a champion of tolerance, reform, aperture and diversification regarding culture."[16] The Warrior for Gringostroika, who also includes a *lucha libre* mask as part of his persona, appears on stage to help spread the prophecies of the New World Border. The character works to tear down traditional borders and hierarchies that marginalize non-whites in neocolonial American culture. The Warrior for Gringostroika is a masked version of Gomez-Peña, who fights his battles through performance and writing. As a champion for marginalized voices, Gomez-Peña uses language to position himself as a cultural warrior: "& I could only fight back in my poetry / [...] See I told you culero, I win most fights in / the streets of my poetry."[17] Together, his poetry, performances, and characters allow him to challenge Western/colonial institutions that traditionally dismantle or dismiss his Latino heritage. Gomez-Peña's masks ease his transition into his champion persona on stage, just as language (and his own language creations) grants him warrior status in his poetry.

For Angel and Numero Cinco, the champion role is not so easily put on, and they rely on masks to avoid, rather than enhance, their heroic identities. In the episode, the title of *champion* is not necessarily positive. Whereas Spike sees Angel as moody and grumpy, Fred makes the point that his attitude is part and parcel with his hero status, stating, "He just gets like that sometimes. Not easy being a champion."[18] Being a champion, in Fred's assessment, entails internal emotional struggles that have an alienating effect. Angel and his companions, with the possible exception of Spike, seem to all accept that fact and tolerate the troubled loneliness that accompanies Angel. His champion status, with all the alienation linked to it, amplifies the guilt Angel feels because of his former crimes. The idea of being a champion, then, is also a punishment; at least, that is how Angel presents it through most of "The Cautionary Tale."

This position sets up his relationship with Numero Cinco. As a defeated fighter and the only survivor of a group of former champions, the Hispanic hero says openly what Angel is clearly thinking. When Angel tries to confront him about always wearing his lucha libre mask, Numero Cinco crosses his arms and states, "It reminds me that only a fool would want to be a champion."[19] The two men have come to a point where they both reject the idea that any good comes from being a champion. Angel enters Season Five as a compromised figure, taking on the leadership of a corrupt company to save his son, and he cannot reconcile his good deeds with the evil works of his company. Numero Cinco, equally compromised from also working at Wolfram & Hart, shares a parallel guilt and hides behind his hostility for the general public and their disrespect for Los Hermanos Numeros. His survivor's guilt allows him to reject the champion persona because he links it directly with the death of his brothers. Both Angel and Numero Cinco labor under their guilty consciences and wallow in the negative qualities of being a champion. They cannot so easily adopt a champion persona to carry out their peace-making agenda, as Gomez-Peña does, because Angel and Numero Cinco are written as complex, realistic individuals while the latter is a performer taking on a non-realistic (almost cartoonish) character of his own creation. However, all three are subject to punishment related to their position in society. Angel and Numero Cinco do, however, utilize masking in their face-offs with evil powers, similar to Gomez-Peña in artistic "fights."

While the plot of "The Cautionary Tale" focuses on the definitions of heroes and resurrecting the desire to fight in both Angel and Numero Cinco, the overarching theme of the episode relates to the nature of masks. Episode writer Jeffery Bell hits on a vital aspect of the hero character inherent in Mexico's tradition of lucha libre and uses it to underscore the masks with which Angel himself wrestles. Mexican lucha libre dates back to the early 1900s, and since its inception, masks have been a central characteristic of the style. The wrestling itself plays out battles of good and evil. According to identifier/contextualizing descriptor Heather Levi, "Observers of Mexican *lucha libre* have tended to account for its appeal to the audience in terms of straightforward catharsis ... where the spectacle of abjection is redeemed through the triumph of good."[20] Levi believes that this is an oversimplification of the tradition, but the theme of triumphant good lends itself to the discussion of heroes and *Angel*. Angel and his friends always look for the triumph of good and come to expect it of Angel. He, as the perpetual hero, fulfills their need over and again in his battles against demons. Numero Cinco, as a member of Los Hermanos Numeros, formerly performed the same task for his community. Men, women, and children all idealized the brothers because of their clear and recurring victories over evil, both in and out of the wrestling ring. The simplification of their battles into good versus evil, however, masks the complexity of the champion identity.

Masks play a vital role in character personification, as the face is a key indicator of identity. Angel hits on just how important masks are in the case of Los Hermanos Numeros as we see a montage of their fights and life. When Angel asks, "So you guys always wore your masks?" we hear Numero Cinco explain in voiceover: "What you are failing to see, my friend, is that we had to be ever-vigilant, ready for action at a moment's notice."[21] The brothers, as with most luchadores (wrestlers), consider the mask not as a prop or set piece but as an extension of the self. The masks do not come off, in the case of Los Hermanos Numeros, because they never take off their hero identities. Levi contends, "To uphold the mask's charisma, wrestlers make a serious commitment never to be seen unmasked."[22] The history of the masking explains the wrestlers' commitment to their faux-identity. As Levi explains, "The introduction of wrestling masks in Mexico coincided with a craze for comics featuring masked heroes. One was the 'Phantom,' whose chief characteristic was that he never removed his mask, not even at home."[23] The popular culture interest of masked avengers directly relates to the use of masks in lucha libre, again tying the idea of heroes and good-versus-evil to the battles in the ring. *Angel* pushes this relationship further by making masked wrestlers actual superheroes who personify the "ever-vigilant" comic book supermen.

For Numero Cinco, however, masking has shifted from a sign of his hero status to a reminder of his dishonor and disappointments. In the episode, he struggles with which identity will win out, the hero or the disgraced mailman. The mask is always on, but it takes on different significance as Numero Cinco shifts personas. Again, in this instance, he and Angel parallel each other. Angel's face has always been a double mask, without a clear indication of his real identity. His human face is, of course, his preference and what the audience sees most of the time. It reminds us of his soul and his hope to be human. However, his human face is a mask because it is not his genuine self. In Whedon's world, vampires use their human faces to attract their prey: actual humans. The eyes, teeth, and forehead all transform to show their vampire nature, and this change usually coincides with violence and predation. Angel is reluctant to show this face throughout the show. He does it in the midst of a fight, to make a point, or to scare bad guys, but in many of his fights, he retains his human features. His vampire face is a reminder of his past shame, just as Numero Cinco's mask is a reminder of his past triumphs. Angel can play at being a human, but he can never truly be one without fulfilling the Shanshu prophecy. He may play at being a vampire — he is a vampire — but he *can* try to hide this identity. As much as he tries to reject his vampire nature, he can never escape it. His human face is a more significant mask in the context of the show. His face, as much as it looks like a normal human's, shows no age, much in the same way Numero Cinco's actual mask has not changed in fifty years, though the face behind it has aged.

Angel's faces represent the overt binary of good and evil that the show wishes to emphasize and often blurs. When the show does seek to emphasize good/evil binaries, it only does so by eroding or upending preconceived notions of good/evil, by removing the masks or appearances of the characters to reveal their true natures. Angel's troubled relationship with his own face exposes how powerful the connection between the self, an internal identity, and external indictors like the face can be. Like Numero Cinco's dual-functioning mask, Angel's human and vampire masks complicate his position as a champion. In his performance art, Gomez-Peña offers his audiences his own take on the complexity of masks and identity construction. In the piece "The New World Border," where he presents himself as El Aztec High-Tech or the Warrior for Gringostroika, he uses masks to move into different personas. In a section of his performance text, *The New World Border,* the stage directions read: "[Gomez-Peña (GP)] puts on a wrestling mask ... GP stands up and boxes with hanging chicken while repeating compulsively, 'I'm beating the Mexican out of myself.' ... GP takes off wrestler mask, puts on 'Caucasian' mask."[24] The switching of masks is not merely a costume change within the context of a performance; these masks symbolize the position of the non-white self having to adapt in order to live in a Euro-American world. More than that, the masks are Gomez-Peña's attempt to reconcile his culture's past, present, and future. The quick changes in character and masking are what scholar José David Saldívar calls a "postmodern shiftiness" to Gomez-Peña's work, and they represent the artist's views of the hybrid identity.[25] Hybridity draws on multiple cultures to create a multicultural world to which people of multiple races can relate.

"The Cautionary Tale" only scratches the surface of what is explored by the complexity of Gomez-Peña's performance and border theory. However, when we consider the intentions of Gomez-Peña, a social wrestler and champion, and his layers of masks, we can draw a theoretical line between our three heroes. Angel and Numero Cinco carry both their past traumas and future hopes in their literal and figurative masks. Gomez-Peña carries a similar trauma, one of racism and stereotyping, in his masks to help establish his ideal hybrid culture. The three men utilize the face, or a disguising of the face, to craft the complexity of a champion, be they fictional or social champions. Angel complicates his position as hero out of guilt, but in the case of Numero Cinco and Gomez-Peña, race dictates just how complicated the hero role is in L.A. or any American city where race and popular culture collide. The episode of *Angel* highlights some characteristics of Chicano culture but grounds itself in certain racial stereotypes that cannot be overlooked. Scholars like Kent A. Ono and Jes Battis discuss the problematic structure of racial hierarchy in the Buffy/Angel-verse and point to the marginalization of non-white characters. In this episode of *Angel*, can we find any progressive agenda for racial issues, or does "The Cautionary Tale" mock non-white cultures on the periphery of American society?

Marginal Performances

The WB's promotional commercial for "The Cautionary Tale" in October 2003 set the tone for the episode and the expectations of the audience. The twenty-second piece starts with Angel in his dark world of demon fighting with the voiceover stating, "Angel has helped all kinds, but nothing will prepare him for this."[26] As soon as the tag line ends, four of the five Hermanos Numeros appear on screen with stereotypical Mariachi music playing in the background. At first glance, the promo indicates a more lighthearted, funny *Angel* episode with Mexican wrestlers in it. However, a closer examination reveals a flippant dismissal of culture that the mainstream audience, for which the promo was intended, could recognize as Chicano. The promoters at the WB, and most likely *not* Bell or Whedon, offer a veiled racism in the implication that among the both dark and virtuous forces Angel has faced, none compare to the strangeness that is Mexican culture. As the promo stresses, no amount of fighting evil or saving good has offered Angel the challenge that Los Hermanos Numeros do. This may appear to be an over-reading of a short promo for a fantasy program that is often humorous (though the humor often alleviates darker themes of the show), but it speaks to the fact that popular culture struggles with non-white culture and finds it difficult not to stereotype when a show like *Angel* focuses on a specific race.

The most obvious example of how the show represents minority characters by stereotyping is the characterization of Charles Gunn. Battis, in his explanation of Gunn's presence, offers his reading of race in *Angel* when he states, "While *Angel* does have Gunn as a non-white character (unless we count Lorne, who is green), his presence on the show veers dangerously close to tokenization, and his inner-city background ... ends up, I think, as merely a stereotypical indicator that white, middle-class audiences can recognize."[27] Following the notion that audiences generally misunderstand racial identity, here exemplified by Gunn, it is not surprising that the promo would paint Mexican wrestling and music as comical, a means of othering the culture by making it seem odd and foreign. The nature of cultural isolation and hierarchy in mainstream America, exactly what Gomez-Peña is fighting, is not easily combated by a popular fantasy television show.

That is not to say that the series did not try legitimately to represent Chicano culture in the episode. Spanish language and Mexican culture pepper "The Cautionary Tale," and the flashbacks of Numero Cinco's life feature spoken Spanish with English subtitles. Language is a predominant signifier of culture and in this context establishes the Mexican L.A. focus of this episode of *Angel*.

Numero Cinco blends Spanish and English together when talking with Angel or taunting the demon, expressing how blurred the borders are between Mexico and America in East L.A. In this instance, the fictional wrestler/demon fighter and Gomez-Peña are most similar as both blend language without thought of translation. In part of *The New World Border* performance, Gomez-Peña challenges his audience's language skills, "Okay, okay. Lección de español numero cinco for advanced English speakers.... Falsa democracia?"[28] His only response is "Translation, please."[29] He embeds his political critiques in Spanish (though many English speakers can understand cognates like "falsa democracia") to make the act of speaking in Spanish as political as the content of the statement. Numero Cinco may not be political, but he does not compromise heritage for Angel's sake. He speaks Spanish because he is Mexican American, and Angel must translate for himself while the audience sees subtitles. When Numero Cinco faces off with Tezcatcatl, he challenges him in Spanish, saying things like "Yo te espero" and "Pues, ven y tomalo. Esta en mi panza."[30] Just as Angel verbally cuffs demons he fights (as does Buffy, marking the importance of language to those who fight evil), Numero Cinco uses his own language to goad the Aztec demon.

Naomi H. Quiñonez, in the article "Re(Riting) the Chicana Postcolonial," states, "Language-use figures prominently as a device, which validates life experience.... Through appropriation, writers may take the language of the dominant culture and replace it with their own, in some cases reconstituting it totally into a 'vehicle for new meanings and adaptations of the cultural experiences of the non-privileged.'"[31] Gomez-Peña and Numero Cinco do not need to translate because they both blend English and Spanish together as a means of reconstructing L.A. culture. They, in poetry, performance, or casual conversation, position Spanish as being as important as English and in turn, place Mexican traditions on par with white American culture. However, when Gomez-Peña uses his mixture of Spanglish and common Mexican-Spanish phrases, he uses his language choices to heighten the focus on cultural borders and a borderless future. In "The Cautionary Tale," the Spanish is not always treated as a means of blending cultures. Echoing the cartoonish nature of the promo, much of the Spanish aimed at Angel amounts to repetitions of "¡Estupido!" and "¡Andale!" These Spanish words do not offer insight into Chicano culture, but rather mock the language by limiting it to words that mainstream (white) audiences can understand and enjoy without concern for broader racial understanding. As much as language in the episode colors the East L.A. setting, the limited vocabulary also highlights the lack of care given to the Chicano culture infused in the episode.

Numero Cinco's role at Wolfram & Hart clarifies the problem of playing to mainstream expectations. He, though a fighter with superhuman strength, does the menial task of interoffice mail delivery. Even with an episode for himself, Numero Cinco is in the end a menial laborer who, in his death, helps

Angel, the white hero, return to his righteous path. His position on the edges of Season Five reflects Ono's view of Whedon's treatment of race in *Buffy*: "In general, characters who are not white are not central to the narrative and are useful only insofar as they somehow enhance some aspect of the main characters. Anything other than Anglo-European cultural values and logic is marginalized."[32] Ono's scathing critique of *Buffy* is severe but does point out the problem that non-white characters are relegated to the margins except when helping a main character. In "The Cautionary Tale," however, Bell acknowledges Latino culture as marginalized and offers moments of social commentary. The most poignant is a passing comment by Numero Cinco when he says, "You need to understand. We were more than just luchadores. No one else cared about Mexicans or Chicanos, so we protected our own."[33] The idea of being isolated by the larger (white) community and the need for Chicano heroes offers the clearest understanding of how *Angel* continues to address race in L.A.

Numero Cinco's lament that no one cared about Chicanos in L.A., combined with his position at Wolfram & Hart and his mask, actually offer a trenchant criticism of modern America. Bell creates in this fictional L.A. a representation of Chicanos that Gomez-Peña discusses at length. According to Gomez-Peña, Chicanos "are being stripped of their humanity and individuality" because of xenophobic fears in mainstream American culture.[34] Latinos are isolated to their communities and condemned by the white majority to function on the margins of society. While "The Cautionary Tale" contains moments of racial misrepresentation, the episode does offer insight into L.A. border identity. Further, we can categorize it as part of a growing trend of introducing Latino culture to mainstream, white audiences. *Dora the Explorer* (first aired in 2000), the last two seasons of *The West Wing* (2004–2006), and *Ugly Betty* (first aired in 2006) all feature Latino/as as influential, powerful, and/or endearing. These popular shows, particularly *Dora* and *Betty*, blend Spanish and Latino traditions into the narratives. *Angel*'s Numero Cinco, from 2003, fits in with this trend of a stronger Latino primetime presence.

At a moment in time when the first Latina Supreme Court Justice, Sonia Sotomayor, faced a nomination process based in large part on racial difference, it is vital for mainstream media to be inclusive of Hispanic culture. Artists like Gomez-Peña represent the margins, pushing and challenging conventional definitions of American culture, especially in relation to the Mexico border. His blurred border composed of hybrid culture does translate, in a diluted way, to shows like *Angel*. "The Cautionary Tale of Numero Cinco" allows a fantasy show to journey into realms unknown to mainstream, white audiences. Numero Cinco proves that being a hero is not limited to white characters and emphasizes that cultural isolation, even in *Angel*'s fictional L.A., is dysfunctional. Cultural crossover in this episode may exoticize Mexican traditions in the same way that the show paints vampires as alien and alluring, yet there is a positive social commentary in Numero Cinco and Angel's relationship that should not be overlooked. In the end, the episode moves us a little closer to Gomez-Peña's ideal worldview: "I see a whole generation / freefalling toward a borderless future / incredible mixtures beyond science fiction: / cholo-punks, pachuno kristnas, / Irish concheros ... I see them all / wandering around / a continent without a name."[35]

Notes

1. For scholarship on these western themes in Whedon's work, see *The Medieval Hero on Screen: Representations from Beowulf to Buffy*, ed. Martha W. Driver and Sid Ray (Jefferson, NC: McFarland, 2004); Allison McCracken, "At Stake: Angel's Body, Fantasy Masculinity, and Queer Desire in Teen TV," in *Undead TV: Essays on* Buffy the Vampire Slayer, ed. Elana Levine and Lisa Parks (Durham: Duke University Press, 2007), 116–44; and scholars who presented at "Greeks and Romans in the Buffyverse: Classical Threads in Fantasy and Science Fiction on Contemporary Television," Open University, Milton Keynes, UK, January 2004.

2. Among Jowett's extensive work on gender in the Buffy/Angelverse, see her book, *Sex and the Slayer: A Gender Studies Primer for the* Buffy *Fan* (Middletown, CT: Wesleyan University Press, 2005). See also Sara Buttsworth, "'Bite Me': Buffy and the Penetration of the Gendered Warrior-Hero," *Continuum: Journal of Media & Cultural Studies* 16.2 (2002): 185–99; Susan A. Owen, "*Buffy the Vampire Slayer*: Vampires, Postmodernity, and Postfeminism," *Journal of Popular Film & Television* 27.2 (1999): 24–31; and AmiJo Comeford, "Cordelia Chase as Failed Feminist Gesture," Buffy *Meets the Academy: Essays on the Episodes and Scripts as Texts*, ed. Kevin K. Durand (Jefferson, NC: McFarland, 2009), 150–60. Also consider Elana Levine's work in *Undead TV: Essays on* Buffy the Vampire Slayer, ed. Elana Levine and Lisa Parks (Durham: Duke University Press, 2007).

3. That is not to say that there is no treatment on issues of race in Whedon's series, only that the field is limited by the lack of representation in the shows themselves. For scholars that do address the issue of race, see Cynthia Fuchs, "'Did Anyone Ever Explain to You What "Secret Identity" Means?': Race and Displacement in *Buffy* and *Dark Angel*," *Undead TV: Essays on* Buffy the Vampire Slayer, ed. Elana Levine and Lisa Parks (Durham: Duke University Press, 2007), 96–115; Candra K. Gill, "Cuz the Black Chick Always Gets It First: Dynamics of Race in *Buffy the Vampire Slayer*," *Girls Who Bite Back: Witches, Mutants, Slayers and Freaks*, ed. Emily Pohl-Weary (Toronto: Sumach Press, 2004), 39–55; and Lynne Y. Edwards, "Slaying in Black and White: Kendra as Tragic Mulatto in *Buffy the Vampire Slayer*," *Fighting the Forces: What's at Stake in* Buffy the Vampire Slayer, ed. Rhonda V. Wilcox and David Lavery (Lanham, MD: Rowman & Littlefield, 2002), 85–97.

4. "Rm w/a Vu," *Angel*, DVD, written by Jane Espenson, directed by Scott McGinnis (1999; 20th Century–Fox,2002).

5. "The Cautionary Tale of Numero Cinco," *Angel*, DVD, written and directed by Jeffery Bell (2003; 20th Century–Fox, 2006).

6. Lisa Wolford, "Introduction: Guillermo Gomez-Peña," in *Extreme Exposure: An Anthology of Solo Performance Texts from the Twentieth Century*, ed. Jo Bonney (New York: Theatre Communications Group, 2000), 276–77 at 277.

7. Guillermo Gomez-Peña, *The New World Border: Prophecies, Poems, and Loqueras for the End of the Century* (San Francisco: City Lights, 1996), 211. All quotations from this work are copyright 1996 by Guillermo Gomez-Peña. Reprinted by permission of City Lights Books.

8. Gomez-Peña refers to L.A. as "Lost Ángeles" throughout many of his poems, essays, and speeches. In both *The New World Border: Prophecies, Poems, and Loqueras for the End of the Century* and *Ethno-techno: Writings on Performance, Activism, and Pedagogy*, he calls the city "Lost Ángeles" throughout the texts. He also referred to Lost Ángeles in his keynote address at the 1998 Association for Theatre in Higher Education (ATHE) conference. The reference here reflects one section of his epic poem, titled "XVIII: Lost Ángeles Diabólicos."

9. Gomez-Peña, *The New World Border*, 208.
10. "Anne," *Buffy the Vampire Slayer*, DVD, written and directed by Joss Whedon (1998; 20th Century–Fox, 2002).
11. Gomez-Peña, *The New World Border*, 208. "Diabólicos" translates to "diabolic." The word "pinche" has many translations, but here Gomez-Peña is using it as an expletive equivalent to "fucking" in English. It can also describe something as worthless.
12. Jes Battis, *Blood Relations: Chosen Families in* Buffy the Vampire Slayer *and* Angel (Jefferson, NC: McFarland, 2005), 118.
13. "The Cautionary Tale of Numero Cinco."
14. "The Thin Dead Line," *Angel*, DVD, written by Jim Kouf and Shawn Ryan, directed by Scott McGinnis (2001; 20th Century–Fox, 2003); "That Old Gang of Mine," *Angel*, DVD, written by Tim Minear, directed by Fred Keller (2001; 20th Century–Fox, 2003).
15. Gomez-Peña, *The New World Border*, 220.
16. Gomez-Peña quoted in Rubén Martínez, "On the North-South Border Patrol, in Art and Life," *New York Times*, October 13, 1991, H5.
17. Gomez-Peña, *The New World Border*, 59.
18. "The Cautionary Tale of Numero Cinco."
19. Ibid.
20. Heather Levi, "Sport and Melodrama: The Case of Mexican Professional Wrestling," *Social Text* 50 (1997): 57–68 at 62.
21. "The Cautionary Tale of Numero Cinco."
22. Levi, "Sport and Melodrama," 65.
23. Ibid., 64.
24. Gomez-Peña, *The New World Border*, 42–43.
25. José David Saldívar, *Border Matters: Remapping American Cultural Studies* (Berkeley: University of California Press, 1997).
26. "'Stupido' WB Promo," Youtube, February 4, 2009, online video, http://www.youtube.com/watch?v=kH8oVNumVqc (accessed July 14, 2009).
27. Battis, *Blood Relations*, 148–49.
28. Gomez-Peña, *The New World Border*, 35.
29. Ibid.
30. "The Cautionary Tale of Numero Cinco." "Yo te espero" translates to "I wait for you" and "Pues, ven y tomalo. Esta en mi panza" translates to "Come and get it. It is in my belly."
31. Naomi H. Quiñonez, "Re(Riting) the Chicana Postcolonial," in *Decolonial Voices: Chicana and Chicano Cultural Studies in the 21st Century*, ed. Arturo J. Aldama and Naomi H. Quiñonez (Bloomington: Indiana University Press, 2002), 129–51 at 141.
32. Kent A. Ono, "To Be a Vampire on *Buffy the Vampire Slayer*: Race and ('Other') Socially Marginalizing Positions on Horror TV," in *Fantasy Girls: Gender in the New Universe of Science Fiction and Fantasy Television*, ed. Elyce Rae Helford (Lanham, MD: Rowman & Littlefield, 2000), 163–86 at 178.
33. "The Cautionary Tale of Numero Cinco."
34. Gomez-Peña, *The New World Border*.
35. Ibid., 1.

Three : Theory & Philosophy

The final score can't be rigged. I don't care how many players you grease, that last shot always comes up a question mark. But here's the thing, you never know when you're taking it.... So you just treat it all like it was up to you, the world in the balance, 'cause you never know when it is.

— Gunn, "Inside Out"

(Re)Negotiating the Dystopian Dilemma: Huxley, Orwell, and *Angel*

MARY ELLEN IATROPOULOS

Dystopian themes resound throughout the world of Joss Whedon's *Angel*. When Wesley Wyndam-Pryce and Charles Gunn, two members of *Angel*'s collective-protagonist superhero investigative team,[1] entreat vigilante vampire Spike to join their team in managing the recently-acquired evil law firm Wolfram & Hart, Spike refers to the firm as "Big Brother's L.A. branch," castigates Wes and Gunn for sucking "the corporate teat" and likens them to the "evil Empire" of *Star Wars*.[2] Spike's allegations presuppose a latent, universal knowledge of classic dystopia, provoking defensiveness from Wes and Gunn precisely because they know and loathe the nightmarish worlds referenced in Spike's comparison.[3] *Angel* here exhibits an acute awareness of the dystopian tradition in which it often operates, and this self-aware participation endows *Angel*'s characters with agency and avenues of action unavailable to their dystopic predecessors. This conscious participation in and manipulation of the dystopian genre enables *Angel* to (re)negotiate the moral dilemma posed by the classic dystopian model, subverting conventions even while engaging them, shifting narrative emphasis from institutional power to individual agency and ultimately pointing the story in a more optimistic direction than the model affords.

Connections to literary and cinematic dystopias run rampant throughout the Whedonverses, and several critical studies have undertaken the task of placing Whedon's works within the dystopic tradition. Sharon Sutherland and Sarah Swan, for example, assert that *Firefly* employs the dystopian model of "an imperfect society" that examines "the political ramifications of its social ordering" though an outlaw's perspective.[4] Lorna Jowett similarly argues for a reading of *Angel*'s L.A. as "a critical dystopia," featuring Team Angel as a utopian enclave symbolizing "hope that the dystopia can be overcome."[5] While these critics convincingly establish a framework for assessing Whedon's works as dystopias unto themselves, no works exist which explicitly analyze points of comparison and divergence between Whedon's works and the classic dystopian model upon which they build. The following comparative analysis between *Angel* and classic dystopian novels by Alduous Huxley and George Orwell aims to fill that gap, by linking previously theorized critical dystopian readings of *Angel* to the classic dystopian literary model.[6] The ways in which *Angel* corresponds to, yet diverges from, these classic dystopian novels enables the show to renegotiate the dystopia's moral dilemma, ultimately subverting the classic model's pessimism to point humanity towards a brighter, more promising future.

Dystopian Dilemma, Moral Negotiation: Identifying the Literary Model

In arguing that *Angel* constitutes a critical dystopia, Jowett posits that the construct of heroism operating in *Angel* revolves around the clash of "utopian impulse against the dystopian reality," in other words, hope vs. despair.[7] Indeed, much of *Angel*'s narrative action lies in the efforts of characters to "live as though the world [is] as it should be, to show it [the world] what it can be."[8] *Angel*, in other words, navigates morally ambiguous territory by embodying idealism in a decidedly less-than-ideal world. *Angel*'s thematic emphasis on negotiating between utopian impulse and dystopian reality connects *Angel* to the literary dystopian model. Yet *Angel* also differs drastically from the model in that it exhibits an awareness of its status as dystopian participant. This awareness changes the process by which moral negotiation occurs, what it signifies, and what options are available to characters, effectively renegotiating the dystopian model on which it builds.

Angel contains but reconfigures four recognizable classic dystopian formal elements: satiric narration, anagnorisis (enlightenment), moral negotiation, and subsequent action. The first common element, satirical introduction to the dystopian landscape, typically exposes conditions which characters experience without judgment but which audiences view as worse than contemporary society. As dystopian novel critic Peter Edgerly Firchow discusses, the dystopian novel cloaks its narrative in rich satire, depicting characters as sincerely oblivious to oppressive conditions that appear to modern audiences as blatant and ridiculous.[9] The eventual progression towards recognizing dystopian reality leads to a second formal characteristic of the classic dystopian novel, anagnorisis. Literally meaning "to discover" in Greek,[10] within the dystopian context anagnorisis describes the moment of enlightenment and/or liberation in which characters recognize the truth of their circumstances. Anagnorisis presents a tremendous threat to dystopic hegemony. Dystopian regimes actively work to suppress its availability by discouraging independent thought. Once enlightened by anagnorisis, characters face the third formal element, moral negotiation, or a period of deliberation over whether to act upon their discovery, or to try to forget the truth as they subside back into illusion. Moral negotiation is self-interrogation, and characters struggle to weigh the comforts afforded to them by the dystopian system against the moral imperative to rebel against oppression. Prompted by anagnorisis, embodied by moral negotiation, their choices are two: take subversive action towards the utopian impulse, or succumb to inevitable dystopian reality. This decision leads to the fourth element common to both classic dystopias and *Angel*: the action that follows moral negotiation. While the classic dystopian novel pessimistically features characters retreating back into complacency, *Angel* again and again prefers to resist dystopia, to use the knowledge gained through anagnorisis to attempt subversion of the dystopic system.

Several episodes appear in *Angel*'s early seasons that feature decidedly dystopian themes. "She" (1.13), for instance, features a band of female demon refugees fleeing a nightmarish home world that oppresses them,[11] and "Reprise" (2.15) depicts Holland Manners, *Angel*'s chief antagonist at the evil law firm Wolfram & Hart, informing Angel that hell exists on earth.[12] More explicitly, the Pylea story arc of Season Two[13] arguably reflects the storylines of the classic dystopian novels *The Time Machine* by H.G. Wells and *Planet of the Apes* by Pierre Boulle.[14] Though dystopian examples abound, two story arcs in particular seem to enter, update, and renegotiate classic dystopian novels: Season Four's Jasmine story arc, and Season Five's Wolfram & Hart takeover/Circle of the Black Thorn story arc. Yet even as *Angel* closely resembles classic dystopian novels in these two story arcs, the show exhibits an awareness of the dystopian model with which it engages, endowing the characters with knowledge and agency unavailable to their literary predecessors, and ultimately enabling *Angel* to subvert the model to point its narrative trajectory in a more hopeful direction than the classic dystopian novel affords.

"We don't even know to fight back": Brave New World *and the Body Jasmine*

Alduous Huxley's *Brave New World*, widely considered the definitive classic dystopian novel, begins with a satiric introduction. A platitudinous, avuncular man called "the Director" proudly escorts a group of schoolchildren through what readers recognize as a eugenics laboratory.[15] As the Director describes the varying fertilization processes for different social classes, the discord between his loving words and the horrific biologically engineered caste system he describes alerts readers to utopian illusion at work. Biological castes, the Director explains, work toward maintaining social order, and in the name of the greater good of the social body, the populace willingly complies. Though the implications of socio-genetic engineering go unrecognized by the inhabitants of *Brave New World*, readers are meant to recognize that the "social body" system is, in the words of critic Keith M. Booker, "little more than a subtle form of tyranny and subjugation," a utopian veil of universal happiness cloaking a coercive agenda of oppression.[16] The government also distributes a drug called *soma* that dopes the populace into blissfully ignorant complacency.[17] People are encouraged to "just forget about" their worries and concerns and take some *soma*, so that "instead of feeling miserable, they'd feel jolly. *So* jolly."[18] The combined efforts of biogenetic oppression and the opiate-induced complacency blend to create, as Huxley describes in his foreword, "a really effective" totalitarian state in which "slaves do not have to be coerced, because they love their servitude."[19] Thus does the government of Huxley's novel manipulate and oppress its subjects, resulting in a dystopian state its inhabitants are conditioned, and willing, to ignore.

Angel similarly explores the dystopian trope of willing slavery with the character of Jasmine, a mystical, mythical goddess who emerges fully-grown from her mother's womb, and enchants everyone who gazes upon her.[20] Once under Jasmine's thrall, her followers find absolute bliss in serving her every whim.[21] The arrival of Jasmine immediately imposes a Huxley-esque dystopic paradigm of willing servitude onto the world of *Angel*. Just as the Director's glowing description of horrific practice reveals dystopia masquerading as utopia, so, too, does Team Angel's absolute and comically sudden devotion underscore Jasmine as oppressively false. Jasmine's stupefying power distracts her victims from recognizing their dystopian circumstances, since, as author Stephen Harper explains, "Once you see Jasmine, you lose all will to do anything but serve her. Still, you'll have no cause for concern — you'll be purely happy every minute."[22] For example, a former conspiracy theorist, once under Jasmine's spell, effuses that Jasmine's blissful thrall erases all his worries.[23] This enchantment serves to regulate Jasmine's body of followers, just as *soma* functions in Huxley's novel. Yet *Angel* also literalizes Huxley's metaphor of the social body. Jasmine becomes able to simultaneously channel herself into each of her worshippers, creating an army of satellite slaves whose minds fuse together to act "like the cells of a single body ... my eyes, my skin, my limbs, and if need be, my fists."[24] *Angel* engages Huxley's rhetoric, in that Jasmine actually refers to herself as the body Jasmine and again makes literal Huxley's metaphor by depicting Jasmine's body being grotesquely slashed and shredded, concurrently with her servants fighting elsewhere and receiving wounds.[25]

Both Huxley and *Angel* feature anagnorisis, the recognition of the oppression behind the charade of the social body. As *Brave New World* unfolds, the character Bernard begins to move towards anagnorisis, exhibiting discontent and gradually becoming aware that the social body robs individuals of crucial freedoms. Although a member of the elite social class Alpha, Bernard physically resembles the underclass Epsilons.[26] His uniqueness alienates him, while allowing him to develop a sense of individual identity. As he expresses to Lenina, a fellow lab worker, he sometimes wishes he were "not just a cell in the social body."[27] Bernard's misgivings stand in stark contrast to Lenina, who effuses with the voice of social conditioning that she is "free to have the most wonderful time. Everybody's happy nowadays."[28] Bernard is clearly upset by the complacency articulated in her response, and as he recognizes the social body as problematic, he undergoes anagnorisis and expresses desire to escape.[29] *Angel*'s Winifred "Fred" Burkle, however, undergoes an instantaneous mystical-induced anagnorisis when she accidentally gets her blood mixed with Jasmine's. Suddenly, the spell is broken, and Fred glimpses the monstrous visage of Jasmine's true form, recognizing the decidedly dystopian slave state lurking behind the utopian illusion.[30] Unlike Bernard's tepid, hesitant misgivings, when Fred recognizes that Jasmine overrides one's "own sense of ideals and values and [replaces] them with an alternative coercive agenda that reduces you to little more than a mindless meat puppet," she instantly rebels.[31] Fred attempts to warn her friends, but they turn on her, forcing her to flee. Fred's anagnorisis renders her dangerous to Jasmine's power, reflecting the social body's deep fear of the individual will. "As long as she's out there, she's a threat," says Wesley, leaving unspoken the question of how Fred, a lonely fugitive, could threaten someone as seemingly powerful as Jasmine.[32] Of course, given the model provided by Huxley's classic dystopian novel, audiences know the source of Fred's threatening status. As the lone holder of truth, the sole possessor of anagnoristic certainty, Fred threatens to liberate the masses from Jasmine's spell, exposing her as a monster.

Once anagnorisis exposes dystopian reality, the ensuing period of moral negotiation features characters questioning how to live under an illusion. In the classic model provided by Huxley, Bernard attempts to bargain his anagnoristic conviction for more power under the dystopian system. He voyages to the so-called "savage land," a territory outside the influence of the social body's eugenics and conditioning. Returning with two savages in tow, Bernard barters his savage specimens for more privilege and status under the dystopian regime. Gone are any thoughts of critiquing the social order. Instead, his newfound scientific celebrity and "success [go] fizzily to Bernard's head, and in the process completely [reconcile] him (as any good intoxicant should do) to a world which, up till then, he had found very unsatisfactory."[33] Bernard, seduced by the comforts now afforded him by the social body, abandons his anagnoristic convictions in the novel's climactic scene. When one of the abducted savages disrupts the weekly distribution of *soma*, Bernard meekly watches. When the police arrive, he merely feigns outrage at the savage so as not to incriminate himself.[34] Bernard's reluctance to challenge the system and his inability to sacrifice his newfound comfort and celebrity cause him to retreat into scared silence and complacency.

Angel updates Huxley's depiction of moral negotiation, shifting the emphasis from the institution's inescapability to individual empowerment. For Fred, no such bargaining option exists. Once anagnorisis liberates her, there is no question for Fred that Jasmine's illusion must be stopped. Empowered by anagnorisis and belief in the ascendancy of individual will, Fred seeks to free her friends, even after they hunt her into the sewers. She soon strategizes a way to prompt the liberation of anagnorisis for Angel, subsequently shattering Jasmine's illusion for the rest of Team Angel. Like Fred, once each team member undergoes anagnorisis, there is no question for them that Jasmine must be destroyed. Though dismantling dystopia requires the seemingly impossible task of "convinc[ing] several million other people that Jasmine's message is false," for Team Angel it is not an issue of whether to rebel, only of how and when.[35] Painfully aware of the peace they have sacrificed in rebelling, they are hunted by the body Jasmine and forced to seek refuge in the sewers, all the while remaining adamant in rebelling her oppression. Functioning as a utopian enclave working to destroy the body Jasmine's dystopia, Team Angel eventually succeeds in breaking Jasmine's spell, revealing her hideous reality to the world.

Interestingly, both *Brave New World* and *Angel*'s Jasmine story arc conclude with dystopian power earnestly engaging the oppressed, articulating the dystopian dilemma in such a way as to re-open the question to the audience. Following Bernard's forfeit of subversive action, he is taken to the office of World Controller Mustapha Mond. Mond explains that people prefer blissful subservience to the terror of war and tragedy that accompany free will: "after the nine year's war, people were ready to have even their appetites controlled then. Anything for a quiet life. We've gone on controlling ever since."[36] *Angel*'s Jasmine arc similarly concludes by addressing the basic question of whether individual free will should be sacrificed for the greater good. While *Brave New World* features the triumph of the blissful social body, *Angel* both exhibits and critiques the privileging of individual will over universal happiness. Team Angel does succeed in defeating Jasmine and revealing the dystopian horror behind her spell, yet once Jasmine is dethroned, *Angel*'s L.A. tumbles into riotous hysteria. Defeated and furious, Jasmine throws open her hands to the burning landscape and howls: "I offered paradise! You chose this! And look where free will has gotten you! This world is doomed to drown in its own blood now."[37] Jasmine's words echo Mustapha Mond's assertion that free will leads to chaos, and that the world is better off with individuality suppressed and the good of the social body exalted. Though Team Angel initially dismisses these panicked ramblings, the disquieting ramifications of Jasmine's words are later underscored by a ghostly visit from Lilah Morgan, liaison to the nefarious interdimensional law firm Wolfram & Hart. Lilah offers Team Angel her employer's L.A. branch as a reward for destroying Jasmine's utopian illusion, which she troublingly refers to as "world peace."[38] Horrified at their possible responsibility for the hell-scape around them, Team Angel wonders whether they might not have made the wrong decision in overthrowing Jasmine. On this note of moral uncertainty, Team Angel accepts custody of Wolfram & Hart, undertaking its own project of creating utopia.

"The compass needle keeps spinning, and the world gets murkier and murkier": Wolfram & Hart as Animal Farm

With the completion of the Jasmine arc, the members of Team Angel find themselves entering another classic dystopian model: the project of transforming an inherited dystopian system into a utopia. Famously portrayed in George Orwell's *Animal Farm*, the "utopian project" literary model entails the takeover of institutional power by those formerly oppressed by the institution, enabling audiences to peek behind the curtain as utopian illusion is manufactured.[39] By featuring glimpses of the mechanisms by which power corrupts and noting the seemingly small decisions that constitute step-by-step moral deterioration, the utopian project showcases its own ultimate futility.[40] Despite the noble intention, the model holds that, in the words of Spike, when one tries to change the system "it doesn't change ... it changes you," thereby denigrating the hopeful reformer to another cog in the self-perpetuating cycle of corruption.[41] As *Angel* engages with the utopian project model, the show seems aware of the model's ultimate futility (as embodied in Spike's aforementioned words), an awareness the characters employ to renegotiate the model's trajectory.

In Orwell's *Animal Farm*, the utopian project unfolds as an ambitious group of pigs galvanize the labor animals of Manor Farm into recognizing their lives as forced slave labor. The animals stage a revolution, and after overthrowing the exploitative humans, they set about to restructure the farm to resemble a utopian ideal.[42] The animals rename the estate "Animal Farm," and create a public list of animal commandments meant to codify utopian conduct. At first, a palpable "positive pleasure" permeates the farm, as the animals revel in eating crops "produced by themselves and not doled out by a grudging master."[43] However, as time passes, the animals notice their rations growing smaller and smaller, causing farm-wide concern over food shortage. The pigs quickly produce statistics that "prove" otherwise, convincing the other animals that "they were not in reality short of food, whatever the appearances might be."[44] As the animals fully believe the pigs' clearly spurious statistics, the classic dystopian trope of satiric narration alerts readers to the pigs' deceit, and the face of false utopia reveals itself.

Angel similarly features the at-first hopeful and later denigrated utopian project with the takeover of Wolfram & Hart. However, unlike Orwell's oblivious animals, *Angel* both exhibits and ignores an awareness of the how the classic model plays out. With Jasmine's dystopia dethroned, the team sees Wolfram & Hart as an opportunity to enact utopian ideals on a larger scale. Their challenge lies in wielding institutional power without exhibiting the same cruelty and corruption as their predecessors, most explicitly symbolized by the late Holland Manners, whose very name signifies all duplicity and corruption associated with the law firm's prior reputation. The homonyms "manor" and "manner" common to both Orwell and *Angel* serve to underscore the predetermined futility of the utopian project. Firmly established both in manor (material resources) and manner (behavior and use of those resources), Wolfram & Hart's power to corrupt very obviously worries Team Angel from the start. While initially deliberating the takeover, for example, Angel cautions his companions, "Before you can cross through their [Wolfram & Hart's] doors, you'll be corrupted."[45] Yet Angel troublingly ignores his own proclamation, ultimately accepting Lilah's offer on the ethically questionable condition that Wolfram & Hart create the illusion of a normal life for his troubled son (while erasing him from the rest of the team's memories). Angel's bargain embodies the classic dystopian model's typical depiction of oppressors manufacturing a "sugar-coated version of events" to weave a web of utopian illusion in order to pacify and subordinate the oppressed.[46] In sugarcoating the past, Angel foreshadows the same hypocrisy and corruption fated to befall the porcine leaders of *Animal Farm*. Other members of Team Angel also criticize and complicate their new mission even as they embrace it.[47] When Fred wonders aloud how they'll ever reform such evil, Angel reminds the team that they "came to Wolfram & Hart because it's a powerful weapon. And we'll figure out how to wield it." Wesley's deadpan, defeatist response, "Or kill ourselves with it," evinces his awareness and skepticism of their morally ambiguous situation.[48] Later, as Fred insists on the feasibility of changing the system from the inside, Gunn informs her that their utopian mission "sounds really naïve."[49] Such awareness serves to distance *Angel* from the classic dystopian novel, in that the characters seem to know corruption is inevitable. This shifts the irony of the classic model from blindness in the face of obvious oppression, to the fact that they proceed while aware of oppression's present influence. This self-aware participation in dystopia endows the characters with agency unavailable to Orwell's pigs. Despite being conscious of the project's inevitability, Team Angel's members insist that their individual agency can triumph over institutional intransigence.

As *Animal Farm* undertakes the task of restructuring a formerly corrupt system, the promise of utopia continues to seduce the pigs into ever-increasing degrees of blatant hypocrisy and manipulation. Several animals express worry over the pigs' behavior, yet as the pigs begin to travel with fierce dogs as bodyguards, criticisms grow scarce. With the "monologue demand for conformity that typically informs dystopian regimes,"[50] the pigs start punishing any dissidents with public execution. At one such bloody display of the pigs' violent authority, the terrified animals recall the cruelty of the humans, but "it seemed to all of them that it was far worse now that it was happening amongst themselves."[51] They remember a commandment outlawing animal-on-animal violence, yet when they consult the wall, the wording has been changed to state that no animal should kill any other animal *without cause*,[52] giving pigs legal grounds to use violence as means of maintaining their power. Angel similarly enforces the rules by breaking them, exhibiting discordance between his confident words and his morally dubious actions. For example, in "Harm's Way" (5.09)[53] moments after Angel decapitates a demon employee as punishment for sacrificing virgins, he justifies his act by stating, deadpan and stern, "No one gets away with murder here. Not anymore."[54] Though Angel's words themselves reiterate the vow to ethically restructure the evil law firm, they also elide Angel's own murder of the wayward Wolfram & Hart employee only moments before. To borrow from the dystopian model, Angel's murderous act signifies that the unspoken rule abolishing murder has been rewritten to add the words "without cause."

The rest of Team Angel implicitly accepts Angel's moral compromise as they negotiate their own newfound power. The murkier the ethics of the issue at hand, the less decisive they seem to be, taking few definitive stances and preferring to voice uneasy questions without answering them. For example, when Wesley asks Fred whether Wolfram & Hart's satellites could assassinate targets from outer space, Fred begins to reason it out, only to quickly back off, stammering "... if we did that sort of thing. Do we do that sort of thing"?[55] Fred, torn between enjoying and fearing the advanced (and potentially dangerous) scientific resources at Wolfram & Hart's disposal, here voices the same uncertainty expressed by Orwell's animals as they struggle to remember the original wording of the commandments. Similarly, a baffled Lorne struggles to understand why Angel leaves Gunn behind in a hell dimension. Grasping at the unprecedented desertion, Lorne stutters, "Stay behind? But you never leave a ... or ... I guess we do. I guess that's what we do now," in a manner that echoes the animals' willingness to overlook the pigs' growing corruption.[56] Though Team Angel's members critically question themselves as they grow accustomed to Wolfram & Hart, their awareness of the dystopian dilemma does not prevent them from allowing moral backsliding to seep into their group dynamic.

Progressive corruption culminates in Orwell's novel in the death of a venerated member of Animal Farm, the old workhorse named Boxer, whose demise signals the anagnoristic moment. Throughout the novel, Boxer's repeated mantras, "I will work harder" and "Napoleon [the head pig] is always right," work to legitimate the pigs' authority, as well as to motivate the other animals to work towards the utopian ideal. When Boxer suddenly collapses in the field one day, the pigs promise to provide him with veterinary care. Oblivious to the pigs' corruption, Boxer blindly embarks into the "hospital" truck that arrives to take him away. The few literate animals realize too late that the words on the truck say "Horse Slaughterer."[57] The devoted Boxer is carted away to the knacker's, a fate that the pigs once promised would await no animal living under the ideals of Animal Farm.[58] The pigs' explicit betrayal of the utopian ideal heralds anagnorisis for Orwell's animals. The dystopian reality lurking behind the utopian illusion presents itself in a manner that seems—to readers, at least—to be undeniable. Yet, when the animals finally voice their protest, the pigs dismiss them, saying the veterinarian had purchased the truck from a slaughterhouse and simply had not removed the ominous lettering. The animals feel tremendous relief at this news, despite anagnorisis and exposure of the pigs' corruption. It is easier for the animals to trust in the pigs than to call the utopian illusion into question. Just as in Huxley's dystopian model, Orwell's animals ignore the revealed reality, choosing instead to forego their suspicions and accept what they know now is an illusion. Boxer's death thus becomes another tool with which the pigs perpetuate their power. Ignoring the dystopian circumstances at work, the animals allow his death to mean nothing, to fade away into the endless charade of feigned paradise.

Angel's progressive moral backsliding also exhibits the death of a beloved team member, Fred. Fred's sunny optimism and cheerful curiosity often serves to motivate and inspire the team, and her untimely death clearly resembles Boxer's downfall, in that she meets her demise as a result of ignoring the dystopian reality that belies their utopian project. While Fred works on decrypting hieroglyphs on an ancient sarcophagus, mysterious vapors suddenly vent forth, infiltrating her lungs and rendering her disabled. That both Fred and Boxer suffer injury to the lungs is significant; living and breathing in the dystopian milieu, the lungs metaphorically function as an interface between the self and the world, and they are the first arena infected by the nightmarish reality lurking behind the illusion. These vapors, we soon learn, comprise the essence of an ancient god-king named Illyria. As Fred succumbs to the infection, Illyria consumes her, destroying Fred's soul and co-opting her body. Worse, Gunn is responsible for bringing the sarcophagus in the team's midst, although every team member feels somewhat responsible for her death. With the loss of such a loveable and dear character, the inevitable falseness of the utopian project reveals itself, and Team Angel faces the anagnoristic moment.

Angel's anagnorisis curiously leads to a bifurcation of the classic dystopian trajectory. On one hand, Fred's death heralds transcendence of the model, as it signals to most of Team Angel how corrupt they have let themselves become, and they use the occasion of her death to make explicit what Orwell leaves unsaid. Gunn, Spike, and Lorne can no longer ignore their misgivings and continue to buy the illusion. They mourn together over all they could have done to prevent Fred's death, "starting with never coming to Wolfram & Hart in the first place."[59] The team also uses the occasion to reflect on the naïveté and folly in attempting to reform institutionalized evil. Gunn, particularly distraught over his guilt, acknowledges their job at Wolfram & Hart as "hiding the horror" of the dystopian deeds they have committed under the guise of reform.[60] In further contrast to Orwell's animals, these members of Team Angel vow not to let Fred's death remain another meaningless casualty of the dystopian regime. Gunn, returning to the baggy clothes and casual language of his former (uncorrupted) self, exhibits a renewed commitment to their original mission, and Spike officially joins the team's efforts because, since "Fred gave her life for it, least I can do is give what's left of mine."[61] Contrary to the fading away of Boxer, Fred's memory remains alive, exerting a powerful posthumous motivation to remain resilient in the face of the crushing oppression of dystopian reality. Once again, awareness of the dystopian model in which they find themselves enables a (re)negotiation of the classic model, enabling the characters' individual agency, rendering their choice to depart from the model significant and optimistic.

Angel's reaction to Fred's death, however, at first appears to adhere to the classic dystopian model. As he negotiates his leadership of Wolfram & Hart, he abandons the rhetoric of utopian promise and embraces the slippery rhetoric of his corrupt predecessors. For example, after Fred's death, Angel compromises the rule outlawing human blood, making an exception for an evil Senator's vampire assistant in order to curry political favor for the firm.[62] Furthermore, Angel allows a group of clients (a demon cult called the Fell Brethren) to adopt and raise a human baby, knowing full well the baby will eventually be ritually slaughtered.[63] Again, the unprecedented act of facilitating human death signals a shift in Angel's priorities from attempting utopian idealism to accepting dystopian pragmatism. Noting Angel's departure from his champion's quest, following the dystopian model provided by *Animal Farm*, suspicion arises amongst Team Angel over whether Angel has turned evil.

As both story arcs draw to their respective closes, corruption seems inevitable. In Orwell, by novel's end the pigs have come full circle, inviting the human owners of neighboring farms to meet and discuss business, fully reneging on Animal Farm's founding principle that "whatever goes on two legs is an enemy."[64] The other farm animals, curious about the meeting but of course denied access to it, watch from outside, huddling around a window to glimpse the intimate circle of power. As the farm animals watch the scene, the men and the pigs appear to be changing and melting. Witnessing the ghastly transformation, the animals look "from pig to man, and from man to pig, and from pig to man again; but already it was impossible to say which was which."[65] On the other side of the glass window, the farm animals' fate is sealed. Revealed to be inevitably futile, the utopian project fails, and so the farm remains mired in dystopia. Emphasizing the intransigent authority of the institution, Orwell's window scene exposes the dystopia as immutable.

In terms of rhetorical positioning, the scene in which Wesley, Gunn, Spike, and Lorne confront Angel about his apparent corruption bears striking resemblance to *Animal Farm*'s climax.[66] The team attacks Angel in his office, and as they shout threats and draw their weapons, the utopian project appears to have failed, the Orwellian cycle of corruption seeming to complete itself. Yet as the narrative soon reveals, Angel's apparent corruption has all been a ruse. Angel casts a spell so that no one outside the room can see what truly is going on within and reveals to the team that he has just been feigning corruption to win the trust of Wolfram & Hart, so that he can infiltrate and assassinate the instruments of the Senior Partners, the Circle of the Black Thorn. He describes his own anagnorisis inspired by Fred's death, stating his intention to make her death more than "another random horrible event in another random horrible world," vowing to resist dystopia even if the utopian project has failed.[67] Though success is uncertain, Angel entreats his team to join his suicidal mission, asserting that "for one, shiny bright moment we [Team Angel] can show them that they don't own us. You need to decide, for yourselves, if that's worth dying for."[68] The camera pans the room, as each slowly raises a hand in unanimous assent to Angel's plan. The camera zooms out through the window, revealing the ironically named Hamilton (liaison to the senior partners) standing just beyond the glass, gazing at the scene unfolding within. Hamilton, outside the reach of Angel's spell, sees only the team at each others' throats.

Angel's use of this window scene shifts its narrative significance; instead of the window portraying inevitable defeat as in Orwell, in *Angel* it serves to frame the subversion of the classic model, opening up the optimistic alternative of truly damaging the system from within. By feigning evil in order to destroy evil, Angel dismantles the master's house with the master's tools, manipulating the expectation of corruption laid out by Orwell's novel in order to subvert the dystopian model. Indeed, it is only because Angel's charade succeeds that he is able to infiltrate the Circle of the Black Thorn and plan to assassinate them all. Moreover, by framing subversion in terms of each team member's personal choice to sacrifice and rebel, *Angel* shifts the classic model's emphasis on institutional power to privileging of individual agency. Though *Angel* could not sustain the utopian project of transforming Wolfram & Hart, neither does *Angel* yield to the inevitability of evil. Though the power of Wolfram & Hart may endure, "they're not there to be beat ... they're there to be fought."[69] Defeat may be inevitable, but in persisting to rebel against the dystopian system, *Angel* remains unbroken.

"The powerful control everything, except our will to choose": Individual Agency and Hopeful Dystopia

In *Angel*'s respective (re)negotiations of classic dystopian novels, special similarities exist between the arcs' endings. Both World Controller Mustapha Mond and Jasmine assert that society benefits from suppression of individual will, and both Orwell and *Angel* employ the window scene framing the apparent inevitability of corruption. Despite these structural similarities, however, *Angel*'s renegotiation of the classic model results in the profound overarching difference of increased emphasis on individual agency within the dystopian system. Whereas the novels display the distinctly pessimistic choice between being either crushed or conquered by dystopia, *Angel* (aware of the dystopian model in which it participates) emphasizes the individual's choice to disrupt the classic cycle, and in doing so, makes available a third option: rebellion. While perhaps futile in changing the system outright, *Angel*'s persistent resistance to dystopia illustrates that the act of refusing to give up still affects powerful and positive change. This optimism, as Jeffrey Bell (director of *Angel*'s final episode) explains, lies at the heart of *Angel*'s message: "The point isn't whether they [Team Angel] win or lose, but ... the fact that these guys will always be fighting."[70] This hopeful response to the despair of the dystopian novel renegotiates and subverts the literary genre's conventions, replacing the model's pessimism with the prospect that individual agency triumphs over dystopia.[71]

Notes

1. Lorna Jowett, "Helping the Hopeless: *Angel* as Critical Dystopia," *Critical Studies in Television* 2 (Spring 2007), 74–89 at 82. Whedon scholar Lorna Jowett convincingly applies Baccolini and Moylan's theories of dystopian protagonists as "collective ex-centric subjects" to *Angel* and its characters.
2. "Soul Purpose," *Angel*, DVD, written by Brent Fletcher, directed by David Boreanaz (2004; 20th Century–Fox, 2004).
3. "Big Brother" alludes to George Orwell's *1984*, a classic dystopian novel wherein the deceptive interface of a kindly, paternal, government-sponsored Big Brother elicits mass compliance towards surveillance, regulation, and oppression of the people. *Star Wars*, as made most famous by George Lucas's 1977 film, similarly depicts a dystopian world in which a ruthless galactic Empire controls its subjects by force and fear.
4. Sharon Sutherland and Sarah Swan, "The Alliance Isn't Some Evil Empire: Dystopia in Joss Whedon's *Firefly/Serenity*," in *Investigating* Firefly, ed. Rhonda V. Wilcox and Tanya Cochran (London: I.B. Tauris, 2008), 89–100 at 90.
5. Jowett, "Helping," 74.
6. Alduous Huxley, *Brave New World* (1932; rpt. New York: Harper & Row, 1989); George Orwell, *Animal Farm* (New York: Harcourt Brace Jovanovich, 1946).
7. Jowett, "Helping," 76.
8. "Deep Down," *Angel*, DVD, written by Stephen S. DeKnight, directed Terrence O'Hara (2002; 20th Century–Fox, 2004).
9. Peter Edgerly Firchow, "Orwell's Dystopias: From *Animal Farm* to *Nineteen-Eighty Four*," in *Modern Utopian Fictions from H.G. Wells to Iris Murdoch* (Washington, D.C.: Catholic University of America Press, 2007), 97–129 at 107.
10. According to the Oxford English Dictionary, the etymology also traces roots to the Greek *gnosis*, knowledge.
11. "She," *Angel*, DVD, written by David Greenwalt and Marti Noxon, directed by David Greenwalt (2000; 20th Century–Fox, 2002).
12. "Reprise," *Angel*, DVD, written by Tim Minear, directed by James Whitmore Jr. (2001; 20th Century–Fox 2003).
13. "Belonging," *Angel*, DVD, written by Shawn Ryan, directed by Turi Meyer (2001; 20th Century–Fox, 2003); "Over the Rainbow," *Angel*, DVD, written by Mere Smith, directed by Frederick King Keller (2001; 20th Century–Fox, 2003); "Through the Looking Glass," *Angel*, DVD, written and directed by Tim Minear (2001; 20th Century–Fox, 2003); "There's No Place Like Plrtz Glrb," *Angel*, DVD, written and directed by David Greenwalt (2001; 20th Century–Fox, 2003).

14. Jowett surmises that Pylea is, in itself, a dystopian landscape insofar as it affects *Angel*'s protagonists ("Helping," 77).
15. Huxley, *Brave New World*, 3–15.
16. Keith M. Booker, *The Dystopian Impulse in Modern Literature: Fiction as Social Criticism* (Westport, CT: Greenwood Press, 1994), 16.
17. *Soma* derives from the Greek work for body (as in psychosomatic), as well as the Latin *somnus*, meaning sleep. Huxley's use of soma conflates these two definitions, as the drug induces a sleepy state of compliance that promotes the conformity necessary to regulating the social body.
18. Huxley, *Brave New World*, 92 (italics in the original).
19. Ibid., xv.
20. "Shiny Happy People," *Angel*, DVD, written by Elizabeth Craft and Sarah Fain, directed by Maria Grabiak (2003; 20th Century–Fox, 2004).
21. Jasmine's gender and race tremendously complicate her role. Though the placement of black/female actors in positions of power does much to improve minority representation in Hollywood, Jasmine as a character is portrayed as insidious and false, which detracts from a reading of the show's casting choices as empowering. The question of what it means for a black woman to be dictatorial master of this short-lived slave state remains an open topic for further scholarly consideration.
22. Steven Harper, "Jasmine: Scariest Villain Ever," in *Five Seasons of* Angel: *Science Fiction and Fantasy Writers Discus Their Favorite Vampire*, ed. Glenn Yeffeth (Dallas: BenBella, 2004), 49–55 at 51.
23. "The Magic Bullet," *Angel*, DVD, written and directed by Jeffrey Bell (2003; 20th Century–Fox, 2004).
24. "Sacrifice," *Angel*, DVD, written by Ben Edlund, directed by David Straiton (2003; 20th Century–Fox, 2004).
25. Ibid.
26. The Epsilons are said to resemble monkeys: short, hairy, and dark. Huxley's satire treats a system of social control that privileges whiteness, as embodied by the fair Alphas (*Brave New World*, 87–89).
27. Ibid., 88.
28. Ibid.
29. Ibid., 92–5.
30. "The Magic Bullet."
31. Ibid.
32. Ibid.
33. Huxley, *Brave New World*, 159.
34. Ibid., 219.
35. "The Magic Bullet."
36. Huxley, *Brave New World*, 235.
37. "Peace Out," *Angel*, DVD, written by David Fury, directed by Jefferson Kibbee (2003; 20th Century–Fox, 2004).
38. "Home," *Angel*, DVD, written and directed by Tim Minear (2003; 20th Century–Fox, 2004).
39. Ibid.
40. Firchow, *Modern Utopian Fictions*, 108.
41. "Soul Purpose."
42. Orwell intended the narrative action of *Animal Farm* to satirize the Soviet socialist/communist project of the early twentieth century. So much scholarly work exists on the political ramifications of *Animal Farm* that, for the sake of space, I limit my discussion to dimensions of Orwell's work that best fit with *Angel*, and omit the more explicit political readings of *Animal Farm*. For a comprehensive political analysis of *Animal Farm*, see Firchow, *Modern Utopian Fictions*.
43. Orwell, *Animal Farm*, 36.
44. Ibid., 105.
45. "Home."
46. Jowett, "Helping," 81.

47. "Conviction," *Angel*, DVD, written and directed by Joss Whedon (2003; 20th Century–Fox, 2004).
48. Ibid.
49. "Soul Purpose."
50. Booker, *The Dystopian Impulse*, 11.
51. Orwell, *Animal Farm*, 84.
52. Ibid., 88, italics in original.
53. "Harm's Way," *Angel*, DVD, written by Sarah Fain and Elizabeth Craft, directed by Vern Gillum (2004; 20th Century–Fox, 2004).
54. Ibid.
55. "Soul Purpose."
56. "Power Play."
57. Orwell, *Animal Farm*, 115.
58. The promise of dignified retirement for labor animals was one of the core tenets of Animal Farm. The fate of the slaughterhouse awaited animals under human rule, and Animal Farm's reversion to its use heralds the pigs' growing resemblance to exploitative humans. Ibid., 20.
59. "Shells," *Angel*, DVD, written and directed by Stephen S. DeKnight (2004; 20th Century–Fox, 2004).
60. "Time Bomb," *Angel*, DVD, written by Ben Edlund, directed by Vern Gillum (2004; 20th Century–Fox, 2004).
61. "Shells."
62. "Power Play," *Angel*, DVD, written by David Fury, directed by James Contner (2004; 20th Century–Fox, 2004).
63. "Time Bomb."
64. Orwell, *Animal Farm*, 33.
65. Ibid.,128.
66. "Power Play."
67. Ibid.
68. Ibid.
69. "Not Fade Away," *Angel*, DVD, written by Jeffrey Bell and Joss Whedon, directed by Jeffrey Bell (2004; 20th Century–Fox, 2004).
70. Ibid., Jeffrey Bell, "Commentary." Disc 6. *Angel*, DVD, directed by Jeffrey Bell, written by Jeffrey Bell and Joss Whedon (2004; 20th Century–Fox 2004).
71. I am indebted to Dr. Heather Hewett of SUNY New Paltz, as well as Barbara Iatropoulos and Daniel E. Madsen, for their invaluable insight and feedback during the writing of this essay.

Angel vs. the Grand Inquisitor
Joss Whedon Re-imagines Dostoevsky[1]
Katia McClain

In the *Angel* episode "Peace Out" (4.21)[2] Angel, the vampire with a soul, and Jasmine, arguably the "scariest villain ever,"[3] begin their final confrontation in a Los Angeles that has erupted into chaos and violence. Jasmine, her power over humanity broken, is furious because Team Angel has destroyed the "perfect" love-filled world she had offered; she shouts at Angel, "Do you have any idea what you've done?"[4] Angel, his face somber, his voice reflecting the full knowledge of the ramifications of his choice, replies over the screeching of cars and the cries of panicked people, "What I had to do."[5] Joss Whedon, his "sneaky existential streak"[6] in full force, uses his champion Angel to insist that humanity must have the freedom to make its own choices, even if these choices lead to the loss of the utopian happiness that Jasmine claims to offer. The scene in *Angel* is a contemporary, albeit streamlined, re-working of Fyodor Dostoevsky's story of the Grand Inquisitor from *The Brothers Karamazov*, something that has not been noted in earlier scholarship on *Angel*.[7] Dostoevsky, like Whedon, used his text to insist on humanity's freedom to make its own choices, rejecting the allegedly happy, but choice-less world offered by the Grand Inquisitor's Catholic Church, just as Whedon, through Angel, rejects Jasmine's paradise.

In this essay, I examine the textual and philosophical parallels between the two scenes, the reasons for those parallels, and other correlations between the texts and philosophy of Whedon,[8] a progressive who considers himself "a very hard-line, angry atheist"[9] and Dostoevsky, who by the 1880s wrote for the conservative *Russian Herald*[10] and felt his beliefs to be "Orthodox ... Christian."[11] Although Whedon's existentialism has been the subject of previous studies,[12] most recently that of J. Michael Richardson and J. Douglas Rabb in *The Existential Joss Whedon*,[13] a direct comparison of the scene in "Peace Out" with Dostoevsky's Grand Inquisitor scene helps illuminate the existentialist character of Whedon's philosophy, which goes beyond the question of free will versus fate to consider freedom of choice versus happiness, and indeed the ramifications of those choices.[14] An analysis of the two texts suggests that what links the existentialism of Whedon and Dostoevsky is a philosophy that insists on a world based on the freedom to make bad choices. In their texts, both authors show that living with the suffering that may result from bad choices is what allows us to follow a path toward redemption, an idea that Whedon says is "one of the most important themes in my work."[15]

Although separated by more than a century, the works of Dostoevsky and Whedon originate in the allegedly "low-brow" popular entertainment of their time period (crime fiction and fantasy/horror television, respectively). Despite the "stigma" of this origin, the works of Dostoevsky, including *The Brothers Karamazov*, have proven their worth to the reading public and as a subject of study to modern scholars and critics.[16] Dostoevsky's novels and their themes "still seem pressingly 'relevant' to the most immediate concerns of the present age...."[17] In a similar vein, Rhonda Wilcox and other scholars of the Whedonverses remind us that we need to take quality television like *Angel* and its creator, Whedon, seriously, as they show "that television can be an art, and deserves to be so studied."[18]

Both Dostoevsky's *The Brothers Karamazov* and Whedon's *Angel* were originally produced as serial entertainment for the popular marketplace of their time, allowing them to draw in readers/viewers with exciting plots and continuing story lines. Whedon's episodes were released as weekly television on the WB network from 1999 to 2004, before being released as DVD boxed sets from 2004 to 2007,[19] while Dostoevsky's novel was first issued in monthly chapters in *The Russian Herald* from 1878 to 1880, before being published as a single volume shortly thereafter.[20] Serial publication of chapters was not unusual in Dostoevsky's day; the same was done with the works of many of his Western contemporaries, such as Dickens.[21]

The public's reaction to "*The Brothers Karamazov* was invariably enthusiastic"[22]; while some contemporary critics disagreed with the public's acclaim, suggesting that the novel "was proof of the decline of Dostoevsky's talent."[23] Years later, Russian novelist Vladimir Nabokov belittled Dostoevsky's work as "the poor relation of Russian literature, unworthy of admission to the pantheon of the great because of his uncouth literary manners and taste for the cheaply melodramatic."[24] This conflict between eager reception by the public and unflattering description by critics bears a resemblance to both the loyal fan following and the early critiques of *Angel* described by Stacey Abbott.[25]

Aside from a common origin in the episodic popular culture of their respective eras, the texts of Dostoevsky and Whedon, with their "increasing moral complexity,"[26] nuanced "representation of good and evil,"[27] and a "world of grays rather than crisp black and white oppositions"[28] have some commonalities in setting, structure, characters, and style. Whedon places *Angel* in the same kind of dark and alienating "nightmare city" that Dostoevsky used to reflect "his characters' souls."[29] Both authors populate their texts with doppelgangers and doubles for their main characters;[30] figures who, as Abbott says of *Angel*, "are damaged or in need of redemption."[31] Both authors layer their narratives with allusions to other texts and cultural products. As those who read Dostoevsky in Russian know, and as the translator Richard Pevear points out,

Dostoevsky uses idiosyncratic language to give distinctive voices to his characters,[32] as does Whedon. This leads to a carnivalesque polyphony in Whedon's narrative, similar to that found by Bakhtin in Dostoevsky's novels.[33] Both authors carefully construct the nuances and style of their texts, even while working within the rapid pace of the episodic format. Both have the ability, as scholar Joseph Frank said of Dostoevsky, "to treat the same material sometimes as tragedy and sometimes as comedy."[34] Both demonstrate, as W. J. Leatherbarrow says of Dostoevsky, the "willingness to entertain and engage with 'high' serious intellectual and emotional issues while simultaneously rewarding any taste we may have for immediately compelling narrative energy and 'low' popular fictional devices."[35] Furthermore, both authors are keenly aware of their role as subtle challengers of the status quo. Frank's description of Dostoevsky applies equally well to Whedon: "His technique had always been to refute the ideas he was combating 'indirectly,' not by explicit argument but by dramatizing their consequences on the fate of his characters."[36]

Given the many similarities, one might suppose that the two authors were writing for identical cultures. This is exactly the conclusion that Richardson and Rabb come to in their otherwise excellent analysis of Whedon's existentialism. Based on an examination of the writings of the Russian philosopher, Lev Shestov, they connect Whedon to an existentialist tradition that stretches back from "Jean-Paul Sartre ... to Dostoevsky."[37] Their claim, what they call "a most extraordinary discovery,"[38] is that the "popular philosophy of contemporary America and that of pre–Marxist Russia, represented in Dostoevsky's writings, are so strikingly similar that it is possible to argue that they are in actual fact one and the same. Pre-Marxist Russia and contemporary America actually share the same philosophy, the same values and the same world views."[39]

While there is a clear parallel between the existentialism of Whedon and Dostoevsky, and while the artistic output of the two writers is part of the popular culture of their time, Richardson and Rabb make an unwarranted leap in claiming that the values and worldview of mid–nineteenth-century Russia and contemporary America are the same.

First, the cultural contexts that Dostoevsky and Whedon work in are almost completely dissimilar. Russia during much of the time that Dostoevsky was writing (1840s-1880) was a country of the harshest government repression of public discourse, in which the only outlet for political and philosophical debate among the tiny intellectual elite was through opaque Aesopian literature.[40]

The costs to writers at that time could include their lives. Dostoevsky himself was sentenced to death, suffered through a nightmarish mock execution, along with twenty-three others, in which they were prepared for death, led out to the firing squad, tied to the posts, and only then told of their "unexpected" reprieve. One of those punished in this way with Dostoevsky went mad as a result.[41] Dostoevsky served four years of hard labor in Siberia, followed by five years of exile in what is now Kazakhstan for being part of the radical Petrashevsky literary circle.[42] The trauma of his experiences, apparently, helped turn Dostoevsky from a moderate progressive with mildly non-religious tendencies into a faithful believer in the Eastern Orthodox religion. Whedon has had only to deal with critics, television ratings, and network executives.[43]

Furthermore, although Richardson and Rabb are correct that Dostoevsky was, at times, immensely popular,[44] there were many other writers and thinkers with views that differed sharply from Dostoevsky who were equally popular. In fact, one of the most interesting features of Russia of this time period is the multiplicity of worldviews and philosophies (utilitarianism, multiple versions of socialism, nihilism, slavophilism, Tolstoyan humanism, mysticism, etc.) that were in conversation and argument with each other among the educated elite, primarily through literature.[45] Richardson and Rabb address this polemic polylogue only briefly. It is not just, as Richardson and Rabb say, that Dostoevsky was "concerned with existential freedom and with rejecting the scientific determinism implicit in studies such as N.G. Chernyshevski's *The Anthropological Principle in Philosophy* (1860)"[46]; rather, Dostoevsky directly attacked the motifs, characters, and even whole passages of Chernyshevsky's novel *What is to be Done* in both *Notes from Underground* and *Crime and Punishment* in order to express his dissatisfaction with Chernyshevsky's philosophical impact on Russian culture and to challenge it with his own worldview. Just as not all Russians of his time period shared Dostoevsky's philosophy and worldview, neither do all Americans share Whedon's.

In fact, this clash with the philosophies of their contemporaries may help explain another possible parallel between the writers—they share a similar artistic philosophy. Like the worldview realized in Dostoevsky's texts, much of the philosophy of the Buffy/Angelverse is set up to challenge cultural and artistic norms. Whedon shares with Dostoevsky the belief that "changing culture is important," and that "it can only be done in a popular medium."[47] Both Dostoevsky and Whedon are in some sense rebels, using innovative, complicated texts to challenge their readers/viewers.

Let us now turn to the parallel texts. The story of the Grand Inquisitor is a "poem" created and feverishly recited by Ivan Karamazov (the atheist, rationalist brother) to Alyosha Karamazov (the spiritual brother) in Part II, Book V, Chapter 5 of *The Brothers Karamazov*, a philosophical novel whose plot centers around the Karamazov brothers and the murder of their father.[48] The poem imagines a confrontation between the Grand Inquisitor and Christ, in which the Grand Inquisitor reports what the Catholic Church has done for humanity in the time since Christ left: "[We] have finally overcome freedom and have done so in order to make people happy."[49] Though these words actually are part of the text of the novel, Dostoevsky's goal in writing the novel was to refute this very philosophy. The Grand Inquisitor passage is the culmination of Dostoevsky's explication of his own anti–Grand Inquisitor philosophy, which he then deconstructs throughout the rest of the novel.

The confrontation between Angel and Jasmine is, arguably, the culmination of Season Four, the season in which the series abandons "the episodic in favor of a sustained story line."[50] From "Slouching Toward Bethlehem" (4.04) to "Peace Out" (4.21) *Angel* tells the story of Team Angel's interaction with Jasmine, an interdimensional "Power that Be," who has arranged to be reborn to Cordelia and Connor in Los Angeles in order to enslave the population into believing her message of peace and love.[51] She explains her goal at a press conference: "To make this the best of all possible worlds, without borders, without hunger, war, or misery. A world built on love, respect, understanding, and, well, just enjoying one another."[52] Of course, nothing is ever so simple in the Whedonverses, as evidenced, for example, by Jasmine's penchant for human snacks. Although her description of a perfect world does not overtly refer to humanity's concomitant loss of freedom, that loss is gradually revealed during Season Four. Once Angel and company free themselves from Jasmine's spell, they must flee her followers, who have turned from love-filled passivity to angry fanaticism.[53] The façade of Jasmine's utopian vision for the world is finally punctured by Angel and company, who find a way to destroy her power over humanity. This leads to the showdown between Angel and Jasmine described at the beginning of this essay.

Like the Angel/Jasmine story that reveals a deeper engagement with more metaphysical concepts, Dostoevsky creates a parable, through Ivan Karamazov, to confront these same concerns. The parable is "set in Spain, in Seville, in the most horrible time of the Inquisition,"[54] some 400 years before Dostoevsky wrote it. Jesus Christ returns to earth on the day after "the Cardinal Grand Inquisitor had burned almost a hundred heretics."[55] The Grand Inquisitor, "an old man, almost ninety ... with a gaunt face" and eyes "that shine with a sinister fire,"[56] has Christ arrested. Although everyone in the crowd has recognized Christ, no one protests. They are, like the crowds hypnotized by Jasmine in *Angel*, "tamed, submissive, and tremblingly obedient to his [the Inquisitor's] will."[57] The Inquisitor later enters the prisoner's cell and tries to find out why he has come to interfere with the work of the Inquisition. He threatens to condemn Christ as a heretic and promises that "the very people who today kissed your feet, tomorrow, at a nod from me, will rush to heap the coals up around your stake."[58]

Forbidding Christ to speak, the Inquisitor initiates a "conversation," in fact a monologue, posing and answering questions highlighting the philosophical differences and differing views of the needs of humankind between Christ and the Catholic Church. Dostoevsky tries to advance his ideas about what humanity needs without having a character voice his side of the argument during the scene except in the infrequent reactions of the "good" brother, Alyosha, as Ivan relates his parable.[59] This lack of explicitness or perhaps the complex nesting of polyphonic narrative voices (Dostoevsky/Ivan/Grand Inquisitor) may have been what misled some critics into suggesting that Dostoevsky's views were those of the Grand Inquisitor.[60] There is no question that Dostoevsky, who had experienced a newly awakened faith in Russian Orthodoxy while imprisoned in Siberia, and who had developed a strong antipathy to the Catholic Church, supported Christ's side in this polemic.[61] Indeed, Dostoevsky emphasizes his arguments against the Inquisitor in the rest of the novel. As Joseph Frank notes, we "should not assume — as ... is too often done by other interpreters as well — that the author here was speaking in his own voice."[62] Whedon's parallel scene avoids this kind of confusion by creating a real dialogue between Angel and Jasmine, with Angel voicing Whedon's message.

The Inquisitor harangues Christ for long passages and accuses him of having made many mistakes[63]: "You rejected the only absolute banner, which was offered to you to make all men bow down to you indisputably — the banner of earthly bread; you rejected it in the name of freedom...."[64] With this, Dostoevsky signals his readers that he is not only attacking the Catholic Church's focus on happiness over freedom, but is specifying that the happiness-filled utopia is a materialist one. This allows Dostoevsky to extend the scope of his attack to also include left-leaning utopianists, who focused on materialist solutions to humanity's poverty and despair.[65] Relying on the reader to pick up on his irony, Dostoevsky writes his Inquisitor continuing, "Instead of taking over men's freedom, you increased it still more for them! Did you forget that peace and even death are dearer to man than free choice in the knowledge of good and evil?"[66] Dostoevsky intends this entire argument to be ironic; he believes that the crucial goal of humanity should be the freedom to make such a choice. Since this is one of the focal points of the Inquisitor's philosophy that he is trying to refute, Dostoevsky has the Inquisitor add to his argument with the same initial refrain as above: "Instead of taking over men's freedom, you ... forever burdened the kingdom of the human soul with its torments."[67]

The Inquisitor attempts to convince Christ that, in his vision of paradise, "everyone will be happy, and they will no longer rebel or destroy each other, as in your freedom...."[68] In other words, if we reject the Inquisitor's argument, as Dostoevsky desires, we need to know that freedom is messy and dangerous, but nonetheless the better option. Given free will, humans may wage war or inflict suffering on each other, yet they must be allowed to make that choice. In continuing his verbal tormenting of Christ, the Inquisitor notes that people will only "become free when they resign their freedom to us, and submit to us ... they will remember to what horrors of slavery and confusion your freedom led them. Freedom, free reason, and science will lead them into such a maze ... that some of them unruly and ferocious will exterminate each other...."[69] Again, Dostoevsky uses the Inquisitor's voice to link submission to the will of the Church and submission to materialism, utilitarianism, and other rationalist philosophies that Dostoevsky rejects.[70]

Finally, the Inquisitor explains to Christ that once the people understand that they "are only pitiful children," they will realize that a "child's happiness is sweeter than any other.... And everyone will be happy, all the millions of creatures...."[71] The Inquisitor, "far from acknowledging the incongruity of burning one's fellow humans in the name of a doctrine of love,[72] ends his "discussion" with the silent Christ figure by saying, "I shall burn you for having come to interfere with us. For if anyone has ever deserved our stake, it is you. Tomorrow I shall burn you."[73] Alyosha is confused by Ivan's poem, which Ivan imagines has proven the validity of the Grand Inquisitor's argument. Alyosha sees what Dostoevsky wants the reader to understand, that the "poem praises Jesus, it doesn't revile him."[74] The Inquisitor has it all wrong. The "paradise" that the Catholic Church and left-leaning groups, according to Dostoevsky, had worked so hard to create provides only a materialistic, constrained happiness, depriving humanity of its freedom to make choices. These choices may be painful—since humanity is forced to see the evil that surrounds it—but they are to be preferred to the blind happiness of the Inquisitor's paradise.

Alyosha's outrage over Ivan's story provokes Ivan to produce a new, less violent, ending to what he now calls "the muddled poem of a muddled student."[75] In this new ending "the Inquisitor fell silent ... he waited for some time for his prisoner to reply.... The old man [the Inquisitor] would have liked him [Christ] to say something, even something bitter, terrible. But suddenly he [Christ] approaches the old man in silence and gently kisses him on his bloodless, ninety-year-old lips. That is the whole answer.... [H]e [the Inquisitor] walks to the door, opens it and says to him: 'Go and do not come again ... do not come at all ... never, never!' And he lets him out into the 'dark squares of the city.'"[76] Despite the forgiving kiss by the Christ figure,[77] and despite the fact that the Inquisitor lets Christ go, Ivan says that the Grand Inquisitor "holds to his former idea."[78]

The final scene between Jasmine and Angel in "Peace Out" re-stages Dostoevsky's Grand Inquisitor/Christ passage. Angel and the "big, bad free will gang"[79] have wrested Los Angeles from Jasmine's control. Angel confronts her on a freeway overpass, lit by the glare of a burning car. The former divinity, her loss of power reflected in her newly visible demonic visage, expresses her outrage, "I offered paradise. You chose this!"[80] Angel, Whedon's vampiric voice for the needs of humanity, explains why he was compelled to act: "Because that's what you took away from us. Choice."[81] Jasmine, who, like the Grand Inquisitor, cannot believe that anyone would choose the chaos, panic, and violence that has replaced her enforced peace, continues: "Look what free will has gotten you."[82] Angel, giving voice to the viewpoint of Dostoevsky's silent Christ, explains why freedom, no matter how messy, is always preferable to its absence, replying, "Hey, I didn't say we were smart. I said it's our right. It's what makes us human."[83] Jasmine argues that what she was offering really was a paradise, by saying, "I could've stopped it, Angel. All of it. War, disease, poverty. How many precious, beautiful lives would've been saved in a handful of years?"[84] Unlike the Grand Inquisitor, Jasmine seems to have some awareness of the incongruity of a loving paradise brought about by murder, but feels justified because, as she says, she "murdered thousands to save billions."[85] Angel forcefully reiterates Whedon's philosophy, as well as that of Dostoevsky: "The price was too high, Jasmine. Our fate has to be our own, or we're nothing."[86] Angel, like Christ, is conciliatory and attempts to persuade Jasmine to join him, saying, "Maybe you can still help us make it [the world] better...."[87] Jasmine, no more persuaded by Angel's argument than was the Grand Inquisitor by Christ's, punches Angel so hard that he flies off the overpass.

Although they vary in narrative details, and although Dostoevsky's original text is dense and convoluted (to the despair of Russian literature students and translators), whereas Whedon's is not, the two texts nevertheless set up parallel arguments.[88] In each case something larger than life — the Church, which has usurped God in Dostoevsky's view, or an interdimensional power that has set itself up as God as in *Angel*— requires followers to give up their freedom of choice, in exchange for some happy, materialistic paradise. The followers will be able live in this paradise free from war and hunger, if they are willing to surrender their freedom to the institution. Of course, in the case of Jasmine, her followers must also be ready to be eaten just as the followers of the Inquisitor's church had to be prepared to trust their safety to a tyrannical authority who burned dissenters at the stake. Offered a constrained happiness versus a potentially very unhappy freedom, Whedon, through Angel, asks us to reject Jasmine's offer of paradise in favor of free will, just as Dostoevsky asked his peers to do 120 years earlier through Christ's response to the Grand Inquisitor.[89]

Scholars who have examined Whedon's existentialism have suggested that the importance of free will and choice is part of what lies at the core of the philosophy of *Angel* and its parent series, *Buffy the Vampire Slayer*.[90] Even though the original mythos of *Buffy* seems to indicate the prominence of fate and lack of choice for the characters — Buffy is fated to be a slayer, Giles a watcher, and Angel a vampire attempting redemption — the Buffy/Angelverse quickly moves beyond that simple formula. Even "seemingly immutable prophecies may be redefined by free will...."[91] The interchange from "Prophecy Girl" (1.12) from the first season of *Buffy* is often used to illustrate this point.[92] Buffy, who had been fated to die at the Master's hand, resists the prophecy enough to allow her revival. When she reappears, The Master (an über-vampire) says to her, "You were destined to die. It was written," and Buffy quips, "What can I say? I flunked the written."[93] The philosophy of choosing to resist or redefine the destiny predicted in prophecies continues in *Angel*; by the finale of the first season, Angel tells Lindsey in typical Whedonspeak, "Don't believe everything you're foretold."[94] This comes about partly because, as Angel observes about prophecies, "you can always interpret them a hundred ways from Sunday."[95] For example, does the Shanshu clause of the Aberjian prophecies — predicting that a vampire with a soul may become human — refer to Angel or Spike (once he too acquires a soul)?[96] Does it predict that the champion of the prophecy will side with the forces of good or evil in the apocalypse? More importantly, however, characters in *Angel* use their free will to actively resist the predetermined fate suggested in the prophecies. Wesley, horrified by a prophecy that he believes predicts Angel's murder of his son Connor, chooses to remove the infant and resist the prediction. And, in Season Five, Angel signs away the Shanshu prophecy to help in his battle against the Circle of the Black Thorn. In the Buffy/Angelverse, as Fred engagingly suggests, "Destiny is just another word for 'inevitable' and nothing's inevitable as long as you stand up, look it in the eye, and say, 'You're evitable!'"[97]

Whedon's characters also use free will to resist "being part of a cosmic puppet show"[98] that would deny them the ability to take Fred's advice. In "Inside Out" (4.17)[99] the demon Skip claims that much of what has happened over the last few years was orchestrated by the Power who will soon appear as Jasmine. In response, Gunn says, "No way. We make our own choices," and Skip retorts, "Yeah, sure. A cheese sandwich here, when to floss, but the big stuff, like two vampires squeezing out a kid?" suggesting that some events are outside the control of an individual's choices.[100] Later in the episode, Fred wonders whether Skip is right and whether they all are "just pieces being moved around a chess board."[101] Gunn sums up Whedon's philosophical stance on the issue, saying, "The final score can't be rigged ... so you just treat it all like it was up to you, the world in the balance, 'cause you never know when it is."[102] Even if the possibility of an unseen puppeteer exists, Whedon's philosophy insists on our right to make choices.

In the Buffy/Angelverse, making choices is typically difficult and often painful. Only these painful choices can lead to redemption, which, as Whedon says, "is really hard and it takes your whole life."[103] Characters frequently make the wrong choices and "often screw up in precisely the same ways they did several seasons ago."[104] As shown in Angel's conversation with Jasmine, Whedon's philosophy demands that they have the freedom to make bad choices. As Angel points out to Faith in "Sanctuary" (1.19), "All that pain, all that suffering ... is coming back on you ... deal with it ... maybe you've got a shot at being free."[105] This is also strikingly parallel to the world of Dostoevsky. Much of *Notes from Underground* and *Crime and Punishment*, for example, is focused on the Underground Man and Raskolnikov's choices (many irrational and contradictory) and the fact that Dostoevsky's characters must be allowed to make them. As the Underground Man says, "Man ... must have the right to wish for himself even what is stupidest of all and not be bound by an obligation to wish for himself only what is intelligent ... it preserves for us the chiefest and dearest thing, that is, our personality and our individuality."[106] In the Buffy/Angelverse characters also make choices that seem to be irrational, or at the very least contradictory—Angel's retreat from his role as champion during his "beige aura" period in Season Two, for example—but they must have the freedom to do so. The parallel scenes between Angel and Jasmine and the Grand Inquisitor and

Jesus Christ suggest that only by having the freedom to make bad choices can we choose between good and evil. Only by suffering with the bad choices we have made can we move toward redemption and reject institutions that limit the freedom to engage in this process.

Still, though Dostoevsky and Whedon share many narrative and philosophical positions, they do not always agree. While Whedon rejects the false happiness provided by all institutions, whether high school or the Initiative in *Buffy*, Jasmine in *Angel*, the Alliance in *Firefly* and *Serenity*, or the blissful state of tabula rasa in *Dollhouse*, Dostoevsky specifically rejects the Catholic Church and the models of socialist utopias that he connects with Western European Catholicism.[107] He has no disagreement with the tenets of Russian Orthodoxy. In fact, at least one critic suggests that the Grand Inquisitor scene is problematic because of what he calls one of Dostoevsky's favorite ideas, "the dubious notion that Catholicism, in arrogating to itself temporal power, had betrayed Christ, and so become the mother of socialism."[108] Dostoevsky links the Catholic Church and socialist utopias, both because they come from the alien West, and because, in his view, they don't trust the freedom of choice that he insists upon. This linked institution assumes that the masses are either too sinful or too corrupted by the current system to make good choices and seeks to control them.

As many scholars have noted, Whedon creates characters that "care passionately about right and wrong, good and evil."[109] The similarity to Dostoevsky in this respect is clear, as noted most recently by Richardson and Rabb, who observe, "Both Whedon and Dostoevsky ... seem preoccupied with the problem of evil and human freedom."[110] I suggest that one key difference is that Whedon asks "probing metaphysical questions and often dares to leave them unanswered,"[111] while Dostoevsky does not leave questions unanswered, but points us toward a single correct answer, in this case, redemption through (Eastern Orthodox) Christian suffering. Dostoevsky asserts that the "most basic spiritual need of the Russian people is the need for suffering, incessant and unslakeable suffering, everywhere and in everything ... without it their happiness is incomplete."[112] The suffering of the characters leads them to the true answers found in the Bible. According to David Bethea, the need among Russian writers to provide the one true answer comes about because Russian writers have seen their role as a kind of "secular saint" and "have long operated under the conviction that they are writing, not one more book, but versions ... of The Book (Bible)."[113]

Although Whedon's characters also suffer greatly along their path to redemption, it is not a path that leads to a single source for answers, although, in general, the path does involve making connections to and sacrifices for others. The nuanced views of the Whedonverses, in fact, emphasize the need to continually ask probing questions and be open to multiple answers. A satire of the dangers of the single answer is shown in "Shiny Happy People" (4.18).[114] Fred, recently de-enchanted from Jasmine's spell, points out that they "all kind of do what she [Jasmine] says"; they "don't ask questions."[115] The still-ensorcelled Angel answers with relief, "Constant questioning, it's finally over."[116] We have the advantage of seeing that Angel's line comes only from his enslavement to Jasmine and understand the interchange as ironic. Whedon further emphasizes his point by showing the witch-hunt — an allusion to the witch-hunts sponsored by the forces of the Inquisition throughout Western Europe in the Early Modern period — that ensues when the other characters realize that Fred has begun to ask questions. Whedon's text again evokes Dostoevsky's Grand Inquisitor, who wants to burn those who, like Christ, disagree with him.

Furthermore, the Buffy/Angelverse has an "ambivalence about organized religion"[117] which is "usually regarded with distance and, at times, irreverence."[118] Unlike Dostoevsky, Whedon is clearly not an advocate of any one or even any religion, as Xander's confusion in "Tabula Rasa" (6.08) reminds us. When faced with possible "death by vampire," he frantically mumbles pieces of Christian, Jewish, and Buddhist prayers, none of which he really knows and none of which are terribly effective.[119] Likewise, Buffy sums up Whedon's ambivalence effectively with her comment, "Note to self, religion freaky."[120] Whedon's characters understand good and evil and the need to have the freedom to choose between them. They can achieve redemption through suffering, but Whedon rejects Dostoevsky's notion of finding the path to redemption in any single way. Richardson and Rabb are correct that "Whedon is defending a radical existential ethics which goes well beyond anything Dostoevsky and Sartre envisaged. Nothing can tell you what to do ... not society, not church, not even divine authority."[121] Whedon's rejection of any one path to redemption, however, does not make his message an empty one of despair. Although institutions are irrelevant or more typically dangerous to redemption, the human act of achieving redemption is a critical part of the Buffy/Angelverse. As Angel says in "Epiphany" (2.16), "If there is no great glorious end to all this, if nothing we do matters, then all that matters is what we do."[122]

Despite some important differences in their philosophy, it should be clear from the discussion above that there is a striking parallel between Whedon's existentialist worldview and that of Dostoevsky. But even Slavists have to admit that Whedon does it, as Spike says in "School Hard" (2.03), "with a little less ritual and a little more fun."[123]

Notes

1. An earlier version of this essay was presented at *SC3: The Slayage Conference on the Whedonverses* (Henderson State University, Arkadelphia, Arkansas, June 5–8, 2008). My thanks to Cynthea Masson for her cogent feedback on that version. This version has benefited greatly from the comments of Hector Javkin, as well as superlative editing by AmiJo Comeford and Tamy Burnett. All remaining errors are, of course, mine.

2. "Peace Out," *Angel*, DVD, written by David Fury, directed by Jefferson Kibbee (2003; 20th Century–Fox, 2004).

3. Steven Harper, "Jasmine: Scariest Villain Ever," in *Five Seasons of* Angel: *Science Fiction and Fantasy Writers Discuss Their Favorite Vampire*, ed. Glenn Yeffeth (Dallas: BenBella, 2004), 49–55 at 49.
4. "Peace Out."
5. Ibid. There is some irony to the scene of a vampire and a demon-god arguing over the fate of humanity.
6. Emily Nussbaum, "Must See Metaphysics," *New York Times Magazine*, September 22, 2002, http://www.nytimes.com/2002/09/22/magazine/must-see-metaphysics.html.
7. I follow the common U.S. spelling conventions for Russian names (e.g., Dostoevsky) in the body of this text. I maintain the original spelling used in other scholarly works, reflecting other conventions (e.g., Dostoevskii) in quotations and citations.
8. I will refer to the philosophy expounded in works created by Joss Whedon as belonging to him, although, as Rhonda Wilcox, *Why Buffy Matters: The Art of* Buffy the Vampire Slayer (New York: I.B. Tauris, 2005), 5–8, and Stacey Abbott, *Angel*, TV Milestones Series (Detroit: Wayne State University Press, 2009), 25–26, among others, point out, the Whedonverses are created not only by Joss Whedon, but by the collaborative collective of writers, actors, and crew he has gathered together and entrusted with carrying out his vision. For contributions of other key writers on Whedon's team see David Perry, "Marti Noxon: Buffy's Other Genius," in *Buffy Goes Dark: Essays on the Final Two Seasons of* Buffy the Vampire Slayer *on Television*, ed. Lynne Y. Edwards, Elizabeth L. Rambo, and James B. South (Jefferson, NC: McFarland, 2009), 13–22, and David Kociemba, "Understanding the Espensode," in *Buffy Goes Dark: Essays on the Final Two Seasons of* Buffy the Vampire Slayer *on Television*, ed. Lynne Y. Edwards, Elizabeth L. Rambo, and James B. South (Jefferson, NC: McFarland, 2009), 23–39.
9. Nussbaum, "Must See."
10. *Russkij vestnik* (sometimes translated as *Russian Messenger*) was published by M. N. Katkov in Moscow from 1856 to 1887 and in Saint Petersburg from 1887 to 1906.
11. Victor Terras, *A Karamazov Companion* (1981; rpt., Madison: The University of Wisconsin Press, 2002), 39. Dostoevsky's growing interest in a kind of populist Russian orthodoxy was complex and possibly connected to his growing anti–Semitism. For further discussion, see Susan McReynolds, *Redemption and the Merchant God: Dostoevsky's Economy of Salvation and Antisemitism* (Evanston: Northwestern University Press, 2008), especially 3–19 and the references therein.
12. For a discussion of the claim that an "existentialist definition of good" might apply to the character of Angel, see Rhonda Wilcox, "'Every Night I Save You': Buffy, Spike, Sex and Redemption," *Slayage: The Online International Journal of Buffy Studies* 2, no. 1 (May 2002), www.slayageonline.com. For a discussion of the tension between free will and fate in the Buffy/Angelverse, see Matthew Pateman, *The Aesthetics of Culture in* Buffy the Vampire Slayer (Jefferson, NC: McFarland, 2006), 190; Thomas Flamson, "Free Will in a Deterministic Whedonverse," in *The Psychology of Joss Whedon: An Unauthorized Exploration of* Buffy, Angel, *and* Firefly, ed. Joy Davidson (Dallas: BenBella, 2007), 35–50; and Gregory Stevenson, *Televised Morality: The Case of* Buffy the Vampire Slayer (Lanham, MD: Hampton Books, 2003). For a discussion of faith and choice see K. Dale Koontz, *Faith and Choice in the Works of Joss Whedon* (Jefferson, NC: McFarland, 2008).
13. J. Michael Richardson and J. Douglas Rabb, *The Existential Joss Whedon: Evil and Human Freedom in* Buffy the Vampire Slayer, Angel, Firefly *and* Serenity (Jefferson, NC: McFarland, 2007).
14. Although most studies focus on free will versus fate, a few earlier studies have commented on the issue of freedom versus happiness in the Jasmine arc, without reference to Dostoevsky's Grand Inquisitor scene. Harper ("Jasmine," 51–2) compares Jasmine's world of hypnotized happiness with that of fanatical evangelists. Richardson and Rabb (*Existential*, 147–149), basing much of their discussion on Harper's essay, compare the loss of freedom in Jasmine's world with that of the Alliance in Whedon's *Firefly* and *Serenity*. Flamson ("Free Will") discusses free will versus happiness.
15. Joss Whedon, "Interview," *The New York Times*. May 16, 2003, http://www.nytimes.com/2003/05/16/readersopinions/16WHED.html. For further discussion of redemption in the Buffy/Angelverse, see Jana Riess, *What Would Buffy Do?* (San Francisco: John Wiley & Sons, 2004); Rhonda Wilcox, *Why Buffy Matters*; and Richardson and Rabb, *Existential*.

16. Vladimir Nabokov is an exception. Nabokov was well-known for his virulent reactions to not only Dostoevsky, but many authors. For example, in a 1966 interview on National Education Television, he famously said, "I have been perplexed and amused by fabricated notions about so-called 'great books.' That, for instance, Mann's asinine 'Death in Venice,' or Pasternak's melodramatic, vilely written 'Dr. Zhivago,' or Faulkner's corn-cobby chronicles can be considered 'masterpieces' or at least what journalists term 'great books,' is to me the sort of absurd delusion as when a hypnotized person makes love to a chair." "Why Nabokov Hates Freud," *New York Times Books*, January 30, 1996, http://www.nytimes.com/books/97/03/02/lifetimes/nab-v-freud.html. For details of Nabokov's dislike of Dostoevsky, see his analysis of Dostoevsky's works in "Fyodor Dostoevski," *Lectures on Russian Literature*, ed. Fredson Bowers (New York: Harcourt, Brace Jovanovich, 1981), 97–135. Simon Karlinsky, in his discussion of reactions to Dostoevsky, speculates that Nabokov's attitude to Dostoevsky (which was not unlike that of other Russian writers including Chekhov, Gorky, Bunin, and Tsvetaeva), "must have acquired its additional polemical bite from the author's decades of residence in the West, where the blind adulation of Dostoevsky can be as irritating as it is universal." Simon Karlinsky, "Dostoevsky as Rorschach Test," in *Crime and Punishment: A Norton Critical Edition*, ed. George Gibian (New York: W.W. Norton, 1989), 612–619 at 618. (Originally published in the *New York Times*, June 13, 1971).

17. W. J. Leatherbarrow, introduction to *The Cambridge Companion to Dostoevskii*, ed. W.J. Leatherbarrow (Cambridge, UK: Cambridge University Press 2002), 1.

18. Wilcox, *Why Buffy Matters*, 13.

19. An interesting subject of further research might be to compare the responses of viewers who watched *Angel* as a weekly series to that of those who first view it as a complete text.

20. Dostoevsky's novel was published serially in the journal *The Russian Herald* from 1878–1880. The novel was then published as a separate edition in 1880, with the publication date given as 1881. For details, see Terras, Karamazov *Companion*, 5–10, and Joseph Frank, *Dostoevsky: The Mantle of the Prophet 1871–1881* (Princeton: Princeton University Press, 2002), 403–408. For details on the publication of the Grand Inquisitor passage, specifically, see Frank, *The Mantle*, 426–438.

21. For more speculation about the links between Whedon and Dickens, see Wilcox, *Why Buffy Matters*, 9–10.

22. Terras, Karamazov *Companion*, 36.

23. Ibid., 34. For a detailed discussion of the negative reaction of contemporary critics, see Victor Terras, "Dostoevsky's Detractors," *Dostoevsky Studies*, 6 (1985), 166–172, http://www.utoronto.ca/tsq/DS/06/165.shtml.

24. Leatherbarrow, "Introduction," 2.

25. Abbott, *Angel*, 1–2.

26. Wilcox, "Every Night."

27. Stacey Abbott, "Walking the Fine Line Between Angel and Angelus," *Slayage: The Online International Journal of Buffy Studies* 3, no. 1 (August 2003), www.slayageonline.com.

28. Ibid.

29. Benjamin Jacob, "Los Angelus: The City of Angel," in *Reading* Angel: *The TV Spin-Off with A Soul*, ed. Stacey Abbott (London: I.B. Tauris, 2005), 75–87 at 83.

30. For an extensive discussion of parodic doubles in the Buffy/Angelverse, see Diane Wilson, "Buffy vs. Bakhtin: Carnival and Dialogism in the Buffyverse"(paper presented at *SC2: The Slayage Conference on the Whedonverses*, Gordon College, Barnesville, GA, May 26–8, 2006), 28–31, http://dianewilson.us/buffy/sc2.paper.pdf.

31. Abbott, "Walking the Fine Line." For a discussion of the connection between a specific "damaged" character from the Buffy/Angelverse (Spike) to Dostoevsky's Underground Man, see Claire Fossey, "Never Hurt the Feelings of a Brutal Killer: Spike and the Underground Man," *Slayage: The Online International Journal of Buffy Studies* 2, no. 4 (March 2003), www.slayageonline.com.

32. Richard Pevear, Introduction to Fyodor Dostoevsky, *Brothers Karamazov*, trans. Richard Pevear and Larissa Volohkhonsky (1990; rpt., New York: Farrar, Straus and Giroux, 2002), xi-xviii. The original translator of Dostoevsky into English, Constance Garnett, smoothed out the text, losing much of Dostoevsky's nuances. For a discussion of Garnett's bland rendering of Dostoevsky, see David Remnick, "The Translation Wars," *The New Yorker*, Novem-

ber 7, 2005, http://www.newyorker.com/archive/2005/11/07/051107fa_fact_remnick?currentPage=all.

33. Wilson, "Buffy vs. Bakhtin."

34. Frank, *Mantle*, 287.

35. Leatherbarrow, "Introduction," 2. For further discussion, see also 1–3 and references therein.

36. Frank, *Mantle*, 430.

37. Richardson and Rabb, *Existential*, 3. Whedon has acknowledged reading Sartre and Camus and mentions Sartre's *Nausea* as being extremely important to him. Joss Whedon, "Commentary" to "Objects in Space," *Firefly*, DVD, written and directed by Joss Whedon (2002; 20th Century–Fox, 2002). For an analysis of Illyria and *Nausea* in *Angel* see Cynthea Masson in this volume. For Masson's earlier analysis of *Angel* episode 5.20 as existential drama, see Cynthea Masson, "What the Hell?—*Angel*'s 'The Girl in Question'" (paper presented at SC3: The Slayage Conference on the Whedonverses, Henderson State University, Arkadelphia, AR, June 5–8, 2008).

38. Richardson and Rabb, *Existential*, 2.

39. Ibid.

40. After the death of Nicholas I in 1855, a somewhat more tolerant era toward intellectual expression ensued (Leatherbarrow, "Introduction," 15).

41. Mock executions are considered among the cruelest of tortures by human rights organizations. See Amnesty International, *Torture Worldwide: An Affront to Human Dignity* (New York: Amnesty International, 2000), 11.

42. Descriptions of these events and Dostoevsky's reaction to them can be found in Frank, *Mantle*, 7–9, and Pevear, "Introduction," xii–xiii, among others.

43. Admittedly, for creative artists, dealing with the capricious behavior of network executives may, at times, feel like being sent into Siberian exile.

44. The popularity of Dostoevsky's writing also varied during his career. For example, *Notes from Underground* attracted very little attention when first published "no critical notice was taken of it in any Russian journal," according to Joseph Frank, "Notes from Underground," in *Notes from Underground: A Norton Critical Edition*, ed. Michael R. Katz (New York: W.W. Norton, 1989), 203. By 1880 Dostoevsky felt that "the public's response to ... readings from *The Brother Karamazov* was invariably enthusiastic" (Terras, *Karamazov Companion*, 3).

45. Perhaps it was this diversity (which parallels the great diversity of American thinking), as well as the claim that "philosophical nourishment" (Richardson and Rabb, *Existential*, 2), was missing from the universities of both Dostoevsky's Russia and Whedon's America that contributed to Richardson and Rabb's claim that the two societies share identical philosophies. In addition, they were misled by certain similarities in the philosophical views of Dostoevsky and Whedon (similarities that can be seen in their existentialist views, not their political or religious ones) and by the popularity of the writers in their own societies. They seem to have generalized from these similarities—saying that "the philosophy [of Dostoevsky] ... may be regarded as *the* popular philosophy, or at the very least, *a* popular philosophy of his Russian readers...." and that "[Whedon's philosophy] we contend is the popular philosophy of contemporary America" (Richardson and Rabb, *Existential*, 2)—in reaching their astonishing, and incorrect, conclusion. The radical difference in the two cultures, the far greater ethnic and cultural diversity of the United States, the widely varying cultural histories, the position of the contemporary United States in the world versus that of Dostoevsky's Russia, the literacy levels, etc. suggest that Dostoevsky's Russia and contemporary America do not share the same culture.

46. Richardson and Rabb, *Existential*, 2.

47. Nussbaum, "Must See."

48. All quotes will be taken from pages 246–264 of Fyodor Dostoevsky, *Brothers Karamazov*, trans. Richard Pevear and Larissa Volohkhonsky (1990; rpt., New York: Farrar, Straus and Giroux, 2002). For the original Russian text, see: http://az.lib.ru/d/dostoewskij_f_m/text_0110.shtml.

49. Dostoevsky, *Brothers Karamazov*, 251.

50. Abbott, *Angel*, 25. For further discussion of the season as an extended narrative arc, see 25–26.

51. "Slouching Toward Bethlehem," *Angel*, DVD, written by Jeffrey Bell, directed by Skip Schoolnik (2002; 20th Century–Fox, 2004). "Peace Out."
52. "Peace Out."
53. The parallel of the fanaticism of Jasmine's followers to that of the mobs in the Inquisition has been noted by Harper ("Jasmine," 54) and, following him, Richardson and Rabb (*Existential*, 147–49). However, the connection to Dostoevsky's passage has not been noted.
54. Dostoevsky, *Brothers Karamazov*, 248.
55. Ibid., 248.
56. Ibid., 249.
57. Ibid.
58. Ibid., 250.
59. Dostoevsky has privileged the views of Alyosha from the beginning of the novel, as he has his first narrative voice (called "the Author") announce on the first page that Alyosha is the "hero" of the novel.
60. Dostoevsky's contemporaries varied widely in their interpretation of both the novel and the Grand Inquisitor scene. See Terras, Karamazov *Companion*, 33–36 for details. A key issue is whether the Grand Inquisitor's words are interpreted as carrying Dostoevsky's authorial message. Dostoevsky himself declared that this is not the case. For discussion see Frank, *Mantle*, 431–432. The issue is further complicated by the fact that the rest of the novel sometimes has a visible (rather chatty, ironic) first person narrator and, at times, a different, and omniscient, narrative voice.
61. For further discussion see Malcolm V. Jones, "Dostoevskii and Religion," in *The Cambridge Companion to Dostoevskii*, ed. W. J. Leatherbarrow (Cambridge: Cambridge University Press, 2002), 148–174 and the references therein.
62. Frank, *Mantle*, 432. See also Terras, Karamazov *Companion*, 34, for further discussion of the issue.
63. Neither Dostoevsky in the original Russian text nor Pevear and Volokhonsky in their translation capitalize "he" or "him" when referring to Christ. I will follow that convention.
64. Dostoevsky, *Brothers Karamazov*, 254.
65. Much of Dostoevsky's work that followed his imprisonment and exile in Siberia was written to counter the ascendancy of various rationalist/utilitarianist philosophies, including utopian socialism and nihilism among his peers, which he felt promoted attention to improving only the material wellbeing of the poor and oppressed of Russia. Dostoevsky parodied another facet of what he perceived as the mistaken focus of these philosophies, lack of appreciation of art, in the oft-quoted phrase from a satirical piece he published in his journal: "a pair of boots are, in every sense, better than Pushkin [the most famous Russian poet]." "Otryvok iz romana [Excerpt from the novel] Shchedrodarov," *Epokha* 5 (May 1864), http://smalt.karelia.ru/~filolog/epokha/1864/Shedryn.htm.
66. Dostoevsky, *Brothers Karamazov*, 254.
67. Ibid., 255.
68. Ibid., 258.
69. Ibid.
70. As Frank points out, socialism for Dostoevsky is merely a secularized version of the Catholic claim to universal earthly domination. Frank, *Mantle*, 271.
71. Dostoevsky, *Brothers Karamazov*, 259.
72. Jones, "Dostoevskii and Religion," 169.
73. Dostoevsky, *Brothers Karamazov*, 260.
74. Ibid.
75. Ibid., 262.
76. Ibid.
77. While the most common interpretation of the kiss is that it is one of forgiveness, Dostoevsky's text is somewhat ambiguous. Other interpretations suggest that the kiss may be evoking the kiss Judas gave to Christ. See discussion in Caryl Emerson, "Zosima's Mysterious Visitor," in *A New Word on* The Brothers Karamzov, ed. Robert Louis Jackson (Evanston: Northwestern University Press, 2004), 155–179 at 156.
78. Dostoevsky, *Brothers Karamazov*, 262.

79. "Sacrifice," *Angel*, DVD, written by Ben Edlund, directed by David Straiton (2003; 20th Century–Fox, 2004).
80. "Peace Out."
81. Ibid.
82. Ibid.
83. Ibid.
84. Ibid.
85. Ibid.
86. Ibid.
87. Ibid.
88. For those reading *The Brothers Karamazov* in an English translation, the 1990 version by Richard Pevear and Larissa Volokhonsky, used for the quotes in this essay, is highly recommended. The translation, with its close attention to the nuances of Dostoevsky's language received the PEN/Book-of-the-Month Club Translation Prize in 1991, as well as enthusiastic endorsement "from some of the country's best Slavic scholars—including Victor Terras, at Brown; Robert Louis Jackson, at Yale; Robert Belknap, from Columbia; and Joseph Frank, Dostoyevsky's supreme biographer, from Stanford" (Remnick, "Translation Wars"). The oldest English translation of *The Brothers Karamazov*, published in 1912 by the Victorian era translator Constance Garnett, has many flaws that are outlined in Remnick's article. Her translation was revised by Ralph Matlaw for the Norton Critical edition of *The Brothers Karamazov* in 1976. Other translations include those by David Magarshak in 1958, David MacAndrew in 1970, David MacDuff in 1993 (revised in 2003), and Ignat Avsey in 1994.
89. Dostoevsky's Grand Inquisitor scene and Whedon's confrontation between Angel and Jasmine encapsulate the arguments that underlie the prototypical dystopian narrative, where a society appears to be perfect, as long as its members relinquish full control of their lives to the state or other entity. Both writers reject the notion that humanity would prefer to live in the "perfect" but choice-less world, instead choosing a world laden with the angst of existential freedom. The frightening dystopian realization of Dostoevsky's philosophy was carried out by the Russian writer Yevgeny Zamyatin in his 1920 novel *We*, http://az.lib.ru/z/zamjatin_e_i/text_0050.shtml. Although published in the West (in translation) earlier, the novel was not published in Russia until 1988. The best translation is Natasha Randall's (New York: The Modern Library, 2006).
90. Stevenson, *Televised Morality*, 70–72; Wilcox, *Why Buffy Matters*, 71–72; Richardson and Rabb, *Existential*, 26–47, 48–62. Alternatively, Flamson ("Free Will") claims that we only imagine we have free will.
91. Stevenson, *Televised Morality*, 71. For further discussion on free will versus prophecy, see also Sharon Sutherland and Sarah Swan, "The Rule of Prophecy: Source of Law in the City of *Angel*," in *Reading* Angel: *The TV Spin-Off with a Soul*, ed. Stacey Abbott (London: I. B. Tauris, 2005), 132–145.
92. "Prophecy Girl," *Buffy the Vampire Slayer*, DVD, written and directed by Joss Whedon (1997; 20th Century–Fox, 2001).
93. Ibid.
94. "To Shanshu in L.A.," *Angel*, DVD, written and directed by David Greenwalt (2000; 20th Century–Fox 2002).
95. "Offspring," *Angel*, DVD, written by David Greenwalt, directed by Turi Meyer (2001; 20th Century–Fox, 2003).
96. Although the prophecy is left ambiguous at the end of the television series, Angel's role as the only one who is eligible to fulfill the Shanshu prophecy is clarified in the comic book continuation. For more details see Brian Lynch, *Angel: After the Fall #13* (September 2008), IDW Publishing.
97. "Offspring."
98. Pateman, *Aesthetics*, 190. See also 243–44.
99. "Inside Out," *Angel*, DVD, written and directed by Stephen S. DeKnight (2003; 20th Century–Fox, 2004).
100. Ibid.
101. Ibid.
102. Ibid.

103. Joss Whedon, "Look Back in *Angel*," interview by Ed Gross, *SFX*, July 2004, 64.
104. Riess, *What Would Buffy*, 129.
105. "Sanctuary," *Angel*, DVD, written by Tim Minear and Joss Whedon, directed by Michael Lange (2000; 20th Century–Fox, 2002).
106. Fyodor Dostoevsky, *Notes from Underground*, trans. Richard Pevear and Larissa Volohkhonsky (New York: Vintage, 1993), 28–29. The Russian original can be found here: http://az.lib.ru/d/dostoewskij_f_m/text_0290.shtml.
107. Note that at least one scholar feels that "it would be wrong to interpret the Grand Inquisitor story as primarily an attack against the Roman Catholic church" (Terras, *Karamazov Companion*, 72).
108. Avrahm Yarmolinsky, introduction to Fyodor Dostoevsky, *The Brothers Karamazov: A Novel in Four Parts & Epilog* (New York: The Heritage Press, 1949), http://www.dartmouth.edu/~karamazo/a_yarmolinsky.html.
109. Riess, *What Would Buffy*, xiii.
110. Richardson and Rabb, *Existential*, 1.
111. Riess, *What Would Buffy*, xii.
112. Frank, *Mantle*, 107.
113. David Bethea, "Literature," in *The Cambridge Companion to Modern Russian Culture*, ed. Nicholas Rzhevsky (Cambridge: Cambridge University Press, 1998), 161–204 at 164. The parenthesis are in Bethea's original text.
114. "Shiny Happy People," *Angel*, DVD, written by Elizabeth Craft and Sarah Fain, directed by Marita Grabiak (2003; 20th Century–Fox, 2004).
115. Ibid.
116. Ibid.
117. Reiss, *What Would Buffy*, xii.
118. Ibid., xv.
119. "Tabula Rasa," *Buffy the Vampire Slayer*, written by Rebecca Rand Kirshner, directed by David Grossman (2002; 20th Century–Fox, 2006).
120. "What's My Line?" (Part 1), *Buffy the Vampire Slayer*, DVD, written by Howard Gordon and Marti Noxon, directed by David Solomon (1997; 20th Century–Fox, 2002).
121. Richardson and Rabb, *Existential*, 4.
122. "Epiphany," *Angel*, DVD, written by Tim Minear, directed by Tom Wright, (2001; 20th Century–Fox, 2003).
123 "School Hard," *Buffy the Vampire Slayer*, DVD, written by Joss Whedon and David Greenwalt, directed by John T. Kretchmer (1997; 20th Century–Fox, 2002).

Charles Gunn, Wolfram & Hart, and Baudrillard's Theory of the Simulacrum

K. SHANNON HOWARD

> *We ain't even lawyers!*
> — Charles Gunn, "Home"[1]

As Stacey Abbott comments in her most recent book on *Angel*, the show's main purpose is to examine how characters remain "human in a corrupt and violent world."[2] By the time the characters reach Season Five, they find that the greatest fear inherent in a struggle against evil is the discovery that at the center of the struggle to be human is an absence of meaning. Further, characters reveal that their search for identity and a sense of belonging throughout the arc of the series threatens to end in this same emptiness. When identity remains in flux due to the corruption of an adult world, as Abbott suggests, characters like Charles Gunn, a former resident of L.A.'s neighborhood street fighters, discover that the emptiness that seems to exist at the core of every struggle against corruption threatens to engulf the hope that keeps them human. Because Gunn consistently negotiates his role within social groups and organizations as he moves from the streets, to a detective agency, and then to the corporate world, he serves as an ideal candidate for succumbing to L.A.'s corruption and materialism—a world that fails to provide substance underneath its seductive image, an image that eventually prompts Gunn's transformation into a hollow shell of his former self.

Gunn's entire being has been transformed by the end of the series, becoming, with each successive season, more vulnerable to the influences of the artificial world around him. By Season Five, Gunn, as a Wolfram & Hart employee, is altered mentally and emotionally by the uploading of legal knowledge into his brain and is, according to Abbott, "transformed into a form of cyborg."[3] In Season Five, this transformation includes simulation of knowledge that previously did not exist; and as the *Oxford English Dictionary* states, "simulation," the kind that occurs when Abbott compares Gunn to a cyborg, is, in part, "a false assumption or display."[4] The show's narrative arc remains built upon the nihilistic premise that Gunn and his fellow detectives must constantly battle a lack of selfhood in a culture that values commodities but not people. They must also, since their previous leader and beacon of identity, Angel, is no longer a free agent, question their own definitions of reality and determine the best way to respond to those definitions. By the time Gunn allies himself with Wolfram & Hart, he is simply a man in a suit, a man who formerly fought with his hands but now fights with artificial knowledge, neglecting both his human body and soul.

Gunn's transformation occurs within a city known for film sets and Hollywood legends, and, at first, Gunn's escape from poverty and ascent into wealth seems like the American dream come true. Nevertheless, as Wolfram & Hart often illustrates, every dream's fulfillment comes at a price. Postmodern theorist Jean Baudrillard also asserts that postmodern life is, indeed, the experience of viewing objects and places in twentieth-century society as simulations — simulations that do not imitate reality but replace it. Put simply, the creation of an illusory world, where streets of Hollywood are characterized by riches and possibilities, does not imitate or build on a real world. Instead, Baudrillard argues that "[i]t is the generation of models of a real without origin or reality: a hyperreal."[5] Gunn, swept up in the materialism of the type of city described by Baudrillard (which embodies a progression of phases of representation before reaching final simulation as discussed below), finds himself lacking moral guidance, unable to differentiate between what is real and what is artificial.

According to Baudrillard, images in contemporary cities like Los Angeles undergo four phases of representation, a study important to *Angel* because, as in film noir, a genre incorporated into this show, sometimes the heroes discover "they have never gotten to the bottom of reality" in their quest to defeat evil.[6] In Baudrillard's first phase, the image is "a reflection of a basic reality," but as it evolves, it begins to "mask and pervert" the real world in the second manifestation of its appearance. When an image reaches its third phase, "it masks the absence of a basic reality" and then will finally, in its fourth incarnation, "bear no relation to any reality whatsoever: it is its own simulacrum."[7] These final stages are most crucial in understanding the evolution of Gunn's character from season to season, culminating in the Season Five arc where Gunn is made into a legal cyborg, a lawyer who fools others with his artificial presentation of a legal background and willingly lies down on the Senior Partners's director's couch to accept this promotion.

In order to gain a basic understanding of Baudrillard's theory of the simulacrum and its application to *Angel* and especially Charles Gunn, a brief analysis of Season Two's "Blood Money" (2.19) illustrates the four stages of the simulacrum.[8] This episode's action includes a charity ball hosted by Wolfram & Hart on behalf of the East Hill Teen Center. The managing director of the law firm appears in a promotional ad projected on the stage. In the ad he sits in a park and tells the audience that "the world can be a dangerous place, especially for our most vulnerable citizens, our children."[9] He pets a collie and takes the hand of a frightened boy who is meant to represent a runaway.

This ad introduces Baudrillard's concept of the simulacrum by first addressing the basic reality of "dangerous" L.A. It also foreshadows the ultimate emptiness that Gunn experiences while employed by the law firm in Season Five. This ad is, at first glance, a genuine attempt to build sympathy and raise funds. Young runaways are, indeed, at risk in large cities. However, the ad also fulfills the second stage, as Baudrillard would argue, because it "masks and perverts" reality as it reveals Wolfram & Hart's desire to extend its influence in L.A. through a subversive representation of charity. Angel's team agrees with the ad's message but recognizes that this advertisement is a ploy by the firm to promote a hidden agenda in which money collected at the charity will be used for evil purposes. Baudrillard's third stage of simulacra, which "marks the absence of a basic reality," is also present, for L.A. is represented as a place where grandfatherly men walk dogs and help the homeless without question, and the notion that L.A. adheres to such imagery opposes the very design of the noirish *Angel* cityscape, where the urban setting frames images of dark alleys, hidden agendas, and Darwinist survival games where people either learn to adapt to a fast-track life or they perish. David Reid and Jayne Walker note that L.A. is not a location characterized by the fulfillment of the American dream in terms of stardom or wealth, but rather a place that is "mad, bad, and dangerous to know," as well as "fallen and inescapable."[10] Such a description is useful in recognizing that in Baudrillard's final stage, the law firm's ad "bears no relation to any reality whatsoever: it's its own pure simulacrum." Wolfram & Hart's display of charity, the park in L. A., the idea of the director representing a guardian to lost children—all of these concepts mask a sinister agenda rooted in the very emptiness that false advertisement signifies, an emptiness that results in despair rather than hope.

The way that Baudrillard's ideas function in relation to Wolfram & Hart's commercial in "Blood Money" is one example of how Baudrillard's theories illuminate layers of simulation in *Angel*. A more complex and significant example may be found in the characterization of Charles Gunn who, as a main character, most significantly represents the phases of Baudrillard's ideas about reality. His character, transformed over time, serves as a concrete manifestation of simulacrum, which is, according to the *Oxford English Dictionary*, like a simulation because it is "a mere image, a specious imitation or likeness."[11] As such "simulation" and "simulacrum" may be used interchangeably to characterize Gunn's development.

To illustrate Gunn's appearance as a simulacrum, it is worthwhile to first examine his appearance in "A Hole in the World" (5.15), an episode that highlights Gunn's compromised identity as one reduced to an absence of self.[12] When Gunn visits Wolfram & Hart's metaphysical gateway, the White Room, he asks the Senior Partners to save Fred, whose fatal illness due to inhalation of sarcophagus dust reveals Gunn's mistake in signing a customs slip that guarantees him additional upgrades to legal knowledge. Although this action is morally compromising, suggesting the presence of a conflicted soul rather than an absence of self, the scene offers an alternative to a more standard reading of this episode. The viewer sees Gunn enter the space of white floors and vanishing walls with feelings of heartache; but then the Conduit, a simulated identity that has always functioned as a shape-shifter rather than a stable presence, appears as Gunn himself. When Gunn questions his reflection, or the Conduit, about Fred's illness, their banter reveals what Baudrillard might describe as a hyperreality as they circle one another, wearing the exact same clothes and using the same mannerisms. The Conduit warns, "You don't want to be here," to which Gunn responds, "I never want to be here. What happened to the cat?" referring to the Conduit's previous panther form in episodes past.[13] Gunn's reflection, the sinister manifestation of what Abbott describes as a "cyborg," asserts, "The physical form of the Conduit is determined by the viewer."[14] The Conduit knocks Gunn against the wall when Gunn dares to quip, "So ... I'm lookin' at me because, what, we're going to play a mirror game?"[15]

When Gunn begs the Conduit to exchange his life for Fred's on account of her illness, the Conduit chuckles and states that he already possesses Gunn's life. In other words, the mirror of Gunn is what he has become, and the real Gunn no longer exists. The Conduit, appearing as Gunn, is now the simulacrum and has full control over reality, but he does not reflect a true self or even a distorted version of a true self. In other words, one cannot, after the exchange of the first few lines of dialogue, tell the mirror image apart from the troubled lawyer who is plagued with guilt over his culpability in Fred's illness. The empty space in the White Room suggests that the real self is fully absent, since it functions as a place that contains no color or shape and does not exist in a physical reality, except as a portal to the disembodied transmission of the Senior Partners's commands.

This appearance of Gunn as Conduit is a culmination of Baudrillard's stages of the image, progressing from a reflection of reality to simulacrum, stages that begin long before he joins Wolfram & Hart. In *Angel*'s early seasons, Gunn reveals a troubled identity, characterized by his inability to fit fully into either Angel's team or his old neighborhood group, remaining torn between the two. Significantly, Gunn's positioning between the two groups coincides with the introduction in the *Angel* mythos of mystical portals through which humans and creatures may be sucked from one dimension to another, thereby prefiguring the White Room as a place in which mysterious binding of separate yet parallel realities occur.[16] Moreover, because the White Room is a metaphorical playground for Baudrillard's theory, showcasing the ephemeral nature of images conjured by the Senior Partners to confuse rather than comfort or even communicate fully with them, it perfectly mirrors the internal transformation Gunn undergoes as his own character continues to shift between realities of life on the street and life in a detective agency.

Indeed, an episode that pivotally illustrates both Gunn's conflicted loyalties and the correlation to the metaphor of mystical portals occurs in "Belonging" (2.19). This episode reflects Baudrillard's ideas as it begins with the shooting of a commercial in which Cordelia must simulate a tan and a perfect figure to please a Hollywood director. Even Angel enjoys basking in the simulated sunlight created by the set when he visits the studio where Cordelia works. However, the mood shifts when Cordelia realizes that the director notes the "circles under her eyes" and cannot stop provoking her to bend farther over so her swimsuit compromises her physical integrity. To the director, Cordelia is just a commodity, reduced to nothing more than another expendable actress. Significantly, the same way that *Angel* utilizes L.A. as a paradoxical cityscape of illusions rather than realities, so does Baudrillard observe L.A. as the model of postmodern simulacrum in its production of artificial images on camera: "Los Angeles is circled by these 'imaginary stations' which feed ... reality-energy, to a town whose mystery is precisely that it is nothing more than a network of endless, unreal circulation: a town of fabulous proportions, but without space or dimensions. As much as electrical and nuclear power stations, as much as film studios, this town, which is nothing more than an immense script and a perpetual motion picture, needs this old [imagery] made up of childhood signals and faked phantasms for its sympathetic nervous system."[17]

Likewise, Gunn, in this same episode, finds that he is treated not as a human being but rather as a series of "childhood signals," representing a Baudrillardian mirror of his basic former reality. George and Rondell's visit to the Hyperion Hotel reminds the viewer that Gunn still has some ties to his former street life. His old friends wish to borrow his "rig," a truck outfitted with weapons designed to kill vampires, significantly, a possession he once paid for with his soul.[18] Although Gunn initially longs to join his old friends in a vampire hunt, he must assist Angel in defeating another demon first. By the time Gunn catches up with his neighborhood friends, he finds them standing around the dead body of one of their own, George. Afraid George has been sired by vampires, the group burns the corpse, and Gunn stands apart from the event, aware that his presence is liminal and that the group needed him only for his commodity, or truck, but not for his fighting skills. As flames engulf George's body, the man's form reduced to ash, Gunn's own persona begins to alter accordingly, changing, as Baudrillard would suggest, from the "mirror of a basic reality" in which he still considers himself a street fighter when actually he is now a detective's sidekick for hire in a less dangerous part of town.

Even George's own corpse foreshadows Gunn's transformation, for George's own image begins as "a good appearance" of an image, with the representation of his character acting like the "order of sacrament" as he dies for his friends' cause with a demonic presence that may have tainted his blood.

This image reflects Baudrillard's emphasis on a key element of the simulacrum and explains why George's body is burned, not buried. The image of George is now associated with Baudrillard's second phase of representation, for, as he says, "in the second [phase], the [image] is an evil appearance: of the order of malefice."[19] Like George, whose body has been replaced by funeral remains, Gunn begins progressing toward a state of absence, for, although not burned at the stake or dead to his friends, he has been replaced by objects because his friends need his truck more than they need him (a pattern that will be repeated in *Angel*'s fifth season). Gunn's separation from his friends at the funeral reinforces this notion of objectification, and his worth as a warrior, already diminishing, will eventually be reduced to ash and replaced by the "cyborg" self who receives downloads of legal information in *Angel*'s final season.

As Season Three of *Angel* commences, particularly in "That Old Gang of Mine" (3.03), Gunn's character undergoes a second transformation.[20] Through encounters with old neighborhood acquaintances Gunn proceeds to the next Baudrillardian phase of imagery because his former activities on the street have become a "perversion" of reality, due to the methods of Gio, Rondell's new friend and partner. The expositional scene of the episode foreshadows this conflict by focusing on Angel delivering a simulated apology to the demon Merle, an act of contrition that the vampire reads off a script rather than speaking out of sincerity. This moment remains significant because Merle's death incites Team Angel to investigate a series of demon murders that lead Gunn straight back to Rondell and his friends. Gio, a recent transplant to the West Coast, says to Gunn, "I know all about you. That *name* is part of the reason I came out here."[21]

The sarcastic stress on *name*, in Baudrillardian terms, demonstrates that beneath the image of Gunn's heroism is an absence of true meaning because Gunn has shifted allegiances and now works with Angel. Gio continually taunts Gunn by using different names throughout the episode to refer to the other man ("G," "Chuck," "Charlie"), suggesting that no name really represents him anymore. Instead of respecting Gunn for his previous work defending the streets from evil, Gio mocks him for working for a vampire and turning away from his role as "alpha vamp hunter" in the neighborhood in which he and his sister grew up. He even mocks Gunn by singing an off-key karaoke version of "Hero" at Caritas when Rondell's team invades the demon bar and takes patrons hostage. When Rondell speaks to Gunn privately, Gunn claims that he had stayed away from his former neighborhood because of the trauma of George's death, to which Rondell replies, "You were gone way before George ... Things ... were never the same after Alonna."[22] Gunn, still haunted by the guilt he carries from staking his sister, is torn because he has submitted his allegiance to a vampire, however soulful that vampire may be.[23]

Therefore, it seems appropriate that Gunn's former friends express confusion regarding his loyalties but still revere him as a founder of their fighting techniques and methods. Gunn takes pride in the fact that he designed the very "rig" or weapon Gio uses to fight monsters. What viewers find in this moment is an addition to the Baudrillardian concept of simulacrum in that once the real image begins to disappear, one finds comfort in "nostalgia" or a "proliferation of myths of origin" in the hope of acquiring a version of reality that has now been lost.[24] Indeed, Gunn clings to his former status as leader even though he knows that his friends have changed since his absence and have altered their mission to include terrorizing all demons and not just those who pose harm to humans.

Indeed, Gio's hostility in Caritas, a perversion of the former mission to keep innocent members of Gunn's neighborhood safe, has become a distortion of reality similar to Baudrillard's second phase of simulation and even borders on the third phase as Gunn disassociates from his roots more completely than ever before. As Gunn vainly searches for a reflection of his former basic reality but finds only violence directed at those with whom he works, he defensively orders Lorne not "to read me" or expose his emotions. Lorne tells Gunn that there is no need for telepathy when Gunn's emotions are clearly evident. He murmurs, "Sweetie, you're a billboard,"[25] which in Lorne's vernacular means that he thinks Gunn is displaying his torment openly; but even more importantly, it foreshadows the idea that Gunn has once again been objectified rather than personified. As his involvement in Angel's group becomes more prominent, Gunn will someday be reduced to nothing more than a site for data behind which no emotional center fully exists (even Gunn's t-shirt in the scene at Caritas says "doubt" on the logo).

During the shootout, Gio taunts Gunn further by saying, "Bet you they won't let you into their little club, huh, Chuck? You ain't even good enough for the vamps, the demons, and the baby-eatin' monsters."[26] Some of Gio's taunt rings true; for next to Cordelia's insight from The Powers That Be, Angel's vampiric strength, Fred's skills as a physicist, and Wesley's intellect, Gunn struggles to define his role in the group. Although, as Michaela Meyer observes, "The narrative frequently emphasizes Gunn's physical strength over his emotional or intellectual abilities,"[27] all members of Team Angel have, over time, developed the physical prowess necessary for fighting. Therefore, it is not a trait that easily sets Gunn apart. Meyer also notes Gunn's willingness to believe he is "the muscle" when other members of Angel's team do not use him for "research or strategy,"[28] reinforcing his lack of unique contribution.

Members of Wolfram & Hart single Gunn out to receive legal knowledge in the Season Five premiere because they sense his insecurity at Angel Investigations.[29] Even before Gunn agrees to mental injections of knowledge, viewers sense that his enthusiasm for joining the law firm is greater than any other character's. Gunn recognizes the opportunity to move farther from the streets where he lived and become a part of a corporate world that once seemed unattainable. Gunn tells Angel and the group, "I'm doin' this. Hope it's not just me, but if it is, that's all right, too."³⁰ Once Gunn moves into Wolfram & Hart, he learns that he is not "dressed for success" and that his current *image* must be retailored. The Senior Partners's liaison Eve suggests that Gunn receive new clothes, thereby literally echoing Baudrillard's focus on image as the major component of hyperrealism. In addition, Joss Whedon's comments on Gunn acquiring legal knowledge also reflect Baudrillard's ideas on simulation: "The reality of the show was we often didn't know what to do with J. [August Richards]'s character [Gunn]. His relationship with Fred had come and gone.... He had a real sort of sense of feeling out of place, so, much as we did with Fred later in making her Illyria, I wanted to show something from J. that people hadn't really seen. I also knew how good he looked in a suit."³¹ While the tail end of Whedon's comment is humorous, it is also significant for its emphasis on the visual image of Gunn rather than the person inside the suit, highlighting the Baudrillardian theory of simulation that characterizes Gunn's gradual change from presence to absence. Ironically, Gunn is the one who exclaims, "We ain't even lawyers!" when Lilah offers Wolfram & Hart's L.A. branch to Angel Investigations.³² The Senior Partners at Wolfram & Hart, like Baudrillard in his study of postmodern simulation, seem to agree that a lack of law experience is not a problem in a hyperreal world, or in Baudrillard's terms, "It is no longer a question of imitation, nor of reduplication, nor even of parody. It is rather a question of substituting signs of the real for the real itself."³³ The real, in this case, may be twofold in its construction of meaning. It first refers to the mission that Gunn, Angel, and the others claim to support: the mission of eradicating forces of darkness in order to make the streets safer for L.A.'s populace. However, that mission is compromised by the re-situation of Team Angel into the firm that supports evil clientele who work against the notion of community peace. Second, the real would also be the presence of a firm where lawyers, with appropriate credentials, utilize conventional protocol to solve cases in a courtroom. With Angel and his friends running the firm, this reality now holds no meaning, for the very managers leading the organization have no real training, nor do they support the original purpose of the firm to represent clients with evil agendas.

Nevertheless, Gunn adapts quickly to his new lifestyle as a legal expert when he receives the upload of data from the firm's scientist, and Fred is first to express her nervousness over this phenomenon: "It's ... what they put into your head.... Maybe you know something more than the rest of us."³⁴ Rather than Gunn actively turning away from his mission to assist Angel in helping the helpless, the character's metamorphosis signals something more sinister: once Gunn operates according to simulated knowledge, he ceases to exist as a person. Instead, he is the simulation of a law book inserted into a fancy suit of clothes.

Here we reach the ultimate symbol of the show's demonstration of Jean Baudrillard's theory of simulacra: the positioning of former lawyer Lindsey and current lawyer Gunn within the "holding dimension" of suburbia during "Underneath" (5.19).[35] The thematic concept of layers, upon which the episode is based, reveals itself during an interdimensional trip to rescue Lindsey from the Senior Partners. When Team Angel members locate Lindsey, Gunn and his friends realize that Lindsey, at the mercy of a sadistic torture schedule, cannot retain memory beyond that of the immediate suburban images enveloping him in simulated domesticity. The former lawyer acknowledges but cannot historicize his experience living with a beautiful wife and child, along with the mundane rituals of retrieving the morning paper and fetching light bulbs from the basement in what appears to be a sunny neighborhood just outside L.A.

Part of this dimension is an image of Lindsey's son, preparing for a science quiz by memorizing the earth's composition. Lindsey reviews the material with his son in the kitchen: "From the top: the earth's outer layer is called?" to which the "child" responds, "The crust." Lindsey then prompts, "And what's underneath that?" The boy pauses and then asks, "The mantle?" Studying continues until Lindsey quips that the final layer is the core, or rather "the soft chewy center." However, the child dismisses this joke, saying instead that the center is "nothing."[36] This "nothing" that seems to suggest a lack of terminology on the child's part to recall science facts actually suggests far more by metaphorically illustrating what is at the center of the hell in which Lindsey suffers. Instead of being fashioned from primeval scenes of fire or ice, this "holding dimension" reinforces the notion of the simulation of a sunny, suburban residence, where houses appear the same and people repeat similar cycles of family chores, and it illustrates Baudrillard's fourth stage of image construction because it bears "no relation to reality whatsoever." This place, rather than imitating L.A., indicates just how unbelievable the concept of suburban bliss is to those who have lived in a corrupt world. Even the son preparing for his science quiz acts as if he is reading from a script, reciting the same lines over and over because he is not a real child but a site of artifice, similar to the Conduit's appearances in the White Room.

To illustrate the horror of this dimension, the prisoner, who at first is Lindsey, must repeatedly fetch an oven light from the basement only to discover that a creature waits below with a carving instrument that will hack out his heart each day; his loss of short-term memory dooms him to repeat this scenario for eternity. When Gunn takes Lindsey's place in this dimension so that his friends may secure the time needed to question Lindsey on the Senior Partners's plans for the apocalypse, Gunn, under the knife, finds himself hollowed out literally and figuratively, an apt metaphor for his gradual evolution into simulation and his reduction into an expendable commodity.

Gunn, still feeling responsible for Fred's death, sacrifices himself by taking Lindsey's place and undergoing the horrific torture reserved for those who defy the Senior Partners, thereby offering a surprise reversal to his character's previous construction as a simulation that cannot act out of a moral or ethical imperative. Abbott observes the significance of violating Gunn's body after violating his mind when injected with legal knowledge: "While the first violation of Gunn, achieved through modern technology, served to compromise Gunn's identity, this experience, hearkening back to medieval torture, facilitates Gunn's gradual recuperation of the 'self' as he is reminded, through the painful and daily penetration of his body, of his humanity. Yet even here there remains a form of alienating intervention as his body is made to mystically restore itself in order to repeat the process."[37] Although his willingness to become part of the simulation exists in order to save his friends, the writers advance the plot while leaving the character subject to a gutted shell of a physical form rather than substance.

While the Senior Partners are the constant threat of danger to Angel and his team, they are also a source of simulation. Angel says, "Everything we do, it's a distraction. Keep us busy, from looking under the surface."[38] The idea of fighting evil is an artificial enterprise according to the Partners's design both at the time Gunn undergoes torture but also long before Fred's death, at which point Team Angel had attempted to solve one "distraction" of a case after another. Although Angel and his friends sense that some evil plan is concealed beneath layers of subterfuge, the vampire temporarily forgets what he had learned in his first years in Los Angeles, a lesson he articulates in "Epiphany" (2.16) when speaking to detective Kate Lockley: "In the greater scheme, in the big picture, nothing we do matters. There's no grand plan. No big win."[39] Again, this admission fits Baudrillard's theory that at an image's core, it bears no resemblance to reality at all. In this case, the image Angel speaks of is the idea of a world at peace, where those who fight evil experience redemption.

Nevertheless, the engagement of characterization and setting with Baudrillard's ideas of simulation in *Angel* does not leave the viewer at odds with the concept of fighting for good. Instead, the effect is quite the opposite: one admires Angel and his friends *more* for acknowledging that their world is corrupt and that it has the power to corrupt *them*. It requires self-awareness to understand that the reality that shapes existence is actually manufactured as simulation and that struggling against it may end in destruction, not victory. Indeed, the final episode of the series, "Not Fade Away " (5.22), implies even by title that the characters intend to struggle, up until the end, against the idea of becoming truly absent.

Gunn spends his last day before this apocalypse at the East Hill Teen Center, the same organization that once used Wolfram & Hart to advertise their cause. Gunn asks Anne, the Center's leader, "What if I told you it doesn't help.... What would you do if you found out that none of it matters? That it's all controlled by forces more powerful and uncaring than we can conceive, and they will never let it get better down here?"[40] Anne considers his words for a brief moment and then replies, "I'd get this truck packed before the next stuff gets here. Want to give me a hand?" The triumph of the show's ingenuity is revealed when Gunn says, "I do." The idea of Gunn existing as mere simulacrum turns on its head when the character chooses to unearth or at least mirror a moral center that once existed inside him and is now momentarily recalled to life. Although Baudrillard's successive phases of imagery suggest that the final moments of reality are characterized by emptiness and "bear no relation to reality whatsoever," Gunn's final choice reveals his ability to transcend simulation and return to the memory of his fully-formed self.

The ultimate triumph of simulated existence occurs when the simulation sees itself and the world for what it is, but still chooses to act upon the idea of a former reality, that, although absent in the present, still exists in memory. Gunn returns to the old neighborhood during this final episode in order to honor the causes of Alonna, Anne, Rondell, and George but also because his return generates an image of the world as it should be, rather than as it is. Like Angel, who assures Kate Lockley of the value of goodness in "Epiphany," Gunn understands that although the world in which he lives is artificial, it is still a place where "if nothing we do matters, then all that matters is what we do."[41]

Notes

1. "Home," *Angel*, DVD, written and directed by Tim Minear (2003; 20th Century–Fox, 2004).
2. Stacey Abbott, *Angel*, TV Milestones Series (Detroit: Wayne State University Press, 2009), 7.
3. Ibid., 57.
4. *Oxford English Dictionary*, s.v. "Simulation."
5. Jean Baudrillard, "Simulacra and Simulations," in *Selected Writings*, ed. Mark Poster, 2d ed. (Stanford: Stanford University Press, 2001), 169–187 at 169.
6. Jean Copjec, "The Phenomenal Nonphenomenal: Private Space in Film Noir," in *Shades of Noir*, ed. Jean Copjec (London: Verso, 1993), 167–197 at 191.
7. Baudrillard, "Simulacra and Simulations," 173.
8. "Blood Money," *Angel*, DVD, written by Shawn Ryan and Mere Smith, directed by R.D. Price (2001; 20th Century–Fox, 2003).
9. Ibid.
10. David Reid and Jayne L. Walker, "Strange Pursuit: Cornell Woolrich and the Abandoned City of the Forties," in *Shades of Noir*, ed. Jean Copjec (London: Verso, 1993), 57–96 at 58.
11. *Oxford English Dictionary*, s.v. "Simulacrum."
12. "A Hole in the World," *Angel*, DVD, written and directed by Joss Whedon (2004; 20th Century–Fox, 2004).
13. Ibid.
14. Ibid.
15. Ibid.
16. "Belonging," *Angel*, DVD, written by Shawn Ryan, directed by Turi Meyer (2001; 20th Century–Fox, 2003).
17. Baudrillard, "Simulacra and Simulations," 175.
18. "Belonging"; "Double or Nothing," *Angel*, DVD, written by David H. Goodman, directed by David Grossman (2002; 20th Century–Fox, 2003).
19. Baudrillard, "Simulacra and Simulations," 173.
20. "That Old Gang of Mine," *Angel*, DVD, written by Tim Minear, directed by Fred Keller (2001; 20th Century–Fox, 2003).

21. Ibid.
22. Ibid.
23. "War Zone," *Angel*, DVD, written by Garry Campbell, directed by David Straiton (2000; 20th Century–Fox, 2006).
24. Baudrillard, "Simulacra and Simulations," 174.
25. "That Old Gang of Mine."
26. Ibid.
27. Michaela Meyer, "From Rogue in the 'Hood to Suave in a Suit: Black Masculinity and the Transformation of Charles Gunn," in *Reading* Angel: *The TV Spin-off with a Soul*, ed. Stacey Abbott (London: I. B. Tauris, 2005), 176–188 at 183.
28. Ibid., 183.
29. "Conviction," *Angel*, DVD, written and directed by Joss Whedon (2003; 20th Century–Fox, 2004).
30. "Home," *Angel*, DVD, written and directed by Tim Minear (2003; 20th Century–Fox, 2004).
31. Joss Whedon, Commentary on "Conviction," *Angel*, DVD, written and directed by Joss Whedon (20th Century–Fox, 2004).
32. "Home."
33. Baudrillard, "Simulacra and Simulations," 170.
34. "Unleashed," *Angel*, DVD, written by Sarah Fain and Elizabeth Craft, directed by Marita Brabiak (2003; 20th Century–Fox, 2004).
35. "Underneath," *Angel*, DVD, written by Sarah Fain and Elizabeth Craft, directed by Skip Schoolnik (2004; 20th Century–Fox, 2004).
36. Ibid.
37. Abbott, *Angel*, 58.
38. "Underneath."
39. "Epiphany," *Angel*, DVD, written by Tim Minear, directed by Thomas J. Wright (2001; 20th Century–Fox, 2003).
40. "Not Fade Away," *Angel*, DVD, written by Jeffrey Bell and Joss Whedon, directed by Jeffrey Bell (2004; 20th Century–Fox, 2004).
41. "Epiphany."

"It's a play on perspective"
A Reading of Whedon's Illyria through Sartre's Nausea

CYNTHEA MASSON

"Something is going to happen: something is waiting for me in the shadow of the Rue Basse-de-Vieille, it is over there, just at the corner of this calm street that my life is going to begin.... I advance, I stretch out my hand and touch the stone."[1] Thus Roquentin, narrator of Jean-Paul Sartre's *Nausea*, approaches both a literal and figurative milestone on his existential journey through the streets of Bouville. *Nausea*, according to philosopher Chris Falzon, "invit[es] us to shake off our ordinary, taken-for-granted presuppositions about the world" and, thereby, "come face to face with brute existence — meaningless, contingent, superfluous, absurd, and nauseating."[2] One might well advance similar claims on various aspects of the Whedonverses even without knowing that Joss Whedon calls *Nausea* "the most important book I ever read."[3] "[T]his book," claims Whedon, "spoke to what I believe more accurately and totally than anything I had ever read."[4] These revelatory statements comprise part of Whedon's DVD commentary on the *Firefly* episode "Objects in Space." Whedon also highlights *Nausea* in the *Buffy* episode "Lover's Walk" (3.08), where Angel is seen reading the novel in its original French (*La Nausée*).[5] Whedon scholars have previously explored Whedon's penchant for existentialism in *Buffy* and *Angel*, but specific parallels with *Nausea* have yet to be drawn.[6] Like *Nausea*'s Roquentin, one Whedon character literally reaches out a hand to touch a stone and thus comes face to face with brute existence. "She was curious," explains Wesley. "That's why Fred didn't put it into containment immediately."[7] "It" is the sarcophagus containing Illyria — a character who challenges our presuppositions of the world and our notions of existence.

In the final eight episodes of the fifth and final televised season of *Angel*, the primordial god-king Illyria invades and appropriates the body of one of the show's beloved major characters, Winifred "Fred" Burkle. The sudden metamorphosis of the smart, gentle, emotional Fred into the powerful, arrogant, inhuman Illyria transforms the whole final story arc of the show, not least by shattering our narrative expectations. The emotions that held so much sway in Fred's life and choices are mere puzzles to Illyria, who is confounded by the restrictions of human embodiment. Yet this very embodiment, however limited, absurd, and contingent allows Illyria consciousness. Like Sartre and the character of Roquentin in *Nausea*, Whedon and the character of Illyria in *Angel* provoke the reader/watcher to engage with existentialism. Whedon invites us to gain new perspective on the human condition by reminding us not only of our limitations but also of our inherent freedom to choose, to change, and to construct meaning.

The fantastical world of *Angel* provides Whedon, through Illyria, the opportunity to explore and even reverse the classic Sartrean conception that "existence precedes essence"—"man first exists: he materializes in the world, encounters himself, and only afterward defines himself."[8] This is the existential Sartrean tenet with which Whedon appears to be playing as *Angel* draws toward its conclusion: What would a being be like in whom essence precedes existence? What would a being be like in whom essence *coincides* with existence?[9] In regard to the first question, Illyria is initially defined by others as an "essence" preceding her existence. For example, in "A Hole in the World" (5.15), Drogyn says to Spike and Angel, "It's been freed—the demon's essence." Likewise, in "Shells" (5.16), the doctor tells Gunn, "The sarcophagus contains the essence of an old one." Even as late as "Time Bomb" (5.19), well after Illyria has established herself within Fred's "shell," Wesley refers to the "demon essence" and its "fusion" with the "host's body"; thereafter, he attempts via sophisticated weaponry to extract from Fred's body Illyria's "radiant essence." Thus, from the perspective of Wesley and others, Illyria's essence not only precedes but supersedes her existence in their preliminary understanding of her. Yet as early as "Shells," Illyria herself claims, "I exist here." Regardless of what she may once have been—whatever "essence" of her originary, primordial self had long ago crystallized within the sarcophagus—now Illyria *exists again* and realizes that she "must learn to walk in this world."[10] Despite the inherent difficulties of adjusting to embodiment, her ontological understanding of the world is arguably Sartrean: "All I am is what I am,"[11] says Illyria—"The world is as it is."[12] In *Nausea*, Roquentin likewise understands that he *exists* only here and now. "I am. I am, I exist," he declares; "it happens that I am myself and that I am here."[13] One cannot *exist* otherwise than here and now. Gradually, Roquentin reaches an existential epiphany: "The true nature of the present revealed itself: it was what exists, and all that was not present did not exist."[14] Through the course of their journeys, both Illyria and Roquentin evaluate their respective worlds and come to acknowledge the absolute presence and intrinsic freedom of their current existence. Whereas Roquentin (via Sartre) confronts existence devoid of originary human essence, Illyria (via Whedon) begins *as* originary essence but must nonetheless enact human existence. Once Illyria *exists*, her originary essence is immaterial—thus existence once again precedes essence.

Illyria, when viewed through the lens of existentialism in *Nausea*, can also be read as a representation of the nature of existence itself—she is superfluous, absurd, and contingent.[15] Her arrival is both unexpected and frightening. "Existence," claims Roquentin, "must invade you suddenly, master you."[16] Thus Illyria invades and masters Fred in a series of events that parallel those of Roquentin in *Nausea*. Roquentin, describing the epiphanic awareness of his existential experience, explains, "It came as an illness does."[17] Wesley similarly refers to Illyria as the "infection" that "consumed" Fred.[18] Where Roquentin experiences "the Nausea," Fred experiences "some monster flu."[19] Like Roquentin, Fred faces a life-altering metamorphosis which begins from a place of fear.[20] Roquentin, in the opening pages of his diary writes, "it was certain that I was afraid" and elaborates shortly thereafter, "I'm afraid of what will be born and take possession of me."[21] Though Fred attempts to be brave when first infected, she too fears that which has taken sudden possession of her, admitting to Wesley, "But I wonder — how very scared I am."[22] Near the end of his journey, Roquentin comes to understand that, "Existence is what I am afraid of."[23] Fred does not survive to reach such a conclusion. Nonetheless, we can read Illyria as Whedon's figurative embodiment of Sartrean existence — that which is feared both by the self and by others because of its potential to disrupt and dislodge the comfort of routine and illusion.

For Sartre, nausea is a symptom of the disorientation one experiences when familiar objects of the world become utterly unfamiliar and incomprehensible. It is the physiological and psychological reaction to the sudden shift in ontological awareness. The epitome of this transformative process occurs during Roquentin's encounters with the tram seat and the chestnut tree root — two of the most pivotal and oft-discussed scenes of the novel — both of which involve a dramatic shift in perspective in relation to once-familiar objects. Roquentin no longer sees merely the red, plush fabric of the tram seat but "thousands of little red paws in the air, all still, little dead paws."[24] Shortly thereafter, he sees a chestnut tree root as transformed into a "black, knotty mass, entirely beastly."[25] Once harmless to Roquentin, these objects are now threatening. Most significantly, explains Roquentin, "I couldn't remember it was a root any more. The words had vanished and with them the significance of things."[26] He neither sees nor understands the world around him as he formerly and habitually had done throughout his life. Language — the human penchant for naming and thus classifying the world — no longer serves its purpose for Roquentin: "Things are divorced from their names. They are there, grotesque, headstrong, gigantic.... I am in the midst of things, nameless things."[27] In this ineffable experience, "existence had suddenly unveiled itself."[28] What remained after the "veneer had melted" was "soft, monstrous masses, all in disorder — naked, in a frightful, obscene nakedness."[29] As Peter Weigel explains in his analysis of the chestnut tree scene, "'Existence' designates the world unmasked of the ordered veneer given in consciousness."[30] For Wesley and others encountering her for the first time, Illyria arguably represents the figurative chestnut tree root. The object (body or shell) formerly known as Fred can no longer be understood or classified as she once had been. Wesley confirms this when he describes to the others his first-hand experience of Fred's death: "I watched it gut her from the inside out. Everything she was is gone."[31] She is not Fred; she is not the woman he loved; she is not even human. "Things have names," says Illyria to Wesley. "The shell — Winifred Burkle — she can't return to you."[32] Illyria challenges, and thereby reveals as illusory, the apparent certainty and permanence of classification through nomenclature. She thus unmasks the ordered assumptions about subjectivity for Wesley and others but also disrupts assumptions about the whole of *Angel* for the series' viewers. Because Illyria physically resembles (but is not) Fred, a radical shift in perspective is suddenly demanded of all who once knew Fred and now encounter Illyria. Instead of Fred, the observer perceives the arguably beastly, monstrous, and (momentarily) naked unveiled being that is Illyria.

Illyria ensures that in *Angel*, as in *Nausea*, the human desire for constancy and predictability is thwarted by the absurdity (and necessity) of contingency. According to George Woods's analysis of *Nausea*, "Roquentin is coming to grips with his brain's penchant for constancy."[33] In other words, the brain prefers the constant, the familiar, the routine. Roquentin's existential experience in *Nausea* shatters the illusion of constancy. As he remarks while watching the people of Bouville, "what they take for constancy is only habit and it can change tomorrow."[34] Through Roquentin, Sartre contends in *Nausea*, "The essential thing is contingency. I mean that one cannot define existence as necessity."[35] Existence, for Sartre, is *unnecessary*; it is contingent and thus absurd. Nothing is *necessarily* constant; nothing *necessarily* exists. Instead, contingency infuses everything and everyone with its threat of disorder, despite attempts "to overcome this contingency by inventing a necessary, causal being."[36] In her analysis of *Nausea*, Elizabeth Rechniewski refers to "the decay and corruption of contingency" in nature, which "threatens at any moment to break through the façade of human constructions to reveal a repugnant, abject, rotting matter."[37] Contingency disrupts and corrupts habits, customs, standards, routines. Where Team Angel and the audience desire or even expect constancy with Fred (as established through Seasons Three, Four, and most of Five), Whedon disrupts this expectation with the contingency of Illyria.[38]

Illyria herself complains to Wesley about human inclination toward constancy: "Your world is so small. And yet you box yourselves in rooms even smaller. You shut yourselves inside — in rooms, in routines."[39] Wesley's response to Illyria is reminiscent of Roquentin's nauseating experience of stark existence: "There are things worse than walls. Terrible and beautiful. If we look at them for too long they will burn right through us. Truths we couldn't bear."[40] For Roquentin, the revelation of the absolute contingency of existence leaves him "motionless and icy, plunged in a horrible ecstasy."[41] As they literally confront existence and its inherent contingency, both Wesley and Roquentin recognize the inevitable compromise of the human condition: the practice of distraction and illusion. "[E]verything we do," says Angel, "it's a distraction to keep us busy from looking under the surface."[42] Roquentin, watching people in a restaurant, likewise acknowledges this aspect of humanity: "Each one of them has his little personal difficulty which keeps him from noticing that he exists."[43] "Usually existence hides itself,"[44] because otherwise, people, plunged into existential ecstasy, would cease to function effectively or practically in the world. In "Origin" (5.19), Wesley goes so far as to advise Illyria, "Try to push reality out of your mind." He specifically suggests she focus on the false memories—those fabricated by Cyvus Vail—rather than on "those that happened." "To hide from the truth?" Illyria asks. "To endure it," Wesley responds. Wesley did not choose to have his memory altered; nonetheless, when given the choice, he chooses to prioritize Vail's fabrication as a coping mechanism—one with which he might mask the reality of his regrettable choice to kidnap Angel's son. Yet in "Not Fade Away," Wesley claims, "The first lesson a watcher learns is to separate truth from illusion—because in the world of magics, it's the hardest thing to do. The truth is that Fred is gone. To pretend anything else would be a lie." *Angel* itself is fabricated—a fictional creation and world of fantasy, a distraction for its viewers (watchers) that provides an escape from day-to-day life and provides the illusion of constancy. Illyria—as the very embodiment of contingency—interrupts routine, requiring Wesley and each of us to acknowledge illusion and choose either to embrace or reject the lie.[45]

Through Illyria, Whedon also challenges Sartre regarding the relationship between existence and death. Not only does Illyria's essence now exist in Fred's body, but Fred's essence likewise continues to exist through Illyria.[46] In Sartre's philosophy, as explained by Lawrence Schehr, "an individual is always changing—and by existence; there is no essence that can be known until after the change has stopped, [that is] after the individual has died."[47] As the Buffy/Angelverse repeatedly illustrates and as its audience is acutely aware, Whedon is not opposed to killing off a beloved or central female character. For Jenny Calendar, Joyce Summers, Tara, Anya, and Cordelia, existence has permanently ceased (or so it appears). Yet, unlike the others' deaths, Fred's death immediately requires the viewer to accept the paradox of the loss of Fred's existence *and* the ongoing, living presence of Fred's body. Thus, to Stacey Abbott, Illyria is "a hybrid ... dead and alive"; to Jennifer A. Hudson, she is "both absent and present" or "literally 'living dead'"; and to Jes Battis, she is both an "exotic surplus of presence" and "a living absence."[48] Most significantly, Illyria maintains and can reproduce Fred's memories. In "Shells," she explains to Wesley that "fragments" of Fred remain: "When her brain collapsed, electrical spasms channeled into my function system—memories." Though Illyria refers to mere *fragments* here and illustrates one such fragment by repeating verbatim Fred's dying words ("Please, Wesley, why can't I stay?"), later episodes reveal that Illyria maintains enough of Fred to replicate her behavior and personality with exquisite precision. Thus, in "The Girl in Question" (5.20), Illyria enacts Fred for her parents (Trish and Roger Burkle), who have not been informed of their daughter's death. She refers to this process as "a simple modulation of my form."[49] The Burkles accept their daughter's apparent existence. In the same episode, Wesley is disturbed enough by Illyria's transformation into Fred to insist, "Change back. Be blue. Be anything. Don't be her. Don't ever be her." Though Wesley knows that Fred is gone, his repeated use of "be"—don't *be* her—suggests that Illyria can, for all intents and purposes, *become* Fred rather than merely reproduce a flawed imitation. Moreover, she can move beyond duplicating verbatim fragments to generating new experiences *as* Fred. In this sense, she creates rather than merely recreates. This is likewise the case at Wesley's death. Though he can "separate truth from illusion," he nonetheless accepts the "lie" that Illyria enacts to comfort him in his final moments of life. If Illyria can manipulate Fred's body and mind (or memories) to create Fred's existence for others, can we justly say that Fred's existence has ceased changing—that her essence has crystallized, that she is *gone*?[50] Illyria has the ability both to reproduce Fred's essence (via the fragments) and to create anew the still changing existence of Winifred Burkle. In this sense, existence and essence *coincide* in the body of Fred/Illyria. Whedon thus offers us a radical revision of Sartre: the philosophical premise of an evolving exchange rather than a fixed correlation between existence and essence.

The memory fragments also make possible and tangible for Fred (via Illyria) an aspect of human consciousness that is impossible and intangible for Roquentin, who "wants his consciousness of his past to be reconstituted in the form of a novel which can be re-viewed."[51] According to Peter Weigel, "Roquentin strives to be what he cannot be, [that is] an object more than or other than mere consciousness.... The impulse to make oneself an object by turning consciousness into something tangible is an impossible desire."[52] Fred's post-death consciousness remains tangible in that it has survived in the form of electrical impulses that can be reviewed or replayed interminably, like pages from a novel or frames in a film. If she desired to do so, Illyria could indeed reconstitute Fred's past. Yet Illyria nonetheless faces a dilemma regarding Fred's tangible memories: "There are two sets of memories," she tells Wesley, "those that happened and those that are fabricated. It's hard to tell which is which."[53] Similarly, Roquentin complains, "I can search the past in vain, I can only find these scraps of images and I am not sure what they represent, whether they are memories or just fiction."[54] The fabricated memories Illyria accesses are those which had been constructed (at the end of Season Four) through the magic of Cyvus Vail. Though she finds it difficult to distinguish between the real and the fabricated, the task is not impossible. If it were, she would neither recognize two distinct sets of memories nor be able to tell that "in places" the original set is "gone" (when Wesley questions her on the topic).[55] Even amidst magical intervention, Illyria can distinguish the real from the illusory. Roquentin, on the other hand, cannot: "There are many cases where even these scraps have disappeared: nothing is left but words.... My words are dreams, that is all."[56] "I am cast out, forsaken in the present," explains Roquentin, "I vainly try to rejoin the past: I cannot escape."[57] Illyria cannot return to her own primordial past — that which long ago turned to dust — but she can access and manipulate the tangible human essence residing within her. Thus Illyria allows Whedon a means of both enacting and counteracting the existential dilemma posed by Roquentin in *Nausea*, thereby again offering to his audience a unique and contemporary revision of classic existentialism.

While she arguably represents contingency and existence for those who encounter (or watch) her, Illyria simultaneously represents and enacts embodied human response to existence. She is, after all, contained within and constrained by a human body — a new and challenging experience for a once-powerful god. In this sense, her responses to being embodied in the world parallel those of Roquentin. Both Illyria and Roquentin gaze into a literal mirror at a barely recognizable physical figure. Indeed, one of the first things Illyria does when she becomes fully conscious within Fred's body is look into a mirror. The mirror had been Fred's, and in it Illyria does not see her original self; instead, she sees the unfamiliar "shell" of Fred, albeit personalized with a tinge of blue. Roquentin, too, is drawn to a mirror near the beginning of his journey: "I draw my face closer until it touches the mirror. The eyes, nose and mouth disappear: nothing human is left.... I cannot say I *recognize* the details."[58] Zahi Zalloua argues, "Roquentin cannot even rely on his own body as a source of knowledge and stability. His hand appears as *other*; as a thing in the midst of the world, from which he finds no escape."[59] For Roquentin, his once-familiar humanity is gone; for Illyria the primordial god-king is gone. Several episodes later, having been stripped of certain powers, Illyria protests that she is now "[c]ondemned to live out existence in a vessel incapable of sustaining [her] true glory."[60] Similarly, Roquentin laments, "I have never before had such a strong feeling that I was devoid of secret dimensions, confined within the limits of my body."[61] They each understand the body as a prison of sorts, one from which they crave escape. Such an escape, however, is a theoretical impossibility for one who *exists*. Gary Cox, in his discussion of Sartre's theories of the body, explains, "embodiment is consciousness's way of being-in-the-world, and its only way. The existence of each and every embodied person is contingent, but given that a person exists, it is absolutely necessary that he be embodied.... Sartre's existentialism rules out disembodied consciousnesses."[62] Though Illyria as *essence* was once a sort of disembodied consciousness — "the mystical equivalent of airborne"[63] — she would not have been able to *exist* in that disembodied state. To exist absolutely requires a body. Indeed, in "A Hole in the World," Drogyn claims of the airborne Illyria, "It will claw into every soul in its path to keep from being trapped." In other words, Illyria would have been trapped *without* a body. Within a body — within Fred's body — she has the luxury of being, as Sartre would say, "condemned to be free."[64] Thus, she must learn that, like Roquentin, she is free to choose *because* she exists—a lesson she does not fully grasp until "Time Bomb."

In both *Nausea* and *Angel*, "time is of the essence."[65] Roquentin states, "I wanted the moments of my life to follow and order themselves like those of a life remembered. You might as well try and catch time by the tail."[66] In other words, he wants the theoretically impossible: to manipulate time in order to make a coherent narrative of his life. Elsewhere, Roquentin ponders the "irreversibility of time," asking, "But why don't we always have it? Is it that time is not always irreversible?"[67] Of course, unlike Roquentin, Illyria can and does manipulate time as she illustrates initially in "Shells." Yet the main plotline of "Time Bomb" involves a disruption of time that threatens to annihilate Illyria (and potentially thousands of others along with her). For Roquentin, time itself inherently includes annihilation: "I think this is what happens: you suddenly feel that time is passing, that each instant leads to another, this one to another one, and so on; that each instant is annihilated."[68] At issue, on the existential level, is the human tendency to cling to the past, to attempt to prevent its annihilation, rather than choosing to exist in the present.[69] In episodes preceding "Time Bomb," Illyria has glorified her past and abhorred her present. For example, in "Underneath" (5.17), she tells Wesley, "I was power and the ecstasy of death. I was god to a god. Now I'm trapped on a roof—just one roof in this time and this place." In "Time Bomb," she finds herself displaced from the relatively (albeit illusory) stability of this time and place—she has been "ripped ... out of linear progression," her timeline "[torn] ... into shreds and stitched ... back together out of sequence." Thus Illyria finds herself "caged ... in this fractured timeframe in moments that repeat themselves over and over without deviation." Roquentin experiences a similar sensation in that he "can no longer distinguish present from future, and yet it lasts, it happens little by little; the old woman advances in the deserted street.... This is time, time laid bare, coming slowly into existence."[70] Illyria literally becomes stuck, repeatedly, in the past—a dilemma that Roquentin encounters with his lover, Anny, who tells him, "I need you to exist and not to change."[71] To expect existence without change is futile. For both Roquentin and Illyria the desire to reclaim an annihilated past, combined with the arbitrary incursions of the past (through Anny or the fractured timeline) culminates in the need—ultimately—to accept the present.

Of course, existentially the only means to escape the past and embrace the present is through one's choice to change. In "Time Bomb," Illyria observes, "Change is constant. Yet things remain the same."[72] This is the paradox from which she must escape, and the only means to do so will be to change her present self. Roquentin observes, "Nothing has changed and yet everything is different.... [A]t last an adventure happens to me and when I question myself I see that it happens *that I am myself and that I am here*."[73] He exists always and only in the present. Indeed, Roquentin's musings on time throughout the novel lead him to conclude that the past does not exist. After his final encounter with Anny, he concludes, "I am free.... My past is dead."[74] Illyria, contemplating time, claims, "It doesn't exist until it cracks apart."[75] Though she literally refers to time, the sentiment could be applied to Illyria herself. Though she understands that she exists in this world (as discussed earlier regarding "Shells"), she does not *choose* to exist fully in the present until she literally begins to crack apart and, thus, is forced to make a choice. "For the existentialist," explains Thomas R. Flynn, "the value and meaning of each temporal dimension of lived time is a function of our attitudes and choices."[76] Sartrean existentialism is fundamentally about choice: "Man is not only that which he conceives himself to be, but that which he wills himself to be."[77] As Roquentin concludes, "Life has a meaning if we choose to give it one. One must first act, throw one's self into some enterprise."[78] Illyria too must learn this lesson. In "Time Bomb" when she is about to explode (*again* in the fractured timeline), Angel pleads with her, "Illyria, the future can change here. You can choose a different path.... Fighting to hold on to what you were, it's destroying you." This is a lesson that Angel understands well: "The powerful control everything — except our will to choose."[79] Falzon explains classic Sartrean existentialism regarding choice: "In *Being and Nothingness*, the only meaning the world and our lives have is the meaning we give to them through our prodigious choices."[80] Or, as Sartre himself explains, "man is nothing other than what he makes of himself. This is the first principle of existentialism."[81] In "Time Bomb," Illyria does indeed choose to change and, with that choice, enacts within the human condition her existential freedom. Notably, Illyria does not revert to the Fred persona until the next episode ("The Girl in Question"). In other words, not until Illyria has chosen to embrace her own humanity does she choose to explore and expose Fred's human essence — thus emphasizing the Fred/Illyria coexistence or co-existential choice.

Near the end of *Nausea*, Roquentin recognizes his freedom and its inherent difficulty: "I am alone.... Alone and free. But this freedom is rather like death."[82] Having chosen to exist and, in the process, having her powers depleted, Illyria likewise claims, "This fate is worse than death.... How am I to function with such limitation?"[83] This appears to be the quintessential question for Whedon.[84] Choices and changes must necessarily be made. According to Sartre, "man is condemned to be free: condemned, because he did not create himself, yet nonetheless free, because once cast into the world, he is responsible for everything he does."[85] The Wesley and Illyria plot of "The Girl in Question" — the antepenultimate episode of *Angel* — emphasizes Illyria's freedom to choose and her progression toward change.[86] Though Illyria claims not to know how to function with these limited powers, within the course of the episode she discovers a potential coping mechanism: her interaction with an Other, that is with Wesley. In her first conversation with Wesley in this episode, Illyria says, "I do not bend to your wishes." In their next conversation (in regard to her physical transformation into Fred), she tells Wesley, "It's a simple modulation of my form. I appear as I choose" and then asks, "Do you wish me to stop?" In their final conversation, in response to Wesley's request, "Change back.... Don't be her," Illyria responds, "As you wish." The repetition of the word "wish" in each instance draws attention to the shift in Illyria's attitude: at first she refuses, then she asks, then she complies. For better or worse, and despite some residual powers, her experiment with a modulation in form leaves her vulnerable to the human condition and to the opinion of others. As Sartre explains in his discussion of the "human *condition*" (as opposed to a "universal essence"), "What never varies is the necessity for him to be in the world, to work in it, to live out his life in it among others."[87] Illyria, conditionally human, is now part of the team. By the series' final episode, Illyria's decisions—first to help Team Angel and then to help Wesley in particular—show Wesley that Illyria is capable of change through personal choice. As Roz Kaveney argues regarding Illyria's transformation to Fred at Wesley's death, "her offer is an outward sign of genuine inward change."[88] Only Cyvus Vail makes the error of assuming Illyria's form is constant, that she's only a "little girl."[89] The slow motion modulation of form from Fred back to Illyria as she delivers the fatal blow to Vail is one that visually articulates the power of existential choice. Coincidence or not, the homonym with "veil" is striking. "And suddenly, suddenly," says Roquentin, "the veil is torn away, I have understood, I have *seen*."[90]

Illyria—as essence and existence—brings to the final episodes of *Angel* a radical and essential transformation, which effectively and abruptly disrupts the constancy of the Buffy/Angelverse. This is not to suggest that Illyria is the only disruption within the Buffy/Angelverse—quite the contrary. However, in *Angel*, Illyria arrives as the series draws toward its end. Where we might have expected solid ground in these final episodes, we find instead "a hole in the world"—"the staggering possibility that someone, a loved someone, could disappear and not come back."[91] At the end of *Nausea*, Roquentin contemplates writing a book: "A story, for example, something that could never happen, an adventure. It would have to be beautiful and hard as steel and make people ashamed of their existence."[92] The parameters of *Angel* enable Whedon to create "something that could never happen" and, thereby, simultaneously explore, challenge, and even revise Sartrean existentialism. In the process, he invites the audience to question the nature of existence. "A Hole in the World"—the episode in which Illyria first invades Fred's body—repeatedly emphasizes the role of the observer in the act of perception and, thus, in the construction of meaning. For example, Gunn is informed by his doppelganger in the White Room, "The physical form of the conduit is determined by the viewer."[93] In the airplane, en route to England in an attempt to save Fred, Spike and Angel share what appears to be typical "Spangel" banter, but which may well encapsulate the existentialism of the Illyria plotline.[94] Spike, looking at a miniature bottle of Jack Daniels that he holds at arm's length says, "Here's a drink, but it's very far away." Angel asks, "What does that mean really?" Spike replies, "It's a play on perspective." But Angel had not meant the Jack Daniels; he had been referring to Fred. "What does it mean," repeats Angel and then clarifies, "that she's gone?" In light of the episode's exploration of existence, one might likewise reply, "It's a play on perspective."[95]

Notes

1. Jean-Paul Sartre, *Nausea*, trans. Lloyd Alexander (Paris: Librairie Gallimard, 1938; New York: New Directions Books, 2007), 54. Citations are to the New Directions edition.

2. Chris Falzon, "Sartre and Meaningful Existence," in *Sartre's Nausea: Text, Context, Intertext*, ed. Alistair Rolls and Elizabeth Rechniewski (Amsterdam and New York: Rodopi, 2005), 105–120 at 105.

3. "Objects in Space," *Firefly*, DVD Commentary by Joss Whedon (2002; 20th Century–Fox, 2003).

4. Ibid.

5. "Lovers Walk," *Buffy the Vampire Slayer*, DVD, written by Dan Vebber, directed by David Semel (1998; 20th Century–Fox, 2006).

6. See, for example, J. Michael Richardson and J. Douglas Rabb, *The Existential Joss Whedon: Evil and Human Freedom in* Buffy the Vampire Slayer, Angel, Firefly *and* Serenity (Jefferson, NC: McFarland, 2007); Stacey Abbott, "Kicking Ass and Singing 'Mandy': A Vampire in L.A.," in *Reading* Angel*: The TV Spin-Off with a Soul*, ed. Stacey Abbott (London: I.B. Tauris, 2005), 1–13; and Stacey Abbott, "Walking the Fine Line Between Angel and Angelus," *Slayage: The Online International Journal of Buffy Studies* 3, no. 1 (August 2003), http://www.slayageonline.com.

7. "Shells," *Angel*, DVD, written and directed by Steven S. DeKnight (2004; 20th Century–Fox, 2006).

8. Jean-Paul Sartre, *Existentialism is a Humanism*, trans. Carol Macomber (Original Lecture, 1945; New Haven, CT: Yale University Press, 2007), 22.

9. In *Buffy*, Whedon also explores the complexities of essence and existence through Dawn — who apparently existed as pure energy prior to being human. However, unlike Illyria, Dawn has no memory of her former self before her existence as human. Thus, in Sartrean terms, Dawn's existence (as human) precedes the *essence* of Dawn (which begins to develop only once she exists as human and will not be complete until her death). One might also argue that the vampire essence, as demon, exists prior to its human embodiment. However (and, again, unlike Illyria), Whedon offers no specific past existence or memories thereof to the demonic essences of vampires. For example, Angel does not discuss his existence as a demon *in and of itself* prior to its embodiment of Liam and existence as Angelus. Illyria, on the other hand, repeatedly contrasts her current embodied existence (and its inherent restrictions) in Fred's "shell" with her former existence as an all-powerful god. Thus, the exploration of essence and existence through Fred/Illyria is unique at this point in the Whedonverses. Of course, *Dollhouse* now complicates matters, providing Whedon with various means of exploring the philosophies of existence.

10. "Shells."

11. "Underneath," *Angel*, DVD, written by Sarah Fain and Elizabeth Craft, directed by Skip Schoolnik (2004; 20th Century–Fox, 2006).

12. "Origin," *Angel*, DVD, written by Drew Goddard, directed by Terrence O'Hara (2004; 20th Century–Fox, 2006).

13. Sartre, *Nausea*, 100; Ibid., 54.

14. Ibid., 95–96.

15. Thomas Martin explains, "Existence, for Roquentin, is characterized by three closely related properties: superfluity, absurdity, and contingency.... Things just are (contingent), bearing no necessary relation to each other (superfluous), and are, hence, devoid of mean-

ing (absurd)." "The Role of Others in Roquentin's *Nausea*," in *Sartre's Nausea: Text, Context, Intertext*, ed. Rolls and Rechniewski, 65–76 at 66–67.

16. Sartre, *Nausea*, 132.
17. Ibid., 4.
18. "Shells."
19. Sartre, *Nausea*, 19; and "A Hole in the World," *Angel*, DVD, written and directed by Joss Whedon (2004; 20th Century–Fox, 2006).
20. In his discussion of Sartre, John K. Simon describes "the antagonism between the inner life of consciousness and the external threat" as a "deadly form of uncontrollable metamorphosis." "Faulkner and Sartre: Metamorphosis and the Obscene," *Comparative Literature* 15, no. 3 (1963), 216–225 at 218.
21. Sartre, *Nausea*, 2; Ibid., 5.
22. "A Hole in the World."
23. Sartre, *Nausea*, 160.
24. Ibid., 125.
25. Ibid., 127.
26. Ibid., 126–7.
27. Ibid., 125.
28. Ibid., 127.
29. Ibid.
30. Peter Weigel, "The Aesthetics of Salvation in Sartre's *Nausea*," in *The Enigma of Good and Evil; The Moral Sentiment in Literature*, ed. Anna-Teresa Tymieniecka (The Dordrecht, Netherlands: Springer, 2005), 473–489 at 474.
31. "Shells."
32. Ibid.
33. George Woods, "'Sounds, Smells, Degrees of Light': Art and Illumination in *Nausea*," in *Sartre's Nausea: Text, Context, Intertext*, ed. Rolls and Rechniewski, 53–63 at 59.
34. Sartre, *Nausea*, 158.
35. Ibid., 131.
36. Ibid.
37. Elizabeth Rechniewski, "Avatars of Contingency: Suarès and Sartre," in *Sartre's Nausea: Text, Context, Intertext*, ed. Rolls and Rechniewski, 93–103 at 101.
38. Of course, contingency and its inherent disruption are not limited to Illyria within the Whedonverses. Indeed, unexpected disruption — especially via death (Joyce, Tara, Anya, Doyle, Cordelia) — is arguably commonplace in the Whedonverses. Nonetheless, the disruption by Illyria is unique in that Illyria struggles with her "birth" and existence within Fred's body even as the others struggle with the death of Fred. The Cordelia/Jasmine plot of Season Four is comparable but not identical. Jasmine may temporarily reside within Cordelia; however, once Jasmine is born, she is a separate entity from Cordelia.
39. "Underneath."
40. Ibid.
41. Sartre, *Nausea*, 131.
42. "Underneath."
43. Sartre, *Nausea*, 111.
44. Ibid., 127.
45. The necessity of making a choice between illusion and reality is also explored in the *Buffy* episode "Normal Again" (6.17). *Buffy*, DVD, written by Diego Guitierrez, directed by Rick Rosenthal (2002; 20th Century–Fox, 2006).
46. Fred's essence is not the equivalent of her soul, which "was consumed by the fires of resurrection" ("Shells"). In Sartrean existentialism, one's essence develops as a result of the choices one makes while existing. Thus, one's essence is complete only at death, once existential choices cease. The choices that Fred made throughout her life comprise the essence of Fred — an essence Illyria is able to access and utilize through memory. For a discussion of the soul in the Whedonverses (including its relation to Sartrean existentialism), see Scott McLaren, "The Evolution of Joss Whedon's Vampire Mythology and the Ontology of the Soul," *Slayage: The Online International Journal of Buffy Studies* 5, no. 2 (September 2005), http://slayageonline.com.

47. Lawrence Schehr, "Sartre's Autodidacticism," in *Sartre's Nausea: Text, Context, Intertext*, ed. Rolls and Rechniewski, 31–51 at 42.
48. Stacey Abbott, *Angel*, TV Milestones Series (Detroit: Wayne State University Press), 60; Jennifer A. Hudson, "'She's Unpredictable': Illyria and the Liberating Potential of Chaotic Postmodern Identity," *Magazine Americana: The American Popular Culture Magazine Online* (March 2005) http://www.americanpopularculture.com/archive/tv/shes_unpredictable.htm; Jes Battis, *Blood Relations: Chosen Families in* Buffy the Vampire Slayer *and* Angel (Jefferson, NC: McFarland, 2005), 124; and Ibid., 129.
49. "The Girl in Question," *Angel*, DVD, written by Steven S. DeKnight and Drew Goddard, directed by David Greenwalt (2004; 20th Century–Fox, 2006).
50. On the topic of Fred's transformation, Stacey Abbott suggestively asks, "Angel and his team are confronted by a being who looks like Fred but is not her—or is it?" *Angel*, 59.
51. Weigel, "The Aesthetics of Salvation in Sartre's *Nausea*," 486.
52. Ibid.
53. "Origin."
54. Sartre, *Nausea*, 32. For a discussion of "Sartre's analysis of memory as interpretive" in relation to Whedon, see Richardson and Rabb, *The Existential Joss Whedon*, 116.
55. "Origin."
56. Sartre, *Nausea*, 33.
57. Ibid.
58. Ibid., 17.
59. Zahi Zalloua, "Roquentin and the Metaphysics of Presence: Philosophy, Literature, Textual Play," *Comparatist: Journal of the Southern Comparative Literature Association*, 25 (2001): 133–150 at 135.
60. "The Girl in Question."
61. Sartre, *Nausea*, 33.
62. Gary Cox, *Sartre: A Guide for the Perplexed* (London: Continuum, 2006), 54.
63. "A Hole in the World."
64. Sartre, *Existentialism*, 29.
65. Thomas R. Flynn, *Existentialism: A Very Short Introduction* (Oxford: Oxford University Press, 2006), 6. Flynn lists "time is of the essence" as one of the "five themes of existentialism," 8.
66. Sartre, *Nausea*, 40.
67. Ibid., 57.
68. Ibid., 56.
69. The continual importance of choice throughout *Angel* has been explored in Richardson and Rabb's *The Existential Joss Whedon*; see chapters eight and nine.
70. Sartre, *Nausea*, 31.
71. Ibid., 137.
72. "Time Bomb," *Angel*, DVD, written by Ben Edlund, directed by Vern Gillum (2004; 20th Century–Fox, 2006).
73. Sartre, *Nausea*, 54.
74. Ibid., 156.
75. "Time Bomb."
76. Flynn, *Existentialism*, 5.
77. Sartre, *Existentialism*, 22.
78. Sartre, *Nausea*, 112.
79. "Power Play," *Angel*, DVD, written by David Fury, directed by James A. Contner (2004; 20th Century–Fox, 2006).
80. Falzon, "Sartre and Meaningful Existence," 112.
81. Sartre, *Existentialism*, 22.
82. Sartre, *Nausea*, 157.
83. "The Girl in Question."
84. Indeed, the question speaks both to the human condition and to television production. How is Whedon to work within the limitation (and contingency) of having his series cancelled?
85. Sartre, *Existentialism*, 29.

86. In "What the Hell? *Angel*'s 'The Girl in Question,'" I discuss choice and change in the Angel and Spike plotline. (This paper was originally presented at *Slayage* Conference on the Whedonverses 3 in 2008 and is currently being considered for publication.)
87. Sartre, *Existentialism*, 42.
88. Roz Kaveney, "A Sense of the Ending: Schrodinger's *Angel*," in *Reading* Angel, ed. Stacey Abbott (London: I.B. Tauris, 2005), 57–72 at 69.
89. "Not Fade Away," *Angel*, DVD, written by Joss Whedon and Jeffrey Bell, directed by Jeffrey Bell (2004; 20th Century–Fox, 2006).
90. Sartre, *Nausea*, 126.
91. Battis, *Blood Relations*, 125.
92. Sartre, *Nausea*, 178.
93. "A Hole in the World."
94. The word "Spangel" derives from the slash fiction about Spike and Angel.
95. Thank you to Marni Stanley and Kathryn Barnwell for invaluable feedback on a draft of this paper.

Four : Genre

You're a bloody puppet! You're a wee little puppet man!
— Spike, "Smile Time"

Helping the Helpless
Medieval Romance in Angel

AmiJo Comeford

"The thing about Angel, he's old-fashioned — old-fashioned like the age of chivalry. He sees you as, pretty much, the damsel in distress." Cordelia's description to Bethany, one of those "damsels" in Season Two's "Untouched" (2.04),[1] reminds viewers that the character is fashioned after a chivalric knight of the medieval order, in addition to being heavily influenced by fantasy, horror, noir, and hard-boiled detective fiction (all of which have received critical attention). Benjamin Jacob makes this observation about Angel and chivalry in his study of how the city of Los Angeles/Los Angelus functions in relation to narrative theme.[2] While the chivalric character construction alone seems obvious and straightforward enough, especially when the writers self-consciously remind us of it, as in Season Two's "Judgment" (2.01),[3] what is less obvious are the ways in which Angel's role as a chivalric knight and the narrative construction embody characteristics of the romance genre (referring to courtly literature focused on knights and their adventures rather than the modern usage of the term "romance" to designate love). The generic twists on the character archetype and the narrative contribute to the creation and resolution of narrative tensions, as well as providing inroads into the ways in which Angel's vampiric humanity provides the ideal form for addressing questions within a romance that remind us of why the genre still "intrigues modern audiences today," to use medieval critic Roberta L. Krueger's words.[4] Krueger's continued response to why romances still interest contemporary audiences could very well sum up the body of scholarship called *Buffy* and *Angel* studies: "The diversity of their form and subject-matter, the complexity of their narrative strategies and perspective, and the many critical responses they invite" all contribute to the popularity of romance today.[5]

We need look no further than high-stakes Hollywood for evidence of how powerful the idea of romance is in the popular mind. Screenwriters have occasionally tried to tap this deeply embedded interest in Western audiences with films like *First Knight* (1995) starring Sean Connery as King Arthur, Richard Gere as Lancelot, and Julia Ormond as Guinevere; *A Knight's Tale* (2001) starring Heath Ledger in the title role of William and Shannyn Sossamon as his love interest Jocelyn; and *Tristan + Isolde* (2006) starring James Franco as Tristan, Rufus Sewell as Marke, and Sophia Myles as Isolde.[6] Significantly, *First Knight* and *A Knight's Tale* both draw part of their narrative lines from Chrétien de Troyes's *Lancelot, the Knight of the Cart*, composed sometime between 1176–1182.[7] Unfortunately for the romance genre and our engagement with it, filmmakers and writers have chosen to place a few pieces here and there as they fit into the dramatic, rather than retaining the romantic genre as a whole. This choice undermines the romance genre, as its strength depends on the unified nature of its elements and themes rather than on its individual parts. What each of these three recent adaptations of the romance have missed is exactly what *Angel* captures—the ultimately irresolvable tensions inherent within the romance tradition of love and adventure, which depend on one identifying aspect of the genre that major filmmakers have yet to capture — the fantastic, exaggerated, and supernatural.[8] *Angel*, however, is different, since it not only allows but normalizes the fantastic as a method of foregrounding the tensions that develop in the romantic hero.

Under the direction of Joss Whedon, *Angel*'s writers sensed—consciously or not is irrelevant — the power of the romance, perhaps because, as Whedon scholar Elizabeth Bridges notes in a recent study of *Buffy*'s relationship to folklore, Joss Whedon has a distinct "ability to tap into deeply shared cultural memory and experience," which might be applied equally well to our deep cultural engagement with the thematic and character elements of romance as to folklore.[9] Because of the pre-established structure of the Buffy/Angelverse and its normalizing of fantastic and exaggerated elements—itself an important characteristic of romance since "at the heart of the romance lies the question of how the unknown, the marvelous, or the demonized are brought into line with normative, idealized chivalric values"[10]— the writers could successfully appropriate the foundational elements of the romance and the romantic hero into the narrative without limiting the show to being a full-fledged romance. Rather, the show incorporates romantic characteristics into its narrative tapestry, sometimes rather self-consciously as in *Angel* Season Two's "Judgment" wherein Angel jousts another demon for the liberation of a woman and her child, and successfully re-introduces the romance, with a twist, of course, to a modern audience.[11] For five seasons, and more since the character originated on *Buffy the Vampire Slayer*, *Angel*'s creative team provided a narrative opening for future television/film writers who are brave enough to step through and wield the romantic sword against the narrative status quo.

In the Preface to *The Cambridge Companion to Medieval Romance*, Krueger writes that romance is "arguably the most influential and enduring secular literary genre of the European Middle Ages."[12] Yet, the genre seems to have suffered from somewhat of a decline in serious interest on the part of average readers or creative writers, as noted earlier, being the stuff of fun bedtime stories and escapist reading/viewing, rather than serious literature that forces audiences to engage with uncomfortable realities on which the romance depends and which it also defies.[13] This is not to say that romance cannot and should not be read for sheer pleasure. After all, romances were part of a medieval tradition of storytelling that was immensely popular as pure entertainment, and in fact once romances were put into writing, they gained even broader audiences.[14] Still, we should not be fooled by the apparent mirth with which the romance has been imbued, much like our viewing of *Angel*. We may find it sheer visual and narrative pleasure, but underneath are the paradoxes, problems, and underpinnings of something more serious.

Romance as a genre dates back to the early twelfth century, with the most "active period" occurring between 1150–1250.[15] The dates are perhaps somewhat easier to determine than any inclusive definition of the genre. Indeed, romance, critic Matilda Tomaryn Bruckner has observed (particularly in reference to romances found in medieval France) that the genre "compel[s], even as it escapes, our urge to define it,"[16] a point on which Simon Gaunt concurs, noting that any attempt to define a romance will lead critics down a path that denies to the genre the complexity and nuance of which it is made.[17] Part of that elusive complexity is also what distinguishes romance from other genres, and for most audiences consists of the same moment of recognition that Supreme Court Justice Potter Stewart famously used in relation to pornography: "I know it when I see it."[18] Still, to recognize a genre is hardly to engage fully with its structure, themes, and relevance, which is what this chapter seeks to do in relation to just two characteristics that make romance identifiable and unique and more importantly add to the complex narrative tapestry in *Angel*, which academics and fans alike have come to expect of Whedon's creations: 1) verisimilitude between the supernatural and the real, and 2) behavioral traits that characterize the courtly lover/hero.

First, a basic working definition of romance as it will be used in this essay is crucial, acknowledging as above that any attempt to define the romance entirely is a troubling endeavor. Still, according to John Finlayson, romance is "a tale in which a knight achieves great feats of arms, almost solely for his own *los et pris* [fame and renown] in a series of adventures which have no social, political, or religious motivation and little or no connection to medieval actuality."[19] Though this definition is useful and a solid beginning, readers are likely to spot one major omission that must be added, what has come to be known as "courtly love."[20] Taking this added characteristic then and Finlayson's definition in tandem, romances can generally be grouped into three categories: the romance of adventure, which works nicely with Finlayson's definition; the romance of love, which recognizes the prominence of love and its consequences; and the romances that encompass both, which is the most relevant to the current *Angel* discussion. Regardless of type, in order to develop the knight's character, both in relation to knightly and lover-like attributes, romance relies heavily on the first of the two characteristics that are the focus of this chapter and so must be addressed here: verisimilitude through the supernatural.

Use of the supernatural is essential in the romance because, as Finlayson writes, "In its proper or best use [the supernatural] creates the special atmosphere of the romance world where elements of social reality and the unnatural commingle, not for the purpose of sensational contrast between the real and the unreal, but to provide a balance between fiction and verisimilitude."[21] The use of verisimilitude is crucial here because it allows the writers to engage social, psychological, and political concerns that would otherwise be problematic for audiences and writers alike but is made safe through the fictional distance. The world of the supernatural provides this option, but in a normalized atmosphere that takes such things for granted, which is what separates the idea of verisimilitude, perhaps, from basic metaphor.

One need go no further into the Buffy/Angelverse than the opening season of *Buffy* to find the writers engaging in this distanced verisimilitude, which at times does comingle with metaphor, in this case with the notion that Sunnydale sits on the Hellmouth, or more popularly worded, "High school is hell."[22] The same is true in *Angel* with episodes like "She" (female genital mutilation) (1.13); "Untouched" (domestic molestation and the accompanying emotional trauma) (2.04); and "Billy" (misogynist violence against women) (3.06), to name a few.[23] And more generally, for critics Michele Greppi and Joyce Millman, the series as a whole functions as "a post-graduate course on coming to grips with life not as you dreamed it but as it unfolds," in addition to being an "astute meditation on what it is to be human."[24] As the seasons continue, viewers discover this verisimilitude over and over again, which becomes more and more thematically ensconced as the narrative arcs intensify, culminating in *Angel*'s fifth season, where the sense of the line between real and imagined is nearly erased for both viewers and characters alike in the move to Wolfram & Hart.[25]

While the normalizing of supernatural or improbable events might be a feature of fantasy in general, the romance's delicate balance between reality and fantasy or exaggeration, and its frequent privileging of the real over the fantastic, is what associates it with *Buffy* and *Angel* more specifically. In other words, the "nature of the action is dependent on the initiating marvel," but it is not necessarily *the* marvel itself that is important but what comes as a result of the knight confronting or seeking out the marvel.[26] One example from a well-known Buffy/Angel moment will stand as illustrative of the many other moments to be found within the two series as they characterize Angel both as character and series.

In *Buffy*'s Season Three two-part finale, "Graduation Day" (3.21–22), Faith shoots Angel with a poisoned arrow to distract Buffy from her slayer duties.[27] The poison has one cure — slayer's blood. In short, for Angel to be cured, he must feed on a slayer. Since Faith has chosen to work with the evil mayor, Buffy decides that to cure Angel, she will bring Faith in and have Angel feed on her. For the current discussion, the initiating marvel is of course the fantasy element of a mystical poison, but the poison itself is not the heart of the issue, as viewers quickly discover. The real question that the moment engages is one of ethical dilemmas worked out in a very real world: sacrificing one wayward human (Faith) to cure another wayward "human" (Angel) whose past deeds are worse than the first's; second, the narrative forces Angel to commit an act he has spent 150 years abhorring and fighting in order to better abhor and fight for another 150 years.

As viewers, we are somewhat stunned to discover that when Buffy returns from her fight with Faith and tells Angel that the only cure for the poison is the blood of a slayer, Angel's weakened response is, "Faith..." — in effect renouncing his "human" side in favor of the demonic — and Buffy calmly replies, "I tried. I killed her."[28] End of story. For all of the emphasis placed on the slayer's and Angel's roles as defenders of human life at all cost, even those lives which seem little deserving of saving,[29] this moment is stunning, a reminder that in the real world, not the world of fantasy and mythology, love and sacrifice sometimes demand of their captives not only allegiance but their very moral natures, a paradox that is ever-present for the chivalric knight of romance.[30]

Eventually, of course, Buffy forces Angel to drink her, which cures him but threatens Buffy with death by blood loss. Again, we are struck by the "commingling" of the "social reality and the unnatural,"[31] as moments after Buffy cures Angel, viewers are presented with the frantic scene of a hospital emergency room and a doctor asking Angel questions that are at odds with the mystical (and erotic) moment audiences have just experienced, "Any allergies...? You two been doing drugs?"[32] The questions seem almost laughable and strangely misplaced; the proximity between the mystical and real is so close that we cannot forget that though Buffy's blood is a mystical cure for Angel, her cure is non-mystical — she needs a blood transfusion not from another slayer but from anyone with a matching blood type. The oddity of the combination of these two moments is illustrated by Angel's reaction to the doctor's mundane questions: he tears the handle from the door in a single frustrated moment. Throughout the Angelverse, the constant reminder that the marvelous and the metaphorical is not *the point* but the initiation to help us reach *the point of the narrative*, in this case moral crossroads for the hero and heroine, is crucial and ever-present. This use of an initiating marvel also foregrounds the one generic factor that most clearly addresses the narrative tensions between reality and fiction, competing ideals and the unavoidable consequences of that competition — the protagonist himself, particularly in his role as courtly lover and chivalric knight, both of which share a symbiotic, though ultimately untenable, opposing bond.

The tension between disparate though intricately intertwined social values within a character functions ideally in Angel given his unique human and vampiric nature, what Stacey Abbott has referred to as his "hybridity" or "well-known" "schizophrenia," as science fiction fantasy writer Laura Resnick has described it.[33] Indeed, we are accustomed to watching the interplay between angel and demon, savior and destroyer, hero and enemy. This normalizing of narrative polarity within one character ideally positions Angel as a de-centered plane for readers to engage the power of the romance and the romantic hero that has embedded itself into Western consciousness in astoundingly potent ways. And here we must move to a discussion of courtly or chivalric love.

For the "foremost poet of twelfth-century France"[34] Chrétien de Troyes, whose highly-developed romances are a tour de force in the trajectory of the romance genre, "not so much invent[ing] romance as guid[ing] it firmly in a direction that it had already taken," not only is love the "source of the hero's new social identity, but also an experience that leads to spiritual progress."[35] This is why Matilda Bruckner's assertion that the romance does indeed "speak to lovers"[36] is a staple for romance and also distinguishes the genre from the vernacular epic adventures that preceded it (like *Beowulf*, for example). W.P. Ker's 1896 study *Epic and Romance* both pre-dates and validates Bruckner's comment: "the value of the best works of the school [of medieval romance] consists in their representation of the passion of love."[37] In other words, feats of great physical prowess are not enough to sustain a knight's honor and nobility. Instead, love acts as an ennobling elixir that raises the knight to new heights of chivalric virtue and uncovers and clarifies his one "true" identity.[38] Under Chrétien's guidance, the romantic hero is one whose physical trials are not just about his individual bravery but rather whose actions are supported by what Finlayson refers to as an "amatory connection,"[39] and here is where we enter the world of what has become known as "courtly love" or the love that we find as the motivating factor for the knight's physical tests. The term itself was first used in 1883 by literary critic and known medievalist Gaston Paris in the French journal *Romania* in connection with *Lancelot, the Knight of the Cart* by Chrétien de Troyes,[40] a tale that has also come to be known simply as *Lancelot*.

That love creates its own virtue, outside of specific social strictures and commentary is evident in *Lancelot*, where love is the driving force behind the narrative, overshadowing adventure. The difficulty, however, is that love itself cannot be separated from a social structure that upholds its idealism in literary terms but nonetheless condemns it as socially unviable.[41] What makes the romance genre so fascinating is that its self-reflexive nature allows it to deal with this paradox of "the role of love within competing value systems," including the tendency for this all-consuming love to endanger social stability and ethics; or put more succinctly in Cordelia Chase's terms, "sex is bad."[42]

For the first time — Chrétien de Troyes's romance being the earliest known text to contain this subject matter — we see the adulterous love affair between Lancelot and Guinevere.[43] The story begins with a challenge from the evil knight

Méléagant to King Arthur that he will exchange the citizens of Arthur's realm whom he has imprisoned for a duel over Guinevere:

> King,
> if you have a single knight
> In this court of yours you can trust
> To take your queen to the woods,
> Where I'll be going when I'm finished
> Here, then I'll agree
> To let him have those prisoners
> I've got in my dungeons, provided
> He can defeat me in battle,
> It being understood
> That possession of your queen is the price
> For victory.[44]

Sir Kay demands the challenge and undertakes the adventure with Guinevere at his side, only to be defeated and allow Méléagant to capture Guinevere. Lancelot soon follows and after having crossed a bridge that is literally the blade of a sword — which severely wounds his hands and feet — he finds Guinevere and they share a passionate night of sexual intimacy.[45] The next morning, Guinevere's infidelity is discovered, though Sir Kay, who had been wounded and captured by Méléagant after having undertaken the challenge, is thought to be the culprit and both now need a champion to defend them. Guinevere even states that Kay is "too honest and loyal / A man to accuse of such things,"[46] identifying those very qualities she most admires about Lancelot, yet in his case courtesy and loyalty are the traits that led to the adulterous affair in the first place. Nonetheless, who else but Lancelot steps in to save her and Kay? Lancelot wholeheartedly upholds the queen's virtue: "May it never please God that such suspicion fall on you or on Kay."[47] Modern readers may find this a moment of extraordinary hypocrisy,[48] but if W.T.H. Jackson is consulted, we discover that foundational to the "treatment of love" in the romances is "the tendency to show the lady as being of superior qualities whose love inspires rather than degrades her lover."[49] Jackson's comment makes this seemingly-hypocritical scene clearer for a modern audience. Love elevates both Lancelot and Guinevere to a level of unquestionable virtue.[50] They are both ennobled by their love for each other, even if it is adulterous. That the same purifying effect is true for Angel and Buffy, minus the adultery, is clear, as we will discover in more depth below in a flashback to Angel's first encounter with Buffy. But first the essential connection between adventure and love must be explored. Lancelot's adventures in reaching Guinevere have qualified him for her love and therefore the virtue that depends on that love, as do Angel's.

The beloved is indeed the motivating and purifying factor behind the adventure. In fact the lady, along with her love and fidelity, is achieved through the knight's physical prowess. This aspect of the romance is made clear in *Angel* throughout its entire run, even pre-dating the events of the first season.

Consider the opening line for the monologue that begins Season One of *Angel*: "It all started with a girl."[51] For audiences who came directly from *Buffy* Season Three, we know that "the girl" is Buffy. However, what we need to see beyond this is that Angel's entire quest in fighting evil and proving his worth (and later that he deserves to shanshu — become human again once he fulfills his destiny) is motivated by Buffy, or in romance terms, his lady, with Angel obviously created throughout the entire series as representative of a knight, a champion who "helps the helpless," a new phrase that could easily replace "saves the damsel."[52] The episode "Judgment" from Season Two is a perfect example.[53] Winifred Burkle (Fred), who joins Team Angel at the end of Season Two, also conceptualizes Angel as a saving knight in her obsessive and frantic illustrations after returning from Pylea.[54] And who can forget Angel as a gladiator/champion in the Season One episode "The Ring" (1.16)?[55]

If Angel, then, is indeed a new type of chivalric knight, we would expect the actions of his life to be motivated by love that purifies, just as Lancelot's does, however disastrous and seemingly socially degrading, for the lovers.[56] And they are, entirely. The final moments in *Buffy*'s first season episode "Angel" (1.07) establish this pattern that will continue to shape Angel's character development, even into the post-television series comic books. When Buffy's cross burns Angel's chest, as she moves close enough to kiss him, she physically marks him as hers.[57] From this point on, he will never be free of Buffy or his connection to her, and the same is true for Buffy, as she never loses the scar from Angel drinking her blood in Season Three's "Graduation Day," significantly the only wound she incurs that never heals.[58]

As Angel and Buffy's relationship continues to build throughout most of *Buffy*'s second and third seasons, he remains only a periphery member of the Scooby Gang, popping in and out when the slayer needs him — not really doing much unless on a mission for Buffy. The tie between them even extends after Angel leaves Sunnydale and strikes out on this own in L.A. After his first entirely self-motivated mission (with some help from The Powers That Be through their emissary Doyle) to save L.A.'s young women from the perverted and sadistic vampire Russell, Angel's first impulse is to call Buffy. Even after accomplishing a feat worthy of her, he requires assurance and needs to let her know he continues to use his skills to earn her love and affection, as a knight seeks adventure to purify and prove himself worthy of the woman's love. In this case he remains tied to Buffy throughout the entire season, roughly reminding her in "Sanctuary" (1.19) that he cannot move on.[59] We are not surprised by either Angel's actions or words when we remember *Buffy*'s Season Two finale "Becoming" (2.21–22).[60] In these episodes, Whedon gave viewers tremendous insight into what drives Angel when the flashback recounts the moment Buffy is called to be a slayer. Angel wanders the streets of L.A., living on rats and looking "disgusting," when Whistler, a messenger from The Powers That Be, appears and suggests that Angel make something of himself, become "someone to be counted."[61]

He takes Angel to witness Buffy's calling. In these few moments, Angel decides to help Buffy, not because he believes in fighting for its own sake, a point made clear by Whistler's first comment to him, "God, jeez, look at you. She must be prettier than the last Slayer."[62] Buffy is what motivates him — not Buffy as slayer — but Buffy as woman. Compounding the issue and taking us back to the knight as the savior of vulnerable women who require champions, is the first image *after* Buffy is told of her destiny — sadness and loneliness. She stands in her bedroom, looking in the mirror, alone while her parents fight. As Angel himself puts it in a later episode in *Buffy*'s third season, "Helpless" (3.12): "I watched you, and I saw you called. It was a bright afternoon out in front of your school. You walked down the steps ... and ... and I loved you ... 'Cause I could see your heart. You held it before you for everyone to see. And I worried that it would be bruised or torn. And more than anything in my life I wanted to keep it safe ... to warm it with my own."[63]

The words are reminiscent of Lancelot, Tristan, or Gawain. This is why Angel fights evil — to both earn and prove his love for Buffy and to act as protector. This seems to be more obviously the case in *Buffy* than in *Angel*, but even in *Angel*, we are reminded that Angel's motivation for continuing to fight is still Buffy.[64] In the final conversation between Cordelia and Angel about Buffy's death, Angel tries to explain his guilt for continuing to live after Buffy has died, guilt that her death did not kill him as well — which it should have given the insistent association between Angel and the courtly lovers/knights like Lancelot and Tristan, both of whom either died of grief or tried to kill themselves after their beloveds had either died or forsaken them.[65] Angel wanted to die fighting by Buffy's side, perhaps even protecting Buffy from that same fate. By the end of the conversation, however, Angel is motivated to continue the good fight as a way of honoring Buffy's name, preserving her memory. So, although Angel finds a certain individual reason to fight — shanshuing and being a hero because it is the right thing to do — his motivation is still his underlying love for Buffy, even when she is dead.[66]

The difficulty is that love and knightly prowess are a much more complex affair than a mere star-crossed lover relationship would have us believe, a complexity summed up succinctly by Yin Liu in her denotation of medieval chivalry in particular: chivalry is a "complex and contentious mix of the ideological, literary, political, military, religious, and quasi-religious."[67] Love, even if the motivating factor for courageous and often superhuman actions, does not in the end lead to a necessarily stable relationship or social order. Rather, what we find is that the end result of love in a modern consciousness — marriage — is often not compatible with the ideals of chivalry. In short, a knight, even if the love was physically consummated, could not remain in any long-term relationship with his beloved. We see this more than once in the romances, the most deadly of which is Tristan and Isolde, and perhaps the most fully dealt with on a pragmatic level in Chrétien de Troyes's *Erec and Enide*, written around 1170.[68]

The hero Erec's securing of Enide as his prize and wife, through illustrating his courage and fighting strength against another knight, is achieved unusually early in the narrative. Post-marriage, Erec and Enide enjoy perfected, passionate love. Erec finds no reason to leave his bed and has no interest in joining other knights in quests and jousting tournaments: "But Erec loved Enide with such love that he cared no more for feats of arms, nor did he attend tournaments. He had no desire to joust. His only wish was to lie beside his wife, whom he made his sweetheart and his mistress. Embracing her and kissing her occupied all his attention, and he longed for no other pleasure ... often it was past noon before he rose from her side."[69] In other words, he renounces being a knight, preferring his new role as full-time lover/husband. However, in renouncing his knightly responsibilities, he is no longer worthy to be Enide's lover, and in the end, only her ill-conceived chastisement on these grounds can force him away from his lover's bower and into the courtly arena again. He vows to prove his prowess once more, with somewhat disastrous consequences for their immediate relationship, all of which must be resolved in the end.

The same paradox also plagues Angel. While the Angel/Buffy pairing could easily be seen as a Romeo/Juliet star-crossed lover relationship, the problem is more complex than that. Angel's role as fighter and champion literally prevents him from having a relationship with Buffy. Consider the Shanshu prophecy: If he fights valiantly, he will be rewarded with humanity (and if she is still available, presumably he gets Buffy in the bargain). Though he cannot fight valiantly and be a champion unless he is other-than-human (the source of his estrangement from Buffy in the first place). We can see the terrible cycle here. In the heart-wrenching *Angel* episode "I Will Remember You" (1.08), when Angel is turned human and then chooses to be restored to his previous form, he explains this very problem to Buffy.[70] She sees his reversion to vampirism as a weak excuse for destroying their idyllic love: "So what? You just took a whole twenty-four hours to weigh the ups and downs of being a regular Joe and decided it was more fun being a superhero?"[71] Angel's comment that prompted this line from Buffy is telling: "If anything I'm a liability to you. You take chances to protect me, and that's not just bad for you, it's bad for the people we were meant to help."[72] He cannot do what he needs to do to be worthy of her love if he is human, but without that humanity, he cannot be with her.

Being a champion who is motivated by love is the very characteristic that prevents the courtly lover from ever really attaining his love. The only way it can work is in an unreal, supernatural setting. We see an example of this necessary and perhaps only available reconciliation in Marie de France's *Lanval*.[73] Lanval is a deserving knight who unaccountably has been passed over for land and gifts by King Arthur. One day, he is out in the forest and meets a beautiful fairy queen. They are immediately smitten with each other and their love is equally and immediately consummated again and again. But there is one catch: Lanval cannot speak of this love or of her to anyone, else she will vanish and never see him again. All is well until Lanval is provoked into speaking of his love's beauty as greater than even that of Guinevere. Consequently, his beloved will not come to him. In the end, Lanval is about to stand trial for treason against Arthur (Guinevere spitefully accuses Lanval of trying to seduce her), and after refusing to speak more of his beloved, repenting his first folly, she arrives just in time to save him. She spirits him away to her fairyland, Avalon, and they live happily ever after—literally.

Unfortunately, this happy ending is not absolute since Arthur's court with its politics and deceit is incapable of holding a love as virtuous and pure as that between Lanval and his lady. Only in the world that does not exist, Avalon, can the ideals of love, marriage, and a knight's courtly courage be reconciled satisfactorily. If we view "I Will Remember You" from this perspective, we can see that the writers are working through the same general ideas, through the verisimilitude that is all-important for the romance genre. The heart-wrenching nature of the episode occurs because of what Buffy says at the very end, "How am I supposed to go on knowing what we had, what we could have had?"[74] What they could have had was perfection, idealized love, the same ideal love of Lanval and the fairy queen—but it could only happen in a non-existent world, in this case, a time that never happened, as Angel reminds Buffy when she whispers that she felt his heart beat and remembers "everything [they] did," to which Angel responds, "It never happened."[75] No, it never did, because his role as lover and his role as champion are incompatible. He cannot earn Buffy's love by giving up his role as champion, which would be necessitated by his humanity—as we see quite clearly in his final fight with the demon in this episode.

This paradox between ideals of chivalric courage and chivalric love is further illustrated in an even more intimate way in the same scene from "Graduation Day" discussed above: Angel drinking Buffy's blood. In this scene viewers witness the complex paradox that the destabilizing and consumptive nature of the lover's love—which is required of him to be a good knight—for his beloved causes: the very suffering that he would most like to alleviate, in effect his ability to be a protector, is compromised because he becomes the persecutor. The powerful nature of his love actually causes suffering and affliction to the beloved and creates within himself an ethical dilemma that compromises his chivalric worth, highlighting the paradox that prevents the happy ending that we so often mistakenly associate with romantic stories of knightly adventure.[76]

The restraint that makes Angel worthy of Buffy's love, his capacity to keep fighting to make amends, is exactly what he has to renounce in order to be in a position to keep making amends—he has to drink her blood. His renunciation in order to be worthy of her affection must itself be renounced if he is to be faithful and keep earning her love—he must not die but keep living in order to prove his worth. The difficulty that this presents for the knight, Angel in this case, is summed up by Xander's harsh chastisement on finding out that

Angel drank Buffy's blood, "Well, it's just good to know that when the chips are down and things look grim you'll feed off the girl who loves you to save your own ass."[77] Angel's obvious distress in this moment and characteristic inability to articulate the situation effectively contributes to the audience's awareness that love and duty are not especially compatible. In fact, we realize that to be a chivalric knight and courtly lover is to face an insurmountable problem of incompatibility.

Angel indeed appears to be an adaptation mirrored on the romantic hero whose love presents an insurmountable object for the attainment of that very love. Such a dilemma forces viewers, as it did readers in the twelfth and thirteenth centuries, to question the value and efficacy of love, duty, identity, and ultimately the place of these values within a society that often is not ideal enough to allow or accept the reconciliation of these paradoxical virtues. As Angel, the character and the series, gains more and more critical attention, the field is wide open for a greater focus on how the show and character successfully take on the fundamental characteristics of powerful and historical literary genres like romance.

Notes

1. "Untouched," *Angel*, DVD, written by Mere Smith, directed by Joss Whedon (2000; 20th Century–Fox, 2003).
2. Benjamin Jacob, "Los Angelus: The City of Angel," in *Reading* Angel: *The TV Spin-Off with a Soul*, ed. Stacey Abbott (London: I.B. Tauris, 2005), 75–87 at 81–82.
3. "Judgment," *Angel*, DVD, written by Joss Whedon and David Greenwalt, directed by Michael Lange (2000; 20th Century–Fox, 2003).
4. Roberta L. Krueger, "Introduction," in *The Cambridge Companion to Medieval Romance*, ed. Roberta L. Krueger (Cambridge: Cambridge University Press, 2000), 1–9 at 1.
5. Ibid.
6. *First Knight*, directed by Jerry Zucker (1995; Columbia Pictures); *A Knight's Tale*, directed by Brian Helgeland (2001; Columbia Pictures and 20th Century–Fox); *Tristan + Isolde*, directed by Kevin Reynolds (2006; 20th Century–Fox). The star-power behind these films speaks to Hollywood's investment in retelling these stories.
7. Joseph J. Duggan, "Afterword," in *Lancelot the Knight of the Cart*, trans. Burton Raffel (New Haven, CT: Yale University Press, 1997), 225–238 at 225.
8. Though one can never be sure about how a film would have been received had it been created differently, significantly here, I think, is that not one of these films received stellar reviews. The reviews for each were generally average or mixed. For a list of reviews see www.metacritic.com.
9. Elizabeth Bridges, "Grimm Realities: *Buffy* and the Use of Folklore," in *Buffy Meets the Academy*, ed. Kevin J. Durand (Jefferson, NC: McFarland, 2009), 91–103 at 91.
10. Thomas Hahn, "Gawain and Popular Chivalric Romance in Britain," in *The Cambridge Companion to Medieval Romance*, ed. Roberta L. Krueger (Cambridge: Cambridge University Press, 2000), 218–234 at 230.
11. "Judgment."
12. Kreuger, *Cambridge Companion*, 1.
13. As just one example, *The Romance of the Rose* by Guillaume de Lorris and Jean de Meun was immensely popular during the twelfth and thirteenth centuries, "a best seller in its day," yet today *The Romance of the Rose* is rarely read by those outside of university courses devoted

to romance or medieval dream visions, perhaps. See Frances Horgan, introduction to *The Romance of the Rose* by Guillaume de Lorris and Jean de Meun (1994; rpt., Oxford: Oxford University Press, 1999), ix–xxii at ix. Clearly as a scholarly field, Medieval English Romance enjoys considerable attention, but I am referring here to the non-scholarly audiences who find little to relate to in the tragedies of Tristan and Lancelot or in the knightly adventures of Yvain or Gawain beyond escapist pleasure reading.

14. Roger Sherman Loomis and Laura Hibbard Loomis, "Introduction: The Origins of Romance," in *Medieval Romances* (New York: The Modern Library, Random House, 1957), vii–xi at vi, ix. See also Gisela Guddat-Figge, "The Audience of the Romances," in *Middle English Romances*, ed. Stephen H.A. Shepherd (New York: W.W. Norton, 1995), 498–506.

15. A.B. Taylor, *An Introduction to Medieval Romance* (1930; rpt. New York: Barnes and Noble, 1969), 7.

16. Matilda Tomaryn Bruckner, "The Shape of Romance in Medieval France," in *The Cambridge Companion to Medieval Romance*, ed. Roberta L. Krueger (Cambridge: Cambridge University Press, 2000), 13–28 at 13.

17. Simon Gaunt, "Romance and Other Genres," in *The Cambridge Companion to Medieval Romance*, ed. Roberta L. Krueger (Cambridge: Cambridge University Press, 2000), 45–59 at 46. For further concerns in terms of the definition of romance and the difficulty in pinning down any one definition that applies to all of the texts that modern scholars or medieval readers and writers refer to as romance see Stephen H.A. Shepherd, "Preface," in *Middle English Romances*, ed. Stephen H.A. Shepherd (New York: W.W. Norton, 1995): xi–xiv; John Finlayson, "Definitions of Middle English Romance," *The Chaucer Review* 15, no. 1 (Summer 1980): 44–62; Yin Liu, "Middle English Romance as Prototype Genre," *Chaucer Review* 40, no. 4 (2006): 335–353.

18. Justice Potter Stewart, *Jacobellis v. Ohio* (1964), http://www.law.cornell.edu/supct/html/historics/USSC_CR_0378_0184_ZC1.html.

19. Finlayson, "Definitions of Middle English Romance," 55. The link between adventure and its use in the romance to help a knight to prove himself is also discussed in Erich Auerbach, "The Knight Sets Forth," in *Middle English Romances*, ed. Stephen H.A. Shepherd (New York: W.W. Norton, 1995): 411–427 at 422–423.

20. Even W.T.H. Jackson, who writes in *The Anatomy of Love* that the term "'courtly love' ... has very little meaning in serious literary criticism," nonetheless goes on to admit that "chivalric romances do possess features in common and show some similarities in the treatment of love...." *The Anatomy of Love* (New York: Columbia University Press, 1971), 2.

21. Finlayson, "Definitions of Middle English Romance," 57. Erich Auerbach makes this point as well, writing that "a self-portrayal of feudal knighthood with its mores and ideals is the fundamental purpose of the courtly romance. Nor are its exterior forms of life neglected— they are portrayed in leisurely fashion, and on these occasions the portrayal abandons the nebulous distance of fairy tale and gives salient pictures of contemporary conditions." Erich Auerbach, "The Knight Sets Forth," in *Middle English Romances*, ed. Stephen H.A. Shepherd (New York: W.W. Norton, 1995), 418.

22. For more on the use of metaphor, see Tracy Little, "High School is Hell: Metaphor Made Literal in *Buffy the Vampire Slayer*," in *Buffy the Vampire Slayer and Philosophy: Fear and Trembling in Sunnydale*, ed. James B. South (Chicago: Open Court, 2003), 282–293.

23. "She," *Angel*, DVD, written by David Greenwalt and Marti Noxon, directed by David Greenwalt (2000; 20th Century–Fox, 2002); "Untouched" and "Billy," *Angel*, DVD, written by Tim Minear and Jeffrey Bell, directed by David Grossman (2001; 20th Century–Fox, 2003).

24. Both critics are quoted in Stacey Abbott, *Angel*, TV Milestones Series (Detroit: Wayne State University Press, 2009), 2.

25. In some ways the comic books restored this line, as the closing sequence of *Angel* the television series refers to slaying a dragon, and *Angel: After the Fall* goes on to detail the battle with the dragon and the restoration of the line between real and imagined, the restoration, in other words, of verisimilitude.

26. Finlayson, "Definitions of Middle English Romance," 58.

27. "Graduation Day" (Part One), *Buffy the Vampire Slayer*, DVD, written and directed by Joss Whedon (1999; 20th Century–Fox, 2002); "Graduation Day" (Part Two), *Buffy the Vampire Slayer*, DVD, written and directed by Joss Whedon (1999; 20th Century–Fox, 2002).

28. "Graduation Day" (Part Two).

29. Viewers see this same issue arise in *Angel* Season Two's "Reunion" when Angel locks a room full of Wolfram & Hart lawyers in with Darla and Drusilla. This moment is specifically coded for the audience as an act that illustrates how far Angel has strayed from his ethical center. No matter how awful the lawyers might be, they are human, and to allow the vampires to slaughter them without a fight is anathema to the "good fight" that is supposed to drive Buffy and Angel. "Reunion," *Angel*, DVD, written by Tim Minear and Shawn Ryan, directed by James A. Contner (2000; 20th Century–Fox, 2003).

30. Most famously both Tristan and Lancelot come to mind, but others like Gawain in *Sir Gawain and the Green Knight* also struggle with this issue.

31. Finlayson, "Definitions of Middle English Romance," 57.

32. "Graduation Day" (Part Two).

33. Stacey Abbott, "Walking the Fine Line Between Angel and Angelus," *Slayage: The Online International Journal of Buffy Studies* 1, no. 3 (June 2001), www.slayageonline.com; Laura Resnick, "That Angel Doesn't Live Here Anymore," in *Five Seasons of* Angel: *Science Fiction and Fantasy Writers Discuss Their Favorite Vampire*, ed. Glenn Yeffeth (Dallas: BenBella, 2004), 15–22 at 16. Resnick goes beyond the Angel/Angelus dichotomy to discuss the Angel who leaves Darla and Drusilla to feed on the lawyers in "Reunion." My own conference paper from the first Slayage Conference also engages this middle persona of Angel, one who is not so clear-cut as Angel and Angelus, but one whose "beige" phrase is crucial to how he develops over the course of the first four seasons. AmiJo Comeford, "Structural Identity, or Saussure Visits *Buffy/Angel's* World: What's the Difference?" (paper presented at *SC1: The Slayage Conference on* Buffy the Vampire Slayer, Nashville, TN, May 28–30, 2004).

34. David Staines, "Introduction," *The Complete Romances of Chrétien de Troyes* (Bloomington: Indiana University Press, 1990), ix–xxviii at ix.

35. Gaunt, "Romance and Other Genres," 52.

36. Bruckner, "The Shape of Romance in Medieval France," 17.

37. W.P. Ker, *Epic and Romance: Essays on Medieval Romance* (New York: Dover, 1957), 328. Quoted in Finlayson, "Definitions of Middle English Romance," 49.

38. Gaunt, "Romance and Other Genres," 47.

39. Finlayson, "Definitions of Middle English Romance," 56.

40. Duggan, "Afterword," 230.

41. Sarah Kay provides an excellent example of this discrepancy between literary and real acceptance of the ideals of courtly love found in *Lancelot*. Chrétien de Troyes writes at the beginning of *Lancelot* that he wrote the work on the request of Marie de Champagne. He is clear that the story and idea came from Marie, and he is the scripter only. Marie, of course, was married at the time to Henry the Liberal, Count of Champagne. Even more interesting is that Philip, Count of Flanders and contemporary to when Chrétien de Troyes is supposed to have been composing *Lancelot*, found out that his wife was having an affair with one of his knights. Philip subsequently, after having plotted a trap to catch the two lovers, had the knight's head held in a sewer until he drowned. After his wife died, having been confined by Philip to her apartment as punishment for adultery, Philip married Mathilda of Portugal. However, before marrying again, he courted Marie de Champagne, a woman who commissioned the writing of *Lancelot*, a romance based entirely around an adulterous affair that mirrored that of Philip's first wife. Sarah Kay, "Courts, Clerks, and Courtly Love," in *The Cambridge Companion to Medieval Romance*, ed. Roberta L. Krueger (Cambridge: Cambridge University Press, 2000), 81–96 at 82–83.

42. Bruckner, "The Shape of Romance in Medieval France," 28; "Expecting," *Angel*, DVD, written by Howard Gordon, directed by David Semel (2000; 20th Century–Fox, 2002).

43. Duggan, "Afterword," 233.

44. Chrétien de Troyes, *Lancelot the Knight of the Cart*, trans. Burton Raffel (New Haven, CT: Yale University Press, 1997), lines 69–80.

45. The Christian symbolism here of Lancelot's wounds is clear. For further reading on the religious implications of Lancelot's wounding and the religious language used in the pursuit of secular love in *Lancelot*, see Sarah Kay, "Courts, Clerks, and Courtly Love."

46. *Lancelot*, trans. Burton Raffel, lines 4849–4850.

47. Chrétien de Troyes, *Lancelot the Knight of the Cart, The Complete Romances of Chrétien de Troyes*, trans. David Staines (Bloomington: Indiana University Press, 1990), 230.
48. Medieval legal documents also identify an adulterous affair between a woman and her husband's knight as a felony. See Duggan, "Afterword," 233.
49. Jackson, *The Anatomy of Love*, 2.
50. Though textual evidence at some points in the romance does indicate the difficulty of this position and suggests that Lancelot's love for Guinevere borders on secular idolatry, even blasphemy.
51. "City of," *Angel*, DVD, written by David Greenwalt and Joss Whedon, directed by Joss Whedon (1999; 20th Century–Fox, 2002).
52. The interchangeability of these two phrases is inherent in the opening quote for this chapter when Cordelia describes Angel's mission to Bethany. The phrase "help the hopeless" first appears in *Angel* Season One's "I Fall to Pieces," and by "Parting Gifts" it had become "help the helpless." See "I Fall to Pieces," *Angel*, DVD, written by Joss Whedon and David Greenwalt, directed by Vern Gillum (1999; 20th Century–Fox, 2002); "Parting Gifts," *Angel*, DVD, written by David Fury and Jeannine Renshaw, directed by James A. Contner (1999; 20th Century–Fox, 2002).
53. Angel functions as a champion for a woman before a mystical tribunal in order to save her baby. The episode ends with jousting, medieval style — with horses and all — an odd sight for a Los Angeles alley.
54. "Fredless," *Angel*, DVD, written by Mere Smith, directed by Marita Grabiak (2001; 20th Century–Fox, 2003).
55. "The Ring," *Angel*, DVD, written by Howard Gordon, directed by Nick Marck (2000; 20th Century–Fox, 2002). Buffy and Angel also have a very "old" feel to them, which often recalls the time period audiences associate with knights, liege lords, and fair maidens. The characters fight with ancient weapons, and Buffy is trained to use a broadsword, not a gun, and indeed when guns are introduced into the stories, our reaction is both horror and a sense of the unreal — even in a world that regularly averts apocalyptic disaster. Hence, Tara's death is more devastating that Doyle's, Anya's, or even Cordelia's because it occurs as a result not of mystical or medieval weaponry, but modern technology. The slayer and her companions are powerless against this type of evil. Buffy and Angel's world only functions if placed within the past.
56. Viewers are reminded of the disastrous potential with Buffy and Angel's relationship from the very beginning, with Buffy noting on more than one occasion that she, the slayer, cannot date Angel, a vampire.
57. "Angel," *Buffy the Vampire Slayer*, DVD, written by David Greenwalt, directed by Scott Brazil (1997; 20th Century–Fox, 2001).
58. Though the opening line for *After the Fall*, "It all started with a girl," could indeed refer to Cordelia or Fred even, we are necessarily taken back to the first line ever uttered in *Angel*, which is identical, and that moment unquestionably referred to Buffy. Janet K. Halfyard has also written about the musical connections between Buffy and Angel and notes that "the similarities of key and motif between *Buffy* and *Angel* are a thinly disguised means of reasserting the eternal bond between the two characters — although they are separated (into two series, apart from anything else), they will always be connected: the shared motif stands as a symbol of their love and also of their separation." See Janet K. Halfyard, "Love, Death, Curses and Reverses (in F minor): Music, Gender, and Identity in *Buffy the Vampire Slayer* and *Angel*," *Slayage: The Online International Journal of Buffy Studies* 1, no. 4 (December 2001), www.slayageonline.com; "Graduation Day" (Part Two).
59. "Sanctuary," Angel, DVD, written by Tim Minear and Joss Whedon, directed by Michael Lange (2000; 20th Century–Fox, 2002).
60. "Becoming" (Part One), *Buffy the Vampire Slayer*, DVD, written and directed by Joss Whedon (1998; 20th Century–Fox, 2002), and "Becoming" (Part Two), *Buffy the Vampire Slayer*, DVD, written and directed by Joss Whedon (1998; 20th Century–Fox, 2002).
61. Ibid.
62. Ibid.
63. "Helpless," *Buffy the Vampire Slayer*, DVD, written by David Fury, directed by James A. Contner (1999; 20th Century–Fox, 2002).

64. "Heartthrob," *Angel*, DVD, written and directed by David Greenwalt (2001; 20th Century–Fox, 2003).

65. Chrétien de Troyes, *Lancelot the Knight of the Cart*; Gottfried von Strassburg, *Tristan with the 'Tristan' of Thomas*, trans. A.T. Hatto (1960; rpt., London: Penguin Group, 2004).

66. Recall Angel's revelation in Season Two's "Epiphany" and his advice to Connor in Season Four's "Deep Down," reiterated again by Connor to a dying Angel in *After the Fall*, Issue #13: "We live as though the world was what it should be, to show it what it can be." See "Epiphany," *Angel*, DVD, written by Tim Minear, directed by Thomas J. Wright (2001; 20th Century–Fox, 2003); "Deep Down," *Angel*, DVD, written by Steven S. DeKnight, directed by Terrence O'Hara (2002; 20th Century–Fox, 2004); and Brian Lynch, *Angel: After the Fall* #13 (October 2008), IDW Publishing, [17].

67. Liu, "Middle English Romance as Prototype Genre," 341.

68. Duggan, "Afterword," 221.

69. Chrétien de Troyes, *Erec and Enide, The Complete Romances of Chrétien de Troyes*, trans. David Staines (Bloomington: Indiana University Press, 1990), 1–86 at 31.

70. "I Will Remember You," *Angel*, DVD, written by David Greenwalt and Jeannine Renshaw, directed by David Grossman (1999; 20th Century–Fox, 2002).

71. Ibid.

72. Ibid.

73. Marie de France, *The Lais of Marie de France* (New York: Penguin, 1986), 73–81.

74. "I Will Remember You."

75. Ibid.

76. *Buffy*'s Season Three episode "Amends" (3.10) states this problem more explicitly than anywhere else in the Buffy/Angelverse, though it is implicit everywhere. Angel stands atop a hill waiting for the sun to rise and kill him, and as they argue Buffy confronts him with the following, "And I hate it! I hate that it's so hard ... and that you can hurt me so much.... Oh, God! I wish that I wished you dead. I don't. I can't." Here Buffy expresses the exact dilemma; their love actually causes her suffering. Buffy tells Willow in Season Four's "Something Blue" (4.09) much the same referring to Angel: "I know it's nuts, but ... part of me believes that real love and passion have to go hand in hand with pain and fighting." And the idea emerges again in Season Five's "Shadow" (5.08) in a conversation between Riley and Dawn. Dawn tells Riley that Buffy "sure cries a lot less with you than she did with Angel.... Everything with him was all ... eee [high pitched crying noise], you know...? Every day was like the end of the world. She doesn't get all worked up like that over you." See "Amends," *Buffy the Vampire Slayer*, DVD, written and directed by Joss Whedon (1998; 20th Century–Fox, 2002); "Something Blue," *Buffy the Vampire Slayer*, DVD, written by Tracey Forbes, directed by Nick Marck (1999; 20th Century–Fox, 2006); "Shadow," *Buffy the Vampire Slayer*, DVD, written by David Fury, directed by James A. Contner (2000; 20th Century–Fox, 2006).

77. "Graduation Day" (Part Two).

Whedon Meets Sophocles
Prophecy and Angel[1]
LAUREL BOWMAN

Doing your mom and trying to kill your dad. Hmm. There should be a play.
— Angelus, "Soulless"[2]

There is hardly a Greek tragedy, and hardly an episode of *Angel*, that does not include a prophecy. The conventions governing the use of prophecy in Western drama were established by the fifth century B.C. in the tragedies where they first appear. These plays were produced before an audience whose makeup, background, and cultural expectations were substantially different from the audience of *Angel*. Still, although our culture has changed radically, the conventions governing the use of prophecy in drama, which were established by the time of Aeschylus, Sophocles, and Euripides, have not materially altered.

Joss Whedon skillfully manipulates his audience's knowledge of those conventions to produce the dramatic effects of prophecy in *Angel*, confounding and subverting the audience's (and the characters') classically-founded expectations in the process. This subversion of the conventions governing the use of prophecy is not merely a result of the series' transparent pleasure in surprising us, but is produced by the profound differences between the worldview of classical drama and that of *Angel*.

Angel initially seems, like Greek tragedy, to portray a universe that operates according to fixed moral rules of hierarchy and order that can be known and understood. As such, prophecy belongs to a universe that can, fundamentally, be known — and known in advance. That perception is, however, consistently undermined by the progress of events as the series unfolds. As *Angel* increasingly evolves into a world that cannot be known entirely, in which hierarchy and order need to be questioned, prophecy, as representative of the "ordered" view of the universe, needs to be questioned as well.[3] Ultimately, though sources of prophecy abound in *Angel*, prophecy is nevertheless increasingly shown to be an unreliable and in fact dangerous guide.[4] A comparison of the use of prophecy in classical drama to its use in *Angel* gives important insights into the narrative techniques and philosophical underpinnings of both imaginary universes.

Much of the tone and content of the prophecies in *Angel* is modeled quite explicitly on Biblical prophecy, particularly the Book of Revelations,[5] but the dramatic function of prophecy, rather than its content, is the primary focus of this paper. All three of the great Athenian tragedians—Aeschylus, Sophocles, and Euripides—use prophecy in their plays. Sophocles's plays make the most varied and lavish use of the device, and thus provide the most useful comparisons for our purposes, especially *Oedipus Rex*, which *Angel* directly references, and which Whedon has also used in other works.[6]

The characteristics of prophecy in classical drama are, broadly speaking, as follows:

1. *The prophecy will come from an authoritative, trustworthy and usually divinely inspired source.* In Sophocles's play *Oedipus Rex*, the prophecies that Oedipus would kill his father and marry his mother, that Oedipus's father King Laius would be killed by his son, and that the plague on Thebes would be lifted when King Laius's killer was found and expelled from the city, are all from the oracle of Apollo at Delphi, the most respected oracular temple in the Greek world.[7] Tiresias, the priest of Apollo, is inspired by Apollo to tell Oedipus the identity of Laius's killer.[8]

2. *The meaning of the prophecy will be somehow obscured for the characters in the drama.* Interpretation is made difficult by various means, of which the two most common are the ambiguity of the language and the desires of the hearers.[9] Attempts to interpret the prophecy may or may not form a large part of the plot, but misunderstanding will always feature one way or another. In *Oedipus Rex*, Oedipus misunderstands the prophecy "you will kill your father and marry your mother" out of the ambiguity of the referents and his own ignorance; he believes his parents are the King and Queen of Corinth.[10] When Oedipus sets out to find Laius's killer, the seer Tiresias tells him plainly, "You are the man you seek," but Oedipus is prevented from understanding out of his own angry determination to stay in power.[11] This causes him to accuse Tiresias of being in the pay of his political adversaries, rather than accepting that Tiresias's speech is divinely inspired.[12]

3. *The prophecy will be fulfilled, but the terms of its fulfillment will come as a surprise to the characters (though not, as a rule, to the audience).* The "true meaning" of the prophecy, though initially ambiguous and capable of multiple resolutions, will be determined by its fulfillment, which will retrospectively provide a pattern to the previous events.[13] In *Oedipus Rex* the prophecies that Oedipus will kill his father and marry his mother, and that Laius's son will kill him, have already been fulfilled as the play begins. Tiresias's prophecy that Oedipus will prove to be the man he seeks for Laius's murder is fulfilled during the play.[14] Oedipus and his mother/wife are horrified to discover who he is and what he has done. She hangs herself, and he stabs out his own eyes with his mother's robe-pins.[15]

4. *The play is not over until the prophecy is shown to have been fulfilled.* In this respect, prophecy constitutes a contract with the audience; once a prophecy has been introduced, it must be fulfilled. Fulfillment brings narrative closure.

These conventions accorded easily with the customs and beliefs of Sophocles's original audience in Athens of the fifth century B.C. Belief in prophecy was widespread, and the use of oracles, divination, auguries, and omens was common in classical Greek culture, not only unofficially by individuals but also officially, by the state.[16] The culture of the target audience of *Angel* does not (at least officially) share in this belief in the utility and reliability of prophecy. However, in order to comprehend and appreciate the use of prophecy in the series, *Angel*'s audience only needs to be aware of the classical conventions governing the use of prophecy in a dramatic text and to accept them as valid within the world of the drama.

The original audiences of Greek tragedy did, however, differ from the audience of *Angel* in one crucial respect: they already knew the general outline of the myths on which the plays were based and how they ended.[17] A tragic playwright could expect his audience to know the main events of the myth. The playwright could change details, but the main plot elements could not be changed. Everyone in the original audience of *Oedipus Rex* already knew the myth that Oedipus had killed his father and married his mother; prophecy did not increase their suspense as to the actual outcome.[18] Rather, prophecy was used to manipulate the emotional impact of the eventual outcome, by leading the characters to consider potential resolutions that the audience knew would not come about. The audience watched the characters be misled by their misinterpretations, and viewers could follow the characters in envisioning a world in which the actual end of the story not only might not, but did not, happen. For example, Anne Carson observes that use of the negative in a poem makes the audience work twice as hard, because first the poem asks them to imagine the scene described, and then, simultaneously, imagine it as described — not.[19] For example, the line "I will not tell you about a shipwreck" causes the reader to imagine a shipwreck and then not imagine it — to draw the picture and simultaneously draw a line through it. Prophecy in classical drama engages the imaginations of the audience in a similar way.

Prophecy, in essence, allowed the classical tragedians to have their cake and eat it too, by producing, in an audience that already knew the end of the story, an emotional reaction to the alternate possibilities that would not be fulfilled, and to the plight of the character who, unlike the audience, did not know the outcome, yet. The audience, knowing that Oedipus was in fact married to his mother, could listen in horrified sympathy as Oedipus considers that perhaps his mother was a slave, and the chorus sings that his father must have been a god.[20] The audience could envisage, along with the characters, an ending in which these hopeful interpretations might prove correct, and simultaneously imagine the emotional impact that the ending they knew was coming would have on the ignorant characters. The ironic tension between the two resolutions, the two mental images held simultaneously — the one the on-stage interpretations of the prophecy enabled characters and audience both to imagine, and the one the audience knew was really in store — gave the actual event a doubled emotional impact, and the use of prophecy to create that impact was crucial.

Although the general outline of the myth will have been known to the classical audience in advance, the prophecies found in the plays generally did not form part of the earlier version of the myth and were added by the playwrights.[21] For example, although the audience knew from other tellings that Oedipus had in fact killed his father and married his mother,[22] Sophocles seems to have invented the Delphic oracle that prophesies these events to Oedipus and inserted the oracle into the story for the purposes of his play. This is not to say that prophecies are never found in earlier versions of the myth. If a prophecy was found in the pre-existing myth, tragic playwrights made use of it; if there was not, they tended to invent one.

Within the play, the primary function of the prophecy was not to inform but rather to mislead the consultant[23] and thereby motivate the action that would bring about the tragic conclusion. In *Oedipus Rex* the prophecy that the plague on Thebes will be lifted if Laius's killer is exiled causes Oedipus's search for the killer, which sets in motion the events that culminate in his discovery of his own identity as his father's murderer and his mother's husband. Narratively, then, the prophecy drives the play's action. From the perspective of the audience, prophecies serve several further functions. Structurally, they give shape to the narrative and tell the audience what the story will be and when it is over. The playwright could produce any number of different plays from a given myth, but the prophecy shaped the particular story the audience saw. From the prophecy, the audience learns what question, when resolved, will bring the end of the play. For the ancient audience, the question in *Oedipus Rex* was not "Who killed Laius?" but "When will Oedipus discover what he's done?" The audience's emotional engagement with the play is then created by following Oedipus's reactions to two prophecies.

The effect of the prophecies, in tragedy, is thus to put the audience in the position of the characters and thereby engage emotionally with the story as it plays out before them. The audience knows what the characters only assume, that the prophecy will be fulfilled, but like the characters, they do not know when or how it will be interpreted or how the characters will react. Prophecy in Greek tragedy thus creates suspense about events within the play, despite the fact that the audience knows the ending. The audience's combination of foreknowledge and sympathy only increases the emotional impact of the unfolding events.

A favorite Whedon technique, the self-fulfilling prophecy specifically, was also frequently used in Greek tragedies to increase emotional impact. Self-fulfilling prophecies always rely on the protagonist's assumption that he knows what the prophecy means and, therefore, how it can be evaded. Had Oedipus not tried to avoid fulfilling the Delphic oracle's prophecy, but simply accepted it and gone back to the king and queen of Corinth — his parents, as he thought — he would never have met his biological parents at all. Only because he tried to evade the prophecy by going to Thebes did he kill his father Laius on the road and marry his mother Jocasta when he arrived there. The wrenching emotional impact on the audience is increased by observing the character's earnest attempts to avoid the very outcome his actions bring about.

The interference caused in characters' fates by self-fulfilling prophecy raises an important question: If the gods lead the protagonists to such catastrophes by giving ambiguous prophecies, does it follow that the gods are malicious or evil? The answer, in Greek tragedy, is no.[24] The noted classical scholar John Peradotto has argued that the author of all of Oedipus's misfortunes in *Oedipus Rex* was not Oedipus, but Apollo himself, who sent the oracles for Oedipus to misunderstand.[25] This interpretation, however congenial to a modern readership, would never have been accepted by the ancient audience. Oedipus misinterprets the oracle, true, but it is his responsibility to go back and ask a clarifying question if he does not understand the first answer; and we are reminded of this duty by the new king Creon's refusal to do anything with the now blinded Oedipus, even exile him from Thebes, before first sending to Delphi to find out what exactly the god wants.[26] Oedipus's father Laius was, moreover, cursed with death at his son's hand for good reason.[27] Human ignorance, desire, and, on occasion, impiety contribute greatly to our woes, but that is not the fault of the gods of Greek tragedy, who are often harsh, but fair and, ultimately, trustworthy.

Though the *Angel* audience does not necessarily share the assumptions of the ancient audience about the efficacy of prophecy in daily life, we quickly learn to suspend our disbelief. In the first episode, the half-demon Doyle arrives bearing visions for Angel directly from The Powers That Be.[28] The first season instructs both the *Angel* protagonists and the series' audience in the conventions governing prophecy within the series. These are identical with the conventions of Greek tragedy: prophecies come from authoritative sources, are usually misinterpreted or otherwise fumbled by the protagonist, and constitute a narrative contract with the audience. They are invariably fulfilled and by their fulfillment provide both closure and a retrospective patterning to previous events.

In Season One, the three sources of prophecy used in *Angel* are strictly the three sources found in classical drama: inspired seers, official oracles, and written texts containing prophecies from unknown but trustworthy sources.[29] The seers, inspired in tragedy by Apollo, are represented in *Angel* by Doyle and, after his death, Cordelia, who are inspired with visions from The Powers That Be. The oracle at Delphi is replaced by the Oracles, in pseudo–Greek costume, statue-like bronze skin paint, archaic diction, and a stone temple background,[30] and the Scroll of Aberjian, a collection of written prophecies of immense age and value, is found locked in the crypt of Wolfram & Hart.[31]

From the use of these sources for prophecy, protagonists and audience learn that prophecies can be trusted and that The Powers That Be, like the gods of tragedy, may be harsh (for example, they let Doyle die), but they are also fair and working on the side of good, wanting only to help Angel help the helpless. If, despite the visions, oracles, or scrolls, Angel fails, it is always because he or his team have misinterpreted or otherwise somehow erred, not because the prophecies were themselves false. For example, in *Angel*'s first episode, Doyle comes to Angel with a vision of Tina, who is trying to escape a powerful, older, evil vampire predator. Tina flees Angel's protection and dies, but Doyle's vision was accurate — she was in mortal and supernatural danger from which she required rescuing. Though Angel fails to save his client's life in this instance, Doyle's and Cordelia's visions throughout Season One direct Angel's efforts to a successful conclusion more often than not.[32] Prophecy is also used in Season One to reassure the audience and Angel himself that there is an overarching design and that he is an important part of it, a warrior for good in the battle between good and evil. Not only do The Powers think that Angel is sufficiently significant to send visions for his use, as Cordelia points out, they even know him by name.[33] The Scroll of Aberjian contains a passage about a "vampire with a soul," about which Wesley comments, "There is a design, Angel. Hidden in the chaos as it may be, but, it's there, and you have your place in it."[34]

Doyle's and Cordelia's visions usually provide the framework for a single episode, as in "City of" (1.01), echoing prophecy's use in the self-contained narratives of Greek tragedies. However, the Scroll of Aberjian introduces a structural function of prophecy that is a logical extension of its use in tragedy, but is not generally found there. Since prophecy forms a narrative contract with the audience — once the prophecy has been introduced, it must be resolved — if a prophecy is not resolved by the end of an episode, it must carry over until it is. A prophecy can thus be used to link several episodes, even whole seasons and beyond.[35] Although Greek tragedies were always produced in groups of three, to be performed on the same day, usually each play of the three was a stand-alone, with no connections between one story and the next, so prophecies rarely performed this linking function.[36] Once Whedon introduces the use of prophecy in *Angel* to link episodes progressively, greater use is made of it. The Shanshu prophecy in the Scroll of Aberjian is not resolved until the last episode of Season Five, and reappears in the post-series comics.[37] Similarly, the complex story woven around the Connor prophecies in the Nyazian Scrolls have enormous significance throughout Seasons Three and Four and are fulfilled — differently — at the ends of both Seasons Four and Five[38]; and Cordelia's "Beast" visions provide the framework for most of Season Four.[39]

Having established the classical conventions governing the use of prophecy in *Angel* in Season One and extended them through the introduction of the multiple-episode prophecies like the Shanshu, Whedon signals the end of his strict reliance on classical principles in the last episode of the season when the demon Voca kills the Oracles in their own temple.[40] From Season Two on, prophecy increases in significance, but variations in its form and function are increasingly introduced. To the traditional classical sources, Whedon adds a number of sources never engaged by classical authors, including Lorne, a musical destiny-reading empath demon, who is introduced in the first episode of Season Two as a new principal character.[41] Other non-traditional sources of prophetic and mystical knowledge include a demon swami; a phone psychic; the Conduit; the Axis of Pythia; Dinza, an Eleusinian mystery and "dark demi-goddess of the lost"; a Hamburger Loa; even a Magic 8-Ball.[42] The classical dramatic functions of prophecy, however, remain essentially the same: to shape the story; to tell the audience what will be significant and what issues will be resolved by the ending; to create suspense; and to engage the audience emotionally, as well as intellectually.

Still, as noted above, the audience of *Angel* differs from the audience of Greek tragedy in one major respect: it does not already know the end of the story. This difference allows Whedon to make a drastic shift in the significance of prophecy in the series. For the tragic audience, prophecy creates a possible alternative path through events. For the audience of Angel, it creates a possible future. Reactions to prophecy in Greek tragedy show the protagonists' efforts to avoid their fate. Reactions to prophecy in *Angel* show the characters' efforts to create a fate for themselves.[43] Prophecy in the two genres thus engages the audience in different ways. Because the tragic audience knows the end of the story, prophecy encourages sympathy which is only increased by ironic foreknowledge. Because the audience of *Angel* does not know the outcome any more than the characters do, prophecy in *Angel* encourages the audience to share the characters' efforts at interpretation and produces an engagement born of identification and shared endeavor.

The audience's ignorance of the end of the story, in *Angel*, is an essential component of the later seasons' destabilization of prophecy as a reliable source of useful information. Even though the audience and characters can continue to assume that prophecies will be fulfilled, the audience participates in the characters' frustration as efforts to interpret prophecy in advance fail again and again. The foreknowledge-equipped tragic audience knows that if the characters could only understand the prophecy, the information would be useful to them. Lacking that foreknowledge, *Angel*'s audience is in a position to feel uncertain of both the meaning of the prophecy and the merits of giving prophecy in general priority over any other source of information. For example, the audience, having seen Wes's successive mistranslations of the Shanshu prophecy in Season One, and having been reminded of those errors earlier in Season Three, has been warned to be dubious about the utility of his enormous efforts to interpret the Nyazian Prophecies later in Season Three, even before it is discovered that the prophecy is a forgery.[44] Similarly, the audience cannot help but wonder why Angel so often runs to Caritas to ask Lorne for help when ordinary detective work would frequently do the job just as well.[45]

This general uncertainty about the utility of prophecy in *Angel* is enhanced by persistent failures of interpretation, as well as by the increasing unreliability of the sources as the series progresses. In tragedy, the sources for prophecy — seers, oracles, and prophetic texts — are unerring, though interpretation often miscarries. In *Angel*, the sources for prophecy themselves become increasingly dubious over the course of the series. No source is invariably reliable, though none is invariably wrong. Cordelia, the infallible source of true visions in Season One, is tormented early in Season Three by a demon psychic who sends her false visions that she cannot distinguish from true ones.[46] Her true visions also become life-threatening, and ultimately she chooses to become part demon in order to keep the visions and survive.[47] This choice makes her later moral corruption possible, and puts her in a position to be hijacked by an evil Higher Power bent on giving birth to itself in this dimension.[48] Her visions, or her accounts of them, become deliberately deceptive in Season Four, even unleashing Angelus into Los Angeles.[49] Likewise, Lorne, whose gift for reading destiny originally seems trustworthy, gives advice that more than once pointlessly risks Angel's life; is generally wrong-headed; or, as the series progresses, simply wrong.[50] He mistakenly identifies Angelus as Angel in Season Four, and in Season Five fatally misreads the deceptively innocent Knox.[51] This last error contributes to the death of Winifred "Fred" Burkle, after which he apparently loses his gift entirely.[52]

In addition to human and/or demon seers, prophecies in *Angel* come from written documents. These records of prophecies on scrolls and papyri prove to be susceptible not only to errors in transmission, mistranslation, and misinterpretation, but also to deliberate fraud. Indeed, a crucial prophecy in the Nyazian Scrolls turns out to have been forged by a time-traveling demon.[53] As the series progresses, it becomes increasingly unclear whether even The Powers themselves are to be trusted, since a renegade Power That Be, Jasmine, tries to destroy the world in Season Four.[54]

The over-reliance on prophecy by Angel Investigations is highlighted by the effort and danger involved in acquiring and interpreting prophecies. These efforts and their consequences frequently form part of the dramatic action in *Angel*. Cordelia's visions nearly kill her.[55] Angel steals the Scroll of Aberjian from the Wolfram & Hart vaults, and Wesley and Gunn steal the Nyazian Scrolls from a private collector, at considerable risk.[56] The Nyazian Scrolls are blown up in an attack on the Hyperion, the fragments stolen and reconstructed by Wolfram & Hart, and the content reconstructed by Wesley from commentaries and translations.[57] Wesley is shown making attempts over several episodes to gradually arrive at and verify a translation and interpretation of the texts of the Prophecies of Aberjian and the Nyazian Scrolls.[58] Despite the extraordinary pains expended, the results tend to be inconclusive, and the correct interpretation will not necessarily be recognized even if it is found.[59]

Despite these issues, Angel Investigations persistently places a high value on prophecy over other sources of information. Wesley spends enormous time and effort on interpretation of the Nyazian Scrolls. Cordelia refuses to give up her visions even though they are increasingly agonizing and debilitating, because she believes they supply her value to the team.[60] When Angel is in need of advice he relies on prophetic sources whenever he can — the Oracles, the Axis of Pythia, Dinza in the Lair of the Lost, and Lorne, even when more conventional methods of investigation would be equally effective, and in spite of the fact that Lorne himself frequently declines to read, usually because the singer should be relying on other sources of advice, a hint Team Angel never seems to take.[61] In short, Angel uses everything, it seems, but his own common sense.

This reliance upon prophecy has dangerous implications. In traditional Greek tragedy there is a clear sense that if the characters only understood a prophecy, they would not make the mistakes they do. In Sophocles's *Oedipus at Colonus*, for example, Oedipus correctly interprets a cluster of prophecies and uses the information successfully to destroy his enemies.[62] In contrast, reliance on prophecy in *Angel*, believing even in the importance of prophecy, seems to lead the characters into far worse error than ignorance or lack of interest would ever have done. Whedon emphasizes the dangers of reliance on prophecy in *Angel* with the use of the technique of the self-fulfilling prophecy in the complex of prophecies surrounding Angel's son Connor. Wesley interprets a crucial line in the Nyazian Prophecies as "the father will kill the son," and he makes strenuous efforts to verify his results in other sources—falling asleep on his books and even consulting the Hamburger Loa.[63] When his efforts to find any other interpretation of the line fail, he kidnaps Connor to save Angel from killing the son he loves. The result of his actions is both disastrous and ultimately self-fulfilling. In the Season Four finale Angel does, in fact, kill his son.[64] This prophecy, however, proves to have been forged by the time-traveling demon Sahjahn, in place of the prophecy originally in the Nyazian Scrolls, which said that Angel's son would kill Sahjahn.[65] Sahjahn's attempt to evade the prophecy of his own death in turn sets in motion the complex two-season-long train of events that leads to his being killed by Connor in Season Five.[66]

Angel's audience does not know what would have happened if Wesley or Sahjahn had simply ignored the prophecies when they first encountered them, though it would be tempting to assume that none of the ensuing disasters would have occurred; all that is certain is that the attempts to evade the prophecies did not succeed. But here *Angel*'s audience is in a very different position from the audience of Greek tragedy. The audience of Greek tragedy knows all along that prophecy will be fulfilled, so it is not tempting to question the utility of prophecy, but only to hope that the protagonist will interpret it correctly. For

Angel's audience, the end of the story is not set in stone; we do not know the final outcome until Angel's knife flashes down across Connor's throat, or Sahjahn's head rolls across the floor. It is, therefore, possible for *Angel*'s audience to believe that these outcomes are not inevitable, and that ignoring the prophecies could have produced different — and better — results. *Angel*'s audience's emotional engagement with the outcome is enhanced by its lack of the ironic intellectual distance of the tragic audience. The audience of *Angel* is thus encouraged by its ignorance of the ending both to believe that the story could have ended differently and to care.

The last and thematically most important prophecy to be considered is the Shanshu prophecy, which spans all five seasons of *Angel*. This prophecy, like all the rest, obeys the conventions laid down in Greek tragedy — it comes from an authoritative source; it is difficult to interpret; it is fulfilled in a surprising way; and the story is not over until it is fulfilled. Despite its adherence to the classical form, this prophecy is used to demonstrate most radically the dangers of reliance on prophecy in *Angel*. The self-fulfillment of the prophecies from the Nyazian Scrolls demonstrates to the audience the dangers of relying on prophecy as a practical guide. The Shanshu prophecy is used more radically, to demonstrate the folly of relying on prophecy to supply meaning to life.

The Shanshu prophecy in the Scroll of Aberjian predicts that the vampire with a soul will "shanshu," a term Wesley progressively translates as "live," "die," and "live until he dies," or "become human."[67] To Angel, the Shanshu means that he will be rewarded with the restoration of his humanity, once he has fulfilled his destiny by fighting for good in an apocalypse. Angel is not interested in becoming human for the pleasures that state offers — indeed, he rejects such an opportunity early in Season One when he becomes human by accident — but he does desire it as a sign of forgiveness for his sins, and as a validation of his role as a hero and a warrior on the side of right.[68] He is eager to accept Wesley's interpretation that the prophecy signifies that he has a destiny and is important in the larger scheme.[69] The Shanshu prophecy is valuable to Angel, in short, as an external validation on which he can base his feeling of self-worth.

In the following three seasons, the audience is increasingly given reasons to be dubious about the reliability of prophecy, and the Shanshu prophecy's renewed significance in Season Five must be read with that in mind. Spike, another souled vampire champion, joins Team Angel in Season Five, and it is not clear which vampire is destined to receive the Shanshu. Although Angel tells Spike that he no longer believes the prophecy, he rereads it in private, and is seriously distressed at the possibility that the prophecy might not refer to him after all.[70] Wesley and the demonic Circle of the Black Thorn, which Angel infiltrates late in Season Five, are both convinced that faith in the Shanshu prophecy is a sign that Angel continues to hope for recognition, forgiveness, and a reward for good behavior from The Powers That Be.[71] Wes thinks this hope is necessary and fears that without it Angel will fall into despair. The Circle of the Black Thorn fears that hope of the Shanshu could cause Angel to betray them, and in the last episode of the series, they force Angel to sign away his interest in the Shanshu to prove his loyalty.[72]

The audience, however, will not have forgotten that Wesley's over-reliance on prophecy has been misguided before. In the context of the dangers of reliance on prophecy that have been increasingly demonstrated over the five seasons of the series, it is clear that Wesley and the Circle of the Black Thorn are both wrong. In fact, for Angel, signing away his prophesied Shanshu is the most hopeful thing he could do. After five years of relying on prophecy not only to tell him what to do but to give him a reason to do it, Angel is ready to fight for good for no reason other than his own hope of making the world a better place through his own efforts. After Angel signs away his hope of Shanshu he leads the team to bring down the Circle and fights for good in the resulting apocalypse.[73]

Whedon has thus used the conventions governing prophecy in Greek tragedy to question the worldview that produces prophecy at all. Prophecies may contain accurate information about the future, but that does not mean that they should be relied upon as a guide for action or external validation of meaning in life. Greek tragedy, using the same conventions, does not ask these questions, much less produce the answers Whedon does. Although Jocasta, Oedipus's doomed wife and mother, says at one point in the play that prophecies are unreliable and that she "would not, for the sake of prophecy, look to her right hand or her left,"[74] the events of the play prove her drastically wrong. However, Jocasta's attitude is validated in *Angel* as overwhelmingly the wisest course.

In *Oedipus Rex*, after all is known, Jocasta is dead; Oedipus has blinded himself; and the new king, Creon, refuses to do anything, even send Oedipus into exile, until he has first consulted Delphi to discover the will of the god. John Peradotto argues that after everything else Apollo has done in the play, this action constitutes a triumph of despair, and the utter breakdown of confidence in the ability of human reason to successfully negotiate the world. The rhetoric of prophecy in the play makes Creon's choice appear the only possible one, but it is, nevertheless, precisely the wrong thing for Creon to do.[75]

No ancient audience would have accepted Peradotto's reading of the *Oedipus*, but Joss Whedon would. Whedon's use of prophecy in *Angel* gave us five televised years of Peradotto's reading of the *Oedipus* made explicit. Reliance on prophecy in *Angel* generally leads to disaster. Much better results are achieved by making your own destiny, day by day.[76]

Notes

1. I would like to thank the editors of this volume, the readers at Tea at the Ford, and Lauren Mayes for their helpful critiques of this paper, and the attendees at the conference

"Classical Threads in Fantasy and Science Fiction on Contemporary Television" (Open University, Milton Keynes, UK, January 7, 2004), for their comments on an earlier version.

2. "Soulless," *Angel*, DVD, written by Sarah Fain and Elizabeth Craft, directed by Sean Astin (2003; 20th Century–Fox, 2004).

3. For the inherent implication of prophecy that a "divine order" exists, see Rebecca W. Bushnell, *Prophesying Tragedy: Sign and Voice in Sophocles's Theban Plays* (Ithaca: Cornell University Press, 1988), 18–19. In this analysis I am implicitly describing *Angel* as a postmodern text. For discussion of the Buffyverse as a postmodern text, see Toby Daspit, "*Buffy* Goes to College, Adam Murders to Dissect: Education and Knowledge in Postmodernity," in Buffy the Vampire Slayer *and Philosophy: Fear and Trembling in Sunnydale*, ed. James B. South (Chicago: Open Court Books, 2003), 117–130. For discussion of postmodern figures in *Angel*, see Jennifer A. Hudson "'She's Unpredictable': Illyria and the Liberating Potential of Chaotic Postmodern Identity," *Americana: The Journal of American Popular Culture* (March 2005), http://www.americanpopularculture.com/archive/tv/shes_unpredictable.htm.

4. A "prophecy" is a statement of accurate knowledge about the past, present, or future, which has been derived from a supernatural source. The prophecy revealed by the Delphic oracle in *Oedipus Rex* that Oedipus will kill his father and marry his mother is a prophecy in that it comes from a supernatural source (the god Apollo, speaking through an inspired priestess), and in that it comes true. The first of many examples of prophecy in *Angel* is Doyle's vision of Tina in "City of," *Angel*, DVD, written and directed by Joss Wheldon (1999; 20th Century–Fox, 2002).

5. Lorne, for example, acknowledges this connection when he remarks of his reading of one of Cordelia's visions, "Well, I haven't read the Book of Revelations lately, but if I was searching for adjectives, I'd probably start there." See "Slouching Towards Bethlehem," *Angel*, DVD written by Jeffrey Bell, directed by Skip Schoolnik (2002; 20th Century–Fox, 2004).

6. The opening epigraph from "Soulless" refers to the plot of Sophocles's *Oedipus Tyrannos*, in *Fabulae*, ed. Hugh Lloyd-Jones and N. G. Wilson (New York: Oxford University Press, 1990). This play will hereafter be cited as "*Oedipus Rex*" as the title most familiar to the readers. The end credits of "The Puppet Show," *Buffy the Vampire Slayer*, DVD, written by Dean Batali and Rob Des Hotel, directed by Ellen Pressman (1997; 20th Century–Fox, 2001) are a pastiche of the same play, performed by Buffy, Willow, and Xander. Classical references abound in Whedon's work: for discussion see Naomi Alderman, "Those Whom the Powers Wish to Destroy, They Must First Make Mad: Gods, Prophecy and Death: The Classical Roots of Madness in *BtVS*" (Paper presented at the *Slayage Conference on* Buffy the Vampire Slayer," Nashville, TN, May 27–30, 2004).

7. Sophocles, *Oedipus Rex*, 792–795, 710–726, 95–106.

8. Ibid., 350, 362.

9. On the difficulty of interpreting prophecy see Bushnell, *Prophesying Tragedy*, 14. On ambiguity of language, see Jan Zwicky, "Oracularity," *Metaphilosophy* 34 (2003): 488–509. On the desires of the hearers, see Steven Lattimore, "Oedipus & Tiresias," *California Studies in Classical Antiquity* 8 (1975): 105–11.

10. Sophocles, *Oedipus Rex*, 774–775.

11. Ibid., 350, 362.

12. Ibid., 378–390.

13. See Deborah H. Roberts, *Apollo and His Oracle in the Oresteia* (Göttingen: Vandenhoeck und Ruprecht, 1984), 31–33, for a full discussion of the function of oracles in tragedy to provide retrospective patterning and thus narrative closure.

14. Sophocles, *Oedipus Rex*, 1185.

15. Ibid., 1265–1280.

16. See Jon D. Mikalson, *Honor Thy Gods: Popular Religion in Greek Tragedy* (Chapel Hill: University of North Carolina Press, 1991); Joseph Fontenrose, *The Delphic Oracle: Its Responses and Operations With a Catalogue of Responses* (Berkeley: University of California Press, 1978); and J.C. Kamerbeek, "Prophecy in Tragedy," *Mnemosyne* 18 (1965): 29–40.

17. See Kamerbeek, "Prophecy in Tragedy" and James V. Morrison, *Homeric Misdirection: False Predictions in the Iliad*, Michigan Monographs in Classical Antiquity (Ann Arbor: University of Michigan Press, 1992), 21–22.

18. For a different view and discussion of, see Erich Bächli, "Sophocles," in *Die Künst-*

lerische Funktion Von Orakelsprüchen, Weissagungen, Träumen Usw. In Der Griechischen Tragödie (Winterthur: Verlag P. G. Keller, 1954), 29–62.

19. Anne Carson, "Simonides Negative," *Arethusa* 21 (1988): 147–57.
20. Sophocles, *Oedipus Rex*, 1062, 1098–1107.
21. See Kamerbeek, "Prophecy in Tragedy," 29.
22. The story of Oedipus's murder of his father and marriage to his mother is first found in Homer's *Odyssey* 11.271–280; See Homer, *The Odyssey, Books 1–12*, vol. 3, Homeri Opera, ed. T. W. Allen (New York: Oxford University Press, 1922).
23. Bushnell, *Prophesying Tragedy*, 14.
24. In Sophocles and Aeschylus, at least; Euripides, the Joss Whedon of his time, asks some harder questions.
25. John Peradotto, "Disauthorizing Prophecy: The Ideological Mapping of Oedipus Tyrannus (the 1990 Presidential Address)," *Tansactions of the American Philological Association (1974–)* 122 (1992): 1–15.
26. Creon announces his intention of consulting the oracle in *Oedipus Rex*, 1438–1439 and 1442–144.
27. Laius was responsible for the death of his host Pelops's son. See Hyginus, "Fabulae," trans. Mary Grant: http://www.theoi.com/Text/HyginusFabulae2.html (accessed December 6, 2009): 85.
28. "City of."
29. Such a collection is used in tragedy in, e.g., Sophocles, "Oedipus Coloneus," in *Fabulae*, ed. Lloyd-Jones and Wilson, 450–455.
30. "I Will Remember You," *Angel*, DVD, written by David Greenwalt and Jeannine Renshaw, directed by David Grossman (1999; 20th Century–Fox, 2002); "Parting Gifts," *Angel*, DVD, written by David Fury and Jeannine Renshaw, directed by James A. Contner (1999; 20th Century–Fox, 2002); "To Shanshu in L.A.," *Angel*, DVD, written and directed by David Greenwalt (2000; 20th Century–Fox, 2002).
31. "Blind Date," *Angel*, DVD, written by Jeannine Renshaw, directed by Thomas J. Wright (2000; 20th Century–Fox, 2002), and "To Shanshu in L.A."
32. For example "Lonely Hearts," *Angel*, DVD, written by David Fury, directed by James A. Contner (1999; 20th Century–Fox, 2002); "I Fall to Pieces," *Angel*, DVD, written by Joss Whedon and David Greenwalt, directed by Vern Gilum (1999; 20th Century–Fox, 2002); "Parting Gifts"; and "She," *Angel*, DVD, written by David Greenwalt and Marti Noxon, directed by David Greenwalt (2000; 20th Century–Fox, 2002).
33. "Somnambulist," *Angel*, DVD, written by Tim Minear, directed by Winrich Kolbe (2000; 20th Century–Fox, 2002).
34. "Blind Date."
35. In fact for this reason, prophecies tend to appear specifically in narrative genres that relate to events extending over a period of time: see Roberts, "Apollo and His Oracle," 17.
36. It's worth noting, though, that in the only tragic trilogy still extant, the *Oresteia* of Aeschylus, the inspired vision of the seer Cassandra in the first play predicts the entire plot arc of all three plays. See Aeschylus, "Agamemnon," in *Septem Quae Supersunt Tragoedias*, ed. Denys Page (USA: Oxford University Press, 1973), 1080–1330.
37. "Not Fade Away," *Angel*, DVD, written by Joss Whedon and Jeffrey Bell, directed by Jeffrey Bell (2004; 20th Century–Fox, 2004). Brian Lynch, *Angel: After the Fall # 12* (September 2008).
38. Introduced in "Offspring," *Angel*, DVD, written by David Greenwalt, directed by Turi Meyer (2001; 20th Century–Fox, 2003).
39. Introduced in "Slouching Towards Bethlehem."
40. "To Shanshu in L.A."
41. "Judgment," *Angel*, DVD, written by David Greenwalt and Joss Whedon, directed by Michael Lange (2000; 20th Century–Fox, 2003).
42. "Guise Will be Guise," *Angel*, DVD, written by Jane Espenson, directed by Krishna Rao (2000; 20th Century–Fox, 2003); "Over the Rainbow," *Angel*, DVD, written by Mere Smith, directed by Fred Keller (2001; 20th Century–Fox, 2003); "Birthday," *Angel*, DVD, written by Mere Smith, directed by Michael Grossman (2001; 20th Century–Fox, 2003); "Loyalty," *Angel*, DVD, written by Mere Smith, directed by James A. Contner (2002; 20th

Century–Fox, 2003); "The House Always Wins," *Angel*, DVD, written by David Fury, directed by Marita Grabiak (2002; 20th Century–Fox, 2004); "Ground State," *Angel*, DVD, written by Mere Smith, directed by Michael Grossman (2002; 20th Century–Fox, 2004); "Players," *Angel*, DVD, written by Jeffrey Bell, Sarah Fain, and Elizabeth Craft, directed by Michael Grossman (2003; 20th Century–Fox, 2004).

43. Other scholars have noted the fundamental existentialist ethics of the Whedonverse and its emphasis on the characters' self-creation of their destinies through their own choices. See most recently J. Douglas Rabb, and J. Michael Richardson, "Myth, Metaphor, Morality and Monsters: The Espenson Factor and Cognitive Science in Joss Whedon's Love Ethic," *Slayage*, 28 (Summer 2009), www.slayageonline.com, and cf. also J. Michael Richardson and J. Douglas Rabb, *The Existential Joss Whedon: Evil and Human Freedom in* Buffy the Vampire Slayer, Angel, Firefly *and* Serenity (Jefferson, NC: McFarland, 2007).

44. "To Shanshu in L.A." in Season One and "Offspring" and "Loyalty" in Season Three. The relevant prophecy is revealed to be a forgery in "Forgiving," *Angel*, DVD, written by Jeffrey Bell, directed by Turi Meyer (2002; 20th Century–Fox, 2003).

45. For example, in "Judgment" Angel goes to Lorne for help locating his client before trying to find her any other way.

46. "That Vision Thing," *Angel*, DVD, written and directed by Jeffrey Bell (2001; 20th Century–Fox, 2003).

47. "Birthday."

48. Skip gives the origins of Cordelia's vulnerability in "Inside Out," *Angel*, DVD, written and directed by Steven S. DeKnight (2003; 20th Century–Fox, 2004). Cordelia explains her hijacking by a higher power in "You're Welcome," *Angel*, DVD, written and directed by David Fury (2004; 20th Century–Fox, 2004).

49. "Calvary," *Angel*, DVD, written by Jeffrey Bell, Stephen S. DeKnight, and Mere Smith, directed by Bill L. Norton (2003; 20th Century–Fox, 2004).

50. Lorne's gift is useful and trustworthy. For example in "Happy Anniversary," *Angel*, DVD, written by David Greenwalt, directed by Bill L. Norton (2001; 20th Century–Fox, 2003), Lorne's chance reading of a client prevents the end of the world. His advice risks Angel's life to no purpose in "Guise Will Be Guise" and "The Trial," *Angel*, DVD, written by David Greenwalt, Tim Minear, and Douglas Petrie, directed by Bruce Seth Green (2000; 20th Century–Fox, 2003). His advice is very much off the mark in "Fredless," *Angel*, DVD, written by Mere Smith, directed by Marita Grabiak (2001; 20th Century–Fox, 2003), and misleading in "Sleep Tight," *Angel*, DVD, written by David Greenwalt, directed by Terrence O'Hara (2002; 20th Century–Fox, 2003).

51. Lorne misreads Angelus in "Calvary" and admits to having misread Knox in "Shells," *Angel*, DVD, written and directed by Steven S. DeKnight (2004; 20th Century–Fox, 2004). See Jennifer Hamilton's essay in this collection for more on Lorne's role in *Angel*.

52. Winifred Burkle dies in "Shells," and Lorne's gift has entirely forsaken him in the next episode, "Underneath," *Angel*, DVD, written by Sarah Fain and Elizabeth Craft, directed by Skip Schoolnik (2004; 20th Century–Fox, 2004).

53. "Forgiving."

54. "Peace Out," *Angel*, DVD, written by David Fury, directed by Jefferson Kibbee (2003; 20th Century–Fox, 2004).

55. "Birthday."

56. "Blind Date" (Scroll of Aberjian); "Offspring" (Nyazian Scrolls).

57. "Lullaby," *Angel*, DVD, written and directed by Tim Minear (2001; 20th Century–Fox, 2003), and "Couplet," *Angel*, DVD, written by Tim Minear and Jeffrey Bell, directed by Tim Minear (2002; 20th Century–Fox, 2003). Sharon Sutherland and Sarah Swan argue that written prophecies in *Angel* are treated like statutes, and visions as interpretive readings, in civil law; and that Wesley and Fred employ the same careful, fine-toothed interpretive strategies used by lawyers. See Sharon Sutherland and Sarah Swan, "The Rule of Prophecy: Source of Law in the City of *Angel*," in *Reading* Angel: The TV Spin-Off With a Soul, ed. Stacey Abbott (London: I.B. Tauris, 2005), 132–145.

58. "Blind Date" and "To Shanshu in L.A."(Scroll of Aberjian); "Couplet" and "Loyalty" (Nyazian Scrolls).

59. When Fred's calculations in "Offspring" reveal that the Nyazian scrolls predict that

the world ended "last March," she exclaims. "That can't be right!" However, her interpretation is correct, since Connor had been conceived the previous March, setting in motion the world-ending events predicted in the scrolls.

60. "There's No Place Like Plrtz Glrb," *Angel*, DVD, written and directed by David Greenwalt (2001; 20th Century–Fox, 2003).

61. Oracles: "I Will Remember You," "Parting Gifts," "To Shanshu in L.A."; Axis of Pythia: "Ground State"; Lorne: "Judgment." Lorne declines to read in "Dear Boy," *Angel*, DVD, written and directed by David Greenwalt (2000; 20th Century–Fox, 2003); "Redefinition," *Angel*, DVD, written by Mere Smith, directed by Michael Grossman (2000; 20th Century–Fox, 2003); "Disharmony," *Angel*, DVD, written by David Fury, directed by Fred Keller (2001; 20th Century–Fox, 2003); and "Offspring."

62. Sophocles, *Oedipus Colonus*, 1384–1392.

63. "Loyalty."

64. Albeit so that Connor can be born into a new life, free from the trauma of his current life. See "Home," *Angel*, DVD, written and directed by Tim Minear (2003; 20th Century–Fox, 2004).

65. "Forgiving."

66. "Origin," *Angel*, DVD, written by Drew Goddard, directed by Terrence O'Hara (2004; 20th Century–Fox, 2004).

67. "To Shanshu in L.A."

68. Angel's interest in the prophecy is frequently shown, e.g., in "Judgment"; "The Cautionary Tale of Numero Cinco," *Angel*, DVD, written and directed by Jeffrey Bell (2004; 20th Century–Fox, 2004); "Destiny," *Angel*, DVD, written by David Fury and Steven S. DeKnight, directed by Skip Schoolnik (2004; 20th Century–Fox, 2004); and "Soul Purpose," *Angel*, written by Brent Fletcher, directed by David Boreanaz (2004; 20th Century–Fox, 2004). He accidentally and briefly becomes human in "I Will Remember You."

69. "Blind Date."

70. "The Cautionary Tale of Numero Cinco," "Destiny," and "Soul Purpose."

71. "The Cautionary Tale of Numero Cinco" (Wes) and "Not Fade Away" (the Circle).

72. "Not Fade Away."

73. Ibid.

74. *Oedipus Rex*, 857–858 (my translation).

75. Peradotto, "Disauthorizing Prophecy."

76. See Wendy Love Anderson, "Prophecy Girl and The Powers That Be: The Philosophy of Religion in the Buffyverse," in Buffy the Vampire Slayer *and Philosophy: Fear and Trembling in Sunnydale*, ed. James B. South (Chicago: Open Court Books, 2003), 212–26, for discussion of the secularization of the spiritual journey in the Buffyverse in general and its effect on the reliability of prophecy.

Detective Fiction/Fictionality from Asmodeus to *Angel*

ALISON JAQUET

When a troubled man, clutching an Angel Investigations business card, consults the detective agency in the Season Two episode "Darla" (2.05), he is visibly dismayed by Angel's lack of interest in his case.¹ Recognizing a pressing financial need for paying clients, Wesley tries to placate the man, reassuring him that Angel's odd demeanor is actually a sign of his investigative genius: "He's an eccentric, all the great ones are. Sherlock Holmes, Philip Marlowe...."² Thus, Wesley likens Angel to two iconic detectives from the pages of nineteenth and twentieth-century literature: Sir Arthur Conan Doyle's masterful logician, Holmes, and Raymond Chandler's hard-boiled hero, Marlowe. Many similar references are made throughout *Angel*, a series that insists upon the fictionality of the detective while being underpinned by investigative discourse. This suggestive preoccupation of *Angel* is reflected in the show's connections to the history of Western detective literature and its collaborative integration of multiple models of detection in order to offer metanarrative commentary on detective fiction/fictionality. Previous *Angel* scholarship has scratched the surface of the detective genre by exploring the noir sensibility of the series.³ In such studies, Lucy Nevitt and Andy William Smith have found "traces of the detective story," and Stacey Abbott identifies screen conventions of "film noir/detective" genre most strongly in Season One of the series.⁴ More recently, Brendan Riley has positioned *Angel* as an exemplar of digital age detection, suggesting that its "collaborative, database-driven modes of inquiry signal new ways of understanding the world."⁵ Thus, *Angel* does not simply privilege the hard-boiled detective, stalking the mean streets in a solitary pursuit of justice. Lorna Jowett points out, "Team Angel are most successful when working together" and argues that although Angel is often compared to superhero figures such as Batman, the series is "not about the individual as hero, rather it presents the group as hero."⁶ This group dynamic is not only a reflection of Joss Whedon's penchant for ensemble casts, but is also reminiscent of the detectives in Bram Stoker's *Dracula* (1897). In *Dracula*, a team of professionals join together, merging their professional knowledge, to track down and destroy the famous Count. In Stoker's novel, Professor Van Helsing speaks of the strength of the group as lying in the "power of combination,"[7] a feature that also underpins detection in *Angel*.

In *Angel* it becomes apparent that detection, as a process of discovery and investigation, is not merely alluded to or found in traces but is central to the series as a whole. Indeed, different types of detection are staged by different characters—Angel, Doyle, Cordelia, Wesley, Fred, Gunn, Spike, and Lorne—in order to demonstrate that detection is an unstable, contested, and, in *Angel*, ideally a collective and collaborative concern. While detection is often underpinned by a desire for knowledge, *Angel* explores the motives that drive this impulse. Ambition, greed, and obsession can transform the pursuit of truth and justice into something much darker. Ultimately, *Angel* suggests that truth may not be discovered by careful investigation or clever deduction alone. This culminates in the final season, when Angel Investigations has been transformed into a large, fragmented corporate operation. While *Angel* toys with the tropes of detection, ultimately, the series depicts detection as a problematic, naïve, or even dangerous enterprise. These metafictional gestures of *Angel* encourage viewers to reconsider and reconceptualize detection and its role in the series, revising previous constructions of the detective genre.

"Locked-door mystery: I've written it a hundred times"[8]

Detection narratives have always been self-reflexive stories.[9] Textual representations of detection often bring into question the act of storytelling itself. That is to say, detectives have been theorized as figurative writers and storytellers as they (re)construct the narrative of a crime.[10] In this vein, Peter Hühn argues that the detective genre "thematizes narrativity itself as a problem, a procedure and an achievement," and Albert D. Hutter suggests that detectives are "inevitably concerned with the problem of knowledge."[11] As such, the very construction of narrative is emphasized within detection stories, and the figure of the detective problematizes assumptions about truth and knowledge. Peter Thoms reflects upon this tendency as one that characterizes the detective genre from its inception: "For the inventors and earliest practitioners of detective fiction, narrative is not what *is*—an unproblematic mirroring of events—but what *is made*, and that process of construction becomes the very subject of these works. In this context, the detective functions as an authorial figure, attempting to uncover the story of the crime, and the 'case' becomes a story about making a story. Thus the resulting solution confronts us as an artifice, as an intelligible chain of narrative constructed from discovered information and, significantly, from other documents."[12] Thus, detective stories provide narratives about constructing narrative, telling stories about storytelling. In *Angel*, the characters organize their investigative efforts by performing the complicated work of interpretation and translation as they encounter diverse narratives such as rare books, prophesies, newspapers, websites, police reports, and psychic visions. Through this work of rewriting, they become storytellers.

In the very first scene of *Angel*, the conceit of storytelling is strongly evident. Over a montage of the city of Los Angeles at night, Angel's voiceover sets the scene, begins the story, and signals a recognizable genre as he says over the image of a downtown bar, "It started with a girl."[13] The use of voiceover and its allusion to the conventions of noir and hard-boiled detective fiction foregrounds the fictionality of this world and stages explicitly the work of storytelling. In the following scene, when the character of Doyle introduces himself to Angel, he explains his role by again alluding to fiction: "Let me tell you a little bedtime story. Once upon a time there was a vampire...."[14] Doyle then launches into a short history of Angel's life as flashbacks to images and scenes from *Buffy* are organized by his narration.[15] While this works as useful exposition for new viewers, Doyle now occupies the role of storyteller, and the construction of narrative is intentionally exposed. From the first scenes of the series, the audience is invited to consider storytelling as a process. The contested nature of storytelling signals that the work of detection will not unproblematically discover truth or provide easy resolution. In *Angel*, detectives tell stories and truth is subjective and contingent.

The casework of Angel Investigations tends to derive either from the ambiguous visions sent to Doyle and eventually Cordelia from The Powers That Be or from the business trade of ordinary people seeking help for extraordinary problems. These problems arise from an urban landscape rife with demons, zombies, werewolves, and myriad other threats. In his analysis of detection, Walter Benjamin suggests that urban modernity creates "times of terror, when everyone is something of a conspirator, everybody will be in a situation where he has to play detective."[16] The team at Angel Investigations are certainly "play[ing] detective" in this mould, always in the act of figuring out how to be investigators, constantly rewriting themselves as detectives, sometimes with little success, since clients, victims, and villains alike are often unconvinced that the members of Angel Investigations *are* real detectives. In particular, Angel's role as a detective is often overtly undermined, not least by Spike when he makes a guest appearance early in the first season. When Angel tells him to leave Los Angeles and go home, Spike retorts: "Why? Because you're Angel, vamp detective, now? I'm so scared. What's next? Vampire cowboy? Vampire fireman? Vampire ballerina?"[17] Spike's list humorously undercuts the role that Angel has adopted, suggesting that his occupation is merely a costumed performance, as easily adopted as cast off and replaced with a tutu or trusted steed. William Patrick Day argues that the modern vampire is "a performer" who is "at times vaguely silly."[18] While Day here refers to the screen cliché of the cloaked figure with glistening fangs, Angel is still implicated. His role as a detective is interpreted as another costumed (and not always credible) performance.

For Angel Investigations, finding solutions to weekly and season-long mysteries is never a straightforward process. The detectives often rely as much on chance and coincidence as deductive reasoning, or as Wesley characterizes their process of detection: "skill, perseverance, luck."[19] Indeed, Wesley is right. Detection in *Angel* does require some luck, as the system is imperfect, and truth is often difficult to pin down. Chelsea Quinn Yarbro criticizes this tendency in the series, arguing that "even with Fred, Wesley, or Cordelia in her prophetess manifestation, on hand to decipher what's happening, they hardly ever [have] much to offer beyond incomplete theories and obscure references."[20] However, while for Yarbro this obscurity might be unsatisfying, I argue that the incompleteness of the detectives' work is intentional. The detective work of Angel, Cordelia, Wesley, and later, Lorne, Fred, Gunn, and Spike alternately complements, contradicts, restricts, and reshapes the deductions and speculations of other group members. The different perspectives coalesce into solutions that are contingent and relational. Each character performs different types of detection and these differing styles have their own histories and implications.

"Stumbling around, playing Agatha Christie"[21]

In many ways, transforming Angel into an investigator recalls an early image of the demon detective figure, Asmodeus. French writer, Alain-René Lesage's 1707 comedy, *Le Diable Boiteux*, depicts the demon Asmodeus as a voyeur who unroofs houses in Madrid to expose the secret crimes occurring within. In Lesage's work, Asmodeus flies a new human companion, Don Cleophas, to the highest tower overlooking the city and explains: "I am about, by my supernatural powers, to take away the roofs from the houses of this great city; and notwithstanding the darkness of the night, to reveal to your eyes whatever is doing within them.... To unlock for you the secret chambers of the human heart, I will explain in what all these persons that you see are engaged. All shall be open to you; I will discover the hidden motives of their deeds, and reveal to you their unbidden thoughts."[22] Asmodeus vows to uncover, reveal, unlock, and explain the secrets of the city-dwellers. What is interesting here is that the etymology of the word "detect" derives from the Latin "detegere" which means to uncover or unroof, and the figure of Asmodeus, the demonic voyeur, was an influential image for nineteenth-century writers of detection.[23] Conan Doyle, in an early Sherlock Holmes story, "A Case of Identity" (1891), engages with this image. In this story, Holmes imagines himself and Watson flying over London, removing the roofs of the houses and peering into the lives of the people who live there. Holmes describes "the queer things which are going on, the strange coincidences, the plannings, the cross-purposes, the wonderful chains of events, working through generations, and leading to the most outré results."[24] While Holmes does not actually possess the supernatural powers of Asmodeus, he is figured as a kind of uncanny super "man" in the series and certainly here in this image. The detective is a powerful, if uncanny, figure in the modern city, and, on the cusp of the twenty-first century, a refiguring of the demon detective, in the form of Angel, arises.

From Victorian London to 1920s L.A., the urban landscape is the hunting ground of the modern detective.[25] David Fine argues that the "tough-guy detective story from Chandler to Mosley has always posited an underground city, a hidden, invisible city beneath the revealed city, one that can be only incompletely known."[26] This emphasis upon the impenetrable and inscrutable façade of the city is a familiar trope of detective fiction also employed in *Angel*. Early in the series, Doyle tells Angel, "You're in the big bad city now, man, where everyone's a stranger, hiding behind walls, keeping secrets."[27] This fictionalized Los Angeles, or what Doyle refers to as the "big bad city," articulates the anxieties of urban modernity and echoes Benjamin's 1938 view of the city in which "everyone is a conspirator."[28] However, unlike the rather voyeuristic versions of the detective hovering above the city, which Le Sage and Conan Doyle depict, Angel learns that he needs to reconnect with the people beneath the roofs and behind the walls. Thus Angel cannot merely aim to explain the "queer things" or "hidden motives" of humans to detect and then purge the criminal threat, but instead, he needs to live among the city-dwellers and to detect from within.

Detectives have always been suspect figures of fiction, often becoming obsessive or corrupt during their investigation of the criminal element. This is particularly true of hardboiled detectives who are haunted by their pasts and who, as Fine puts it, "dig for answers in the urban muck."[29] Even the early figure of Le Sage's Asmodeus tells his companion that he has "good and bad qualities" that are "equally useful."[30] Like these detectives, Angel is also an unstable, though productive, amalgam of good and evil. Much is made in the series of his liminal status as a vampire who is at constant risk of losing his soul and returning to the monstrous Angelus. However this demonic aspect of Angel is what enhances his proficiency as a detective. His vampiric sensitivity to the smell of blood often assists in investigating violent crimes. This skill is something that resonates with what has been considered the earliest detective novel in English fiction, Charles Dickens's *Bleak House* (1853). In this novel, Inspector Bucket is a watchful and persistent police detective who is on the trail of a murderer and follows, as Dickens puts it, "the narrow track of blood" to solve the crime.[31] In *Angel* this metaphor is literalized as Angel becomes the detective-as-bloodhound.[32] Useful as this is, it also becomes a rather unsettling ability. At certain points Angel reveals that his heightened sense of smell alerts him to sexual relationships between the characters, in one instance, detecting Wolfram & Hart lawyer Lilah's scent on Wesley, revealing that the other man has been sleeping with the enemy.[33] Like Asmodeus, there is something unsavory about the access Angel has to the lives of people around him, and so the detective remains an ambiguous figure.

Angel's status as a detective is, early on, also juxtaposed against the official police force. Angel's police contact, Detective Kate Lockley, assists his investigations, providing police reports and witness statements, but she also constantly questions his credentials, including his lack of license, resume, and surname. This depiction of the police professional, in contrast to the detective's less certain role, echoes another revolutionary piece of detective fiction, Edgar Allan Poe's "Murders in the Rue Morgue" (1841), where the small-minded police prefect is trumped by Dupin's cleverness.[34] This depiction has continued into modern screen texts, as Sharon Sutherland and Sarah Swan point out; the private detective of film and television always operates outside dominant forms of justice that tend to be corrupt or inadequate.[35] In *Angel*, Kate falls into the latter category of the inadequate police detective. Her limited viewpoint renders her unable to unravel crimes to which Angel provides uncanny solutions. He encourages her to see what is really going on in the streets of the city, to expand her interpretation to include supernatural explanations, something that she resists. However, when she finally accepts this new knowledge, she is alienated from her police colleagues and finally dismissed from her job. This suggests that the official detectives construct truths as much by exclusion of certain knowledge as by inclusion of other information.

The character of Cordelia is, perhaps, a less obvious detective figure than Angel, but she nevertheless plays an important role in detection. She begins the series as a blunt, materialistic, and unsuccessful actress who largely tracks down lost invoices and occasionally uses her craft to elicit information from witnesses and suspects during investigations. She is initially a reluctant investigator, but early in the first season, she demonstrates her ability to read people as a corollary of her training as an actress. In "Lonely Hearts" (1.02), Doyle receives a portent of danger and directs the team to a crowded nightclub. Here, Cordelia indicates that she can do more than just hand out business cards, telling Doyle, "I am an actress, a student of the human animal. I don't have to talk to people to know their story."[36] She then cleverly picks out the killer's next victim by identifying a mismatched couple and assuming that a relatively plain-looking woman must be wealthy to have snared her attractive male companion. The audience already knows him to be a sinister figure and very probably the danger that Doyle perceived. While neither Cordelia nor Doyle register this, the viewer can perceive at least the partial accuracy of her deduction — there is something suspect about this couple's activities and only Cordelia's analysis has detected this.

Cordelia's style of detection is directly compared to Angel's in the Season Three episode "Billy" (3.06). Stacey Abbott argues that in this episode, "the conventions of horror are built on an investigative narrative."[37] Moreover, in keeping with the concerns of the episode, this investigation becomes a gendered contest between Angel and Cordelia, who are both trying to track down the dangerous suspect, Billy, who transforms regular men into violent misogynists with a touch of his hand. In her investigation, Cordelia employs feminine knowledge. She detects that Billy's lawyer, Lilah, has been crying when she notices the other woman's hastily reapplied makeup. Cordelia then banters with Lilah, traversing a diverse discursive field from fashion to male violence. In so doing, she creates a particularly female bond, appealing to the power that underpins Lilah's identity as a "vicious bitch," a label that Cordelia herself once wore proudly.[38] At the same time, Angel is able to track the blood trail left in Billy's wake and is also given direct access to male witnesses who are more candid in his presence.[39] Both methods are shown to be successful, but Angel ultimately resorts to following Cordelia's trail in order to find their suspect.

During the first season the writers transformed Cordelia into her key role in the series: a medium figure, guiding the team at Angel Investigations to people in need. The evolution of Cordelia results in a shift from her rather tactless and selfish outlook into a more sincere and open outlook. Given that she is bestowed with prophetic visions, she seems to be drawing closer to her namesake, the brave, truth-telling Cordelia of Shakespeare's *King Lear*. However, in *Angel*, this aspect of truth is both signaled and problematized. The ambiguous visions of the future transmitted to her by The Powers That Be are often only partial or, as she describes them, "so vague they require closed captions."[40] Thus although they wear the mantle of truth or prophecy, the vivid, quickly-cut sequences that represent the visions display a confusing montage of sight and sound. In vision-mode, the camera lurches from side-to-side and the images are sudden, horrific intrusions into the visual field; as Karen Sayer reflects: "Cordy and Doyle shatter the show with their visions."[41] The sequences are intentionally inexplicable to a viewer, mirroring the difficulty of interpretation for the detectives. In addition, at certain points in the series, the visions that Cordelia receives are not merely confusing but completely fabricated. In "That Vision Thing" (3.02),[42] Wolfram & Hart uses a psychic to transmit false images to Cordelia, and in Season Four, when Cordelia is possessed, she intentionally misleads the team with a staple of the detective genre: the red herring. Hence, these visions are always ambiguous and occasionally fictitious. They are not altogether trustworthy narratives.

Cordelia's roles as visionary and detective have an important historical conjunction. Chris Willis points to the coterminous arrival of the fictional detective with the rise of spiritualism in nineteenth-century Western culture. Willis argues that both detective fiction and spiritualism "attempt to explain mysteries" using the figures of the medium and the detective "to make the dead speak in order to reveal a truth."[43] This conjunction is also reflected in *Angel*, where the role of medium and detective is combined in the figure of Cordelia. However, while being a receiver of visions gives Cordelia a role in the team, this does not necessarily give her power. Fred voices this anxiety when she compares Cordelia to a well-known television dog: "You're like Angel's Lassie. Sure, he does most of the saving, but it's your visions that tell him that Timmy's trapped in the well, the robbers are hiding in the barn...."[44] As the receiver of painful visions, Cordelia's mind and body are under perpetual threat of invasion and, at times, hers is an uncomfortably passive role. When her human body falters under the strain of the visions, Cordelia is forced to either relinquish her role or become part demon. This produces a sequence of events that leads to her possession by the rouge Power Jasmine and her eventual coma and death. For Doyle too, the visions are an affliction that constrains his life choices and produces alcoholic tendencies. In later seasons, the character of Lorne tends to stand in for the seer figure. Lorne's psychic skills also give him a privileged status, but, like Cordelia and Doyle, this ability makes him and his karaoke bar vulnerable to attack. Thus, these prophetic messages, that seem to resemble truth, are unreliable and ultimately damaging to those who convey them.

The characterization of Wesley Wyndam-Pryce draws on another recognizable figure from the gothic detective tradition: the scholar-detective. From early seasons, the Mutant Enemy creative team depicts Wesley as fluent in many languages: foreign, dead, and demon, and viewers often see him clutching a dusty tome or buried under stacks of rare volumes. In this way he harks back to the scholar-detectives or occult experts like Stoker's Van Helsing or the amateur detectives of M.R. James or H.P. Lovecraft's uncanny tales. In a particularly funny scene, from Season Two, Wesley is cast in the role of gentleman-detective. While leading the team on a case involving a wealthy family, he performs a textbook detective's revelatory speech. In a scene reminiscent of an Agatha Christie denouement, he tells the gathered family that the murderer "is someone in this room."[45] As he stalks around the well-furnished parlor, he reconstructs the crime, listing motives and evidence and theorizing the guilt of each family member in turn until he identifies the elderly Aunt Helen as the murderer. He reframes the domestic homicide into an intellectual puzzle, insisting, "You just have to keep sifting the evidence until the truth finally hits you."[46] This scene is played for comic effect, but Wesley takes on the role of a genteel, rational detective, adding yet another permutation of the detective archetype to the repertoire of Angel Investigations.

As the series continues, the detective agency expands to include the scientific skills of unstable physicist, Winifred "Fred" Burkle, and the street knowledge of local vampire fighter, Charles Gunn. With the combination of these different modes of knowledge, detection becomes, emphatically, a collaborative concern. Gunn often finds practical solutions to what Wesley and Fred perceive to be intellectual puzzles, and Wesley's scholarly-historical style of detection is often juxtaposed with Cordelia's modern approach. In "The Ring" (1.16), while Cordelia relies heavily on a website database titled "Demons, Demons, Demons," Wesley emphasizes the importance of "traditional research."[47] However, it is precisely Wesley's faith in the superiority of these scholarly traditions and the sanctity of the printed word that is forcefully undermined during the series. *Angel* promotes the benefits of a mixed methodology of detection and solution; thus single-minded approaches to complex problems often fail.

The use of prophecy in *Angel* suggests that the work of representation and interpretation inherent to detection is a difficult and treacherous enterprise. During the third season, the team, led by Wesley, try to decipher the Nyazian scrolls, prophecies that concern Angel and his newborn son. One scene in the episode "Offspring" (3.07) emphasizes the importance of collaborative work. Cordelia works at her computer and warns Wesley about his previous mistakes with the Shanshu prophecy translation. Simultaneously, Fred works alongside him to decode some mathematical equations linked to the prophecy, and Gunn walks between them, asking questions, looking for connections. Wesley explains that, in his translation, a particular word translates to "purification" in Aramaic and "ruination" in ancient Greek but "in the lost Ga-shundi language, it's both."[48] Hence, there is an acknowledgement that the signs are slippery and uncertain, that the "clues" to this mystery do not offer one sole truth. Ultimately, only a collaborative approach to detection proves to be an effective strategy in the face of shifting meanings and uncertain knowledge — a lesson reinforced later when Wesley's individual work on the prophecies wrongly leads him to kidnap Angel's son and effectively ostracizes him from the group.

In the later episode "Couplet" (3.14), Wesley is still working on the prophecies, but this time he is alone. While the other members of the team are preoccupied with romantic or family matters, Wesley remains at work on the translation. In the final scene of the episode, a close-up of his written notes reveals the ominous words "The Father will kill The Son."[49] Wesley seems to have come to the conclusion that Angel presents a danger to his child, but as the camera draws in to frame only the final translated words, it excludes the work of translation that has gone before.[50] This working-out includes the phrase: "second part of manuscript coordinates only slightly with this theory," emphasizing the speculative nature of the conclusion. Thus, when Wesley acts on this interpretation without consulting the group, a disastrous sequence of events ensues, leading to betrayal, abduction, and murder.[51] This suggests that an attempt to pin-down meaning, to simplify without considering the gaps, the inconsistencies, and the alternative explanations is a dangerous exercise. Wesley's scholarly approach is shown to be problematic in this instance due to its narrow application. And, the prophecy is ultimately found to be a fabrication — a rewriting.

"The world gets murkier and murkier"[52]

In the final season of *Angel*, the emphasis upon collaborative detection and cautious solution is underlined by the Season Five arc, which depicts the fracture and fragmentation of Angel Investigations. After spending the first four seasons fighting the international and pandimensional law firm, Wolfram & Hart, the team at Angel Investigations accepts the offer from the faceless "Senior Partners" to run the L.A. Branch and continue their work on a larger scale. Stan Beeler reflects this change as "a move from the marginal detective lifestyle appropriate to the film noir homage of earlier seasons to an office tower at the corporate heart of Los Angeles."[53] Angel is Chief Executive Officer and each character is put in charge of his/her own fully-staffed department, allowing specialization of their unique skills and interests.

The benefits of these added resources to their work seem clear but are ultimately revealed to offer no clear advantage to Team Angel. In "Unleashed" (5.03), team members combine their skills to track down a girl who is bitten by a werewolf and subsequently abducted.[54] Gunn, who has received legal knowledge via a brain enhancement, pulls police files; Fred and her practical science department analyze forensic evidence; Wesley, as head of Research and Intelligence, has psychics tracking the missing girl. Given that it appears to be an inside job, Lorne has the staff sing to him in the boardroom, and Angel oversees his team. But even with these resources, the solution to the crime relies on chance. When following the wandering specter of Spike, Fred enters the office of a staff member and finds a vial of chemicals that implicates him in the crime. The girl is rescued from her abductors, but the solution is achieved by coincidence and serendipity, something that is emphasized in the episode. The coincidental nature of this incident suggests that despite a wealth of documentary evidence and resources, recovering knowledge or solving crime may not be assured. This emphasis on chance represents a subversion of the traditional detective formula. Stephen Knight argues that this is a common feature of postmodern crime narratives and their emphasis upon "coincidence, overlapping accounts [and] indeterminacy."[55] Moreover, the importance of serendipity to the investigation in this episode indicates that even the collaborative model of detection has its own limitations. In the final season of *Angel*, unraveling mysteries still relies as much on chance and luck as on skill and deduction.

Season Five continues the series' preoccupation with juxtaposing different kinds of knowledge. In "The Cautionary Tale of Numero Cinco" (5.06) the team is trying to track down a seemingly invulnerable creature that eats the hearts of heroes.[56] The scene begins in Fred's laboratory, with a shot of a computer screen displaying blood cultures. In the lab, surrounded by microscopes, petri dishes, harsh blue light, and hard clinical surfaces, the team discusses how to kill the creature. When Spike interjects with his theory that the creature's Achilles heel must be its heart, Fred looks skeptically at her computer. She asks, "You see that in the science?" to which Spike says: "No, love, in the poetry. We're dealing with a mythic creature here, a kill-or-be-killed kind of creature."[57] Gunn confirms that Spike is correct, finding the details of a contract in the archives. But what is staged for us here is the failure of empirical measures to derive meaning from the situation. Spike, using a different framework, based in myth and his own experience, is more successful in deduction than Fred with her scientific approach. The series still seems to insist upon the importance of the collaborative model as it juxtaposes and considers alternative forms of knowledge.

The desire for knowledge, the impetus underpinning detection, is ultimately critiqued through the characters of Gunn and Fred. Gunn has been transformed into a suit-wearing legal expert, fighting courtroom battles and negotiating tricky contracts.[58] However, his legal certificates are clever forgeries and his new knowledge causes his colleagues to regard him with suspicion. When his abilities start to deteriorate, he makes a deal to upgrade his knowledge that leads to Fred's death and the fracturing of the group. Knowledge seeking — or detection — thus also becomes a treacherous enterprise for Fred. However, after she is infected in her laboratory and dies, Wesley reflects upon how it was her own desire for knowledge, not Gunn's ambition, that killed her: "She was curious.... How things work, what makes them special. She was always searching for what other people couldn't see. She was just curious. I think I hate her a little for that."[59] Fred's innocent curiosity, her strong desire to learn about the mysteries of the world, was, in Wesley's summation, her undoing.[60] Had she followed safety procedures upon receiving Illyria's sarcophagus rather than begin immediate investigation into it, Fred may not have died. Fred's death when Illyria overtakes her body reinforce one of Season Five's themes: the single-minded pursuit of knowledge remains a dangerous and corrupting one.

The problem in Season Five is that the work of detection valorized by Angel Investigations only works on a small scale. When Angel tells his team that they will figure out how to wield the "powerful weapon" of Wolfram & Hart,[61] he is mistaken from the outset. Corporatizing their work empties it of significance. The point is the struggle, the work, the collaborative process. In contrast to the detection-in-process approach established at Angel Investigations, Wolfram & Hart embraces values of domination and mastery. When the group has employees to delegate to, their own efforts begin to lose meaning, and as each character's skills and knowledge are specialized even further, this leads to the fragmentation of the group and their isolation from each other. Angel calls boardroom meetings complete with bullet-point agendas that nobody attends. No one quite trusts Gunn anymore because they cannot be sure what else Wolfram & Hart has implanted in his brain with his legal upgrade. The presence of Spike, another ensouled vampire, further unsettles Angel's investment in the Shanshu prophecy that promises a souled vampire redemption in the form of being made human, and it becomes for him merely a consoling fairytale.[62] Under the pressure of his position, instead of reading people's destinies, Lorne starts to write them.[63] And the team members all start to use the invasive and totalitarian techniques for gathering information that have until now been the methods of their enemies.[64] With increased power, the detectives become as sinister as the threats they aim to contain.

The group grapples with these problems of power and corruption throughout the final season as they work to utilize the resources of Wolfram & Hart's L.A. branch for their detection. In "Soul Purpose" (5.10), when Fred reflects on their position, she says defiantly, "We haven't sold out, we're changing the system from the inside," to which Gunn responds, "You know when you say it out loud, it sounds really naïve."[65] This tension culminates in the final battle of the series, when Angel's plan to double-cross the Senior Partners is carried out. In the final moments of the episode, the remaining members of the team are trapped in an alley with a horde of demons descending upon them, facing (almost) certain death. While the Senior Partners have unleashed Hell upon L.A., Angel's final words are: "Let's go to work."[66] Thus, the end refuses closure. Not only do viewers never discover the identity of the Senior Partners of Wolfram & Hart or The Powers That Be, we also do not bear witness to the outcomes of Angel, Spike, Illyria, and Gunn.[67] The final moments of the television series deny full disclosure, explication, or solution.[68]

At its conclusion, *Angel* resists the viewer's desire for knowledge and for the fantasy of order that this knowledge will restore. Thus, although the series constantly alludes to detective stories, it ultimately suggests that truth may not be accessible via investigation or deduction. Detection in *Angel* draws from various traditions, and the characters of Angel Investigations stage the convergence of knowledge to form unstable truths. In this way, *Angel* undermines faith in the efficacy of detection and situates the act of detection firmly in the realm of fiction.

Notes

1. "Darla," *Angel*, DVD, written and directed by Tim Minear (2000; 20th Century–Fox, 2003).
2. "Dear Boy," *Angel*, DVD, written and directed by David Greenwalt (2000; 20th Century–Fox, 2003).
3. See Stacey Abbott, "Kicking Ass and Singing 'Mandy': A Vampire in L.A.," in *Reading* Angel: *The TV Spin-off with a Soul*, ed. Stacey Abbott (London: I.B Tauris, 2005), 1–13; Jennifer Stoy, "'And Her Tears Flowed Like Wine': Wesley/Lilah and the Complicated(?) Role of the Female Agent on *Angel*," in *Reading* Angel: *The TV Spin-off with a Soul*, ed. Stacey Abbott (London: I.B Tauris, 2005), 163–175; and Boyd Tonkin, "Entropy as Demon: Buffy in Southern California," in *Reading the Vampire Slayer: The New, Updated Unofficial Guide to Buffy and Angel*, 2d ed. Roz Kaveney (London: I.B. Tauris, 2004), 83–99.
4. Lucy Nevitt and Andy William Smith, "'Family Blood Is Always the Sweetest': The Gothic Transgressions of Angel/Angelus," *Refractory: A Journal of Entertainment Media* 2 (2003), http://blogs.arts.unimelb.edu.au/refractory/2003/03/18/family-blood-is-always-the-sweetest-the-gothic-transgressions-of-angelangelus-lucy-nevitt-andy-william-smith/; Stacey Abbott, *Angel*, TV Milestones Series (Detroit: Wayne State University Press, 2009), 35.
5. Brendan Riley, "From Sherlock to Angel: The Twenty-First Century Detective," *The Journal of Popular Culture* 42, no. 5 (2009): 908–922 at 921.

6. Lorna Jowett, "Helping the Hopeless: *Angel* as Critical Dystopia," *Critical Studies in Television* 2, no. 1 (Spring 2007): 74–88 at 83–4.
7. Bram Stoker, *Dracula* (1897; rpt. New York: Penguin, 2009), 254.
8. "Are You Now or Have You Ever Been," *Angel*, DVD, written by Tim Minear, directed by David Semel (2000; 20th Century–Fox, 2003).
9. Here I wish to extend the analysis of Abbott as she designates "Spin the Bottle" (4.06) as "a stand-alone experiment in postmodern storytelling in which the process of telling a story is the story being told" (*Angel*, 95). Abbott argues that the episode draws "attention to its construction" in order to invite the audience to "consider the processes of storytelling" (*Angel*, 91). However, I want to suggest that this is a function of detection narratives in general and while this episode is remarkable for the reasons that Abbott outlines, this tendency permeates the entire series.
10. This emphasis on storytelling and narrative (re)construction follows such works as Tzvetan Todorov, *The Poetics of Prose*, trans. Richard Howard (Oxford: Basil Blackwell, 1977). Todorov argues that detective fiction necessarily involves two stories: the story of the crime and the story of the investigation (44–45). See also: Dennis Porter, *The Pursuit of Crime: Art and Ideology in Detective Fiction* (New Haven, CT: Yale University Press, 1981).
11. Peter Hühn, "The Detective as Reader: Narrativity and Reading Concepts in Detective Fiction," *Modern Fiction Studies* 33, no. 3 (Autumn 1987): 451–666 at 451; Albert D. Hutter, "Dreams, Transformations and Literature: the Implications of Detective Fiction," *Victorian Studies* (December 1975): 181–209 at 194.
12. Peter Thoms, *Detection and its Designs: Narrative and Power in Nineteenth-Century Detective Fiction* (Athens: Ohio University Press, 1998), 1.
13. "City of," *Angel*, DVD, written and directed by Joss Whedon (1999; 20th Century–Fox, 2002).
14. Ibid.
15. Doyle has an authoritative presence in the early episodes of *Angel*. He guides Angel and later, Cordelia, to whom he bestows his visions. Thus, Doyle's name might be interpreted as another allusion to Arthur Conan Doyle. Doyle in *Angel* is part-demon, but has a human mother, possibly the origin of his Irish accent. Conan Doyle also had an Irish mother, Mary Foley. For a discussion of Conan Doyle's Irishness, see Catherine Wynne, *The Colonial Conan Doyle: British Imperialism, Irish Nationalism and the Gothic* (Westport, CT: Greenwood Press, 2002), 3.
16. Walter Benjamin, *Charles Baudelaire: A Lyric Poet in the Era of Hight Capitalism*, trans. Harry Zohn (London: N.L.B., 1973), 40.
17. "In the Dark," *Angel*, DVD, written by Douglas Petrie, directed by Bruce Seth Green (1999; 20th Century–Fox, 2002).
18. William Patrick Day, *Vampire Legends in Contemporary American Culture: What Becomes a Legend Most* (Lexington: The University Press of Kentucky, 2002), vii.
19. "Calvary," *Angel*, DVD, written by Jeffrey Bell, Steven S. DeKnight, and Mere Smith, directed by Bill Norton (2003; 20th Century–Fox, 2006).
20. Chelsea Quinn Yarbro, "*Angel*: An Identity Crisis," in *Five Seasons of* Angel: *Science Fiction and Fantasy Authors Discuss Their Favourite Vampire*, ed. Glenn Yeffeth (Dallas: BenBella, 2004), 79–86 at 84.
21. Spike characterizes the detection of the group in these terms in the Season Five episode, "The Cautionary Tale of Numero Cinco," *Angel*, DVD, written and directed by Jeffrey Bell (2003; 20th Century–Fox, 2004).
22. Alain René Le Sage, *Asmodeus or The Devel on Two Sticks*, trans. Joseph Thomas (London: Hutchison, 1924), 13–14.
23. See Charles Dickens, *Dombey and Son* (Oxford: Oxford University Press, 1974), 620, "Oh for a good spirit who would take the house-tops off, with a more potent and benignant hand than the lame demon in the tale, and show a Christian people what dark shapes issue from amidst their homes"; Anthea Trodd, *Domestic Crime in the Victorian Novel* (London: Macmillan, 1989), 3–5, who points to the figure of Asmodeus, as an influential image for Victorian writers to depict the private and yet suspiciously secretive home; and Kate Summerscale, *The Suspicions of Mr. Whicher or The Murder at Road Hill House* (London: Bloomsbury, 2008), 157.

24. Arthur Conan Doyle, "A Case of Identity," in *The Complete Sherlock Holmes* (London: Penguin, 1981), 190–191.
25. For a useful discussion of Angel as noir detective, see Benjamin Jacob, "Los Angelus: The City of Angel," in *Reading* Angel: *The TV Spin-off with a Soul*, ed. Stacey Abbott (London: I.B. Tauris, 2005), 75–87.
26. David Fine, *Imagining Los Angeles: A City in Fiction* (Reno: University of Nevada Press, 2000), 147.
27. "Lonely Hearts," *Angel*, DVD, written by David Fury, directed by James A. Contner (1999; 20th Century–Fox, 2002).
28. Benjamin, *Charles Baudelaire*, 40.
29. Fine, *Imagining Los Angeles*, 119. Fine also reflects that the hardboiled detective often "comes away without really 'solving' anything" (119).
30. Le Sage, *Asmodeus*, 6.
31. Charles Dickens, *Bleak House* (1853; rpt. New York: Norton, 1977), 628. See Thoms, *Detection and its Designs*, 71–92, for an extended discussion of this metaphor in the novel.
32. An important early work in the history of detection literature is Ian Ousby, *Bloodhounds of Heaven: The Detective in English Fiction from Godwin to Doyle* (Cambridge: Harvard University Press, 1976). The title of Ousby's work is strangely resonant for Angel, who may not be a "bloodhound of heaven" but is certainly linked to the god-like Powers That Be.
33. "Ground State," *Angel*, DVD, written by Mere Smith, directed by Michael Grossman (2002; 20th Century–Fox, 2006).
34. Edgar Allan Poe, "Murders in the Rue Morgue," in *Tales of Mystery and Imagination* (London: J. M. Dent, 1984), 411–444 at 444.
35. Sharon Sutherland and Sarah Swan, "The Rule of Prophecy: Source of Law in the City of *Angel*," in *Reading* Angel: *The TV Spin-off with a Soul*, ed. Stacey Abbott (London: I.B. Tauris, 2005), 132–145 at 133.
36. "Lonely Hearts."
37. Abbott, *Angel*, 32.
38. "Billy," *Angel*, DVD, written by David Greenwalt, directed by Turi Meyer (2001; 20th Century–Fox Home Entertainment, 2003). For Cordelia's display of the powerful "bitch" persona, see "Rm w/a Vu," *Angel*, DVD, written by Jane Espenson, directed by Scott McGinnis (1999; 20th Century–Fox, 2002), and Anika Stafford's chapter in this volume.
39. "Billy."
40. "Parting Gifts," *Angel*, DVD, written by David Fury and Jeannine Renshaw, directed by James A. Contner (1999; 20th Century–Fox, 2002).
41. Karen Sayer, "'This Was Our World and They Made it Theirs': Reading Space and Place in *Buffy the Vampire Slayer* and *Angel*," in *Reading the Vampire Slayer: The New, Updated Unofficial Guide to* Buffy *and* Angel, 2d ed., ed. Roz Kaveney (London: I.B. Tauris, 2004), 132–155 at 155.
42. "That Vision Thing," *Angel*, DVD, written by Jeffrey Bell, directed by Bill Norton (2001; 20th Century–Fox, 2003).
43. Chris Willis, "Making the Dead Speak: Spiritualism and Detective Fiction," in *The Art of Detective Fiction*, ed. Warren Chernaik, Martin Swales, and Robert Vilain (Basingstoke, UK: Macmillan, 2000), 60–74 at 60.
44. "That Vision Thing."
45. "Happy Anniversary," *Angel*, DVD, story by Joss Whedon and David Greenwalt, teleplay by David Greenwalt, directed by Bill Norton (2001; 20th Century–Fox, 2003).
46. Ibid.
47. "The Ring," *Angel*, DVD, written by Howard Gordon, directed by Nick Marck (2000; 20th Century–Fox, 2002).
48. "Offspring," *Angel*, DVD, written by David Greenwalt, directed by Turi Meyer (2001; 20th Century–Fox, 2003).
49. "Couplet," *Angel*, DVD, written by Tim Minear and Jeffrey Bell, directed by Tim Minear (2002; 20th Century–Fox, 2003).
50. In this scene, the camera reveals initially that the page is littered with phrases such as "passage unclear refer to Greek text p.631." The notes indicate that Wesley has cross-referenced a number of different languages to come to his final solution.

51. Following this, Wesley's characterization darkens. See Jennifer Stoy ("And Her Tears Flowed Like Wine") for an analysis of Wesley and Lilah as versions of the noir detective and femme fatale. See also Sharon Sutherland and Sarah Shaw's chapter in this collection for more on Lilah as femme fatale.

52. Spike utters these words in the Season Five episode "Soul Purpose," *Angel*, DVD, written by Brent Fletcher, directed by David Boreanaz (2004; 20th Century–Fox, 2004).

53. Stan Beeler, "Outing Lorne: Performance for the Performers," in *Reading* Angel: *The TV Spin-off with a Soul*, ed. Stacey Abbott (London: I.B. Tauris, 2005), 88–100 at 98.

54. "Unleashed," *Angel*, DVD, written by Elizabeth Craft and Sarah Fain, directed by Marita Grabiak (2003; 20th Century–Fox, 2004).

55. Stephen Knight, *Crime Fiction 1800–2000: Detection, Death, Diversity* (London: Palgrave Macmillan, 2004), 95.

56. "The Cautionary Tale of Numero Cinco."

57. Ibid.

58. See Sara Upstone, "'L.A.'s got it all': Hybridity and Otherness in *Angel*'s Postmodern City," in *Reading* Angel: *The TV Spin-off with a Soul*, ed. Stacey Abbott (London: I.B Tauris, 2005), 101–113. Upstone describes Gunn's transformation as "a startling erasure of his black identity" (109). See also Michaela D. E. Meyer, "From Rogue in the 'Hood to Suave in a Suit: Black Masculinity and the Transformation of Charles Gunn," in *Reading* Angel: *The TV Spin-off with a Soul*, ed. Stacey Abbott (London: I.B. Tauris, 2005), 176–188, for further discussion of the problematics of this depiction; and Shannon Howard's chapter in this volume for a consideration of what Gunn's transformation means for his characterization in a Baudrillardian context.

59. "Shells," *Angel*, DVD, written and directed by Stephen S. DeKnight (2004; 20th Century–Fox, 2005).

60. Writing prior to the release of the final season of *Angel*, Roz Kaveney correctly speculates that Fred "shares with Wesley and Willow a pride of intellect, which may be her downfall," in "'She Saved the World a Lot': An Introduction to the Themes and Structures of *Buffy* and *Angel*," in *Reading the Vampire Slayer Reading the Vampire Slayer: The New, Updated Unofficial Guide to* Buffy *and* Angel, 2d ed., ed. Roz Kaveney (London: I.B. Tauris, 2004), 1–82 at 72.

61. "Conviction," *Angel*, DVD, written and directed by Joss Whedon (2003; 20th Century–Fox, 2004).

62. Angel is seen in the final scene of "The Cautionary Tale of Numero Cinco" (5.06) reading the prophecy before bed.

63. "Life of the Party," *Angel*, DVD, written by Ben Edlund, directed by Bill Norton (2003; 20th Century–Fox, 2004).

64. The whole season is shadowed by the secret pact Angel makes with Wolfram & Hart to alter reality in order to save his son.

65. "Soul Purpose."

66. "Not Fade Away," *Angel*, DVD, written by Jeffrey Bell and Joss Whedon, directed by Jeffrey Bell (2004; 20th Century–Fox, 2004).

67. While Wesley does dies in "Not Fade Away," the Buffy/Angelverse's penchant for resurrecting characters leaves viewers without full closure in relation to his character also.

68. The *Angel: After the Fall* comic series (IDW Publishing), while resolving some of these issues, nevertheless creates a further deferral of closure.

It (Re-)Started with a Girl
The Creative Interplay Between TV and Comics in Angel: After the Fall

STACEY ABBOTT

Long held to be a lesser form of literature largely characterized as simplistic adventure stories aimed at pre-adolescent boys, the comic book industry has in recent years challenged these stereotypes by demonstrating that there is a growing adult readership for comics drawn to their increasingly mature and complex storylines. As Mila Bongco argues, a new era of comic books began in the 1980s with such works as *Batman: The Dark Knight Returns* and *Watchmen* that "tackle complex moral dilemmas and diverse political shifts."[1] As a result of these changes, as well as the synergistic quality of modern multimedia industries, the comic book has found itself playing an increasingly high profile role within the contemporary media landscape. There is a long history of crossovers between film, television and comic books/graphic novels. For instance, as early as 1940, only two years after his first appearance in comics, *Superman* was adapted into a radio serial, which was followed in 1951 by a live action television series, an animated series in 1973, and of course onto cinema screens in 1978 with Christopher Reeve starring as the man of steel. Cinema continues to regularly draw upon graphic novels as source material, as evidenced by such films as *Sin City* (Robert Rodriguez/Frank Miller, 2005), and *300* (Zach Snyder, 2006). Likewise, since its early days, television has repeatedly based series, both live action and animated, upon classic superhero comics such as *Superman, Batman, Spiderman, The Incredible Hulk,* and *The X-Men.*

Similarly, comic book companies, recognizing a market for cult media, have a history of producing comics based upon popular films and TV series such as *Planet of the Apes* (Franklyn J. Schaffner, 1968), *Star Wars* (George Lucas, 1977), *Star Trek* (NBC, 1966–69), *Alien/Aliens* (Ridley Scott, 1979/James Cameron, 1986), *Buffy the Vampire Slayer* (WB/UPN, 1997–2003), *Battlestar Galactica* (SciFi Channel, 2004–2009) and *Angel* (WB, 1999–2004). These comics have always stood as creative and lucrative ancillary texts, existing parallel to the canonical texts, telling the further adventures of their main or peripheral characters. As they are parallel texts, they often risk recounting events that run contrary to stories that eventually unfold within the main series.

For instance, the Dark Horse comics based upon Twentieth Century–Fox's *Alien* films were published in between *Aliens* and *Alien*[3] (David Fincher, 1992). Since the company was sold the license to the series but not the main character Ripley, they chose to build their narrative around the two other surviving characters from *Aliens*, Corporal Hicks and Newt. Unfortunately, the next film in the series, *Alien*[3], begins with their deaths, effectively invalidating the narrative from the Dark Horse series.[2] This highlights the difference between canonical and non-canonical texts, a subject of great importance for many fans of cult media from film to TV to comics. A canonical text is officially sanctioned by the creators of the original show, comic, or film series. Furthermore, as many of these types of cult products involve a coherently developed alternate universe with slowly unraveling narrative arcs, a canonical text fits within the logic of that universe and narrative. While numerous other products such as tie-in novels, comics, and fan-fiction may be encouraged and welcomed by the creators of the primary text, they are usually not accepted as canon as they often contradict the continuity of the original product. As Joss Whedon explains:

> Canon is key, as is continuity. If you are massive nerd. Which I am. I believe there's a demarcation between the creation and ancillary creations by different people. I'm all for that stuff, just like fanfic, but I like to know what's there's [sic] an absolutely official story-so-far, especially when something changes mediums, which my stuff seems to do a lot.[3]

Furthermore, the appreciation of canonical texts is often linked to notions of authorship, presuming that the comic, film, or TV series is produced by an overarching creative artist such as George Lucas, Ron Moore, Frank Miller, or Joss Whedon who maintains the "true vision" for the series as well as the ability to tell these stories in a specific style. This is particularly the case with Joss Whedon, who has an extensive fan following. Loyalty to these auteurs and their "official texts" is often a significant part of cult fandom.

The recent comic book series *Buffy Season Eight* and *Angel: After the Fall* (*Angel: ATF*), however, are not ancillary texts but rather canonical texts, penned or plotted by Joss Whedon himself. These comics are specifically designed to continue the narrative where the original shows, now off the air, ended. For *Angel*, this narrative extension enabled Whedon to tell the story that he and the team at Mutant Enemy had planned for a sixth season before the show was cancelled. This chapter will, however, demonstrate that *Angel: ATF*, plotted by Whedon and written by Brian Lynch, is more than simply the continuation of the show's story arc as envisioned by Whedon; it is also a reworking of *Angel*'s narrative that interrogates the relationship between television and comics in terms of narrative structure and generic conventions. *Angel: ATF* merges stylistic, narrative, and generic conventions of the comic book with those of the original show, while also drawing the reader back into the world of the television series through narrative allusion. This comic book demands to be considered and read alongside *Angel* as well as earlier traditions of comic book superheroes.

Often described as a third generation television writer, Joss Whedon is also a highly skilled multimedia creator.[4] While his greatest successes have arguably been achieved through television (*Buffy*, *Angel*, *Firefly*/Fox 2002–2003, and *Dollhouse*/Fox 2009–2010), Whedon has worked across a range of media as a writer, producer, and director, including cinema: *Toy Story* (John Lasseter, 1995), *Alien Resurrection* (Jean-Pierre Jeunet, 1997), *The Cabin in the Woods* (Drew Goddard, 2011); the internet: *Dr. Horrible's Sing-Along Blog* (Joss Whedon, 2008); and comics: *The Astonishing X-Men* (Marvel Comics). More significantly, he has repeatedly reinvented existing works for new media. *Buffy the Vampire Slayer* (Fran Rubel Kuzui, 1992) began its life as a cinema feature and was subsequently reinvented for television while *Firefly* began on television and was later rebooted as *Serenity* (Joss Whedon, 2005) for the cinema.[5] It is therefore not surprising that in deciding to continue both *Buffy* and *Angel* Whedon chose to reinvent them through a different media, in this case comic books. The official canon of the Buffyverse had already extended into comic book form through such titles as *Fray*, *Tales of the Slayer*, and *Tales of the Vampire* penned by Whedon and other *Buffy* writers.[6] Whedon's involvement in *Angel: ATF* is, however, less direct than in these earlier comics or with *Buffy Season Eight*. On *Buffy*, Whedon serves as "Executive Producer," overseeing the series and writing numerous installments, including the opening and closing issues. On *Angel: ATF*, however, he is credited with plotting the series. Unable to make the same commitment as with *Buffy*, Whedon chose to turn over the "showrunning" of the comic series to a like-minded writer who shares his vision, Brian Lynch, author of earlier *Angel* tie-in comics *Spike: Asylum* and *Spike: Shadow Puppets*.[7]

The leap to comic from television is in many ways not a giant one. In terms of narrative structure, comics are quite compatible with television, utilizing a serialized form of narration that allows the story to unfold gradually over time and enables greater character detail and development, key characteristics of Whedon's television programs. In fact, the comic book is in some ways even more suited to this approach to narrative. While the pressures of commercial television meant that *Angel* was forced to become more episodic in its fifth season, as broader narrative arcs were seen to be alienating to the casual viewer, the serialized comic book is built around the notion of building a loyal fandom that will follow the narrative from issue to issue. Each installment of *Angel: ATF* ends on a cliff-hanger or a startling revelation, requiring the reader to pick up the next issue to find out what happened. Furthermore, much space in the comics is devoted to what Henrik Örnebrig describes in relation to television as "character showcasing," that is moments that provide "discursive opportunities not to develop and change the character but to let the character do 'what he/she does best.'"[8] So space is given over for Spike to bicker with Angel; for Lorne in his brightly colored suits to drink Sea Breezes and shower Angel with homo-erotic pet names such as Angelcakes; for the Groosalugg (Groo) to bravely pursue honorable battle; and for the revelation that both

Angel and Groo have named their mighty steeds, a dragon and a winged horse respectively, after their mutual love — Cordelia. It is, therefore, through these character moments that the loyal following of the series, and not the casual reader, is being targeted.

Having said this, comics do have distinct differences from television on both a narrative and aesthetic level. In terms of narrative structure, *Angel: ATF* is episodic, taking the form of seventeen issues published over sixteen months, but, quite unlike *Angel* (which interspersed stand-alone episodes within its broader serialized narrative) it is one long continuous storyline with one notable interruption. Having climaxed issue #5 with Illyria transforming into Fred at the sight of a now ghostly Wesley, the series interrupted this momentous reunion by devoting the next three issues to the self-contained "First Night" narratives that recount what happened to each of the *Angel* regulars on the first night after the confrontation with Wolfram & Hart in the alley that concluded "Not Fade Away" (5.22).[9] These stories disrupt the overall narrative of *Angel: ATF*, leaving readers for months on a cliff-hanger with the re-emergence of Fred in the midst of a heated battle between Team Angel and the demons of hell. Yet these episodic "First Night" tales also deliberately bring us back to the final episode of *Angel* and another apocalyptic battle, revealing for the first time how that episode's cliff hanger had concluded for each of the characters.[10] Here the series demonstrates a playful engagement with the original television show by creating drama and suspense by freezing the cliff-hanger — the return of Fred — and returning to a previously unresolved climax. It also highlights the comic series' difference by interrupting the main Angel-centered narrative, in which, like the TV show, Angel appeared in every issue, in order to focus upon the other characters — Spike, Connor, Lorne, Wesley, Kate, Gwen, and Gunn.

In a similar vein the series has spawned two spin-off mini-series, *Spike: After the Fall* and *Angel: Only Human*, self-contained narratives that tell the stories of favorite characters, Spike, Gunn, and Illyria. The comic book format, where comic book characters often find their origins in one series before being spun off into their own, enabled the Angelverse to expand beyond the television show's narrative focus on the vampire with a soul. *Angel: ATF* and its spin-offs could now encompass a range of character-based narratives that, due to the television convention where the central character is traditionally the driving force in the story, would not have been possible on TV.

In fact, while Angel is present in the narrative from the beginning of issue #1, a significant proportion of the narrational structure of *Angel: ATF* is built around the appearance of each of the characters from the series and revelations of what has happened to them since the fall of Los Angeles. More importantly, these revelations are focused upon character development and operate in a creative interplay with the television series as these characters are clearly presented as having undergone a process of transformation from where they were at the end of "Not Fade Away." Minor characters like Nina, Gwen, and Connor — no longer isolated in the "real world" by their superhuman hybrid natures—reconcile their identity issues in hell by banding together. Similarly, Lorne's identity seems to be quite self-consciously restored through his sojourn in hell. Many fans were unhappy with the noirish transformation of Lorne at the end of *Angel*'s final season in which Fred's death and Angel's final request that Lorne shoot Lindsey leave Lorne a broken and melancholic figure, walking away from his friends in the series finale. In *Angel: ATF* he has seemingly been restored. His first appearance in issue #4, as Lord of Silver Lake, the one location in L.A. protected from the violence of hell and where humans and demons co-exist in harmony, deliberately stands in stark contrast with his final appearance in "Not Fade Away." When last seen, Lorne, dressed in uncharacteristic brown suit and leather coat, shoots Lindsey McDonald, drops the gun, and morosely walks out of the room with the parting line "Good Night Folks." In *Angel: ATF* he is re-introduced as the ruler over the one part of L.A. where the sky is blue and the sun is shining, and he makes an entrance in a more typical yellow suit and cape.[11] More importantly, where in "Not Fade Away" Lorne refuses to join the final fight because the work has become "unsavoury," in issue #5 it is Lorne who reconstitutes the Angel Investigations team so that they can join Angel in his planned confrontation with the Lords of Hell.[12]

In contrast, Angel, Wesley, and Gunn are plummeted into their own personal depths of hell where their entire identities are redefined. Angel has been made human just when he needs his vampire powers to protect those he unwittingly plunged into hell; Gunn has become what he loathes most of all — a vampire; and Wesley, having seemingly found peace in death and the possibility of a reunion with Fred, is forced to return not only as a ghost but now contracted to Wolfram & Hart, serving as a form of mystical—and potentially evil—Watcher over Angel. Having previously failed as a Watcher but grown as a Rogue Demon Hunter through his work with Angel, Wesley's enslavement by Wolfram & Hart is all the more painful because of this return to his earlier foppish persona, replete with the all too familiar spectacles and three piece suit of his first appearance on *Buffy*. Even worse is the fact that having banded together against Wolfram & Hart in the show's finale, the three demon-hunters are separated in hell, each isolated and positioned to distrust the other. The way in which the characters are presented and developed in the comic book series, therefore, requires the reader to engage with how their characters developed on the show. Furthermore, each character is later restored to their original selves as last seen in "Not Fade Away" when, at the climax of *Angel: ATF*, Angel's death forces Wolfram & Hart, still determined to keep Angel alive, to return everyone to "the very last moment before all of this started," that is, the alley behind their L.A. offices. At least, the characters are almost restored to their original selves.[13] Bearing the memory of their time in hell, each character is unalterably changed by the experience of violence, torture, betrayal, and death.[14] *Angel*'s narrative, therefore, undergoes a reboot, as the comic takes us back to the end of the television series, and forges a new path for these characters in the next series, *Angel: Aftermath* and any subsequent series and spin-offs.

Aesthetically, the lack of sound is a particularly significant difference between the television and comic spheres that impacts the conception of *Angel: ATF*. Sound in audio-visual media is a key conveyer of meaning, often providing clues to the audience about how to read the images. As a result, the comic book artists need to find visual expression for aural moments. For instance, the character of Lorne is defined on *Angel* by music and Andy Hallet's singing voice, with his first appearances in the television series taking place on stage at the demon karaoke bar, Caritas. To capture this musical aspect to his character, both in terms of the lilting quality to Hallet's vocal delivery as well as the aesthetic and generic associations with the musical, Lorne's "First Night" story is told in Dr. Seuss–style verse:

> The taxi conveyed him as far as it could
> but was tromped by a Golem, right there in the hood!
> Our Lorne ran for cover, "Oh, this takes the cake!"
> He'd arrived in a town they had named Silverlake.
> This once was a happy place, all 'bout the arts.
> But when things went to hell.
> Demons tore it apart!
> But ... Lorne witnessed something he didn't expect.
> People are People — although they're in heck![15]

The presence of sound is replaced by this lyrical approach to the narration, juxtaposed with John Byrne's far more cartoon-like and colorful drawings, all of which serves to capture the musical and camp qualities associated with Lorne.

Furthermore, the importance of sound in the transition of *Angel* from television to comic is emphasized by the significance placed upon the capturing of voices in the process of adapting *Angel* to comic book — more important even than capturing visual likenesses. While the written scripts of a television series are brought to life by the performances of actors, the scripts and drawings in a comic book are brought to life by the reader, for as Scott McCloud explains, the reader of comics is "a willing and conscious collaborator" in the construction of meaning.[16] The fans of the series bring their familiarity with the voices of *Angel* actors to the comics, but Lynch, in addition to capturing the writing style of the series' creators, must get the rhythms and the cadence of the character/actors' voices right. When the Groosalugg (Mark Lutz) is reunited with Angel and Wesley in issue #4, the rhythm of his welcome speech calls to mind Lutz's comically enthusiastic and sincere performance-style: "Hell has been kind to you, old friend! And Wesley! I heard you were without mass! Good for you, always keep your enemies guessing."[17] Similarly, Spike's response to the revelation that Angel is now human evokes James Marsters's vocal intonations as he displays his familiar jealousy of Angel: "I knew he gained weight!

Spider told me I was just being catty! Catty or bloody not, I was right and he is human and chunky! Dowdy, even — ."[18]

The success of Brian Lynch as an *Angel* writer has been predicated upon his ability to capture voices. For instance, Joss Whedon explained that he specifically chose Brian Lynch to helm the new series because his previous work in *Spike: Asylum* and *Spike: Shadow Puppets* showed that he could capture "[t]he voices. Not just of the characters from the show but everybody."[19] Fans of the series have, similarly, commented on Lynch's success in this area. In the "letters to the editor" pages of *Angel: ATF*, Josh Stafford explained that when reading Lynch's Spike comics that "I could hear the voices of James Marsters and Andy Hallet as I read the dialog spoken by the characters they played on TV,"[20] and Angela Morningstar comments that when reading *Angel: After the Fall*, "I can hear the voices in my head, so I agree with the choice of writer for this project."[21] An anonymous poster to Brian Lynch's blog commented that "[y]our skill in moving them [the characters] from one media to another and yet managing to maintain each individual voice is a rare talent and one that I much appreciate,"[22] while Artemis praised Lynch for capturing "all of the characters' voices perfectly (this is particularly difficult to do with Angel, who's so reserved compared to, say, Spike, but you did it wonderfully)."[23] Here the expectations of television, and Whedon's programs in particular where dialogue and character voices are a crucial element of fan enjoyment, impact upon the form of the comic.

Another significant aural element of the new series is the extensive use of voiceover conveyed through the presence of text balloons. *Angel: ATF* opens with the line "It all started with a girl" written at the top of the first page.[24] This opening initiates a narrational device that is used consistently throughout much of the series, in which Angel narrates the unfolding story of his time in hell as a form of internal monologue. This line also positions the voiceover as an homage to the original series by referencing the show's film noir influences. *Angel* opens with a visual montage of Los Angeles at night, over which Angel delivers the following narration: "Los Angeles. You see it at night and it shines. A beacon. People are drawn to it. People and other things. They come for all sorts of reasons. My reason? No surprise there. *It started with a girl.*"[25] As I've argued elsewhere, this monologue married with a montage of night time images of Los Angeles establishes film noir as one of the show's primary generic influences.[26] Yet the use of voiceover throughout much of *Angel: ATF* also separates the comic book from the TV series as this seemingly noirish technique is used quite sparingly in the television show. In addition to the narration quoted above, voiceover by Angel is only used in "Redefinition" (2.11).[27] Instead, Angel's perspective is conveyed through narrative, cinematography, mise-en-scène and performance. Furthermore, his is but one of many points of view that are privileged within this ensemble series. So while initially the voiceover seems to be a means of recreating the style of the TV show, it is actually reworking *Angel* to comic book form since the first person narration is, according to Bongco, a key component of the superhero comic books. As Bongco argues, "Specific narrative devices grant superheroes narrative centrality and often cede to them narrative authority through point-of-view frames, first person narration, and other textual and graphic cues which foster reader identification with them and their exploits."[28] So here in the first issue of *Angel: ATF*, the line "it started with a girl" takes us back to the first episode of *Angel* but also restarts the new series in a style that is compatible with its new medium.

Similarly, the opening images of the comic also establish its connection to and difference from the TV show. Both the pre-credit sequence in "City of" (1.01) and the pre-title panels in *Angel: ATF* issue #1, show Angel saving a young woman from a demon in an alley, avoiding her questions about the monsters attacking her and then disappearing in a rather mysterious fashion. In "City of" this takes place in a dark, claustrophobic Los Angeles alley as the girl is attacked by a group of vampires which Angel dispatches with wooden stakes. In *Angel: ATF*, however, the girl is attacked by a group of winged demons set against a seemingly post-apocalyptic L.A., surrounded as they are by fire, crumbling buildings, and debris. No longer is Angel fighting the hidden world of demons and monsters that lurks beneath the veneer of civility in contemporary L.A. that characterized *Angel*; rather L.A. has been transformed into the hellish world of fantasy novels, comics, and role-playing games. No longer armed with wooden stakes, hidden up his sleeves à la *Batman*, Angel is now armed with a sword and a dragon. When we turn to the title page — which is marked by an epic image of Angel flying on the back of a dragon across a burning and demon infested Los Angeles, not confined by the frames of the panel but bleeding across both pages — we are clear that we are no longer within the realm of television but entering the fantastic possibilities of the graphic novel.[29] This may be the story that Whedon had in mind for a sixth season, but its comic book imagery presents a vision for this series that would have been impossible on television.

The allusions to "City of" in these opening pages also remind the reader that all is not as it seems and Angel's role as a hero is potentially questionable. In "City of" Angel dismisses the gratitude of the young woman and retreats down the dark alley because the vampire in him is drawn to the smell of her blood. He may save her life, but in that alley, he is as much a danger to her as the vampires he has dispatched. In *Angel: ATF*, he disappears on the back of his dragon and avoids the girl's questions about why the citizens of L.A. are being punished because he cannot admit the truth — that they are in hell because he took a stand against Wolfram & Hart, who subsequently sent "Los Angeles to Hell." In this manner, the comic establishes that the new series will continue the television show's preoccupation with discursively challenging Angel's position as a hero as well as deconstructing the notion of heroism more broadly.

These themes are not, however, new to comic books but are a crucial element of the revisionist superhero genre that emerged in the 1980s with

Watchmen and *Batman: The Dark Knight Returns* and have continued in other series such as *Hellblazer* and *Preacher*.[30] As Bongco argues, "The new comics dealt simultaneously with something very familiar and very strange: heroes who have ceased to be superhuman; who sometimes have problems with drugs, alcohol, and sex; and above all, who grapple with notions of authority, power, and evil that are not always clear and against which they do not always win."[31] The approach to *Angel*'s morally ambiguous universe clearly situates the series within this comic book tradition. While Janet K. Halfyard has argued that characteristics of the cinematic superhero, particularly *Superman* (Richard Donner, 1978), *Superman 2* (Richard Lester, 1980), and *Batman* (Tim Burton, 1989), were "woven into Angel's identity in Season One" as a means of "establishing his superheroic credentials at the outset of the series," there are also strong parallels with recent revisionist comic books.[32] Like *The Watchmen*, Angel's position as a superhero is undermined by the series' emphasis upon his human nature. From the first episode he is presented as socially awkward, romantically challenged, and, much like an alcoholic, struggling against the demon inside him. He is plagued by guilt for his past as a vampire and while his desire to atone for that past is morally sound, often his attempts to do so are marked by all too human failure or mistaken choices. Throughout the series, he is often presented as being unable to save the characters he is trying to protect: Tina in "City of," Darla in "Reunion" (2.10), Connor in "Sleep Tight" (3.16), Cordelia in "Inside Out" (4.17), and Fred in "A Hole in the World" (5.15).[33] Furthermore, much like comic book anti-hero John Constantine (*Hellblazer*)—a demon hunter who battles the forces of evil but is haunted by the friends who have been sacrificed to this mission — Angel must often make morally ambiguous choices with sinister ramifications. In "Reunion" he decides to let vampires Darla and Drusilla murder the evil but human Wolfram & Hart lawyers; in "Peace Out" (4.21)[34] he kills the goddess Jasmine who has robbed humanity of free will but brought about world peace in the process; and in "A Hole in the World" he chooses to let Fred die because the act of saving her would kill too many others. Furthermore, Angel, like Batman, Constantine, and Jesse in *Preacher* before him, lives in a world where moral lines initially seem to be clear as he is positioned within an epic battle between good and evil. But upon further examination those lines become blurred. Frank Miller explains that in *The Dark Knight Returns* "the key transition is his recognition he's no longer part of the authority. That's really the transition at the end of *Dark Knight*, this knowledge that he's no longer on the side of the *powers that be* anymore, because the powers that be are wrong."[35] Much like Batman, Angel's mission initially appears to be grounded in good as he too is supported by The Powers That Be — in his case god-like beings who send visions to Angel through Doyle and Cordelia to assist Angel's mission. In Season Four's "Inside Out," however, it is revealed that The Powers That Be are manipulating Angel and his team to achieve their own ends, shattering his moral compass and overturning established notions of good and evil — reaffirmed by Angel himself taking over the L.A. branch of Wolfram & Hart in its fifth season in order to fight the evil from within the belly of the beast. These parallels demonstrate that before *Angel* moved to comic books, it was already in dialogue with the comic book superhero genre. Even the cinematic adaptation of *Hellblazer*, Francis Lawrence's *Constantine* (2005), contains parallels with *Angel*, with its near-apocalyptic narrative relocated from the comic's original London location to Los Angeles and the transformation of Constantine's iconic brown raincoat to a highly Angel-like black overcoat.

Angel: ATF continues this revisionist approach by revealing in issue #3 that Angel is now human and therefore ultimately vulnerable in his battle against evil.[36] Furthermore, within the series, Angel is regularly forced to confront the often violent consequences (to strangers, friends, and family) of his choice to enter into the showdown with Wolfram & Hart that damned them all to hell. Finally, in this series Whedon and Lynch reveal that the previously ambiguous Shanshu prophecy about the vampire with a soul who will play a pivotal role in the apocalypse does refer to Angel (rather than Spike), but the role he is destined to play will be on the side of evil, although the fact that this revelation is made by Wesley speaking on behalf of Wolfram & Hart maintains the program's moral ambiguity as Wolfram & Hart are never to be trusted. While this earth shattering revelation almost brings the series to an end with Angel's decision to allow himself to die rather than face a future where he will be the harbinger of death, it is once again an allusion to the original series that places Angel back on his mission. Leaning over a dying (human) Angel, Connor urges his father to hold on and relays a familiar message passed on to him by Kate, former police officer from Season One and Season Two of *Angel* and now turned demon-hunter: "A friend of a friend once said something that might help you now. I'm paraphrasing because we're short on time and the dude was a blowhard. It doesn't matter what you were, doesn't matter what people think you're going to be. It's not all building to something so we should stop living like it is. All that counts — is what you do now."[37] The allusion to Angel's Season Two epiphany that "if nothing you do matters, then all that matters is what you do" restores the sense of hope that is inherent in *Angel* whereby the revisionist superhero genre does not merely deconstruct notions of heroism but offers new templates for a modern understanding of heroism within a morally complicated world.[38]

This analysis of the *Angel: After the Fall* comic book series in relation to the original television show *Angel* demonstrates that the interplay between television and comic is not a one way process of adaptation or simply a narrative continuation. Rather, this process of transforming *Angel* from television to comic book highlights the aesthetic challenges of both media and the interdependency of intertextual references across the Angelverse. The manner in which *Angel: ATF* alludes to and reworks specific moments from the television series demonstrates that the comic is in dialogue with its own televisual past. Temporally, the comic takes us back to "Not Fade Away" to conclude its story with the team winning the battle against Wolfram & Hart, but visually it goes back further. The last image in the final issue calls to mind the visual landscape of "City of."[39] In it Angel is alone, walking down a dark, empty LA street, framed in film noir chiaroscuro as he renews his commitment to his original mission to "help the helpless" by declaring: "My name is Angel. I've done very bad things. I've been told I'm destined to do worse. But for now ... I'm here to help."[40] To develop *Angel* as a comic book series, Joss Whedon and Brian Lynch have gone back to the beginning as a means of paving a narrative way forward ... or back.

Notes

1. Mila Bongco, *Reading Comics: Language, Culture, and the Concept of the Superhero in Comic Books* (New York & London: Garland, 2000), 94.
2. Kerry Gough, "Translation Creativity and Alien Econ(c)omics: From Hollywood Blockbuster to Dark Horse Comic Book," in *Film and Comic Books*, ed. Ian Gordon, Mark Jancovich, and Matthew P. McAllister (Jackson: University of Mississippi Press), 37–63.
3. Joss Whedon interviewed by Chris Ryall, *Newsarama.com*, "Joss Whedon Talks Angel After the Fall," April 26, 2007, http://forum.newsarama.com/showthread.php?t=110457 (accessed July 17, 2009).
4. David Lavery, *Joss: A Creative Portrait of Joss Whedon, Maker of the Whedonverses* (London: I.B. Tauris, 2009).
5. For a closer discussion of the transition of *Firefly* from television to big screen see Stacey Abbott, "'Can't Stop the Signal': The Resurrection/Regeneration of *Serenity*," in *Investigating* Firefly *and* Serenity*: Science Fiction on the Frontier*, ed. Rhonda V. Wilcox and Tanya R. Cochran (London: I.B. Tauris, 2008), 227–238.
6. Joss Whedon, *Fray* (Milwaukie, OR: Dark Horse, 2003); Joss Whedon, *Tales of the Slayers* (Milwaukie, OR: Dark Horse, 2002); Joss Whedon, *Tales of the Vampires* (Milwaukie, OR: Dark Horse, 2004).
7. Whedon, "Joss Whedon Talks Angel After the Fall"; Brian Lynch, *Spike: Asylum* (San Diego: IDW, 2007); Brian Lynch, *Spike: Shadow Puppets* (San Diego: IDW Publishing, 2009).
8. Henrik Örnebrig, "The Show Must Go On ... And On: Narrative and Seriality in *Alias*," in *Investigating Alias: Secrets and Spies*, ed. Stacey Abbott and Simon Brown (London: I.B. Tauris, 2007), 25.
9. "Not Fade Away," *Angel*, DVD, written by Jeffrey Bell and Joss Whedon, directed by Jeffrey Bell (2004, 20th Century–Fox Home Entertainment, 2004).
10. The "First Night" stories are collected in the followings issues: Brian Lynch, *Angel: After the Fall* #6 (April 2008); #7 (May 2008); #8 (June 2008), IDW Publishing. Note: *Angel: After the Fall* is written by Brian Lynch and plotted by Joss Whedon and Brian Lynch, as such all references to the specific issues of the series are to the writer, Lynch.
11. Brian Lynch, *Angel: After the Fall* # 4 (February 2008), IDW Publishing, [14].
12. Brian Lynch, *Angel: After the Fall* #5 (March 2008), IDW Publishing, [18].
13. Brian Lynch, *Angel: After the Fall* #16 (January 2009), IDW Publishing, [10].
14. A number of characters die in these final pages of the series only to be returned to life through the reboot, including Angel, Connor, Gwen, Groo, and Cordelia the dragon.
15. Brian Lynch, *Angel: After the Fall* #6 (April 2008), IDW Publishing, [16–17].
16. Scott McCloud, *Understanding Comics: The Invisible Art* (New York: Harper Perennial, 1993), 65.
17. Brian Lynch, *Angel: After the Fall* # 4 (February 2008), IDW Publishing, [17].

18. Brian Lynch, *Angel: After the Fall* # 14 (November 2008), [3].
19. Whedon, "Joss Whedon Talks Angel After the Fall."
20. Josh Stafford, letter printed in "The Powers-that-Read," *Angel: After the Fall* #4 (February 2008), [27].
21. Angela Morningstar, letter printed in "The Powers-that-Read," *Angel: After the Fall* #4 (February 2008),[26].
22. Anon, comment on "Angel 17 Tomorrow," *Brian Lynch: Blog for You Specifically*, comment posted February 10, 2009, http://bloglynch.blogspot.com/2009/02/angel-17-tomorrow.html (accessed July 19, 2009).
23. Artemis, comment on "Angel 17 Tomorrow," *Brian Lynch: Blog for You Specifically*, comment posted February 12, 2009, http://bloglynch.blogspot.com/2009/02/angel-17-tomorrow.html (accessed July 19, 2009).
24. Brian Lynch, *Angel: After the Fall* #1 (November 2007), [1].
25. "City of," *Angel*, DVD, written by David Greenwalt and Joss Whedon, directed by Joss Whedon (1999, 20th Century–Fox Home Entertainment, 2002). My emphasis.
26. Stacey Abbott, "Kicking Ass and Singing 'Mandy': A Vampire in L.A.," *Reading* Angel: *The TV Spin-Off with a Soul*, ed. Stacey Abbott (London: I.B. Tauris, 2005), 1
27. "Redefinition," *Angel*, DVD, written by Mere Smith, directed by Michael Grossman (2000, 20th Century–Fox Home Entertainment, 2003).
28. Bongco, *Reading Comics*, 65.
29. Brian Lynch, *Angel: After the Fall* #1 (November 2007), [4–5]. The artist for this issue is Franco Urru.
30. Alan Moore, *Watchmen* (DC Comics, 1987); Frank Miller, *Batman: The Dark Knight Returns* (DC Comics, 1997); Garth Ennis, *Hellblazer: Dangerous Habits* (Vertigo/DC Comics, 1996); Garth Ennis, *Preacher: Gone to Texas* (Vertigo/DC Comics, 1996).
31. Bongco, *Reading Comics*, 141.
32. Janet K. Halfyard, "The Dark Avenger: Angel and the Cinematic Superhero," in *Reading* Angel: *The TV Spin-Off With a Soul*, ed. Stacey Abbott (London: I.B. Tauris, 2005), 150.
33. "Reunion," *Angel*, DVD, written by Tim Minear and Shawn Ryan, directed by James A. Contner (2000, 20th Century–Fox Home Entertainment, 2003); "Sleep Tight," *Angel*, DVD, written by David Greenwalt, directed by Terrence O'Hara (2002, 20th Century–Fox Home Entertainment, 2003); "Inside Out," *Angel*, DVD, written and directed by Steven S. DeKnight (2003, 20th Century–Fox Home Entertainment, 2004); "A Hole in the World," *Angel*, DVD, written and directed by Joss Whedon (2004, 20th Century–Fox Home Entertainment, 2004).
34. "Peace Out," *Angel*, DVD, written by David Fury, directed by Jefferson Kibbee (2003, 20th Century–Fox Home Entertainment, 2004).
35. Frank Miller cited in Bongco, *Reading Comics*, 142. My emphasis.
36. Brian Lynch, *Angel: After the Fall* #3 (January 2008), [22].
37. Brian Lynch, *Angel: After the Fall* # 13 (October 2008), [17].
38. "Epiphany," *Angel*, DVD, written by Tim Minear, directed by Tom Wright (2001, 20th Century–Fox Home Entertainment, 2003).
39. Issue #16 is the conclusion of the *Angel: After the Fall* main narrative although it was followed by an epilogue issue #23. I am not referring to this here as the epilogue is a follow up to the narrative in *Angel: ATF* about Gunn and serves as a bridge to the mini-series *Angel: Only Human*.
40. Brian Lynch, *Angel: After the Fall* #16 (January 2009), [22].

About the Contributors

Stacey Abbott is a reader in film and television studies at Roehampton University where she teaches courses on film genres as well as world cinema and textual analysis. She is the author of *Angel* (Wayne State University Press, 2009) and *Celluloid Vampires* (University of Texas Press, 2007). Her current research is focused on developments within cult television. She is the editor of *The Cult TV Book* (2010) and *Reading* Angel (2005) and co-editor of *Investigating* Alias (2007) and *Falling in Love Again* (2009), all from I.B. Tauris.

Angel Anderson graduated with a master's degree in English in December of 2008 and will begin her PhD in composition at Indiana University of Pennsylvania in the fall of 2010. Beyond composition studies, Angel's research interests lie primarily in contemporary fiction and popular culture.

Laurel Bowman is an assistant professor of Greek and Roman studies at the University of Victoria, British Columbia, specializing in myth and Greek literature, especially tragedy. She has published on *Medea*, prophecy in Sophocles and Hellenistic women poets, and believes that Joss Whedon is the next Euripides. She still misses Illyria.

Tamy Burnett is a lecturer at the University of Nebraska–Lincoln in English and women's and gender studies. She received her PhD in English, with a specialization in women's and gender studies, from the University of Nebraska–Lincoln, and most of her research focuses on 20th century American literature and 20th and 21st century television and popular culture. Tamy has also written on *Buffy the Vampire Slayer*, *Veronica Mars*, and *The X-Files*, and she is currently working on a book exploring issues of community and feminism in relation to turn-of-the-21st-century heroines of cult television.

AmiJo Comeford is an assistant professor of English at Dixie State College of Utah. She received her PhD in English from the University of Nevada–Las Vegas. Her essay "Cordelia Chase as Failed Feminist Gesture" appeared in *Buffy Meets the Academy* (ed. Kevin K. Durand; McFarland, 2009). When she is not focused on her popular culture interests, AmiJo studies American Civil War poetry and prose and early British literature. She is researching Herman Melville's Civil War poetry and its relevance to a more comprehensive study of the war's aftermath through the nation's literary consciousness.

Jennifer Hamilton is a professor of English at Modesto Junior College, teaching composition, poetry, and British literature. She did her graduate work at the University of Aberdeen, earning her MLitt in Scottish and Irish studies and her PhD in English. Her academic work focuses on the writing of Scottish author Naomi Mitchison, and she has written about popular culture's influence on American identity. She also writes poetry, which has recently appeared in galleries in New York and California.

K. Shannon Howard is currently a lecturer at the University of South Alabama, having earned her MA last spring. Her ultimate goal is to complete a PhD in rhetoric and composition. She has taught high school English and theatre for eight years and served as an education fellow at Berkeley Repertory Theatre in 2008. Her research interests include late Victorian and early modern literature as well as the pedagogical practices of teaching composition to first-year college students.

Mary Ellen Iatropoulos is a media educator and project manager at the Children's Media Project in Poughkeepsie, New York, where she designs and teaches professional development seminars for school educators that focus on integrating media production into traditional English and ESL/ELL curricula. She also develops and teaches media and technology-oriented workshops for youth, among them the youth-produced radio show Radio Uprising and the after-school writing and zine-making program Nightwriters. She holds a BA in English from Vassar College and an MA in English from the State University of New York–New Paltz, and she is currently working towards a master's degree in secondary education.

Alison Jaquet recently received her PhD from the University of Western Australia with a dissertation titled "Detection and the Domestic: Discursive Practices in the Writing of Ellen Wood." She is researching ideas of detection in Victorian domestic and sensation fiction, and new approaches to the oeuvre of novelist, editor and journalist Ellen Wood (1814–1887). Her interests include gothic and detective fiction, popular culture, women's writing, and pedagogy. She is an award-winning teacher in the fields of Victorian and Romantic literature.

Lorna Jowett is a senior lecturer in film and television studies and American studies at the University of Northampton, where she teaches horror, science fiction, contemporary fiction, and television. She received her PhD in American literature from Durham University. For nearly ten years she has published on horror and the fantastic, with much of her research dealing directly with genre and its operations in fiction, television, and film. She wrote *Sex and the Slayer: A Gender Studies Primer for the* Buffy *Fan* (Wesleyan University Press, 2005) and is a member of the editorial board of *Slayage: The International Online Journal of Buffy Studies*.

Victoria Pettersen Lantz recently received her PhD in theatre and drama from the University of Wisconsin–Madison. In 2009, she was awarded both a Dissertator Fellowship and Vilas Travel Grant from the University of Wisconsin–Madison Graduate School to finish her dissertation, "Locating Cultures, Constructing Identities: The Caribbean Diaspora, Black Britain, and the Theatre of Mustapha Matura." Her work primarily focuses on postcolonial theatre in the Caribbean and England, but she is also interested in postcolonial representations in popular culture.

Cynthea Masson holds a PhD in English from McMaster University. She teaches medieval literature and composition in the English Department at Vancouver Island University (British Columbia). She has published works on medieval visionary literature, medieval alchemical poetry, and the contemporary works of Joss Whedon. Her paper "What the Hell?—*Angel*'s 'The Girl in Question'" won the Mr. Pointy Award at the *Slayage Conference on the Whedonverses 3* (2008).

Katia McClain holds a PhD in Slavic languages and literatures from the University of California–Los Angeles and teaches in the Department of Germanic, Slavic and Semitic

Studies at the University's Santa Barbara campus. Her interests focus on Eastern Europe and the Balkans and include the areas of language acquisition, language pedagogy, linguistics, literature, folklore, marginalized populations, media representation, science fiction, and gender studies. She presents work on popular media representations of Eastern Europe on *Third World News Review*, a television/radio program broadcast in the Santa Barbara area, and she has presented papers on the Whedonverses at three *Slayage* conferences.

Anika Stafford is a PhD student in women's and gender studies at the University of British Columbia, where she determinedly writes and publishes articles on education, critical disability studies, and queer theory. Her previous publications include "Beyond Normalization: Challenging Heteronormativity in Children's Picture Books" in *Who's Your Daddy? And Other Writings on Queer Parenting* (Sumach Press, 2009). For fifteen years she has been organizing events on a myriad of anti-oppression topics.

Sharon Sutherland is an assistant professor at the University of British Columbia in the Faculty of Law, where she teaches mediation, law and theatre, and torts. She practices as a civil and child protection mediator and acts as clinic supervisor for the CoRe Conflict Resolution Clinic at UBC. Sharon's current research examines the applications of drama and theatre to conflict resolution pedagogy and practice. She is the editor of *Masks: The Online Journal of Law and Theatre*.

Sarah Swan is an attorney and frequent contributor to collections on law and popular culture. She has written on a variety of topics in that area, including the portrayal of female attorneys on television, issues of morality in post–9/11 works, and dystopic elements in popular texts. She has also contributed to collections on cult television, *The Sopranos*, and *Grey's Anatomy*. Together with Sharon Sutherland, she is working on a book focused on law in the works of Joss Whedon.

Bibliography

Abbott, Stacey. *Angel*. TV Milestones Series. Detroit: Wayne State University Press, 2009.

———. "'Can't Stop the Signal': The Resurrection/Regeneration of *Serenity*." In *Investigating* Firefly *and* Serenity: *Science Fiction on the Frontier*, edited by Rhonda V. Wilcox and Tanya R. Cochran, 227–238. London: I.B. Tauris, 2008.

———. "Kicking Ass and Singing 'Mandy': A Vampire in L.A." In *Reading* Angel: *The TV Spin-Off with a Soul*, edited by Stacey Abbott, 1–13. London: I.B. Tauris, 2005.

———. "'Nobody Scream ... or Touch My Arms': The Comic Stylings of Wesley Wyndam-Pryce." In *Reading* Angel: *The TV Spin-off with a Soul*, edited by Stacey Abbott, 189–202. London: I.B. Tauris, 2005.

———. "Walking the Fine Line Between Angel and Angelus." *Slayage: The Online International Journal of Buffy Studies* 3, no. 1 (August 2003). www.slayageonline.com.

———, ed. *Reading* Angel: *The TV Spin-off with a Soul*. London: I.B. Tauris, 2005.

Aeschylus. "Agamemnon." In *Septem Quae Supersunt Tragoedias*, edited by Denys Page, 1080–1330. New York: Oxford University Press, 1973.

Alcoff, Linda, and Laura Gray. "Survivor Discourse: Transgression or Recuperation?" *Signs: Journal of Women in Culture and Society* 18, no. 2 (1993): 284.

Alderman, Naomi. "Those Whom the Powers Wish to Destroy, They Must First Make Mad: Gods, Prophecy and Death: The Classical Roots of Madness in *BtVS*." Paper presentation, Slayage Conference on Buffy the Vampire Slayer, Nashville, TN, May 27–30, 2004.

Amnesty International. *Torture Worldwide: An Affront to Human Dignity*. New York: Amnesty International, 2000.

Anderson, Wendy Love. "Prophecy Girl and The Powers That Be: The Philosophy of Religion in the Buffyverse." In Buffy the Vampire Slayer *and Philosophy: Fear and Trembling in Sunnydale*, edited by James B. South, 212–26. Chicago: Open Court Books, 2003.

"Angel 17 Tomorrow" (anonymous comment). *Brian Lynch: Blog for You Specifically*. Comment posted February 10, 2009. http://bloglynch.blogspot.com/2009/02/angel-17-tomorrow.html (accessed July 19, 2009).

Artemis. Comment on "Angel 17 Tomorrow." *Brian Lynch: Blog for You Specifically*. Comment posted February 12, 2009. http://bloglynch.blogspot.com/2009/02/angel-17-tomorrow.html (accessed July 19, 2009).

Auerbach, Erich. "The Knight Sets Forth." In *Middle English Romances*, edited by Stephen H.A. Shepherd, 411–427. New York: W.W. Norton, 1995.

Auerbach, Nina. *Our Vampires, Our Selves*. Chicago: University of Chicago Press, 1995.

Bächli, Erich. "Sophocles." In *Die Künstlerische Funktion Von Orakelsprüchen, Weissagungen, Träumen Usw. In Der Griechischen Tragödie*, 29–62. Winterthur: Verlag P. G. Keller, 1954.

Barringer, Carol E. "The Survivor's Voice: Breaking the Incest Taboo." *NWSA Journal* 4, no.1 (1992): 4–22.

Battis, Jes. *Blood Relations: Chosen Families in* Buffy the Vampire Slayer *and* Angel. Jefferson, NC: McFarland, 2005.

Baudrillard, Jean. "Simulacra and Simulations." In *Selected Writings*, 2d ed., edited by Mark Poster, 169–87. Stanford: Stanford University Press, 2001.

Beeler, Stan. "Outing Lorne: Performance for the Performers." In *Reading* Angel: *The TV Spin-off with a Soul*, edited by Stacey Abbott, London: I.B. Tauris, 2005: 88–100.

Benjamin, Walter. *Charles Baudelaire: A Lyric Poet in the Era of Hight Capitalism*, translated by Harry Zohn. London: N.L.B., 1973.

Bennett, Juda. *The Passing Figure: Racial Confusion in Modern American Literature*. New York: Peter Lang, 1996.

Bethea, David. "Literature." In *The Cambridge Companion to Modern Russian Culture*, edited by Nicholas Rzhevsky, 161–204. Cambridge, UK: Cambridge University Press, 1998.

Blade. Directed by Stephen Norrington. London: Amen Ra Films, 1998.

Bongco, Mila. *Reading Comics: Language, Culture, and the Concept of the Superhero in Comic Books*. London: Garland, 2000.

Booker, Keith M. *The Dystopian Impulse in Modern Literature: Fiction as Social Criticism*. Westport, CT: Greenwood Press, 1994.

Bridges, Elizabeth. "Grimm Realities: *Buffy* and the Use of Folklore." In Buffy *Meets the Academy*, edited by Kevin K. Durand, 91–103. Jefferson, NC: McFarland, 2009.

Bruckner, Matilda Tomaryn. "The Shape of Romance in Medieval France." In *The Cambridge Companion to Medieval Romance*, edited by Roberta L. Krueger, 13–28. Cambridge: Cambridge University Press, 2000.

Bruner, Jerome. *Making Stories*. New York: Farrar, Straus and Giroux, 2002.

Bushnell, Rebecca W. *Prophesying Tragedy: Sign and Voice in Sophocles's Theban Plays*. Ithaca, NY: Cornell University Press, 1988.

Buttsworth, Sara. "'Bite Me': Buffy and the Penetration of the Gendered Warrior-Hero." *Continuum: Journal of Media & Cultural Studies* 16, no. 2 (2002): 185–99.

Carson, Anne. "Simonides Negative." *Arethusa* 21 (1988): 147–57.

"Cause I'm a Blonde—Harmony." YouTube. http://www.youtube.com/watch?v=xD85NlE5blw (accessed May 2009).

Collins, Jim. "Postmodernism and Television." In *Channels of Discourse, Reassembled: Television and Contemporary Criticism*, edited by Robert C. Allen, 327–353. Chapel Hill: University of North Carolina, 1992.

Comeford, AmiJo. "Cordelia Chase as Failed Feminist Gesture." In Buffy *Meets the Academy: Essays on the Episodes and Scripts as Texts*, edited by Kevin K. Durand, 150–60. Jefferson, NC: McFarland, 2009.

_____. "Structural Identity, or Saussure Visits *Buffy/Angel's* World: What's the Difference?" Paper presented at *SC1: The Slayage Conference on* Buffy the Vampire Slayer, Nashville, TN, May 28–30, 2004.

Conan Doyle, Arthur. "A Case of Identity." In *The Complete Sherlock Holmes*. London: Penguin, 1981.

Copjec, Jean. "The Phenomenal Nonphenomenal: Private Space in Film Noir." In *Shades of Noir*, edited by Jean Copjec, 167–97. London: Verso, 1993.

Cox, Gary. *Sartre: A Guide for the Perplexed*. London: Continuum, 2006.

Creed, Barbara. *The Monstrous-Feminine: Film, Feminism, Psychoanalysis*. London: Routledge, 1993.

Curry, Agnes B. "'We Don't Say "Indian"': On the Paradoxical Construction of the Reavers." *Slayage: The Online International Journal of Buffy Studies* 7, no. 1 (Winter 2008), www.slayageonline.com.

Daniels, Sarah. *Beside Herself*. In *Daniels Plays: 2: The Gut Girls, Beside Herself, Head-Rot Holiday, and The Madness of Esme and Shaz*, 95–188. London: A&C Black, 2003.

Daspit, Toby. "*Buffy* Goes to College, Adam Murders to Dissect: Education and Knowledge in Postmodernity." In Buffy the Vampire Slayer *and Philosophy: Fear and Trembling in Sunnydale*, edited by James B. South, 117–130. Chicago: Open Court Books, 2003.

Day, William Patrick. *Vampire Legends In Contemporary American Culture: What Becomes a Legend Most*. Lexington: University Press of Kentucky, 2002.

de Troyes, Chrétien. *Erec and Enide*. In *The Complete Romances of Chrétien de Troyes*, translated by David Staines, 1–86. Bloomington: Indiana University Press, 1990.

———. *Lancelot the Knight of the Cart*, translated by Burton Raffel. New Haven, CT: Yale University Press, 1997.

———. *Lancelot the Knight of the Cart*. In *The Complete Romances of Chrétien de Troyes*, translated by David Staines, 170–256. Bloomington: Indiana University Press, 1990.

Derounian-Stodola, Kathryn Zabelle, and James Arthur Levernier. *The Indian Captivity Narrative, 1550–1900*. New York: Twayne Press, 1993.

Dickens, Charles. *Bleak House*. 1853. Reprint, New York: Norton, 1977.

———. *Dombey and Son*. Oxford: Oxford University Press, 1974.

Dostoevsky, Fyodor. *Brothers Karamazov*, translated by Richard Pevear and Larissa Volohkhonsky. 1990. Reprint. New York: Farrar, Straus and Giroux, 2002.

———. *Notes from Underground*, translated by Richard Pevear and Larissa Volohkhonsky. New York: Vintage, 1993.

———. "Otryvok iz romana [Excerpt from the novel] Shchedrodarov." *Epokha* 5 (May 1864), http://smalt.karelia.ru/~filolog/epokha/1864/Shedryn.htm.

Dracula: Dead and Loving It. Directed by Mel Brooks. Culver City, CA: Castle Rock Entertainment, 1995.

Driver, Martha W., and Sid Ray, ed. *The Medieval Hero on Screen: Representations from Beowulf to Buffy*. Jefferson, NC: McFarland, 2004.

Duggan, Joseph J. "Afterword." In *Lancelot the Knight of the Cart*, translated by Burton Raffel, 225–38. New Haven, CT: Yale University Press, 1997.

Edwards, Lynne Y. "Slaying in Black and White: Kendra as Tragic Mulatto in *Buffy the Vampire Slayer*." In *Fighting the Forces: What's at Stake in* Buffy the Vampire Slayer, edited by Rhonda V. Wilcox and David Lavery, 85–97. Lanham, MD: Rowman & Littlefield, 2002.

Emerson, Caryl. "Zosima's Mysterious Visitor." In *A New Word on* The Brothers Karamazov, edited by Robert Louis Jackson, 155–179. Evanston: Northwestern University Press, 2004.

Emmons-Featherston, Sally. "Is that Stereotype Dead? Working With and Against 'Western' Stereotypes in *Buffy*." In *The Truth of* Buffy: *Essays on Fiction Illuminating Reality*, edited by Emily Dial-Driver, Sally Emmons-Featherston, Jim Ford, and Carolyn Anne Taylor, 55–66. Jefferson, NC: McFarland, 2008.

Ennis, Garth. *Hellblazer: Dangerous Habits*. New York: Vertigo/DC Comics, 1996.

———. *Preacher: Gone to Texas*. New York: Vertigo/DC Comics, 1996.

Faery, Rebecca Blevins. *Cartographies of Desire: Captivity, Race, and Sex in the Shaping of an American Nation*. Norman: University of Oklahoma Press, 1999.

Falzon, Chris. "Sartre and Meaningful Existence." In *Sartre's Nausea: Text, Context, Intertext*, edited by Alistair Rolls and Elizabeth Rechniewski, 105–120. Amsterdam and New York: Rodopi, 2005.

"The Femme Fatale Throughout History." *History Television*. www.history.ca/content/ContentDetail.aspx?ContentId=73.

Feuer, Jane, et al., ed. *MTM Quality Television*. London: BFI, 1985.

Fine, David. *Imagining Los Angeles: A City in Fiction*. Reno: University of Nevada Press, 2000.

Finlayson, John. "Definitions of Middle English Romance." *The Chaucer Review* 15, no. 1 (Summer 1980): 44–62.

Firchow, Peter Edgerly. "Orwell's Dystopias: From *Animal Farm* to *Nineteen-Eighty Four*." In *Modern Utopian Fictions from H.G. Wells to Iris Murdoch*, 97–129. Washington, D.C.: Catholic University of America Press, 2007.

Flamson, Thomas. "Free Will in a Deterministic Whedonverse." In *The Psychology of Joss Whedon: An Unauthorized Exploration of* Buffy, Angel, *and* Firefly, edited by Joy Davidson, 35–50. Dallas: BenBella, 2007.

Flynn, Thomas R. *Existentialism: A Very Short Introduction.* Oxford: Oxford University Press, 2006.

Fontenrose, Joseph. *The Delphic Oracle: Its Responses and Operations With a Catalogue of Responses.* Berkeley: University of California Press, 1978.

Fossey, Claire. "Never Hurt the Feelings of a Brutal Killer: Spike and the Underground Man." *Slayage: The Online International Journal of Buffy Studies* 2, no. 4 (March 2003), www.slayageonline.com.

Frank, Joseph. *Dostoevsky: The Mantle of the Prophet 1871–1881.* Princeton: Princeton University Press, 2002.

_____. "Notes from Underground." In *Notes from Underground: A Norton Critical Edition*, edited by Michael R. Katz, 202–237. New York: W.W. Norton, 1989.

Fuchs, Cynthia. "'Did Anyone Ever Explain to You What "Secret Identity" Means?': Race and Displacement in *Buffy* and *Dark Angel.*" In *Undead TV: Essays on* Buffy the Vampire Slayer, edited by Elana Levine and Lisa Parks, 96–115. Durham: Duke University Press, 2007.

Gaunt, Simon. "Romance and Other Genres." In *The Cambridge Companion to Medieval Romance*, edited by Roberta L. Krueger, 45–59. Cambridge: Cambridge University Press, 2000.

Gelder, Ken. *Reading the Vampire.* New York: Routledge, 1994.

Gill, Candra K. "Cuz the Black Chick Always Gets It First: Dynamics of Race in *Buffy the Vampire Slayer.*" *Girls Who Bite Back: Witches, Mutants, Slayers and Freaks*, edited by Emily Pohl-Weary, 39–55. Toronto: Sumach Press, 2004.

Ginsburg, Elaine K. "Introduction: The Politics of Passing." In *Passing and the Fictions of Identity*, edited by Elaine K. Ginsburg and Donald E. Pease, 1–18. Durham: Duke University Press, 1996.

A Glossary of Literary Terms. 5th ed. New York: Holt, Rinehart, and Winston, 1970.

Gomez-Peña, Guillermo. *The New World Border: Prophecies, Poems, and Loqueras for the End of the Century.* San Francisco: City Lights, 1996.

Gough, Kerry. "Translation Creativity and Alien Econ(c)omics: From Hollywood Blockbuster to Dark Horse Comic Book." In *Film and Comic Books*, edited by Ian Gordon, Mark Jancovich, and Matthew P. McAllister, 37–63. Jackson: University Press of Mississippi, 2007.

"Greeks and Romans in the Buffyverse: Classical Threads in Fantasy and Science Fiction on Contemporary Television." Open University, Milton Keynes, UK, January 2004.

Guddat-Figge, Gisela. "The Audience of the Romances." In *Middle English Romances*, edited by Stephen H.A. Shepherd, 498–506. New York: W.W. Norton, 1995.

Hahn, Thomas. "Gawain and Popular Chivalric Romance in Britain." In *The Cambridge Companion to Medieval Romance*, edited by Roberta L. Krueger, 218–234. Cambridge: Cambridge University Press, 2000.

Halfyard, Janet K. "The Dark Avenger: Angel and the Cinematic Superhero." In *Reading* Angel: *The TV Spin-Off With a Soul*, edited by Stacey Abbott, 149–62. London: I.B. Tauris, 2005.

_____. "Love, Death, Curses and Reverses (in F minor): Music, Gender, and Identity in *Buffy the Vampire Slayer* and *Angel.*" *Slayage: The Online International Journal of Buffy Studies* 1, no. 4 (December 2001). www.slayageonline.com.

Harper, Steven. "Jasmine: Scariest Villain Ever." In *Five Seasons of* Angel: *Science Fiction and Fantasy Writers Discus Their Favorite Vampire*, edited by Glenn Yeffeth, 49–55. Dallas: BenBella, 2004.

Harrison, Janine R. "Gender Politics in *Angel*: Traditional vs. Non-traditional Corporate Climates." In *Reading* Angel: *The TV Spin-off with a Soul*, edited by

Stacey Abbott, 118–131. London: I.B. Tauris, 2005.

Hartman, James D. *Providence Tales and the Birth of American Literature*. Baltimore: The Johns Hopkins University Press, 1999.

Homer. *The Odyssey, Books 1–12. Homeri Opera*, vol. 3, edited by. T. W. Allen. New York: Oxford University Press, 1922.

Horgan, Frances. Introduction to *The Romance of the Rose* by Guillaume de Lorris and Jean de Meun, ix–xxii. 1994. Reprint, Oxford: Oxford University Press, 1999.

Horton, Andrew, ed. *Comedy/ Cinema/ Theory*. Berkeley: University of California Press, 1991.

Hudson, Jennifer A. "'She's Unpredictable': Illyria and the Liberating Potential of Chaotic Postmodern Identity." *Americana: The Journal of American Popular Culture* (March 2005). http://www.americanpopularculture.com/archive/tv/shes_unpredictable.htm.

Hühn, Peter. "The Detective as Reader: Narrativity and Reading Concepts in Detective Fiction." *Modern Fiction Studies* 33, no. 3 (Autumn 1987): 451–666.

The Hunger. Directed by Tony Scott. London: MGM, 1983.

Hutter, Albert D. "Dreams, Transformations and Literature: the Implications of Detective Fiction." *Victorian Studies* (December 1975): 181–209.

Huxley, Alduous. *Brave New World*. 1932. Reprint, New York: Harper & Row, 1989.

Hyginus. "Fabulae." Translated by Mary Grant. http://www.theoi.com/Text/HyginusFabulae2.html (accessed December 6, 2009).

Jackson, W. T. H. *The Anatomy of Love*. New York: Columbia University Press, 1971.

Jacob, Benjamin. "Los Angelus: The City of Angel." In *Reading* Angel: *The TV Spin-Off with a Soul*, edited by Stacey Abbott, 75–87. London: I.B. Tauris, 2005.

Jancovich, Mark, and James Lyons, ed. *Quality Popular Television*. London: BFI, 2003.

Johnson, James Weldon. *The Autobiography of an Ex-Colored Man*. New York: Penguin Books, 1990.

Jones, Malcolm V. "Dostoevskii and Religion." In *The Cambridge Companion to Dostoevskii*, edited by W. J. Leatherbarrow, 148–74. Cambridge: Cambridge University Press, 2002.

Jowett, Lorna. "Helping the Hopeless: Angel as Critical Dystopia." *Critical Studies in Television* 2, no. 1 (Spring 2007): 74–89.

_____. *Sex and the Slayer*. Middleton: Wesleyan University Press, 2005.

Kamerbeek, J.C. "Prophecy in Tragedy." *Mnemosyne* 18 (1965): 29–40.

Kane, Christian. "L.A. Song." *Live Fast, Die Never: Music from the TV Series*, Fox Music, 2007.

Karlinsky, Simon. "Dostoevsky as Rorschach Test." *New York Times*, June 13, 1971. Reprinted in *Crime and Punishment: A Norton Critical Edition*, edited by George Gibian, 612–19. New York: W.W. Norton, 1989.

Kaveney, Roz. "A Sense of the Ending: Schrodinger's *Angel*." In *Reading* Angel: *The TV Spin-off with a Soul*, edited by Stacey Abbott, 57–72. London: I.B. Tauris, 2005.

_____. "'She Saved the World a Lot': An Introduction to the Themes and Structures of *Buffy* and *Angel*." In *Reading the Vampire Slayer: The New, Updated Unofficial Guide to* Buffy *and* Angel, 2d ed., edited by Roz Kaveney, 1–82. London: I.B. Tauris, 2004.

Kay, Sarah. "Courts, Clerks, and Courtly Love." In *The Cambridge Companion to Medieval Romance*, edited by Roberta L. Krueger, 81–96. Cambridge: Cambridge University Press, 2000.

Ker, W. P. *Epic and Romance: Essays on Medieval Romance*. New York: Dover, 1957.

Kirkland, Ewan. "The Caucasian Persuasion in *Buffy the Vampire Slayer*." *Slayage: The Online International Journal of Buffy Studies* 5, no. 1 (June 2003), www.slayageonline.com.

Knight, Stephen. *Crime Fiction 1800–2000: Detection, Death, Diversity*. London: Palgrave Macmillan, 2004.

Kociemba, David. "Understanding the Espensode." In *Buffy Goes Dark: Essays on the Final Two Seasons of* Buffy the Vampire Slayer *on Television*, edited by Lynne Y. Edwards, Elizabeth L. Rambo, and James B. South, 23–39. Jefferson, NC: McFarland, 2009.

Koontz, K. Dale. *Faith and Choice in the Works of Joss Whedon*. Jefferson, NC: McFarland, 2008.

Krueger, Roberta L. "Introduction." In *The Cambridge Companion to Medieval Romance*, edited by Roberta L. Krueger, 1–9. Cambridge: Cambridge University Press, 2000.

Larsen, Nella. *Passing*. 1929. Reprint, New York: Dover, 2004.

Latham, Rob. *Consuming Youth: Vampire, Cyborgs, & the Culture of Consumption*. Chicago: University of Chicago Press, 2002.

Lattimore, Steven. "Oedipus & Tiresias." *California Studies in Classical Antiquity* 8 (1975): 105–11.

Lavery, David. "The Allusions of Television." *Flow* 3, no. 10. http://davidlavery.net/writings/Television/Flow/Allusions_of_TV.pdf.

_____. *Joss: A Creative Portrait of Joss Whedon, Maker of the Whedonverses*. London: I.B. Tauris, 2009.

Leatherbarrow, W.J. "Introduction." In *The Cambridge Companion to Dostoevskii*, edited by W.J. Leatherbarrow, 1–20. Cambridge: Cambridge University Press, 2002.

Le Sage, Alain René. *Asmodeus or The Devel on Two Sticks*. Translated by Joseph Thomas. London: Hutchison, 1924.

Levi, Heather. "Sport and Melodrama: The Case of Mexican Professional Wrestling." *Social Text* 50 (1997): 57–68.

Levine, Elana, and Lisa Parks, ed. *Undead TV: Essays on* Buffy the Vampire Slayer. Durham: Duke University Press, 2007.

Little, Tracy. "High School is Hell: Metaphor Made Literal in *Buffy the Vampire Slayer*." In Buffy the Vampire Slayer *and Philosophy: Fear and Trembling in Sunnydale*, edited by James B. South, 282–293. Chicago: Open Court, 2003.

Liu, Yin. "Middle English Romance as Prototype Genre." *Chaucer Review* 40, no. 4 (2006): 335–353.

Loomis, Roger Sherman, and Laura Hibbard Loomis. "Introduction: The Origins of Romance." In *Medieval Romances*, vii-xi. New York: Random House, 1957.

Lynch, Brian. *Angel: After the Fall*. San Diego: IDW, 2007–2009.

Marc, David. *Comic Visions: Television Comedy and American Culture*, 2d ed. Malden, MA: Blackwell, 1997.

Marie de France. *The Lais of Marie de France*. New York: Penguin Books, 1986.

Martin, Thomas. "The Role of Others in Roquentin's *Nausea*." In *Sartre's Nausea: Text, Context, Intertext*, edited by Alistair Rolls and Elizabeth Rechniewski, 65–76. New York: Rodopi, 2005.

Martínez, Rubén. "On the North-South Border Patrol, in Art and Life." *New York Times*, October 13, 1991, H5.

Masson, Cynthea. "What the Hell?— *Angel*'s 'The Girl in Question.'" Paper presented at *SC3: The Slayage Conference on the Whedonverses*, Henderson State University, Arkadelphia, AR, June 5–8, 2008.

McCabe, Janet, and Kim Akass, ed. *Quality TV: Contemporary American Television and Beyond*. London: I. B. Tauris, 2007.

McCloud, Scott. *Understanding Comics: The Invisible Art*. New York: Harper Perennial, 1993.

McCracken, Allison. "At Stake: Angel's Body, Fantasy Masculinity, and Queer Desire in Teen TV." In *Undead TV: Essays on* Buffy the Vampire Slayer, edited by Elana Levine and Lisa Parks, 116–44. Durham: Duke University Press, 2007.

McLaren, Scott. "The Evolution of Joss Whedon's Vampire Mythology and the Ontology of the Soul." *Slayage: The Online International Journal of Buffy Studies* 5, no. 2 (September 2005), www.slayageonline.com.

McReynolds, Susan. *Redemption and the Merchant God: Dostoevsky's Economy of*

Salvation and Antisemitism. Evanston: Northwestern University Press, 2008.

Meyer, Michaela D. E. "From Rogue in the 'Hood to Suave in a Suit: Black Masculinity and the Transformation of Charles Gunn." In *Reading* Angel: *The TV Spin-off with a Soul,* edited by Stacey Abbott, 176–88. London: I.B. Tauris, 2005.

Meyer, Stephenie. *Twilight.* Boston: Little, Brown and Company, 2005.

Mikalson, Jon D. *Honor Thy Gods: Popular Religion in Greek Tragedy.* Chapel Hill: University of North Carolina Press, 1991.

Miller, Frank. *Batman: The Dark Knight Returns.* New York: DC Comics, 1997.

Mills, Matthew. "Ubi Caritas? Music as Narrative Agent in *Angel.*" In *Reading* Angel: *The TV Spin-off with a Soul,* edited by Stacey Abbott, 31–43. London: I.B. Tauris, 2005.

Moore, Alan. *Watchmen.* New York: DC Comics, 1987.

Morningstar, Angela. Letter printed in "The Powers-that-Read." *Angel: After the Fall* #4. San Diego: IDW, February 2008.

Morrison, James V. *Homeric Misdirection: False Predictions in the Iliad,* Michigan Monographs in Classical Antiquity. Ann Arbor: University of Michigan Press, 1992.

Nabokov, Vladimir. "Fyodor Dostoevski." In *Lectures on Russian Literature,* edited by Fredson Bowers, 97–135. New York: Harcourt Brace Jovanovich, 1981.

_____. "Why Nabokov Hates Freud." *New York Times Books,* January 30, 1996. http://www.nytimes.com/books/97/03/02/lifetimes/nab-v-freud.html.

Nadja. Directed by Michael Almereyda. Kino Link Company, 1994.

Naples, Nancy. *Feminism and Method: Ethnography, Discourse Analysis, and Activist Research.* New York: Routledge, 2003.

Neale, Steve, and Frank Krutnik. *Popular Film and Television Comedy.* London: Routledge, 1990.

Nevitt, Lucy, and Andy William Smith. "'Family Blood is Always the Sweetest': The Gothic Transgressions of Angel/Angelus." *Refractory: A Journal of Entertainment Media* 2 (2003). http://blogs.arts.unimelb.edu.au/refractory/2003/03/18/family-blood-is-always-the-sweetest-the-gothic-transgressions-of-angelangelus-lucy-nevitt-andy-william-smith/.

Nussbaum, Emily. "Must See Metaphysics." *New York Times Magazine,* September 22, 2002. http://www.nytimes.com/2002/09/22/magazine/must-see-metaphysics.html.

Ono, Kent A. "To Be a Vampire on *Buffy the Vampire Slayer*: Race and ('Other') Socially Marginalizing Positions on Horror TV." In *Fantasy Girls: Gender in the New Universe of Science Fiction and Fantasy Television,* edited by Elyce Rae Helford, 163–86. Lanham, MD: Rowman & Littlefield, 2000.

Örnebrig, Henrik. "The Show Must Go On ... and On: Narrative and Seriality in *Alias.*" In *Investigating* Alias: *Secrets and Spies,* edited by Stacey Abbott and Simon Brown, 11–26. London and New York: I.B. Tauris, 2007.

Orwell, George. *Animal Farm.* New York: Harcourt Brace Jovanovich, 1946.

Ousby, Ian. *Bloodhounds of Heaven: The Detective in English Fiction from Godwin to Doyle.* Cambridge: Harvard University Press, 1976.

Owen, Susan A. "*Buffy the Vampire Slayer*: Vampires, Postmodernity, and Postfeminism." *Journal of Popular Film & Television* 27, no. 2 (1999): 24–31.

Pateman, Matthew. *The Aesthetics of Culture in* Buffy the Vampire Slayer. Jefferson, NC: McFarland, 2006.

Peradotto, John. "Disauthorizing Prophecy: The Ideological Mapping of Oedipus Tyrannus (the 1990 Presidential Address)." Transactions of the American Philological Association (1974-) 122 (1992): 1–15.

Perry, David. "Marti Noxon: Buffy's Other Genius." In *Buffy Goes Dark: Essays on the Final Two Seasons of* Buffy the Vampire Slayer *on Television,* edited by Lynne Y. Edwards, Elizabeth L. Rambo, and James B. South, 13–22. Jefferson, NC: McFarland, 2009.

Pevear, Richard. "Introduction." In *Brothers Karamazov*, by Fyodor Dostoevsky, translated by Richard Pevear and Larissa Volohkhonsky, xi–xviii. 1990. Reprint, New York: Farrar, Straus and Giroux, 2002.

Poe, Edgar Allan. "Murders in the Rue Morgue." In *Tales of Mystery and Imagination*, 411–444. London: J. M. Dent, 1984.

Porter, Dennis. *The Pursuit of Crime: Art and Ideology in Detective Fiction.* New Haven, CT: Yale University Press, 1981.

Quiñonez, Naomi H. "Re(Riting) the Chicana Postcolonial." In *Decolonial Voices: Chicana and Chicano Cultural Studies in the 21st Century,* edited by Arturo J. Aldama and Naomi H. Quiñonez, 129–51. Bloomington: Indiana University Press, 2002.

Rabb, J. Douglas, and J. Michael Richardson. "Myth, Metaphor, Morality and Monsters: The Espenson Factor and Cognitive Science in Joss Whedon's Love Ethic." *Slayage: The Online International Journal of Buffy Studies* 7, no. 4 (Summer 2009). www.slayageonline.com.

———. "Reavers and Redskins: Creating the Frontier Savage." In *Investigating Firefly and* Serenity: *Science Fiction on the Frontier,* edited by Rhonda V. Wilcox and Tanya R. Cochran, 127–38. London: I.B. Tauris, 2008.

Rechniewski, Elizabeth. "Avatars of Contingency: Suarès and Sartre." In *Sartre's Nausea: Text, Context, Intertext,* edited by Alistair Rolls and Elizabeth Rechniewski, 93–103. Amsterdam and New York: Rodopi, 2005.

Reid, David, and Jayne L. Walker. "Strange Pursuit: Cornell Woolrich and the Abandoned City of the Forties." In *Shades of Noir*, edited by Jean Copjec, 57–96. London: Verso, 1993.

Remnick, David. "The Translation Wars." *The New Yorker*, November 7, 2005. http://www.newyorker.com/archive/2005/11/07/051107fa_fact_remnick?currentPage=all.

Resnick, Laura. "That Angel Doesn't Live Here Anymore." In *Five Seasons of* Angel: *Science Fiction and Fantasy Writers Discuss Their Favorite Vampire,* edited by Glenn Yeffeth, 15–22. Dallas: BenBella, 2004.

Richardson, J. Michael, and J. Douglas Rabb. *The Existential Joss Whedon: Evil and Human Freedom in* Buffy the Vampire Slayer, Angel, Firefly *and* Serenity. Jefferson, NC: McFarland, 2007.

Riess, Jana. *What Would Buffy Do? The Vampire Slayer as Spiritual Guide.* San Francisco: John Wiley & Sons, 2004.

Riley, Brendan. "From Sherlock to Angel: The Twenty-First Century Detective." *The Journal of Popular Culture* 42, no. 5 (2009): 908–922.

Roberts, Deborah H. *Apollo and His Oracle in the Oresteia.* Göttingen: Vandenhoeck und Ruprecht, 1984.

Roe Kestler, Frances. Introduction to *The Indian Captivity Narrative: A Woman's View,* xxiii. New York: Garland Press, 1990.

Rorty, Richard. *Philosophy and the Mirror of Nature.* Princeton: Princeton University Press, 1981.

Rowe, Kathleen. *The Unruly Woman: Gender and the Genres of Laughter.* Austin: University of Texas Press, 1995.

Rowlandson, Mary. "The Sovereignty and Goodness of God." In *The Sovereignty and Goodness of God, Together with the Faithfulness of His Promises Displayed: Being a Narrative of the Captivity and Restoration of Mrs. Mary Rowlandson and Related Documents,* edited by Neal Salisbury, 62–112. Boston: Bedford Books, 1997.

Saldívar, José David. *Border Matters: Remapping American Cultural Studies.* Berkeley: University of California Press, 1997.

Salisbury, Neal. "Introduction: Mary Rowlandson and Her Removes." In *The Sovereignty and Goodness of God, Together with the Faithfulness of His Promises Displayed: Being a Narrative of the Captivity and Restoration of Mrs. Mary Rowlandson and Related Documents,* edited by Neal Salisbury, 1–60. Boston: Bedford Books, 1997.

Sartre, Jean-Paul. *Existentialism is a Humanism.* 1945. Translated by Carol Macomber. New Haven, CT: Yale University Press, 2007.

_____. *Nausea,* trans. Lloyd Alexander. Paris: Librairie Gallimard, 1938. Reprint, New York: New Directions Books, 2007.

Sasa, Ghada Suleiman. *The Femme Fatale in American Literature.* New York: Cambria Press, 2008.

Sayer, Karen. "'This Was Our World and They Made It Theirs': Reading Space and Place in *Buffy the Vampire Slayer* and *Angel.*" In *Reading the Vampire Slayer: The New, Updated Unofficial Guide to* Buffy *and* Angel, 2d ed., edited by Roz Kaveney, 132–155. London: I.B. Tauris, 2004.

Schehr, Lawrence. "Sartre's Autodidacticism." In *Sartre's Nausea: Text, Context, Intertext,* edited by Alistair Rolls and Elizabeth Rechniewski, 31–51. New York: Rodopi, 2005.

Serenity: The Official Visual Companion. London: Titan, 2005.

Shaun of the Dead. Directed by Edgar Wright. London: Studio Canal, 2004.

Shepherd, Stephen H.A. "Preface." In *Middle English Romances,* edited by Stephen H.A. Shepherd, xi–xiv. New York: W.W. Norton, 1995.

Simon, John K. "Faulkner and Sartre: Metamorphosis and the Obscene." *Comparative Literature* 15, no. 3 (1963): 216–225.

Sophocles's Oedipus Tyrannos. In *Fabulae,* edited by Hugh Lloyd-Jones and N. G. Wilson. Oxford: Oxford University Press, 1990.

Stafford, Josh. Letter to the Editor in "The Powers-that-Read." In *Angel: After the Fall* #4. San Diego: IDW, February, 2008.

Stafford, Nikki. *Once Bitten.* Toronto: ECW Press, 2004.

Staines, David. Introduction to *The Complete Romances of Chrétien de Troyes,* ix–xxviii. Bloomington: Indiana University Press, 1990.

Stevenson, Gregory. *Televised Morality: The Case of* Buffy the Vampire Slayer. Dallas: Hamilton Books, 2003.

Stewart, Potter. *Jacobellis v. Ohio.* 1964. http://www.law.cornell.edu/supct/html/historics/USSC_CR_0378_0184_ZC1.html.

Stoker, Bram. *Dracula.* 1897. Reprint, New York: Penguin, 2009.

Stoy, Jennifer. "'And Her Tears Flowed Like Wine': Wesley/Lilah and the Complicated(?) Role of the Female Agent on *Angel.*" In *Reading* Angel: *The TV Spin-off with a Soul,* edited by Stacey Abbott, 163–175. London: I. B. Tauris, 2005.

Strieber, Whitley. *The Hunger.* 1981. Reprint, New York: Pocket, 2007.

"'Stupido' WB Promo." YouTube. February 4, 2009, online video, http://www.youtube.com/watch?v=kH8oVNumVqc (accessed July 14, 2009).

Summerscale, Kate. *The Suspicions of Mr. Whicher or The Murder at Road Hill House.* London: Bloomsbury, 2008.

Sutherland, Sharon, and Sarah Swan. "The Alliance Isn't Some Evil Empire: Dystopia in Joss Whedon's *Firefly/Serenity.*" In *Investigating* Firefly, edited by Rhonda V. Wilcox and Tanya Cochran, 89–100. London: I.B. Tauris, 2008.

_____. "The Rule of Prophecy: Source of Law in the City of *Angel.*" In *Reading* Angel: *The TV Spin-Off with a Soul,* edited by Stacey Abbott, 132–145. London: I. B. Tauris, 2005.

Taylor, A.B. *An Introduction to Medieval Romance.* 1930. Reprint, New York: Barnes and Noble, 1969.

Terras, Victor. "Dostoevsky's Detractors." *Dostoevsky Studies* 6 (1985): 166–172. http://www.utoronto.ca/tsq/DS/06/165.shtml.

_____. *A Karamazov Companion.* 1981. Reprint, Madison: The University of Wisconsin Press, 2002.

Thompson, Robert J. *Television's Second Golden Age:* From Hill Street Blues *to* ER. Syracuse: Syracuse University Press, 1997.

Thoms, Peter. *Detection and its Designs: Narrative and Power in Nineteenth-Century Detective Fiction.* Athens: Ohio University Press, 1998.

Todorov, Tzvetan. *The Poetics of Prose,*

translated by Richard Howard. Oxford: Basil Blackwell, 1977.

Tonkin, Boyd. "Entropy as Demon: Buffy in Southern California." In *Reading the Vampire Slayer: The New, Updated Unofficial Guide to Buffy and* Angel, 2d ed., edited by Roz Kaveney, 83–99. London: I.B. Tauris, 2004.

Trodd, Anthea. *Domestic Crime in the Victorian Novel*. London: Macmillan, 1989.

Trumpener, Katie. *Bardic Nationalism: The Romantic Novel and the British Empire*. Princeton: Princeton University Press, 1997.

Twilight. Directed by Catherine Hardwicke. Summit Entertainment, 2008.

Twitchell, James B. *The Living Dead: A Study of the Vampire in Romantic Literature*. Durham: Duke University Press, 1981.

Upstone, Sara. "'L.A.'s Got it All': Hybridity and Otherness in Angel's Postmodern City." In *Reading* Angel: *The TV Spin-off with a Soul*, edited by Stacey Abbott, 101–13. London: I. B. Tauris, 2005.

The Vampire Lovers. Directed by Roy Ward Baker. England: American International Pictures, 1970.

VanDerBeets, Richard. *Held Captive by Indians: Selected Narratives 1642–1836*. Knoxville: University of Tennessee Press, 1973.

_____. *The Indian Captivity Narrative: An American Genre*. New York: University Press of America, 1984.

von Strassburg, Gottfried. *Tristan with the "Tristan" of Thomas*. Translated by A.T. Hatto. 1960. Reprint, London: Penguin Group, 2004.

Weigel, Peter. "The Aesthetics of Salvation in Sartre's *Nausea*." In *The Enigma of Good and Evil: The Moral Sentiment in Literature*, edited by Anna-Teresa Tymieniecka, 473–89. The Netherlands: Springer, 2005.

Whedon, Joss. *Fray*. Milwaukie, OR: Dark Horse, 2003.

_____. "Interview." *The New York Times*, May 16, 2003. http://www.nytimes.com/2003/05/16/readersopinions/16WHED.html.

_____. "Joss Whedon Talks Angel After the Fall." Interview by Brian Lynch. *Spike: Asylum*. San Diego: IDW, 2007.

_____. "Joss Whedon Talks Angel After the Fall." Interview by Chris Ryall. Newsarama.com, April 26, 2007, http://forum.newsarama.com/showthread.php?t=110457.

_____. "Look Back in *Angel*." Interview by Ed Gross. *SFX*, July 2004.

_____. *Tales of the Slayers*. Milwaukie, OR: Dark Horse, 2002.

_____. *Tales of the Vampires*. Milwaukie, OR: Dark Horse, 2004.

Wilcox, Rhonda V. "'Every Night I Save You': Buffy, Spike, Sex and Redemption." *Slayage: The Online International Journal of Buffy Studies* 2, no. 1 (May 2002). www.slayageonline.com.

_____. *Why Buffy Matters: The Art of Buffy the Vampire Slayer*. New York: I.B. Tauris, 2005.

_____, and David Lavery, "Afterward: The Depths of *Angel*." In *Reading* Angel: *The TV Spin-Off with a Soul*, edited by Stacey Abbott, 221–29. London: I.B. Tauris, 2005.

Williamson, Milly. *The Lure of the Vampire*. London: Wallflower, 2005.

Willis, Chris. "Making the Dead Speak: Spiritualism and Detective Fiction." In *The Art of Detective Fiction*, edited by Warren Chernaik, Martin Swales, and Robert Vilain, 60–74. Basingstoke, UK: Macmillan, 2000.

Wilson, Diane. "Buffy vs. Bakhtin: Carnival and Dialogism in the Buffyverse." Paper presented at *SC2: The Slayage Conference on the Whedonverses*, Gordon College, Barnesville, GA, May 26–8, 2006: 28–31, http://dianewilson.us/buffy/sc2.paper.pdf.

Wilson, Steve. "Laugh, Spawn of Hell, Laugh." In *Reading the Vampire Slayer*, 1st ed., edited by Roz Kaveney, 78–97. London: I. B. Tauris, 2001.

Wolford, Lisa. "Introduction: Guillermo Gomez-Peña." In *Extreme Exposure: An Anthology of Solo Performance Texts from the Twentieth Century*, edited by Jo Bonney, 276–77. New York: Theatre Communications Group, 2000.

Woods, George. "'Sounds, Smells, Degrees of Light': Art and Illumination in *Nausea*." In *Sartre's Nausea: Text, Context, Intertext*, edited by Alistair Rolls and Elizabeth Rechniewski, 53–63. Amsterdam and New York: Rodopi, 2005.

Wynne, Catherine. *The Colonial Conan Doyle: British Imperialism, Irish Nationalism and the Gothic*. Westport, CT: Greenwood Press, 2002.

Yarbro, Chelsea Quinn. "*Angel*: An Identity Crisis." In *Five Seasons of* Angel*: Science Fiction and Fantasy Authors Discuss Their Favorite Vampire*, edited by Glenn Yeffeth, 79–86. Dallas: BenBella, 2004.

Yarmolinsky, Avrahm. "Introduction to Fyodor Dostoevsky." In *The Brothers Karamazov: A Novel in Four Parts & Epilog*. New York: The Heritage Press, 1949. http://www.dartmouth.edu/~karamazo/a_yarmolinsky.html.

Yeats, William Butler. "The Second Coming." In *Yeats's Poetry, Drama, and Prose*, edited by James Pethica, 76. New York: W.W. Norton, 2000.

Zalloua, Zahi. *Comparatist: Journal of the Southern Comparative Literature Association* 25 (2001): 133–150.

Zamyatin, Yevgeny. *We*. 1920. Translated by Natasha Randall. New York: The Modern Library, 2006. http://az.lib.ru/z/zamjatin_e_i/text_0050.shtml.

Zwicky, Jan. "Oracularity." *Metaphilosophy* 34 (2003): 488–509.

Index

Abbott, Stacey 2, 4, 5, 6, 18, 53n26, 64n4, 81n4, 131, 141n8, 147, 150, 156, 163, 169n6, 171n50, 180, 206, 211, 217n3, 218n9
Acker, Amy 6
Adam (Biblical) *see* Bible/Biblical
Aeschylus 191, 192, 203n24, 203n36
Alien 221; *Alien Resurrection* 223; *Alien3* 222; *Aliens* 221, 222
Alighieri, Dante 3
The Alliance 139, 141n14
Alonna 152, 156, 157
America/American 4, 9, 12, 30, 38, 54, 64n5, 69, 70, 71, 72, 77, 78, 79, 80, 81, 81n4, 98, 99, 100, 103, 106, 107, 108, 109, 132, 133, 145n45, 148
American Indian 9, 70, 71, 72, 73, 75, 77, 78, 79, 80, 81n21, 83n52
Angel: After the Fall 4, 12, 13, 52n7, 220n68, 222, 223, 224, 225, 226, 227, 228, 230, 231
Angel: Aftermath 226
Angel: Only Human 224, 232n39
Angel Investigations 6, 7, 11, 41, 43, 44, 45, 47, 48, 49, 52n12, 57, 74, 93, 96, 198, 199, 206, 207, 208, 209, 212, 213, 215, 216, 225; *see also* Team Angel
Angelus 2, 3, 52n9, 169n9, 198, 204n51, 210
Animal Farm 10, 121, 122, 128n42
Anne 156
Anya 24, 163, 170n38, 189n55
Apocalypse/Apocalyptic 48, 138, 155, 189n55, 200, 201, 224, 228, 230
Aristotle 24
The Astonishing X-Men 223; *see also The X-Men*

"The Bachelor Party" 34, 37, 40n34
Bakhtin, Mikhail 132
Batman (character) 206, 229
Batman (comic) 221, 228
Batman (1989 film) 229
Batman: The Dark Knight Returns 221, 229
Battis, Jes 43, 70, 101, 106, 107, 163
Battlestar Galactica 221
Baudrillard, Jean 148, 149, 150, 151, 152, 153, 154, 155, 157

Beeler, Stan 215
Bell, Jeffrey 99, 104, 107, 109, 127
"Belonging" 151
Benz, Julie 7
Beowulf 180
Beside Herself 9, 86, 87, 88, 89, 90, 91, 94, 95, 96
Bethany 9, 58, 59, 64n14, 86, 93, 94, 95, 96, 175, 189n52
Bible 71, 139, 192; Adam 55, 60, 92; Book of Judges 55; Book of Revelation 192, 202n5; Delilah 55, 60; Eve 54, 60, 92; Judas Iscariot 3; Samson 60
"Billy" 55, 62, 178, 211
Billy (character) 56, 57, 62, 63, 90, 212
bitch 9, 24, 56, 57, 58, 62, 88, 90, 91
Black Thorn *see* Circle of the Black Thorn
Blade (character) 20; *Blade* (film) 19
"Blind Date" 59, 204n58
"Blood Money" 148, 149
Bongco, Mila 221, 227, 228
Book of Judges *see* Bible
Book of Revelation *see* Bible
Boreanaz, David 6, 52n12
Brave New World 10, 117, 118, 120
Bridges, Elizabeth 176
The Brothers Karamazov 10, 130, 131, 133, 145n88
Buffy Season Eight 222, 223
Buffy the Vampire Slayer (television series) 4, 6, 7, 11, 18, 19, 20, 22, 23, 24, 25, 26, 27, 13n11, 52n12, 62, 80, 83n52, 85, 98, 109, 137, 139, 159, 176, 178, 182, 208, 221, 223, 225
Buffy/Buffy the Vampire Slayer (character) *see* Summers, Buffy
Burkle, Roger and Trish 77, 164
Burkle, Winifred "Fred" 6, 9, 11, 21, 23, 25, 26, 45, 49, 50, 51, 53n33, 62, 64n12, 69–81, 103, 119, 120, 122, 123, 124, 125, 126, 138, 139, 150, 153, 154, 155, 156, 159, 161, 162, 163, 164, 165, 167, 168, 169, 169n9, 170n38, 170n46, 182, 189n58, 198, 204n52, 204n57, 204n59, 207, 209, 213, 214, 215, 216, 217, 220n60, 225, 229

Buttsworth, Sara 98
Byrne, John 226

The Cabin in the Woods 223
Calendar, Jenny 163
"Calvary" 52n9, 57, 204n51
Caritas 18, 43, 44, 46, 47, 152, 198, 226
Carmilla (character) 21, 22, 28n31
Carmilla (novella) 17
"Carpe Noctem" 64n12
Carpenter, Charisma 6
Catholic Church 130, 133, 134, 135, 136, 139, 146n107
"The Cautionary Tale of Numero Cinco" 10, 99, 100, 102, 104, 106, 107, 108, 109, 204n68, 215, 218n21, 220n62
Chandler, Raymond 206, 210
Chase, Cordelia/Cordy 2, 6, 9, 20, 21, 22, 23, 24, 33, 34, 35, 37, 38, 40n34, 45, 46, 47, 48, 52n9, 56, 57, 58, 62, 63, 69, 70, 72, 73, 74, 77, 78, 79, 86, 88, 89, 90, 91, 94, 95, 96, 134, 151, 153, 163, 170n38, 175, 180, 183, 189n52, 189n55, 189n58, 195, 196, 198, 199, 202n5, 204n48, 207, 208, 209, 211, 212, 213, 224, 229
Chicano/a 10, 99, 100, 101, 106, 107, 109; see also Latino/a; Mexico/Mexican
Choice(s), freedom of/right to make 10, 12, 61, 127, 130, 131, 135, 136, 137, 138, 139, 141n12, 167
Christ/Jesus 3, 133, 134, 135, 136, 137, 139, 140; Anti-Christ 1
Circle of the Black Thorn 10, 50, 51, 117, 126, 138, 200, 201
"City of" 4, 67, 196, 202n4, 228, 229, 231
Classical Drama 191, 192, 193, 195
Coleridge, Samuel Taylor 27n1
Collins, Jim 44, 45
Comedy Genre 1, 17, 18, 19, 20, 24, 26
Comeford, AmiJo 98
Comics 12, 196, 221–235
Conan Doyle, Arthur 12, 206, 209, 210, 218n15
The Conduit 150, 168
Connor 48, 59, 65n26, 134, 138, 190n66, 196, 199, 200, 204n59, 205n61, 205n64, 214, 224, 225, 229, 230
"Conviction" 49
Cordelia *see* Chase, Cordelia/Cordy
Cordy *see* Chase, Cordelia/Cordy
"Couplet" 204n58, 214
Crime and Punishment 133, 138

Daniels, Sarah 9, 86, 88, 91, 93, 96
Dante *see* Alighieri, Dante
Darla 7, 46, 63, 188n29, 188n33, 229
"Darla" 204

Dawn (character) *see* Summers, Dawn
Day, William Patrick 208
"Dear Boy" 52n9, 205n61
"Deep Down" 190n66
"Destiny" 23, 205n68
De Troyes, Chrétien 176, 180, 183
Delilah *see* Bible
Denisof, Alexis 6
Dennis (ghost) 22, 89
detective fiction genre 206–220; hardboiled 175, 206, 208, 210, 219n29
Dickens, Charles 131, 142n21, 210, 218n23
"Disharmony" 21, 22, 25, 205n61
Dollhouse 85, 98, 139, 169n9, 223
doppelganger 131, 168
Dostoevsky, Fyodor 10, 130–146; Mock execution of 132
Doyle, Allen Francis 6, 8, 30–38, 39n11, 39n23, 40n34, 40n41, 67, 89, 170n38, 182, 189n55, 195, 196, 202n4, 207, 208, 211, 212, 213, 218n15, 229
Doyle, Harriet "Harry" 35, 36, 37, 38
Dracula (character) 20
Dracula (novel) 17, 27, 206; Lucy 17, 19, 25, 27
Dracula: Dead and Loving It 18
Drogyn 160, 165
Drusilla 7, 188n29, 188n33, 229
dystopia(n) 10, 115–127, 128n14, 145n89

Early Modern period 79, 140
"Epiphany" 140, 156, 190n66
episodes (serials) of *Angel: After the Fall*: #1 224; #4 226; #5 224, 225; #13 145n96, 190n66
episodes of *Angel* see name of episode
episodes of *Buffy the Vampire Slayer*: "Amends" 190n76; "Angel" 182; "Becoming" 182; "Graduation Day" 178, 182, 185; "Helpless" 183; "Lover's Walk" 159; "Normal Again" 170n45; "Pangs" 80, 83n52; "Prophecy Girl" 137; "The Puppet Show" 46, 202n6; "School Hard" 140; "Shadow" 190n76; "Something Blue" 190n76; "Tabula Rasa" 140;
episodes of *Firefly*: "Objects in Space" 159
Euripides 191, 192, 203n24
Eve (Biblical) *see* Bible
Eve (character in *Angel*) 50, 154
The Existential Joss Whedon 52n10, 130, 171n54, 171n69
Existentialism 11, 130, 132, 133, 137, 140, 141n12, 160, 162, 165, 166, 167, 168, 170n46, 203n43

Faith (character) 60, 138, 178, 179
Falzon, Chris 159, 167

Index

fate 52*n*10, 130, 132, 137, 138, 141*n*12, 141*n*14, 183
Faulkner, William 39*n*14
feminism/feminist 9, 54, 58, 59, 61, 62, 63, 85, 86, 87, 88, 89, 91, 93, 96, 98
femme fatale 8, 9, 54, 55, 56, 57, 58, 59, 60, 63, 64*n*12, 220*n*51
Finn, Riley 190*n*76
Firefly 4, 80, 83*n*52, 85, 98, 115, 139, 141*n*14, 223
"First Impressions" 52*n*9
Flamson, Thomas 43, 52*n*10, 141*n*12, 141*n*14, 145*n*90
"Forgiving" 60
Foucault, Michel 87
Fray 223
Fred *see* Burkle, Winifred "Fred"
"Fredless" 77, 204*n*50
free will 1, 7, 10, 44, 48, 52*n*10, 120, 130, 137, 138, 141*n*12, 141*n*14, 145*n*91, 229

Gavin *see* Park, Gavin
George 151, 152, 157
Giles, Rupert 137
"The Girl in Question" 163, 167
Gomez-Peña, Guillermo 10, 98, 99, 100, 101, 102, 103, 104, 105, 106, 107, 108, 109, 110, 110*n*8, 111*n*11
Greenwalt, David 6, 98
Groosalugg/Groo 69, 81*n*4, 223, 224, 226
"Groundstate" 205*n*61
Gunn, Charles 2, 6, 11, 25, 26, 49, 50, 51, 53*n*33, 62, 63, 69, 102, 107, 113, 115, 122, 123, 124, 125, 138, 147, 148, 149, 150, 151, 152, 153, 154, 155, 156, 157, 160, 168, 198, 209, 213, 215, 216, 217, 220*n*58, 224, 225, 232*n*39
Gwen 224, 225

Halfyard, Janet K. 189*n*58, 229
Hallet, Andy 6, 226, 227
Hamilton 23, 27, 126
Harlem Renaissance 31
Harmony 8, 17–27
"Harm's Way" 21, 23, 24, 25, 26, 123
Harper, Stephen 118, 141*n*14, 144*n*53
Harris, Xander 25, 26, 140, 185, 202*n*6
Harrison, Janine R. 77
Harry *see* Doyle, Harriet "Harry"
Hellblazer 229, 230
"Hero" 34, 36, 40*n*41
"A Hole in the World" 49, 149, 160, 165, 168, 229
Holmes, Sherlock 206, 209
"Home" 60, 61, 205*n*64
Horror Genre 1, 17, 18, 131, 175, 211
Horton, Andrew 18, 19, 20, 27

The Host *see* Lorne
hotel *see* Hyperion Hotel
Hughes, Langston 39*n*14
Huxley, Aldous 10, 116, 117, 118, 119, 124, 128*n*17, 128*n*26
Hyperion Hotel (Angel's hotel) 5, 46, 76, 95, 151, 198

"I Will Remember You" 184, 185, 204*n*61, 205*n*68
Illyria 6, 11, 45, 49, 51, 70, 81*n*5, 124, 143*n*37, 159, 160, 161, 162, 163, 164, 165, 166, 167, 168, 169*n*9, 170*n*46, 216, 217, 224
"In the Dark" 37
Indian *see* American Indian
The Inferno 3
The Initiative 139
"Inside Out" 113, 138, 204*n*48, 229

Jasmine 10, 48, 117, 118, 119, 120, 121, 126, 128*n*21, 130, 134, 136, 137, 138, 139, 140, 141*n*14, 170*n*38, 198, 213, 229
Jesus *see* Christ/Jesus
Jowett, Lorna 7, 98, 115, 116, 127*n*1, 128*n*14, 206
Joyce *see* Summers, Joyce
Judas Iscariot *see* Bible
"Judgment" 41, 43, 60, 175, 176, 182, 205*n*61, 205*n*68

Kane, Christian 7
Kartheiser, Vincent 7
Kaveney, Roz 23, 26, 27, 168, 220*n*60
Keats, John 27*n*1
Knox 49, 198, 204*n*51
Kociemba, David 141*n*8
Koontz, K. Dale 52*n*10, 141*n*12

Lancelot, the Knight of the Cart 176, 180
Landau, Juliet 7
Landock 79
Lanval 184
Larsen, Nella 8, 30, 32, 35, 37, 39*n*7
Latino/a 10, 99, 100, 102, 103, 109; *see also* Chicano/a; Mexico/Mexican
Lavery, David 5, 13*n*11, 13*n*13, 18
LeFanu, Sheridan 17, 21, 22
Lehane, Faith *see* Faith, character
Lesage, Alain-René 209, 210
Liam 169*n*9; *see also* Angelus
"Life of the Party" 24, 49
Lilah *see* Morgan, Lilah
Lindsey *see* McDonald, Lindsey
Linwood *see* Murrow, Linwood
Little, Tracy 187*n*22
Lockley, Kate 156, 157, 210, 224, 230

"Lonely Hearts" 33, 211
Lorne 3, 6, 8, 26, 41–51, 52n7, 52n9, 57, 70, 78, 79, 83n50, 99, 107, 123, 124, 125, 153, 196, 198, 199, 202n5, 204n45, 204n50, 204n51, 204n52, 205n61, 207, 209, 213, 215, 216, 219, 224, 225, 226
Los Angeles/L.A. 1, 4, 6, 8, 10, 11, 13, 41, 43, 48, 51, 52n7, 70, 72, 73, 74, 76, 77, 99, 100, 101, 102, 103, 106, 107, 108, 109, 110n8, 115, 120, 130. 136, 147, 149, 151, 154, 155, 182, 208, 210, 215, 217, 224, 225, 227, 228, 230
Lovecraft, H.P. 213
"Loyalty" 60, 204n58
Lucas, George 127n3, 222
Lucy (character in *Dracula*) *see* Dracula (novel)
Lutz, Mark 226
Lynch, Brian 145n96, 190n66, 222, 223, 226, 227, 230, 231

Maclay, Tara 163, 170n38, 189n55
Manners, Holland 58, 117, 121
Marsters, James 6, 226, 227
The Master 137
McDonald, Lindsey 7, 50, 51, 57, 58, 59, 137, 154, 155, 225
McNab, Mercedes 24
Melville, Herman 71
Mexico/Mexican 98, 99, 100, 102, 104, 105, 106, 107, 108, 109; *see also* Latino/a; Chicano/a
Meyer, Michaela D.E. 26, 153, 220n58
Miller, Frank 222, 229
mise-en-scène 227
Miss Piggy 19, 20, 26
Moore, Ron 222
Morgan, Lilah 3, 7, 8, 9, 54–63, 90, 91, 120, 154, 210, 212, 220n51
Murrow, Linwood 59, 60
Mutant Enemy 213

Nabokov, Vladimir 131, 142n16
Native American *see* American Indian
Nausea 11, 143n37, 159, 160, 161, 162, 165, 166, 167, 168
Nina 225
Noir 1, 5, 54, 56, 64n4, 64n12, 98, 148, 175, 206, 208, 219n25, 220n51, 225, 227, 231
"Not Fade Away" 4, 12, 50, 51, 156, 163, 224, 225, 231
Notes from Underground 133, 138, 143n44
Numero Cinco (character) 98, 100, 102, 104, 105, 106, 107, 108, 109; *see also* "The Cautionary Tale of Numero Cinco"
Nyazian Scrolls 196, 197, 198, 199, 200, 204n59, 214

Oedipus 192, 193, 194, 195, 201, 202n4
Oedipus at Colonus 199
Oedipus Rex 3, 192, 193, 194, 195, 201, 202n4, 202n6
"Offspring" 46, 204n59, 205n61, 214
Ono, Kent A. 106, 109
Orwell, George 10, 116, 121, 122, 123, 124, 125, 126, 127n3, 128n42
"Over the Rainbow" 52n9, 59n9, 81
Owen, Susan A 98

Park, Gavin 59, 62
"Parting Gifts" 15, 204n61
Passing 8, 30–38, 39n7
Pateman, Matthew 141n12
"Peace Out" 130, 136, 229
Planet of the Apes 117, 221
Poe, Edgar Allan 12, 71, 211
Postmodern(ism) 8, 11, 41, 43, 44, 45, 46, 106, 148, 151, 202n3
"Power Play" 50
The Powers That Be 6, 30, 45, 56, 134, 153, 182, 195, 196, 198, 200, 208, 212, 213, 217, 219n32, 229
prophecy 1, 3, 12, 53n33, 103, 105, 137, 138, 145n91, 191, 192, 193, 194, 195, 196, 197, 198, 199, 200, 201, 204n44, 204n57, 205n68, 212, 220n62
Pylea/Pylean 2, 8, 9, 41, 43, 50, 51, 69, 70, 72, 73, 76, 78, 79, 80, 81n4, 83n50, 117, 128n14, 182

Quinn, Glenn 6

Rabb, J. Douglas 52n10, 130, 132, 133, 139, 140, 141n14, 141n15, 143n45, 169n6, 171n69, 204n43
Reavers 80, 83n52
Rechniewski, Elizabeth 162
"Redefinition" 205n61, 227
redemption 1, 6, 27, 58, 61, 63, 130, 131, 137, 138, 139, 140, 141n15, 156, 216
"Reprise" 117
"Reunion" 188n29, 188n33, 229
Revelation (Book of) *see* Bible
Rice, Anne 20
Richards, J. August 6, 154
Richardson, J. Michael 52n10, 130, 132, 133, 139, 140, 141n14, 141n15, 143n45, 169n6, 171n69, 204n43
Riess, Jana 141n15
Riley, Brendan 206
"The Ring" 55, 60, 182, 213
"Rm w/a Vu" 9, 88, 89, 95
Romance Genre 175–186
Romanov, Stephanie 7, 55
Rondell 151, 152, 157

Rosenberg, Willow 22, 190n76, 202n6, 220n60
Rowlandson, Mary 9, 70, 71, 72, 73, 74, 75, 76, 77, 78, 79, 80, 81, 82n8, 82n12, 81n21, 81n24, 83n31

Sahjahn 57, 199, 200
"Sanctuary" 138, 182
sarcophagus 159, 160; Fred's death from 49, 124, 150, 216
Sartre, Jean-Paul 11, 132, 140, 143n37, 159–169, 170n46
Scroll of Aberjian/prophecy of 137, 196, 198, 200
"The Second Coming" 3, 46, 48
Senior Partners 23, 45, 48, 49, 50, 51, 56, 57, 60, 61, 126, 148, 150, 154, 155, 156, 215, 217
Serenity 4, 83n52, 139, 141n14, 223
Shakespeare, William 3; *King Lear* 212; *The Merchant of Venice* 55; *Romeo and Juliet* 11
Shanshu prophecy 1, 12, 53n33, 105, 137, 138, 145n96, 182, 183, 184, 196, 197, 200, 201, 214, 216, 230
"She" 117, 178
"Shells" 49, 160, 163, 166, 170n46, 204n51, 204n52
"Shiny Happy People" 139
simulacrum/simulacra/simulation 11, 148, 149, 150, 151, 153, 154, 155, 157
Skip 138, 204n48
slayer 6, 25, 137, 178, 179,182, 183, 189n55, 189n56
"Sleep Tight" 64n12, 229
"Slouching Toward Bethlehem" 46, 134, 202n5
"Smile Time" 173
Sophocles 12, 191, 192, 194, 199, 203n24
"Soul Purpose" 217, 220n52
"Soulless" 202n6, 205n68
The Sovereignty and Goodness of God 71, 80
Spiderman (Comic) 221
Spike 6, 7, 18, 21, 22, 23, 25, 26, 51, 53n33, 63, 103, 115, 121, 124, 125, 137, 142n31, 160, 168, 169, 200, 207, 208, 215, 216, 218n21, 220n52, 223, 224, 226, 227
Spike: Asylum 223, 227
Spike: After the Fall 224
Spike: Shadow Puppets 223, 227
"Spin the Bottle" 2, 47, 218n9
Stafford, Nikki 24, 26
Star Trek 21, 221
Star Wars 115, 127n3, 221
Stevenson, Gregory 52n10, 141n12
Stoker, Bram 17, 25, 206, 213; *see also Dracula* (novel)

Stoy, Jennifer 62, 63, 217n3, 220n51
Summers, Buffy 6, 11, 20, 23, 52n12, 76, 101, 108, 137, 140, 178, 181, 182, 183, 184, 185, 186n55, 190n76, 202n6
Summers, Dawn 169n9, 190n76
Summers, Joyce 163, 170n38
Sunnydale 22, 46, 89, 90, 101, 178
Superman 221, 229
Superman II 229
"Supersymmetry" 52n9, 83n35
Sutherland, Sharon 115, 145n91, 204n57, 211, 220n51
Swan, Sarah 115, 145n91, 204n57, 211, 220n51

Tales of the Slayer 223
Tales of the Vampire Slayer 223
Tara *see* Maclay, Tara
Team Angel 1, 2, 3, 5, 6, 7, 13, 26, 43, 48, 69, 70, 76, 77, 79, 80, 81n5, 93, 99, 115, 118, 120, 121, 124, 125, 126, 130, 134, 152, 153, 155, 156, 168, 182, 206, 215; *see also* Angel Investigations
"That Old Gang of Mine" 102, 152
"That Vision Thing" 45, 57, 212
"There's No Place Like Plrtz Glrb" 69, 81
"The Thin Dead Line" 102
"Through the Looking Glass" 81, 81n4
"Time Bomb" 160, 166, 167
"To Shanshu in L.A." 204n58, 204n61
Toy Story 223
Tragedy 12, 18, 24, 120,191, 193, 194, 195, 196, 197, 198, 199, 200, 201
"The Trial" 41
Twilight (novel/film) 19

"Underneath" 24, 155, 166, 204n52
"Untouched" 9, 59, 86, 93, 175, 178
Utopia(n) 115, 116, 117,120, 121, 122, 123, 124, 125, 126, 130, 134, 135, 139, 144n65

Vail, Cyvus 163, 164, 168
The Vampire Lovers 17, 22

watcher 6, 137, 163, 225
Watchmen 221, 229
Wells, H.G. 117
werewolf 208, 215
Wes/Wesley *see* Wyndam-Pryce, Wesley
Westerna, Lucy *see Dracula* (novel)
Whedon, Joss 2, 3, 4, 5, 6, 7, 8, 10, 11, 12, 13, 38, 43, 44, 48, 52n12, 54, 63, 69, 71, 79, 80, 85, 86, 89, 93, 94, 96, 98, 99, 101, 105, 107, 109, 110n1, 110n3, 115, 130, 131, 132, 133, 136, 137, 138, 139, 140, 141n8, 154, 159, 160, 162, 163, 164, 165, 167, 168, 169n9, 171n84, 176, 177, 191, 194, 196,

197, 199, 201, 203n24, 206, 222, 223, 227, 228, 230, 231
Whistler 182
White Room 11, 149, 150, 155, 168
Wilcox, Rhonda V. 4, 13n11, 18, 131, 141n8, 141n12, 141n15, 142n21
Willow *see* Rosenberg, Willow
Wolfram & Hart 2, 3, 7, 11, 21, 23, 24, 25, 26, 27, 45, 46, 47, 48, 49, 50, 51, 52n9, 53n33, 56, 57, 58, 60, 61, 62, 65n26, 79, 104, 108, 109, 115, 117, 120, 121, 122, 123, 124, 125, 147, 148, 149, 150, 153, 154, 156, 178, 188n29, 196, 198, 210, 212, 215, 216, 217, 220n64, 224, 225, 228, 229, 230, 231

Wyndam-Pryce, Wesley 2, 3, 6, 7, 11, 18, 45, 50, 51, 53n33, 57, 62, 63, 69, 115, 119, 125, 138, 153, 159, 161, 162, 163, 164, 166, 167, 168, 195, 197, 198, 199, 200, 201, 204n57, 206, 207, 209, 210, 213, 214, 215, 216, 219n50, 220n51, 220n60, 220n67, 224, 225, 226

Xander *see* Harris, Xander
The X-Men (comic) 221

Yeats, William Butler 3, 46, 48

www.ingramcontent.com/pod-product-compliance
Ingram Content Group UK Ltd.
Pitfield, Milton Keynes, MK11 3LW, UK
UKHW041934140426
5217IPUK00014B/474